Code for interior lighting 1994

D1514140

© The Chartered Institution of
Building Services Engineers
Delta House
222 Balham High Road
London SW12 9BS

ISBN 0 900953 64 0

First published	1936
Revised	1938
Revised	1941
Revised	1942
Revised	1944
Revised	1945
Revised	1946
Revised	1949
Revised	1955
Revised	1961
Revised	1968
Revised	1973
Revised	1977
Revised	1984
Reprinted with amendments	1985
New edition	1994

© The Chartered Institution of Building Services Engineers

Charity number 278104

London 1994

Typeset by CIBSE Technical Department

Printed in Great Britain by Multiplex Techniques Ltd, St Mary Cray, Kent

Foreword

In 1988 the Lighting Division Technical Committee of the Chartered Institution of Building Services Engineers appointed a Task Group to revise the 1984 *Code for Interior Lighting*. Extensive enquiries were made with users to ensure that the categories of tasks used in the recommendations were still valid and useful. The replies received helped to set the aims of this edition and expanded its scope. The Institution is indebted to the various government and local authority departments, professional and trade associations, academic institutions and individuals in the UK and overseas for their constructive comments on the previous editions and drafts of this document.

Task Group

R C Aldworth (Chairman)	C M Parry
J E Baker	K B Pike (Secretary)
R I Bell	A I Slater
D J Carter	A Tammes
E T Glenny	P R Tregenza
B D Jacob	A Wilson
R M Kerswill	A P Wilson

Publications Secretary	**Editor**
K J Butcher	R Yarham

The Institution wishes to acknowledge the following organisations for their valuable assistance in the preparation of this publication: BhS, Building Research Establishment, Electricity Association, Engineering, Design and Procurement Ltd, Facet Ltd, Lighting Design Partnership, Philips Lighting Ltd, Siemens Lighting Ltd, Thorn Lighting Ltd, University of Liverpool, University of Sheffield, University of Wales. Other contributors were M B Halstead, M R Pointer (Kodak Ltd,) M J Whillock (National Radiological Protection Board), A B Wilkins (Medical Research Council).

The members of the Task Group wish to thank P R Boyce, J A Lynes, A M Marsden, J C Procter and P T Stone for their detailed and constructive contributions. The authors also wish to thank many other colleagues and organisations for their responses at the public comment draft stage before this document was finalised. Finally, a special vote of thanks goes to Joanne O'Connor who typed the five drafts involved in the preparation of this *Code*.

Cover illustrations: (clockwise from top) Imperial war museum (reproduced with kind permission of Nicholas Gentilli); use of colour to enhance office interior (see page 21); Stansted Airport interior (lit by ERCO Lighting Limited, reproduced with kind permission); car factory production line; display lighting (see page 35).

Note from the publisher

This publication is primarily intended to provide guidance to those responsible for the design, installation, commissioning, operation and maintenance of building services. It is not intended to be exhaustive or definitive and it will be necessary for users of the guidance given to exercise their own professional judgement when deciding whether to abide by or depart from it. For this reason also, departure from the guidance contained in this publication should not necessarily be regarded as a departure from best practice.

Contents

Preface

Lighting affects almost every aspect of our lives. It is used in places as diverse as factories, offices, libraries, restaurants, schools and shops, to produce conditions which enable us to see what we are doing, and to create an ambience appropriate to the setting. This *Code* has been prepared with the aims of:

(*a*) specifying the lighting conditions appropriate for a wide range of interiors

(*b*) offering guidance on design methods for obtaining those conditions.

It is organised in six parts, the first four constituting the main body of the *Code*:

— Part 1 summarises the effect of lighting conditions on the performance of tasks, the appearance of the interior and the comfort of the occupants

— Part 2 contains recommendations of maintained illuminance and other design criteria, both general and specific, which are suitable for a large number of interior and exterior applications

— Part 3 describes the properties of interior lighting equipment which is generally available

— Part 4 sets out suitable design procedures.

Further information is given in:

— Part 5: Appendices

— Part 6: Glossary, bibliography and references.

Lighting is an art and a science. It can provide both a visual experience for the observer of a scene and conditions to enable a task to be performed, though the relative importance of these aspects will vary with the application. Given the differences in visual tasks, building form and surface finish that occur, and the different light sources, luminaires and control systems that are available, there is plenty of opportunity for variety in design. For this reason the recommendations made in this *Code* are given in terms of the end result rather than the means of producing it, which must be determined by the designer.

The recommendations given in this *Code* are representative of good practice. They are the result of considering scientific knowledge, practical experience, technical feasibility and economic reality. Although the *Code* has no statutory standing, some of the recommendations are cited as references in certain mandatory standards. Taken together, the recommendations represent a base for designers to build on.

Changes in the *Code*

This edition of the *Code* contains many changes, but the layout and structure of the previous edition have been retained. There are many more cross-references within the text and a fuller index. It is recommended that users read the *Code* at least once before using it as a reference document. The major changes in this edition are summarised on the next two pages.

Maintained illuminance replaces service illuminance

The illuminance recommendations are based on 'maintained' illuminance rather than 'service' illuminance. This alters the value and the definition of 'maintenance factor' used in calculations; the term now includes lamp luminous flux (lumen) maintenance and life survival. This change is in response to the CIBSE Lighting Division policy statement of June 1989. This established that the basis of lighting design is that the illuminance provided by an installation should not fall below the recommended value. This should also ensure harmonisation, during the life of this edition, with European lighting recommendations currently being drawn up within the European Committee for Standardisation (CEN).

The maintained illuminance values in the schedule in section 2.6.4 are now true minima which result in higher initial illuminance and installed loads. To minimise these increases, maintenance procedures become a more important element in the design process. The flow chart (Figure 2.3, page 43) has also been revised to include intermediate steps in the illuminance scale which designers and users can apply when setting the design maintained illuminance.

Generic information on lamps and luminaires

This has been updated to include developments since the last edition. To assist designers in the calculation of maintained illuminance some typical lamp, luminaire and room maintenance data have been included. However, the manufacturer's data must be used when they are available.

Energy and green issues

Since 1984 the importance of these issues has come to the fore in response to the environmental concerns about 'global warming' and emissions from fossil fuel power stations (see section 5.11). This edition places more emphasis throughout on energy load and use. The section on energy (section 2.5) has been substantially revised and now includes in Table 2.2 (page 39) target ranges of installed power density ($W/m^2/100$ lux). The information on the range, design and availability of lighting control systems has also been expanded.

European Community (EC) directives and standardisation

New European Community directives for the working environment have been published since the last edition. These are taken into consideration in this *Code*. In particular, legislation controlling the use of visual displays now has a significant impact on the design of commercial and industrial lighting. Throughout, new references to relevant EC directives and associated standards have been added. A new appendix (section 5.10), covering this area, has been introduced. Reference to quality assurance (*BS 5750/ISO 9000/EN 29000*) has also been included in Part 3.

Recommendations for all interiors and activities

Users of previous editions of the *Code* have not always appreciated that the lighting schedule provided only specific recommendations which varied with the activity or interior. This resulted in the schedule being adopted without taking account of the general recommendations. The intention was that the schedule should be applied in addition to the other recommendations in Part 2.

The new Part 2 of this *Code* emphasises that there are 'core recommendations' which apply to all areas and the lighting schedule and flowchart give extra recommendations tailored to specific tasks, interiors and activities.

Illuminance selection

In response to requests from users, section 5.6 has been added to explain how illuminance recommendations can be related to visual performance.

Illuminance variation

This edition gives more detailed advice and recommendations about the variation of illuminance in an interior in terms of uniformity and diversity.

Daylighting

Separate recommendations are now given for daylighting to enhance the general brightness of a room and daylight for tasks. The *Code* assumes that daylighting and electric lighting are used together in many buildings but that most users of the *Code* have little influence on window design. The CIBSE Applications Manual: *Window design* is referred to for specific guidance on window design.

Financial appraisal

A new appendix (section 5.1) describes methods of financial appraisal of a lighting installation.

Uplighting

A new appendix (section 5.14) describes indirect lighting and calculation methods.

'Art of lighting'

Based on the argument that 'art' cannot be codified, previous editions have consciously avoided this topic. In this edition the first steps have been taken to provide advice on lighting design, which goes beyond purely task-orientated concepts, for the purpose of expressing architecture, creating a mood or providing emphasis. For the future, it is hoped that this subject will be developed and more guidance given in supplementary publications.

Part 1   Visual effects of lighting

1.1   Introduction

The lighting of an interior should fulfil three functions. It should:

(*a*) ensure the safety of people in the interior (Figure 1.1)

(*b*) facilitate the performance of visual tasks (Figure 1.2)

(*c*) aid the creation of an appropriate visual environment (Figure 1.3).

Safety is always important but the emphasis given to task performance and the appearance of the interior will depend on the nature of the interior. For example, the lighting considered suitable for a factory tool room will place much more emphasis on lighting the task than on the appearance of the room, but in a hotel lounge the priorities will be reversed. This variation in emphasis should not be taken to imply that either task performance or visual appearance can be completely neglected. In almost all situations the designer should give consideration to both these aspects of lighting.

Lighting affects safety, task performance and the visual environment by changing the extent to which, and the manner in which, different elements of the interior are revealed. Safety is ensured by making any hazards visible. Task performance is facilitated by making the relevant details of the task easy to see. Different visual environments can be created by changing the relative emphasis given to the various objects and surfaces in an interior. Different aspects of lighting influence the appearance of the elements in an interior in different ways.

This part of the *Code* discusses the influence of each important aspect of lighting separately. However, it should always be remembered that lighting design involves integrating the various aspects of lighting into a unity appropriate to the design objectives. This process is discussed in Part 4.

Figure 1.1   Lighting for safety

Figure 1.2   Lighting for task performance (reproduced with kind permission of Muirhead Vactric Components Ltd)

Figure 1.3   Lighting the visual environment (Imperial War Museum, reproduced with kind permission of Nicholas Gentilli)

1.2   Daylight and electric light

1.2.1   General

People prefer a room with daylight to one that is windowless, unless the function of the room makes this impracticable. Few buildings are in fact windowless but it is also true that in the majority of present-day buildings some of the electric lighting is in continuous use during daytime hours. For efficient use of energy and for lighting of high quality, the electric lighting and the daylighting should be complementary (Figure 1.4).

The use of daylight with good electric lighting controls can lead to a significant saving in the primary energy used by a building to national advantage and to the benefit of the environment and building users.

A window or rooflight may serve one or more of three main visual purposes: to provide a view, to increase the general brightness of a room, and to provide illumination for task performance. These three functions must be considered separately by the designer. A window or electrical installation which serves one purpose well may not be adequate for another. For instance, an opening which provides a good view might give good task lighting but not enhance the general appearance of the room.

Recommendations for daylighting and supplementary electric lighting are given in *BS 8206* Part 2[1].

1.2.2   Providing a view

A room which does not have a view to the outside, where this could reasonably be expected, will be considered unsatisfactory by its users. Unless an activity requires the exclusion of daylight, a view should be provided. Sometimes a view is essential for security or supervision; but all occupants of a building should have the opportunity for the refreshment and relaxation offered by a change of scene and focus. Even a limited view to the outside is valuable. If

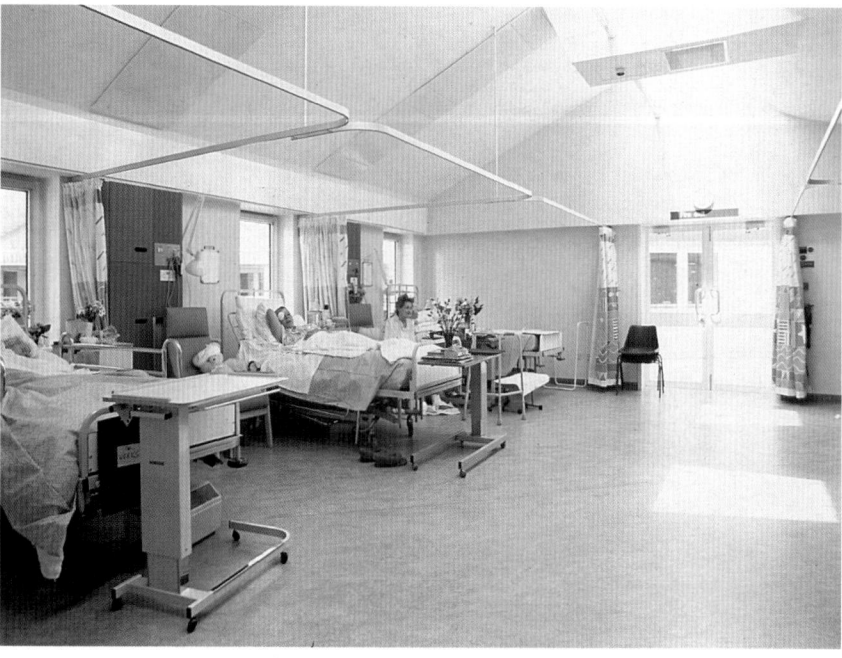

Figure 1.4   Integration of daylight and electric lighting

this is not possible, an internal view possessing some of the qualities of an outdoor view could be available, into an atrium, for example. Sometimes a view into a room is required, for display or for security. More often there is a need for privacy, and this must be taken into account when windows are planned for an external view.

The design of windows for view is covered in the CIBSE Applications Manual: *Window design*[2].

1.2.3   Increasing general room brightness

A user's perception of the character of a room is related to the brightness and colour of all the visible surfaces, inside and outside. The general lighting in a room is a separate consideration from the task illumination but it is as important. It can be achieved by using daylight or electric light, or both, but the natural variation of daylight is valuable. The light from a side window, in particular, enhances the architectural modelling of a room, but its variation with time gives information about the weather and the time of day.

The character of a naturally-lit room is often considered valuable by users. A room can appear daylit even though the principal illumination on the working plane is from electric sources. Contrast between inside and outside is reduced when there is a high level of diffuse daylight internally and when light from luminaires falls on the walls and ceiling. The detailed design of the window frames or surrounds is also important.

Provided that it does not cause thermal or visual discomfort, or deterioration of materials, direct sunlight is appreciated by users. It is especially welcomed in habitable rooms used for long periods during the day and in buildings, such as those used by the elderly, where occupants have little direct contact with the outside. Good control of the sunlight is, however, essential, particularly in working interiors. Generally, sunlight should not fall on visual tasks or directly on people at work. Criteria of window size to achieve good general lighting are given in section 2.3. Direct sunlight is covered in detail in the CIBSE Applications Manual: *Window design*[2].

1.2.4   Illumination for task performance

When there are visual tasks to be carried out, the principles of lighting design using daylight are the same as those for electric lighting: it is necessary both to achieve a given quantity of illumination and to take account of the circumstances that determine its quality. Daylight has particular characteristics as a task illuminant:

(a) A constant illuminance on the task cannot be maintained. When the sky becomes brighter, the interior illuminance increases and, although control is possible with louvres, blinds and other methods, fluctuations cannot be avoided. Conversely, in poor weather and at the end of the working day, daylighting may need to be supplemented with electric lighting.

(b) Windows, acting as large diffuse light sources to the side of a worker, give excellent three-dimensional modelling. Rooflights which give a greater downward lighting component give similar modelling to large ceiling-mounted luminaires.

(c) The spectral distribution of daylight varies significantly during the course of a day, but the colour rendering is usually considered to be excellent.

(d) When tasks are seen in the same field of view as the bright sky, performance can be impaired by disability glare. If surfaces are placed so that the view of the window is mirrored in them (as when pictures are on a wall which faces a window), visibility can be impaired by the glossy reflections.

The use of windows to provide task lighting in working interiors is economically valuable in many buildings, but the success is dependent on good control of the electric lighting. This is described in sections 3.4 and 4.4.4.

1.3 Lighting levels

The human eye can only perceive surfaces, objects and people through light which is emitted from them. Surface characteristics, reflection factors and the quantity and quality of light determine the appearance of the environment.

These variables create unlimited permutations between the physical elements and the light which strikes them. Nevertheless, when dealing with an interior, it is useful to quantify the luminous flux received per unit of area i.e. the illuminance measured in lumens per square metre or lux. The illuminance can be specified and measured as planar, scalar, cylindrical and vector illuminance. These are explained elsewhere in this *Code* (sections 5.2 and 5.3). The commonly used planar illuminance relates to tasks which lie in a horizontal, inclined or vertical plane. The plane within which the task is seen is called the reference plane. It is assumed that many critical tasks take place on the flat surface of a desk or bench and this establishes a horizontal reference plane at the height of the desk or bench tops. This is referred to as the working plane.

This *Code* deals principally with recommendations relating to the task(s) and requires that each task is correctly illuminated and that extreme variation is avoided both across the task and within the space. For the sake of convenience the recommendations are often applied to the entire working plane, but the designer should be aware of those many tasks which do not lie on the horizontal plane and therefore require separate consideration (see section 1.3.2 and Figures 1.8(a) and (b)).

Measures of illuminance are important because they influence three key aspects of the visual environment.

1.3.1 Task performance

The ability to see degrees of detail is substantially determined by size, contrast and the viewer's vision. Improvement to lighting quantity and quality makes an important contribution to improved visual performance. The effect of lighting on task performance depends on the size of the critical details of the task and on the contrast with their background (Figure 1.5). Figure 1.6 shows the effect of illuminance on the performance of tasks carried out under laboratory conditions. Three important points should be noted:

— Increasing the illuminance on the task produces an increase in performance following a law of diminishing returns.

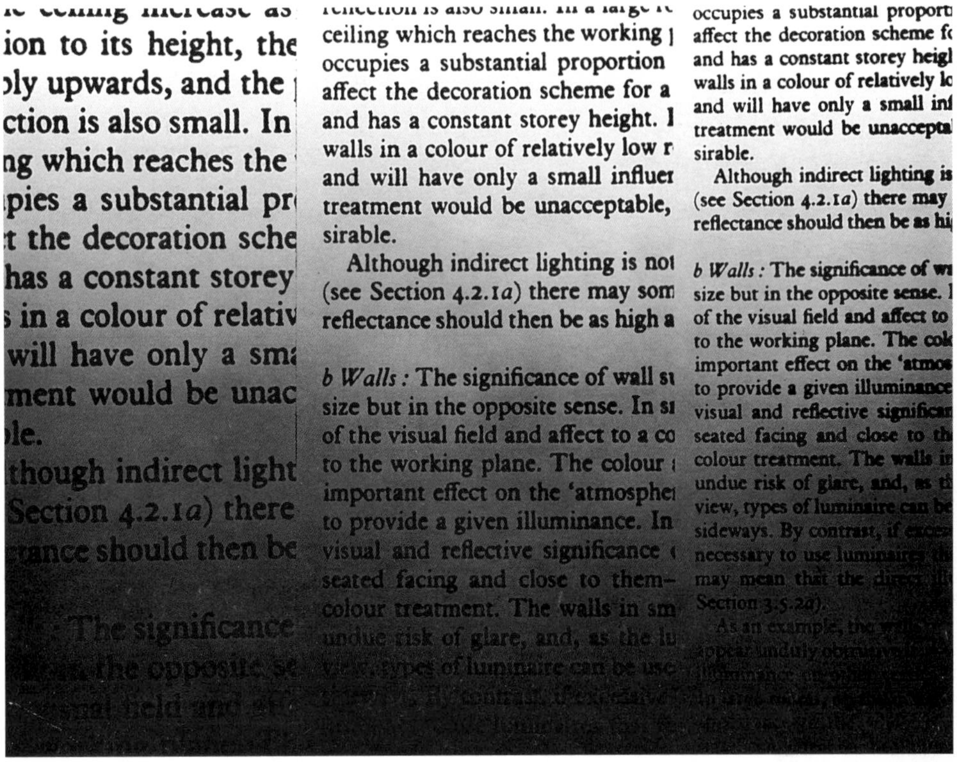

Figure 1.5   Effect of varying size and contrast of task details on ease of reading

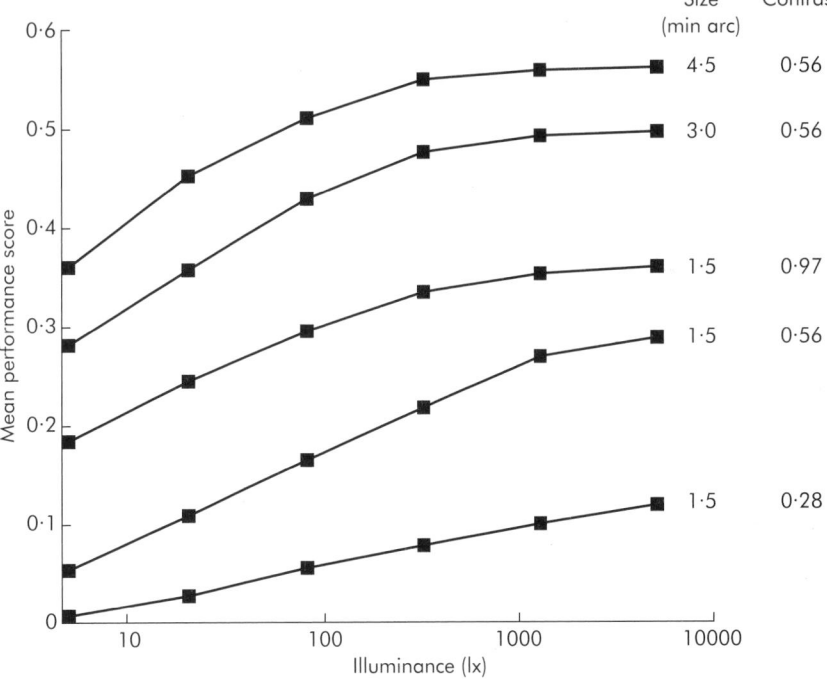

Figure 1.6   Mean performance scores for Landolt ring charts[3]

— The illuminance at which performance levels off is dependent on the visual difficulty of the task, i.e. the smaller the size and the less the contrast of the task the higher the illuminance at which performance saturates.

— Although increasing illuminance can increase task performance, it is not possible to bring a difficult visual task to the same level of performance as an easy visual task simply by increasing the illuminance.

In principle these effects occur for all tasks, although the exact relationship between the illuminance on the task and the performance achieved will vary with the nature of the task. Another aspect is the extent to which the visual part of the task determines the overall performance. Where there is only a small visual component, as in audio typing, the influence of illuminance on overall task performance is likely to be small but where the visual component is a major element of the complete task, as in copy typing, the illuminance provided will have a greater influence.

A model of visual performance based on reaction times is given in section 5.6. This can be used to examine the effect of changes in illuminance on task performance for tasks of different size and contrast.

1.3.2 Satisfaction

Subjective response to a space depends on more than task illuminance and the vocabulary which expresses such responses includes 'bright', 'dull', 'gloomy', 'under-lit' and 'well lit'. The spatial distribution of light, particularly on vertical surfaces, determines these reactions and influences adaptation (see section 1.4.6) which affects visual performance. The ratios between task, wall and ceiling luminances have a strong influence on satisfaction (see sections 2.4.4–2.4.5)[4].

Figure 1.7 shows mean assessments of the quality of lighting obtained in an office lit uniformly by a regular array of luminaires. Increasing the illuminance on the plane of the desk increases the perceived quality of the lighting until it saturates at about 800 lux. This demonstrates the importance of the illuminance as one factor in determining people's satisfaction with an interior.

There is no sharp cut-off where lighting conditions move from 'bad' to 'good'. Figure 1.7, like Figure 1.6, shows that as illuminance increases from a low level there is initially a rapid improvement, but as illuminance continues to increase, the im-

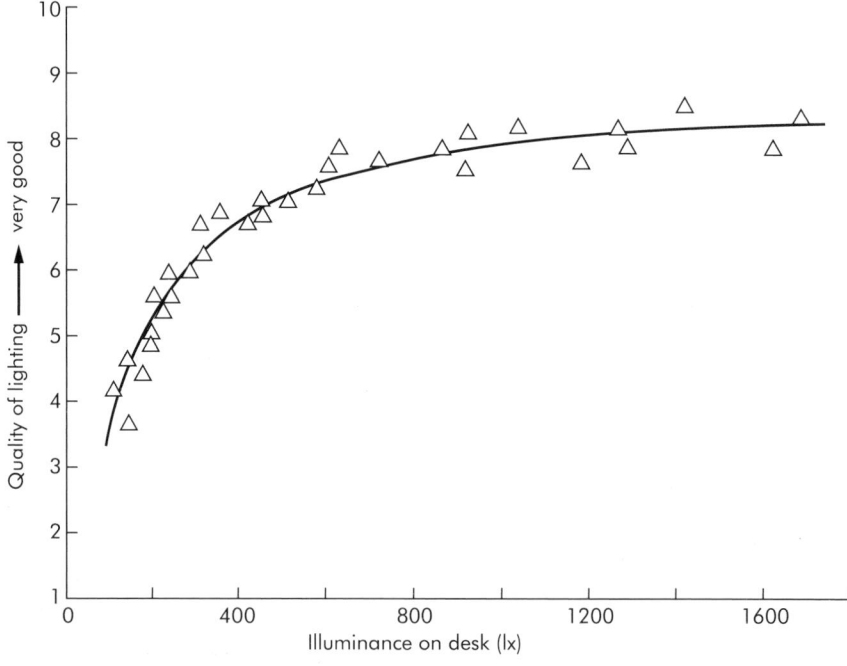

Figure 1.7 Mean assessment of quality of lighting[5]

Figure 1.8(a)   Not all working planes are horizontal: vertical task lighting in an industrial application

Figure 1.8(b)   Not all working planes are horizontal: vertical task lighting in a supermarket

provement becomes smaller, until eventually it ceases altogether. So, identifying a suitable illuminance for an interior is a matter of judgement. The recommended 'standard maintained illuminance' on an appropriate plane (Figure 1.8(a) and (b)) for each specific application is given in section 2.6.4. This is converted to the 'design maintained illuminance' by referring to Figure 2.3 (page 43) and the associated notes in section 2.6.3.1.

1.3.3   Appearance

Any space can be revealed in a variety of ways and the degree of visual stimulus will depend on the use(s) of the space. Some lighting, especially in non-working environments, will not have a direct, task-related, function. Such lighting will express the architecture, create appropriate mood, provide emphasis and establish visual coherence. Integrating these non-functional lighting elements within the total lighting design and deciding how to interpret the architecture, requires the designer to move beyond pure engineering considerations, taking account of form, colour, texture, and architectural intent. To light a space in a manner which is sympathetic to changes in daylight, function and mood will require the designer to anticipate such changes and develop an appropriate lighting solution.

1.4   Variation in lighting

1.4.1   Illuminance variation: definition

When applied to lighting, 'variation' can be in either time or space and can have at least three meanings:

(a) Short term variation occurs either naturally with daylight or with controllable lighting equipment which may change automatically, prompted by changes in daylighting in response to various signals or user manual control.

(b) Long term variation which occurs as a result of light loss as lamps age and dirt accumulates over a period of months. Some modern lighting control equipment can counteract this effect. (See section 4.4.4.1.)

(c) Spatial variation means the uniformity or diversity of illuminance over the task and room surfaces throughout an interior space. This can also include the gradation of light revealing texture or the form of objects.

Topics related to (a) and (b) are discussed in Parts 3 and 4 of this *Code*. Spatial variation will be discussed here in more detail with the terms 'uniformity' related to variation in illuminance over the task area and 'diversity' to changes throughout the interior.

1.4.2   Spatial variation of illuminance in working locations

Variation of illuminance can be considered over two areas: on and around the visual task itself and over the whole interior. The task area may be considered as the area containing those details and objects necessary for the performance of the given activity and includes the immediate surround, or background, to the details or objects. Excessive rates of change of illuminance over the task area can be distracting and cause changes in visual adaptation across the task which will reduce visual performance. Excessive variations of illuminance within an interior may affect comfort levels and visual performance by causing transient adaptation problems. These problems are partly addressed by other recommendations such as those governing the wall-to-task and ceiling-to-task illuminance ratios, and the surface reflectance recommendations (see sections 2.4.4–2.4.5). Excessive variation in horizontal illuminance will also contribute to these problems and should be avoided (see section 2.4.3).

General lighting installations lit by ceiling-mounted arrays of luminaires will usually provide acceptable uniformity conditions over the task areas if luminaires are installed within their recommended spacing-to-height ratios as published by lighting manufacturers (see sections 3.3.2 and 4.5.3.4).

Further information on the effects of obstructions and illuminance variation when using local or localised lighting will be found in sections 2.4.3, 4.5.4 and 5.3.

1.4.3   Illuminance variation in non-task locations

There are many lighting applications which do not demand the performance of an exacting visual task for long periods. In public and private areas the lighting design may be required to entertain and stimulate those using the space. In other areas leisure, relaxation or even contemplation may be required. To achieve this the lighting designer may be justified in introducing more or less variation. This approach is discussed further in sections 1.4.6 and 2.4.8.

Figure 1.9(a)   Luminance is an objective quantity

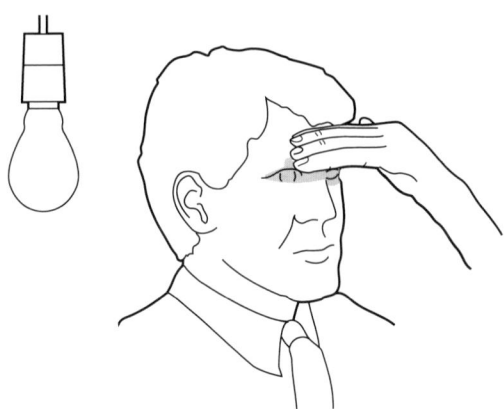

Figure 1.9(b)   Brightness is a subjective experience

1.4.4   Illuminance, luminance and brightness

The calculation and measurement of the amount of luminous flux (lumens) per unit area reaching various surfaces is the basis of most lighting design. This is primarily because illuminance is relatively simple to calculate and measure. The disadvantage is that the visual system responds physiologically to the luminance distribution in the field of view, but does not perceive the image in this way. The viewer is able to interpret the scene by differentiating between surface colour, surface reflectance and illumination. This process involves the phenomena known as brightness and colour constancy[6]. For example, if a brown wall is illuminated from one side resulting in a strong gradation of luminance across the wall it will still be perceived as a wall of constant colour and reflectance with a variation in illuminance across it. If constancy did not apply, the colour of the wall would appear to change.

The quantity, luminance, depends on both the illuminance and the reflectance of the surface. Illuminance and luminance are both objective quantities but neither relate directly to the subjective response to the 'brightness' which is what the eye and brain 'see' (see Figure 1.9(a) and (b)).

Luminance, however, provides an important objective link between the illuminance provided and the apparent brightness of the scene.

1.4.5   Luminance in the visual field

The lighting system will produce patterns of luminance over the task, the immediate surroundings and the peripheral field of view. For reasons of visual satisfaction, comfort and performance, the luminances within the visual field need to be correctly balanced. Too low a luminance surrounding a critical visual task, involving high reflectance white paper, can produce uncomfortable viewing conditions. Low reflectance office desk tops can certainly give rise to this problem (see section 2.4.5.3). Similar poor viewing conditions can result from the reverse situation of too high a luminance alongside the visual task, when for example the use of a high reflectance wall finish in an art gallery reduces the detail that can be seen in a dark coloured painting.

The lumen method (see section 4.5.3) of design provides the average horizontal plane illuminance at the floor or working plane and can be extended to give average illuminance values over the walls and ceiling. Examples of illuminance ratios between the task and the walls or ceiling are given in section 2.4.4 for typical office workplace lighting. However, when lighting the architectural structure is the main design objective, these illuminance ratios need not apply. The average illuminance can be converted to average luminance values by applying the mean reflectance of the main room surfaces. This gives no detail of the luminance pattern in the field of view. Point by point computation methods (sections 4.5.5 and 5.13) with data on the reflectance characteristics of all relevant surfaces and objects (section 5.7) can be used to predict the more detailed and complex luminance pattern. To interpret these results in terms of the visual appearance produced, account must be taken of the visual mechanism known as adaptation.

1.4.6 Adaptation

The subjective visual appearance will depend upon adaptation which is governed by the luminances of the various elements within the field of view, the sizes of the areas involved and their location with respect to the lines of sight of observers. Levels of adaptation continually change as the eyes move.

The eye can adapt to a wide range of lighting conditions. For example, headlines in a newspaper can be read under moonlight, providing some 0.2 lux, or by day where the illuminance may be of the order of 100 000 lux. However, the eye cannot adapt to the whole of this range at one time. At night a dark-adapted viewer will be dazzled by the headlights of an on-coming car, whereas on a sunny day these lights will be barely noticeable. Inside a room daylit by large windows, conditions might allow all objects and surfaces to be viewed comfortably, but looking into the room from the outside, when adapted to the bright daylight conditions, the windows will appear black and no internal objects or surfaces will be visible.

Our eyes are drawn to the brightest part of a scene. Within work areas, therefore, higher luminance values usually occur at the task areas, but if this is taken to extremes, brightness constancy could break down. This can be avoided by providing adequate illuminance with good colour rendering and glare control. Sharp shadows, sudden large changes in luminance and excessively bright and frequent highlights should be avoided.

With a uniform electric lighting system and medium to high reflectances of the main surfaces of an interior, the range of luminance will usually be satisfactory. Light ceilings and floors will ensure a high proportion of inter-reflected light and will avoid dark corners.

Reflectance of room surfaces strongly affects the perceived atmosphere in the room. In section 2.4.5 typical ranges of reflectance are given for major room surfaces.

In comparison with electric lighting, the luminance range produced by sunlight and daylight in an interior will vary enormously. The ranges of luminance in an interior will remain relatively constant for overcast daylight conditions, despite changes in the external illumination, but this will not be the case with sunlight penetration. Here control will be needed, particularly in working areas, because of adaptation problems that can occur.

Within many working interiors there will be areas intended for circulation or relaxation. It may be desirable here to provide a wider range of luminance values for variety and visual stimulation. Some specular reflections and a limited amount of sparkle would be welcomed from sunlight or display lighting.

1.5 Glare

Glare occurs whenever one part of an interior is much brighter than the general brightness in the interior. The most common sources of excessive brightness are luminaires and windows, seen directly or by reflection. Glare can have two effects. It can impair vision, in which case it is called disability glare (Figure 1.10) and it can cause discomfort, in which case it is called discomfort glare (Figure 1.11). Disability glare and discomfort glare can occur simultaneously or separately.

Figure 1.10   Disability glare from bright sky in front of VDT operator makes the screen difficult to read

Figure 1.11   Discomfort glare from bright luminaire

Figure 1.12(a) Effect of veiling reflections from electric lighting on VDT screen

Figure 1.12(b) VDT screen without veiling reflections

1.5.1 Disability glare

Disability glare is most likely to occur when there is an area close to the line of sight which has a much higher luminance than the object of regard. Then, scattering of light in the eye and changes in local adaptation can cause a reduction in the contrast of the object. This reduction in contrast may be sufficient to make important details invisible and hence may influence task performance. Alternatively, if the source of high luminance is viewed directly, noticeable after-images may be created. The most common sources of disability glare indoors are the sun and sky seen through windows (Figure 1.10) and electric light sources seen directly or by reflection (Figure 1.12(a)). Care should be taken to avoid disability glare in interiors by providing some method of screening windows and avoiding the use of highly specular surfaces. A formula which can be used to estimate the effect of disability glare on contrast is given in section 5.4.1.

1.5.2 Discomfort glare from electric lighting

The discomfort experienced when some elements of an interior have a much higher luminance than others can be immediate but sometimes may only become evident after prolonged exposure. The degree of discomfort experienced will depend on the luminance and size of the glare source, the luminance of the background against which it is seen and the position of the glare source relative to the line of sight. A high source luminance, large source area, low background luminance and a position close to the line of sight all increase discomfort glare. Unfortunately most of the variables available to the designer alter more than one factor. For example, changing the luminaire to reduce the source luminance may also reduce the background luminance. These factors could counteract each other, resulting in no reduction of discomfort glare. However, as a general rule, discomfort glare can be avoided by the choice of

Figure 1.13 Effect of veiling reflections from daylight

luminaire layout and orientation, and the use of high reflectance surfaces for the ceiling and upper walls. In any proposed lighting installation the likelihood of discomfort glare being experienced can be estimated by calculating the glare index (GI) (see sections 4.5.6 and 5.4.2). Recommended limiting glare indices for specific applications are given in section 2.6.4 and for luminous ceilings and indirect lighting installations maximum luminances are given in section 2.4.5.1.

1.5.3   Discomfort glare from windows

Severe visual discomfort arises when a person is looking through a window in the direction of the sun or when direct sunlight falls on a light-coloured surface in the immediate field of view. In such circumstances there may also be thermal discomfort. Solar control is essential in most buildings: this may be in the design of the building's overall form and orientation, or in the use of external screens and louvres, glass of low transmittance, or internal blinds and curtains. All of these reduce the total amount of light entering a room and this must be considered by the lighting designer.

Glare can also arise when an overcast sky is viewed through a window. It may be reduced by solar control devices or by other means of decreasing the contrast between the interior and the view of the sky. These include the use of splayed window reveals to give areas of intermediate brightness, by ensuring that the window wall is light-coloured, and by using electric lighting to increase the luminance of the window wall.

1.5.4   Veiling reflections

Veiling reflections are high luminance reflections which overlay the detail of the task (Figure 1.13). Such reflections may be sharp-edged or vague in outline, but regardless of form they may affect task performance and cause discomfort. Task performance will be affected because veiling reflections usually reduce the contrast of a task, making task details difficult to see and may give rise to discomfort. Two conditions have to be met before veiling reflections occur:

— part of the task, task detail or background, or both, has to be glossy to some degree

— part of the interior, called the 'offending zone' (see section 5.5.2.3), which specularly reflects towards the observer has to have a high luminance.

The most common sources of veiling reflections are windows and luminaires. Generally applicable methods of avoiding veiling reflections are to use matt materials in task areas, to arrange the geometry of the viewing situation so that the luminance of the offending zone is low or reduce the luminance by, for example, using curtains or blinds on windows.

The magnitude of the veiling reflections occurring on a flat task at a particular position can be quantified by the contrast rendering factor. Details of this quantity are given in section 5.5.

It should be noted that although veiling reflections are usually detrimental to task performance there are some circumstances in which they are useful. Lighting Guide *LG1*[7] contains examples of the use of high luminance reflections in inspection lighting.

1.6   Directional qualities and modelling

The direction and distribution of light within a space substantially influence the perception of the space as well as objects or persons within it. Decisions which determine such perception relate partly to the provision of desirable illuminance values and partly to the subjective issues of architectural interpretation, style and visual emphasis. Good lighting design results both from an appreciation of the nature and qualities of the surfaces upon which light falls and of the methods of providing such light. The visual characteristics of surfaces and sources of light are interrelated and interdependent. The appearance of a surface or object will depend on the following:

(a) Its colour and reflectance and whether it is specular or diffuse, smooth or textured, flat or curved. All surfaces reflect some portion of the light falling on them and so become sources of light. Depending on their degree of specularity, texture and shape, their appearance will also vary with the direction of view.

(b) The layout and orientation of luminaires and sources of reflected light. Single sources of relatively small size will produce harsh modelling, the effect becoming softer as the number and size of the sources increase. The predominant direction of light has a fundamental effect on appearance; lighting from above provides a distinct character that is totally different to that achieved by lighting from the side or lower angles. In addition, colour differences between sources of light of various distributions and orientation strongly influence the lit appearance of spaces, surfaces and objects. With so many variables, luminance patterns become too complex to predict in detail.

This element of unpredictability is generally acceptable, or even desirable, providing that the basic rules of good lighting practice are observed, such as the limitation of extremes of glare, contrast and veiling reflection. The importance of modelling is obvious for retail display, exhibition work and the creation of mood. However, any lighting installation which fails to create appropriate degrees of modelling will provide visual results which are perceived as bland and monotonous. Virtually all environments can benefit from a lighting approach which considers the question of direction and the resulting revelation of architectural form, texture and facial modelling. The designer must decide where in the range from harsh or dramatic to soft or subtle modelling the design aim should be set. Further information is given on specification of modelling in section 2.4.8 and modelling design in section 4.4.3.3.

1.6.1 Revealing form

The revelation of the form of an object or structure is determined by the relationship of the incident angle and intensity of light to the surface in question, the position of the viewer relative to the surface and the nature or composition of the surface.

Light reveals surfaces by three basic methods: emission, silhouette and reflection. Figures 1.14(a)–(e) show an identical form revealed by these methods. Revelation by emission (Figure 1.14(a)) or silhouette (Figure 1.14(b) exposes little or none of the three-dimensional quality of the form. However, the white vase (Figure 1.14(c)) is dramatically revealed as three-dimensional by the gradation of reflected light over its surface. The same visual message is provided by the highlight on the surface of the glossy black vase (Figure 1.14(d)). The vase (Figure 1.14(e)) is lit to provide a balanced rendering of the form by the use of a strong rear 'key' light and a less intense frontal 'fill' light.

The relationship between the intensity of strongly directional, emphatic lighting and the ambient or general illuminance level within a space is critical. In an otherwise dark space, a relatively low intensity of directional light will strongly reveal an object whilst the same degree of emphasis in a brightly lit space will require considerably greater intensity from the directional highlighting. Subtle and pleasant modelling is usually favoured in general working areas and public spaces where more extreme ratios, especially when combined with unusual angles of directional light, will produce an increasingly dramatic and distorted effect on faces. However, this may prove appropriate for other circumstances such as architectural detailing, sculpture, museum artefacts and some types of retail display (see section 2.4.8).

Since much electric lighting emanates from ceiling locations it is important to consider the relationship between predominantly vertical downlighting and light reflected from the surrounding walls and floor. Insufficient reflected light will result in harsh facial shadowing. The lighting designer should consider the reflection factor of the walls and their illuminance to ensure a satisfactory balance.

1.6.2 Revealing texture

The revelation of the texture of a material can have both aesthetic and functional value. Figure 1.15 shows an example of lighting used to reveal surface texture. By lighting at oblique angles, the texture of the shuttered concrete is revealed as an architectural feature of the building. The deliberate use of a non-uniform luminance pattern provides greater visual impact without losing structural coherence. If the spotlights had been directed at near right angles to

Figure 1.14(a)

Figure 1.14(b)

Figure 1.14(c)

Figure 1.14(d)

Figure 1.14(e)

Figure 1.14 Appearance of identically shaped vase changes depending on its surface finish and lighting set-up: (a) frosted glass vase lit internally from below to give subtle rendering of the form; (b) matt black vase silhouetted against the lighted background appears only as a two-dimensional shape (note that a highlight has been added immediately behind the vase in (b) and (d) to prevent the base of vase merging with the dark surface); (c) matt white vase lit from front and right at about 45° with backlighting added from left; (d) same front and back lighting positions used as in (c) but smaller narrow beam spotlights have been used to produce highlights in the glossy black finish (these provide the three-dimensional information which is lacking, for example, in (b)); (e) positions of light sources are again unchanged with matt white vase but, compared with (c), intensity of backlight has been doubled and a lower intensity, diffused front lighting has been used.

the surfaces, or diffused lighting had been used, the interior would have lost vitality and interest.

The texture can be suppressed or expressed by applying light at an appropriate angle. The decision to reveal the texture or not is one related to style and architectural expression. The functional revelation of texture is illustrated in Figure 1.16 which shows the effect of light at glancing angles over fabric in order to detect a pulled thread.

Not all revelation of texture is desirable. A common problem arises with uplighting on badly finished ceiling surfaces which reveals unwanted 'texture' or a degree of unevenness which other angles of light would not reveal. Shadows and highlights can reveal too much textural detail which can result in a reduction of task visibility; the degree to which texture is revealed should therefore be related to the particular requirements of the task.

1.6.3 Display lighting

The preceding comments about the directional qualities of lighting are particularly relevant to display lighting techniques. Revelation of form, dimension and texture are objectives which are invariably encountered in retail and other forms of display work. Additionally the question of colour appearance and colour rendering is critical. Figure 1.17 illustrates some of the basic techniques for revealing a three-dimensional model to best effect when viewed from one angle. The illustration shows six basic approaches and the associated optimum incident lighting angles. In practice numerous combinations of these can be used to achieve the required balance of emphasis and revelation (see section 2.4.8).

1.7 Surfaces

The effect a lighting installation creates in an interior is strongly influenced by the properties of the major room surfaces. For this

Figure 1.15 Lighting to reveal texture of shuttered concrete

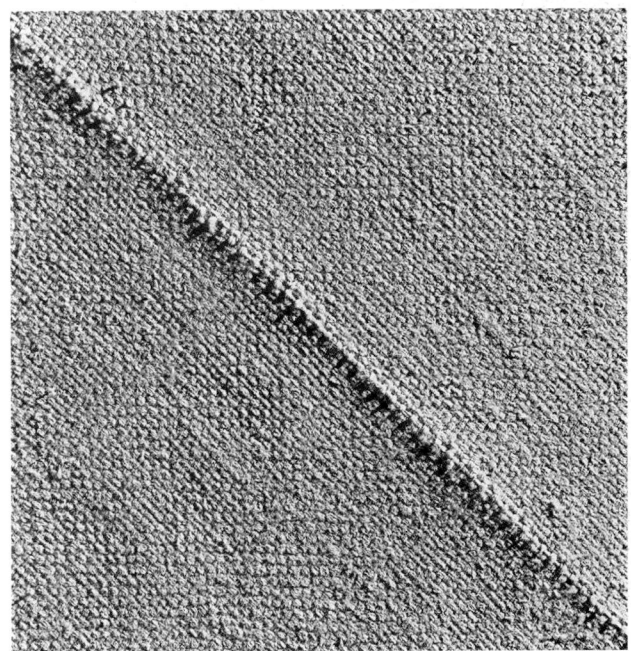

Figure 1.16 Directional lighting indicating pulled thread in material

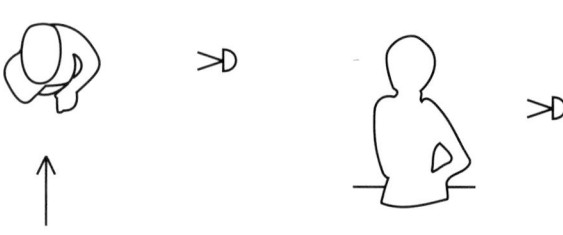

Figure 1.17(a)   Low-level side lighting from the right of the picture

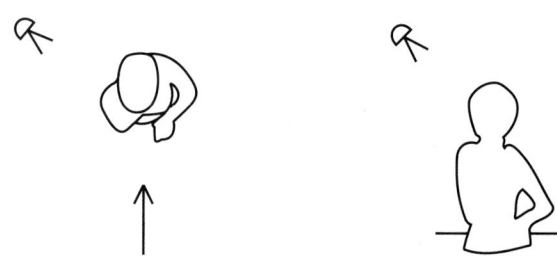

Figure 1.17(b)   High level side lighting from the left at approximately 45°

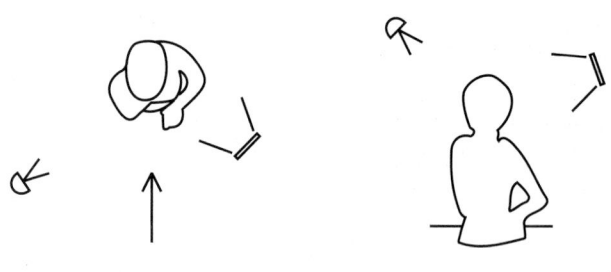

Figure 1.17(c)   Combination of high intensity 'key' lighting from the front and left of the picture at about 40° and a diffused 'fill' light of lower intensity from the right

Figure 1.17   Examples of the modelling effects that can be produced by some basic display lighting techniques. These illustrations are limited to one viewing direction and the lighting of the background is unchanged. The lighting arrangement is indicated by the plan and elevation diagrams with each picture.

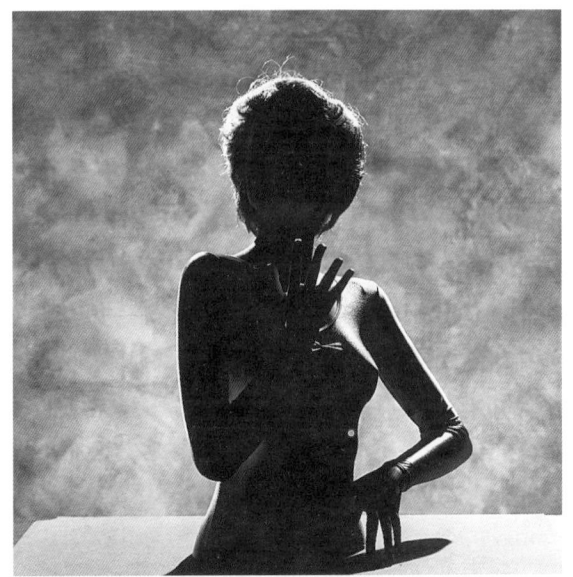

Figure 1.17(d)   'Backlighting' from above and slightly to the right

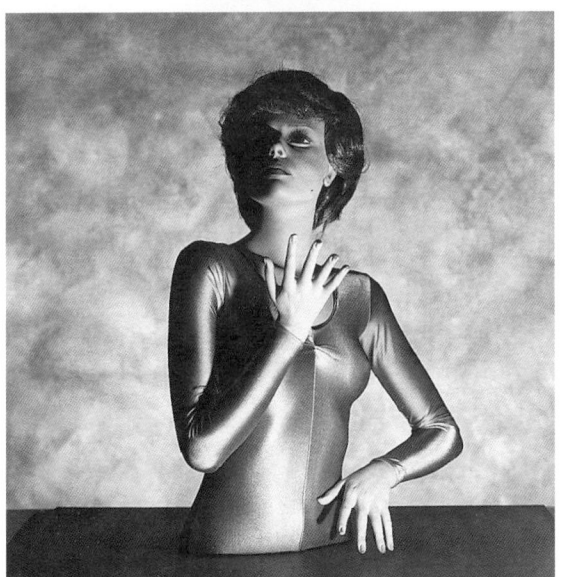

FIgure 1.17(e)   Front lighting at a low angle from the right

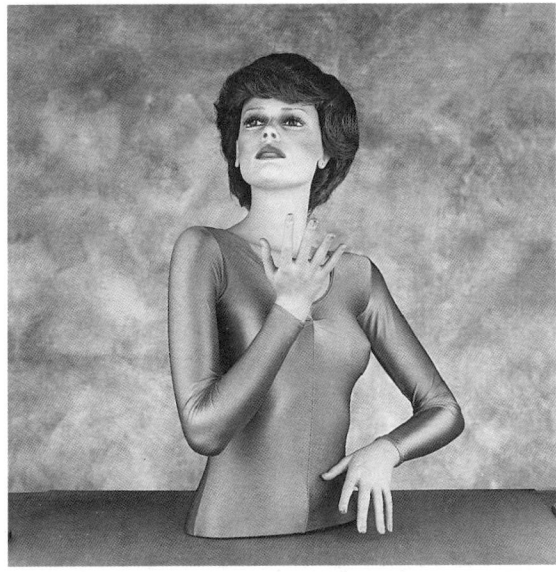

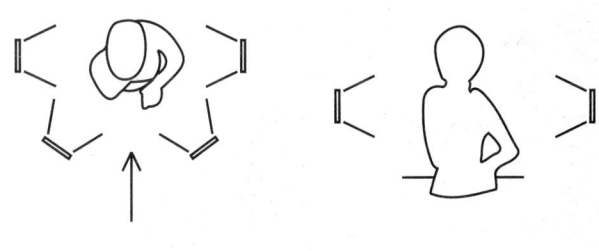

Figure 1.17(f)   Diffused lighting from the front and sides

reason, if for no other, the lighting designer should always attempt to identify the proposed surface finishes early in the design process. The main properties of the room surfaces which are relevant to the appearance of the space are their reflectance and their colour.

1.7.1   Surface reflectances

For interiors lit from the ceiling, the significance of the ceiling reflectance increases as the room area increases. In small rooms the ceiling is not conspicuous and its contribution to the illuminance on the working plane is usually small. In a large room the contribution of light reflected from the ceiling to the total illuminance on the working plane is usually large and the ceiling occupies a substantial proportion of the visual field. Achieving an acceptable reflectance for the ceiling cavity requires a white or near-white ceiling. In small rooms a low reflectance ceiling may be acceptable, although if the room is predominantly lit by daylight from side windows the room may appear gloomy if too low a reflectance is chosen. Where indirect lighting is used a white or near-white ceiling is essential, regardless of room size.

Wall reflectance is usually unimportant to the lighting of a large room except for positions close to the wall. If low wall reflectances are used the illuminance in the adjacent areas may be too low. In small rooms wall reflectance is always important. High wall reflectances will enhance the illuminance on the working plane and increase the inter-reflected component of the lighting, thereby improving uniformity. The importance of having a high wall reflectance is increased when the room is predominantly lit by daylight from side windows. In all rooms, unless a high reflectance finish is applied to the window wall, the luminance difference between the window wall and the daytime view through the window may be excessive and uncomfortable.

All this suggests that a high reflectance finish to walls is highly desirable. However, the use of high reflectance wall finishes should be treated with caution. Large areas of high reflectance may compete for attention with the task areas and may lead to eyestrain and feelings of discomfort. Further, if the high reflectance surfaces are produced using gloss paint, reflected glare is likely to occur. The effective reflectance of the wall finish will be reduced by windows, unless light coloured blinds or curtains are used. Dark wall hangings, cupboards or other equipment, above the working plane, will also reduce the effective wall reflectance. Where the perception of people's faces is important, e.g. lecture theatres and conference rooms, the brightness of the walls needs to be controlled as these form the background against which people are seen.

Dark floor cavities will tend to make ceilings and walls look underlit, especially when daylight from side windows is used, but using very light floors tends to create a maintenance problem. Recommendations for room surface reflectance are given in section 2.4.5 and the effect on installed load is discussed in sections 2.5 and 4.5.3.3.

1.7.2   Surface colours

Surface colour can be classified by the use of a colour system. This allows colour to be specified unambiguously. For the purposes of lighting design and calculation, information on the reflectance of surface colours is required. Several colour systems exist, some of which can be used to estimate reflectance. Further information on the most commonly used systems is given in section 5.7 together with Table 5.8 and 5.9 (pages 215–217) of approximate reflectances for colours and typical building materials and finishes. In the Munsell system for example, each colour is specified by three quantities: hue, value, and chroma. Hue describes whether a colour is basically red, yellow, green, blue, purple etc. Value describes the lightness of the colour and is related to its reflectance. Chroma describes the strength of the colour. This classification forms a convenient basis on which to discuss the effects of room surface colour on the appearance of space.

By choosing different values for different components of the interior it is possible to dramatise or to buffer the pattern of light and shade created by the lighting. An example of this is the use of a high reflectance (high value) wall opposite a window wall.

By choosing colours of different chromas it is possible to create a pattern of emphasis. Strong emphasis requires strong chromas but their use calls for caution. An area of awkward shape, which might pass unnoticed at weak chroma, can looked unsightly at strong chroma. Also a small area of strong chroma might be stimulating but the same chroma over a large area could be overpowering.

The selection of hue is partly a matter of fashion and partly a matter of emotion. By choosing a predominant hue for a space it is possible to create a 'cool' or a 'warm', a 'restful' or an 'active' atmosphere. Figures 1.18 and 1.19 illustrate the use of surface colours in public and commercial interiors[8]. The children's room in the library in Figure 1.18 uses upholstery in strong primary colours to provide a vibrant and stimulating atmosphere. This contrasts with the use of cooler blues and greens in the office in Figure 1.19, where a calmer and more sophisticated ambience is required.

All rooms will have a mixture of colours. This fact raises the question of colour harmony. There are a number of so-called rules of colour harmony which are little understood. However, it is

Figure 1.18   Use of colour to enhance the appearance of an interior: children's play area

Figure 1.19   Use of colour to enhance the appearance of an interior: office

widely believed that the main variable influencing pleasant colour harmonies is the difference in value for the two colours compared; the greater the difference in value the greater the chances of achieving a pleasant colour combination. The effect of chroma differences is thought to be similar, combinations of colours with large differences in chroma tending to be pleasant. As for hue differences, there is not believed to be any consistent effect, all the same hues, closely related hues, or complementary hues, being capable of creating either pleasant or unpleasant colour combinations.

These observations suggest that when selecting colours for an interior the first aspect to consider is the value of colours, then the chroma and finally the hue. However, once the pattern of light, shade and emphasis has been established by the choice of the value and chroma for different surfaces, the range of hues that are available may be limited. For example, if a given surface is to have both strong chroma and high value, then it must inevitably have a yellowish hue. Conversely, when a surface is required to have low value and strong chroma, a colour from the red to blue part of the hue circle must be used. Once the level of chroma is reduced from a high level the whole range of colours is available.

The light reflected from a surface of strong chroma will be coloured and may influence the colour of other surfaces. The most common situation where this is seen is the case of a floor covering of strong chroma lit by a lighting installation which does not light the ceiling directly. In this situation, the ceiling will mainly be lit by light reflected from the floor which will tend to colour the ceiling.

1.7.3   Object colours

The colours of objects within an interior can have a marked effect on the appearance of the space. In choosing a combination of colours for both the surfaces and equipment within a space it is preferable if the elements can be considered as a whole so that a degree of visual co-ordination can be achieved. The actual choice of a combination of colours to produce a co-ordinated colour scheme is probably one of the most elusive design tasks and at present there is no single widely accepted design procedure.

There are limitations to the choice of colours of some objects within the space. These arise from the use of colour for the coding of services and to indicate potential hazards. The use of colour for the coding of services is governed by *BS 1710*[9] and should be undertaken sparingly with emphasis given to identification of outlets, junctions and valves. The use of colour to identify potential hazards is governed by *BS 5378*[10]. Care should be taken to avoid confusion between *BS 5378* on hazard warning colours, *BS 1710* on service colours and other colours in the interior. The lighting should not unduly distort the colours reserved for services or hazard indication in such a way as to be confusing.

1.8   Light source radiation

This *Code* is primarily concerned with light source radiation in that small part of the electromagnetic spectrum from 400 nm to 780 nm which stimulates the sense of sight and colour. However, all light sources radiate energy at shorter wavelengths in the ultraviolet as well as the longer wavelengths in the infra-red parts of the spectrum. This radiation can promote physiological effects which are either a benefit or a hazard. The basic function of luminaires is to control the visible radiation (light) but they can also concentrate, diffuse or attenuate the non-visible radiation from lamps. The lighting designer needs to be aware of the effects of all radiation that is being emitted. Details of the non-visible physiological effects of lighting are discussed in section 5.9.

Light has two colour properties: the apparent colour of the light that the source emits and the effect that the light has on the colours of surfaces. The latter effect is called colour rendering.

1.8.1 Apparent colour of emitted light

The colour of the light emitted by a near-white source can be indicated by its correlated colour temperature (CCT). Each lamp type has a specific correlated colour temperature but for practical use, the correlated colour temperatures have been grouped into three classes by the Commission Internationale de l'Eclairage (CIE) (Table 1.1)[11].

The choice of an appropriate colour appearance of a light source for a room is largely determined by the function of the room. This may involve such psychological aspects of colour as the impression given of warmth, relaxation, clarity etc., and more mundane considerations such as the need to have a colour appearance compatible with daylight and yet to provide a 'white' colour at night.

1.8.2 Colour rendering

The ability of a light source to render colours of surfaces accurately can be conveniently quantified by the CIE general colour rendering

Table 1.1 Correlated colour temperature classes and colour rendering groups used in the *Code for interior lighting*

Correlated colour temperature (CCT)	CCT class
below 3300 K	Warm
3300 K to 5300 K	Intermediate†
above 5300 K	Cold

Colour rendering groups	CIE general colour rendering index (R_a)	Typical application
1A	$R_a \geq 90$	Wherever accurate colour matching is required, e.g. colour printing inspection
1B	$90 \geq R_a \geq 80$	Wherever accurate colour judgements are necessary or good colour rendering is required for reasons of appearance, e.g. shops and other commercial premises
2	$80 \leq R_a \leq 60$	Wherever moderate colour rendering is required
3	$60 \leq R_a \leq 40$	Wherever colour rendering is of little significance but marked distortion of colour is unacceptable
4	$40 \leq R_a \leq 20$	Wherever colour rendering is of no importance at all and marked distortion of colour is acceptable

† This class covers a large range of correlated colour temperatures. Experience in the United Kingdom suggests that light sources with correlated colour temperatures approaching the 5300 K end of the range will usually be considered to have a 'cool' colour appearance.

index[12]. This index is based on the accuracy with which a set of test colours is reproduced by the lamp of interest relative to how they are reproduced by an appropriate standard light source, perfect agreement being given a value of 100. The CIE general colour rendering index has some limitations but it is the most widely accepted measure of the colour rendering properties of light sources (see section 5.8). Table 1.1 shows the groups of the CIE general colour rendering index used by the CIE and in this *Code*. For recommendations see section 2.4.7.

1.9   Light modulation

All electric lamps operated on an AC supply (50 Hz in Europe) have an inherent modulation in light output at twice the supply frequency (see Figure 1.20[13]). With most discharge lamps there is also a small component at the supply frequency itself which can increase as the lamp ages (see Figure 1.21). The 100 Hz modulation in light output is not perceptible by the great majority of people and the light appears steady. The percentage modulation of flux (ϕ) is defined as:

$$\frac{\phi_{max} - \phi_{min}}{\phi_{max} + \phi_{min}} \times 100$$

and depends on the lamp type. Incandescent lamps only show a small modulation because of thermal inertia; discharge lamps can show a modulation between 17% and 100%.

If lamps with a large modulation are used to light rotating machinery, coincidence between the modulation frequency and the frequency of rotation may cause moving parts to appear stationary. This is called the stroboscopic effect and can be dangerous (see section 4.4.3.1).

Light modulation at lower frequencies (about 50 Hz or less) which is visible to most people, is called flicker. Flicker is a source of both discomfort and distraction and may even cause epileptic seizures in some people. Sensitivity to flicker varies widely between individuals. The perceptibility of flicker is influenced by the frequency and amplitude of the modulation and the area of vision over which it occurs. Large amplitude variations over large areas at low frequencies are the most uncomfortable conditions. The eye is most sensitive to flicker at the edge of the field of view; thus visibly flickering overhead lights can be a source of great discomfort.

Lamps driven by high frequency power supplies (e.g. 35 kHz) overcome these drawbacks in that all significant low frequency modulation below 100 Hz is eliminated. Although 100 Hz modulation of appreciable amplitude does affect a very small minority of the population[14], the modulation from well designed electronic ballasts (Figure 1.22) is similar in shape and amplitude to that of incandescent sources.

Recent research[15] has shown that the use of electronic ballast over conventional types reduces the incidence of headaches and other symptoms in office workers.

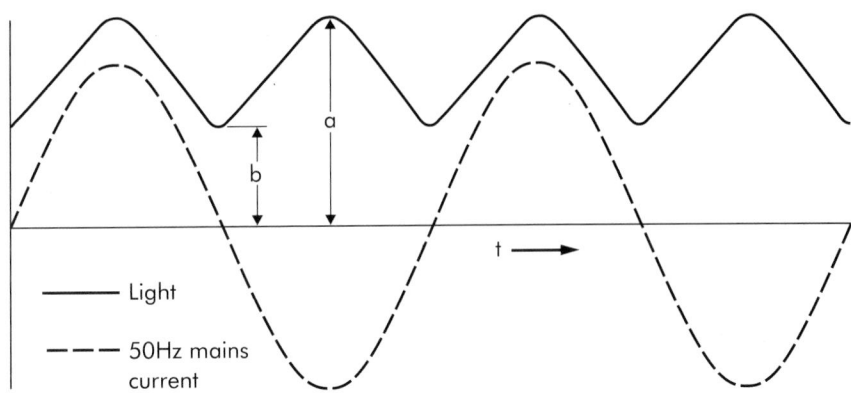

Figure 1.20   100 Hz light output waveform from typical fluorescent lamp operating on conventional wire wound control gear: (a) peak light output coinciding with peak lamp and mains current, (b) minimum light output due to 'after-glow' of phosphors when supply current is zero

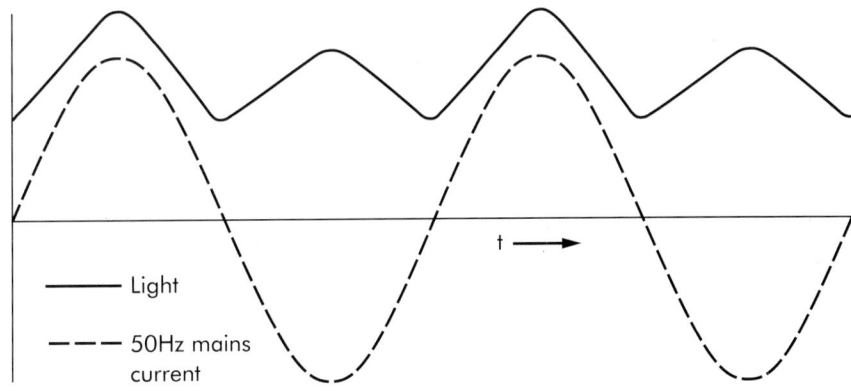

Figure 1.21   Changes in electrode characteristics at end of life can produce 50 Hz ripple on 100 Hz light output waveform

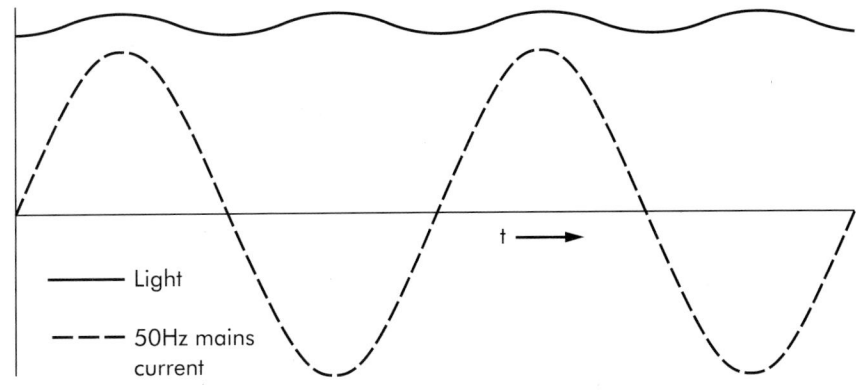

Figure 1.22   7% modulation of 100 Hz light output of fluorescent tube operating on electronic ballast connected to 50 Hz mains supply. The high frequency lamp current is not shown.

Part 2

Recommendations

2.1   Introduction

The recommendations are presented in four sections. The first (section 2.3) covers daylighting and the second (section 2.4) general electric lighting recommendations for interiors. The third (section 2.5) discusses the energy implication of design with recommendations for installed power density. The fourth (section 2.6) defines the lighting conditions appropriate for specific typical interior and exterior areas or activities, where the lighting is used to aid task performance or to create an appropriate and comfortable appearance.

During the preparation of this edition, work has been continuing in CEN/TC/169 on harmonised European lighting design standards and, in CIE, revisions to international recommendations for illuminance, glare and colour have also been undertaken. None of this had been approved and published before this edition was printed. Nevertheless, a number of the drafting committee members are involved in these European and international activities and so, based on their advice, the most likely changes have been noted at appropriate points throughout this document.

2.2   Status

The recommendations are representative of good lighting practice. They are judged to hold an appropriate balance between the benefits of lighting, in terms of task performance and visual comfort, and the costs of both equipment and energy. They have no statutory standing in their own right but may be adopted by appropriate authorities.

2.3   Recommendations for daylighting[1,2]

2.3.1 Daylight for general room lighting

In most types of buildings, users prefer rooms to have a daylit appearance during daytime hours. This appearance can be achieved, even though there is a significant amount of daytime electric lighting, by ensuring that the changing brightness of daylight is clearly noticeable on walls and other interior surfaces. It is also necessary to achieve sufficiently bright interior surfaces to avoid glare from contrast with the sky.

The following values should be adopted where a daylit appearance is required.

2.3.1.1 Interiors without supplementary electric lighting during daytime

If electric lighting is not normally to be used during daytime hours, the average daylight factor should be not less than 5%.

The internal reflectances and the positions of windows should be such that inter-reflected lighting in the space is strong and even. When the shape of the room causes the distribution of daylight to be very uneven (such as when a large area lies behind the no-sky line—see section 4.4.1.1 (*a*)) supplementary electric lighting may still be necessary.

2.3.1.2 Interiors with supplementary electric lighting during daytime

If electric lighting is to be used during daytime the average daylight factor should be not less than 2%.

In a room where the average daylight factor is significantly less than 2%, the general appearance is of an electrically lit interior. Daylight will be noticeable only on room surfaces immediately adjacent to windows, although the windows may still provide adequate views out for occupants throughout the room.

2.3.2 Daylight for task illumination

Where daylight alone provides the illumination for a visual task, the illuminance should not fall below that given in the schedule in section 2.6.4. The uniformity of illuminance within the immediate task area should be similar to that acceptable with electric lighting, (section 2.4.3) although there may be differences in the level of daylight in different parts of an interior.

2.3.3 Supplementary electric lighting design

The two distinct functions of electric lighting used in conjunction with daylight are to enhance the general room brightness and to supplement the daylight illuminance on visual tasks (see sections 4.5.1.4 and 4.5.1.5).

Where there is a significant amount of daylight (an average daylight factor of 2% or more), electric lighting may be required to reduce the contrast between internal surfaces and the external view. It needs to fall on the walls and other surroundings of the window opening. The brighter the view, the higher the luminance required of the surfaces surrounding the window. Electric lighting may be required also to increase the general illumination of parts of the room distant from a window. *If this is the case, the average working plane illuminance from electric lighting in the poorly daylit areas should not be less than 300 lux.* If a lower illuminance is used, in circulation areas for example, there may be noticeable contrast between areas near windows and other parts of the room, with a corresponding impression of harshness or gloominess.

As far as possible, the electric lighting should not mask either the natural variations of daylight across surfaces or the way in which natural lighting changes with time and weather.

When a room is daylit only to a low level, the electric lighting is required to give the general illumination over all room surfaces. Particular illumination may still be required on surfaces around windows as, for instance, in the case of a small pierced window through which an area of bright sky is visible.

Where both daylight and electric light provide task lighting, the combined illuminance should satisfy the criteria given in the schedule. The directionality of daylight is usually an advantage in achieving good modelling, but electric lighting may be required to increase the luminance of surfaces in shadow. Care should be taken, in the provision of daylight, that tasks are not viewed against the sky or a very bright area of the interior (Figure 1.10, page 11). If this is unavoidable, the background luminance should be such that there is a satisfactory brightness contrast between task and background (see section 2.4.4).

2.3.4 Colour

The sky varies in colour with time, azimuth and altitude. These variations are very great, and no electric lamp matches continuously the colour appearance of daylight. *In general room lighting, apparent discrepancies between the colour of electric light and daylight can be reduced by using lamps of intermediate colour temperature (3300–5300 K)* and screening lamps from the view of the occupants, using opaque louvres rather than translucent diffusers[16].

When discrimination of surface colour is essential for task performance, the choice of lamp should be that recommended for the task under entirely electric lighting (section 2.4.7). It may be necessary for the user to see whether the task is illuminated primarily with electric light or with daylight.

2.4 General recommendations for electric lighting

2.4.1 Introduction

These recommendations form the foundation for the specification and design of all electric lighting to ensure visual comfort and satisfaction.

The supplementary guidance on energy use (see section 2.5) and the detailed lighting requirements for specific interiors and activities in the schedule and flow chart (in section 2.6) are intended to be complementary. The information given in the schedule in section 2.6.4 should, therefore, only be applied after considering the basic recommendations in this section.

2.4.2 Illuminance

The maintained illuminance for specific applications can be obtained from the schedule and flow chart in section 2.6. *The recommendations given are consistent with the rule that working spaces which are to be occupied for long periods should have a maintained illuminance of not less than 200 lux on the working plane.*

With the introduction of maintained illuminance recommendations in the lighting schedule (section 2.6.4), the flow chart (Figure 2.3, page 43) and the associated notes have been augmented. The implications of this change for design and calculation are covered in section 4.5.2.

It is also assumed that the people doing the work have normal vision. If a significant number of building occupants have some degree of visual impairment, the maintained illuminance could be increased. The most common effects of old age on vision are an increase in the shortest distance at which an object can be focused, reduced light transmission through the eye and an increase in the scattering of light in the eye (see section 5.6). Spectacles or contact lenses can be used to correct the first effect. Increasing the illuminance will offset the loss in transmission and will increase visual sensitivity. A 70-year old person can require around three times the illuminance needed by a 20-year old person, to achieve similar visual performance[17]. The recommendations (section 2.6.4) generally assume an age of 40–50 years.

Although increasing the illuminance and avoiding glare will benefit most people with some degree of visual impairment, there are some severe forms of visual defect, e.g. cataract, for which increasing the illuminance may be detrimental. It is essential to match the lighting conditions to the nature of the visual defect.

Neither the schedule nor the flow chart are intended to cover lighting for the visually handicapped. Further information can be obtained on this from the *Lighting for partial sight handbook*[18].

2.4.3 Illuminance variation

For the task area and immediate surround, uniformity is important. A task area is not usually the entire area of a workstation. On an office desk, for example, the task area may only be about the size of a desk blotter, but in interiors such as drawing offices, for example, the visual task may cover the whole area of a drawing board. The range of task areas is even wider in industry, e.g. from a micro-electronics assembly line to a car body production line. However, when the precise size of the task area is not known, calculations can be based on an area measuring $0.5 \text{ m} \times 0.5 \text{ m}$ located immediately in front of the observer at the edge of the desk or working surface.

It is recommended that the uniformity of illuminance (minimum to average illuminance) over any task area and immediate surround should not be less than 0.8, (sections 4.5.4 and 5.3.3.3) and that the average illuminance on the task must be appropriate to that of the activity as set out in the schedule in section 2.6.4. Where task areas may be located anywhere over an area of a room then the recommendation applies to that area. The uniformity recommendation does not necessarily have to apply to the entire room.

In most spaces there are various visual tasks with differing degrees of difficulty. Although general lighting systems (section 4.4.2.1) provide flexibility of task location the average illuminance is determined by the needs of the most exacting task. It is often wasteful to illuminate all areas to the same level and non-uniform lighting may be provided by local or localised lighting systems (sections 4.4.2.2–4.4.2.3). If control systems (sections 3.4 and 4.4.4.1) are used, individuals may be able to adjust their levels of supplementary task lighting, and presence detection may also switch off luminaires in unoccupied areas. Whatever lighting system is used excessive variations of horizontal illuminance across an interior must be avoided: *the diversity of illuminance expressed as the ratio of the maximum illuminance to the minimum illuminance at any point in the 'core area' of the interior should not exceed 5:1.* The core area is that area of the working plane having a boundary 0.5 m from the walls (see section 5.3.3.2, Figure 5.1, page 195).

Installations lit by ceiling-mounted arrays of luminaires designed by the lumen method (section 4.5.3) following the conventional spacing and layout criteria will usually satisfy the uniformity requirements. It is normal in such installations for the horizontal illuminance at the perimeter to be significantly less than the average value over the working plane. This is particularly marked in interiors having low-reflectance walls (hence, the earlier reference to the 'core area'). Local reductions in illuminance, due to shadowing, may also be caused by large items of furniture or equipment which project substantially above the working plane.

Both in these areas and at the perimeter of the room local or localised lighting may be necessary if critical visual tasks are to be performed.

In a localised or local lighting system, the normal design method is to establish the highest recommended task illuminance, then to set the average 'ambient' level at one third of this value or to the requirement of the non-task areas (whichever is greater). The illuminance at the task is then 'topped up' with localised or local lighting to the appropriate task level, the usual uniformity requirements for the task area must be satisfied. Calculation methods are given in sections 4.5.5. and 5.13. The design of uplighting to provide suitable conditions of uniformity is covered in section 5.14.

2.4.4 Luminance and illuminance ratios

Research which has attempted to find the preferred balances of luminances between the task, the immediate surround and the general background has identified that performance will be reduced and that attention will be harder to maintain if the task is dimmer than the immediate surround, while a sharp contrast between the two makes visual conditions uncomfortable.

Luminance differences may be specified or measured in terms of the ratio between one luminance and another. Suggested targets are: task-to-immediate surround 3:1, and task-to-general background 10:1.

It has become the convention to translate luminance ratios into relative illuminances, since it is the illuminance which is used in lighting design practice. Figure 2.1 illustrates ranges of relative illuminances for general lighting using ceiling-mounted luminaires with a predominately downward light distribution for a typical office. The values shown are based on research findings modified by design application and experience.

Recommendations are also made for a range of reflectances for each of the major room surfaces.

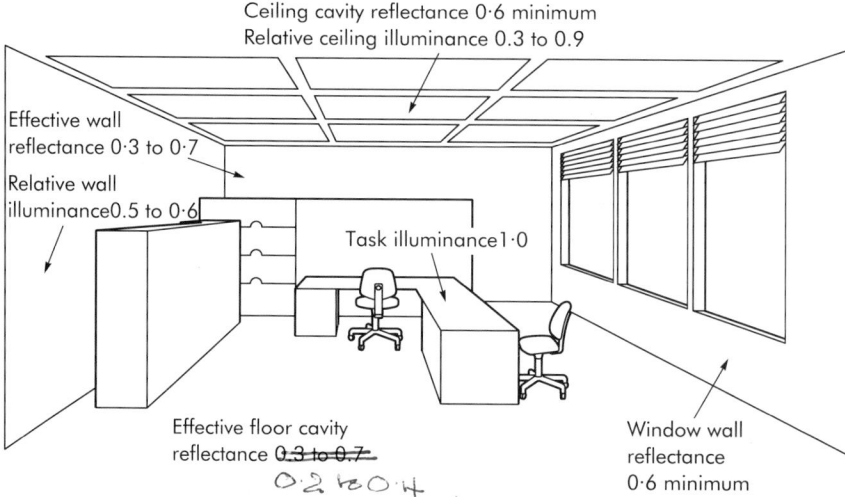

Figure 2.1   Relative illuminances from a ceiling-mounted direct general lighting system for the main surfaces in a commercial working interior with suggested reflectances

2.4.5 Room surfaces

The lighting system should play a role in reinforcing the architectural character of the interior, using daylight where possible as part of an energy strategy. Spatial clarity, mood and the visual nature of the space may be emphasised by the choice of light distribution and use of colour as discussed in sections 1.6, 1.7 and 4.4.3.3.

The reflectance and finish of the major surfaces in an interior will play an important part in the use of light. High reflectance surfaces will help inter-reflection and are normally recommended for working interiors. This does not preclude the judicious use of colour and lower reflectance as part of the décor to give visual interest.

Matt finishes are normally recommended to avoid specular reflections or disguise surface imperfections.

2.4.5.1 Ceilings

The ceiling cavity (Figure 4.14, page 162) will play a less significant role in a small room than it will in a large one where it can occupy a substantial part of the field of view.

The recommendation for general lighting with a predominantly downward distribution is for the ratio of average illuminance on the ceiling to the average illuminance on the horizontal working plane to be within the range 0.3 to 0.9.

In general the ceiling cavity reflectance should be as high as practicable, at least 0.6. The reflectance of the surface finish therefore should be of the order of 0.8 (see section 4.5.3.3).

*Luminous ceilings utilising large diffusing panels are not recommended for lighting interiors for which the recommended unified glare rating is less than 19. In any case, the average luminance of such luminous ceilings should not be greater than 500 cd/m². *

For indirect lighting, the average luminance of all surfaces forming the ceiling cavity should not be more than 500 cd/m². However, small areas of luminance of up to 1500 cd/m² will generally be acceptable, provided sharp changes from high to low luminance are avoided (see section 5.14).

2.4.5.2 Walls

Higher reflectance of wall and partition surfaces will increase the perception of lightness in the interior. Walls with windows are a particular case. The surfaces surrounding the windows should have a reflectance not less than 0.6 in order to reduce the contrast with the relatively bright outdoor view through the window during daytime. Windows at night form a dark specular surface which should be covered with suitable curtains or blinds. Sharply defined patterns of light and shade, 'scalloping', caused by hard-edged downlighting or wall-washing luminaires can cause a breakdown of brightness constancy which can disrupt the visual continuity of wall surfaces.

The ratio of the average illuminance on the walls to the average illuminance on the horizontal working plane is related to the average vertical plane illuminance throughout the space. This has been shown to give good correlation with visual satisfaction for office lighting[4].

The recommendation is for the ratio of the average illuminance on any wall or major partition surface to the average illuminance on the horizontal working plane to be within the range 0.5 to 0.8.

In general the effective reflectance of the principal walls should be between 0.3 and 0.7. The reflectance of window wall surface finishes should be at least 0.6. See section 5.4.3.

2.4.5.3   Floor and working plane

The reflectance of the floor cavity plays an important role in the visual appearance of a room. With most lighting installations, a proportion of the light on the ceiling will have been reflected from the floor cavity and, where this has a low reflectance, it may be difficult to obtain satisfactory modelling effects without directly lighting other surfaces and so changing the luminance balance. Conversely, as the floor cavity may be one of the largest planes in a space, it is important that its luminance should not be so high as to dominate the appearance of the scene. It is, therefore, undesirable for the floor cavity to have an average reflectance of less than 0.20 or greater than 0.40.

The floor cavity consists of a number of surfaces: the floor, the lower parts of the walls (i.e. those below the level of the working plane) the top and sides of desks or benches and the surfaces of other furniture or equipment. Each of these surfaces will have a particular reflectance and its effect on the average reflectance will be in proportion to the unobscured area of the surface. It should be noted that in practical interiors it is extremely unlikely that the floor space will be unobstructed by furniture or machinery and allowance should be made in calculating the average floor cavity reflectance (see Table 4.10, pages 164–165). Low-reflectance bench and desk tops should generally be avoided as these surfaces have a major influence on the average floor cavity reflectance as well as usually forming the immediate surround to the task.

In general, it is undesirable for the average floor cavity reflectance to exceed 0.40 or fall below 0.20, although it is recognised that in 'dirty' industries or heavily obstructed areas this latter figure may be difficult to achieve. In such cases steps should be taken to avoid dark coloured furniture and to keep working and other surfaces clean so that the average reflectance is maintained at 0.10 or above.

The reflectance of the area immediately surrounding the task should not be less than one third of the task itself. In the case of office tasks involving white paper this will require desk tops to have a reflectance of at least 0.30.

2.4.6   Colour appearance

In addition to the comments in section 1.8.1 the only general rules to help with the selection of light source colour are as follows:

(*a*) for rooms lit to an illuminance of 300 lux or less, a warm or intermediate colour is preferred; cold apparent colour lamps tending to give rooms a gloomy appearance at lower illuminance

(*b*) where it is desirable to blend with daylight, intermediate correlated colour temperature (CCT) sources should be used.

(*c*) different colour lamps should not be used haphazardly in the same room.

However, where light sources with good colour rendering are used, there is no evidence of a simple relationship between CCT and people's preference of the space[19, 20].

2.4.7   Colour rendering

Where work involving accurate colour judgement is to be undertaken, electric light sources with high CIE general colour rendering indices (Table 1.1 Groups 1A or 1B) are necessary. Where exact colour matching is to be undertaken, lamps of colour rendering group 1A should be used and the recommendations of *BS 950*[21] should be followed as appropriate. *The surfaces surrounding areas where accurate colour judgements are being made should be of weak chroma (not greater than 1 on the Munsell scale, see section 5.7.1) and medium reflectance (not less than 0.4). An illuminance of at least 500 lux should be provided on the task.*

Where the main consideration is the appearance of the space and objects within it, light sources with a high CIE general colour rendering index may be desirable. In general, light sources with good colour rendering properties (Group 1B) make surfaces of objects appear more colourful than do light sources with moderate or poor colour rendering properties (Groups 2, 3 and 4). In addition, light sources with poor colour rendering properties may distort some colours to a marked extent. Thus, where a colourful appearance is desirable, lamps with good colour rendering properties are appropriate. However, the exact level of colour rendering desirable in any particular circumstance remains a matter of individual judgement. Ultimately the CIE general colour rendering index is no substitute for actually seeing the effect of different light sources when it comes to assessing their contribution to the appearance of an interior (see section 5.8.2).

2.4.8   Modelling and emphasis

Illumination, which falls on an object from all directions, enables the object to be seen, but does not reveal much of its form or texture because there are few, if any, shadows. Lighting, from a dominant direction, will emphasise shape, form and texture. The relationship between the intensity of the directional lighting and the diffuse illuminance is expressed as the vector/scalar ratio (see section 4.4.3.3). This objective ratio is a useful criterion when considering the relative values of directional lighting to non-directional or reflected lighting. *A vector/scalar ratio from 1.2 to 1.8 will prove satisfactory in normal general lighting conditions where perception of faces is important. Under such conditions facial modelling will usually appear balanced and natural.*

Display lighting calls for greater impact and emphasis. Table 2.1 is intended to give general guidance on the display illuminance ratios (DIR) that must be provided to achieve increasing degrees of emphasis from 'subtle' to 'dramatic'. The display illuminance ratio is that between the general horizontal plane illuminance in the room and the value of local illuminance in the plane of the object to be displayed. Greater degrees of emphasis are likely to require lower values of general diffused lighting to avoid the need for excessive values of local display illuminance.

The table also shows that, because of visual adaptation, the apparent brightness difference between the object on display and its surroundings is less than the measured illuminance difference.

Table 2.1   General guidance on the display illuminance ratios to achieve increasing degrees of impact and emphasis

Display effect	Objective display illuminance ratio (DIR)	Subjective apparent brightness ratio
Subtle	5:1	2.5:1
Moderate	15:1	5:1
Strong	30:1	7:1
Dramatic	50:1	10:1

The values given in Table 2.1 indicate only the degree of emphasis achieved due to the apparent brightness ratio between an object and its surroundings. The values are based on a difference in reflectance between the object and the background not greater than 2:1 and a ratio between the average horizontal and vertical components of the general lighting of approximately 3:1. Increasing the difference in the reflectance or the hue of the object and its background or reducing the average vertical component of the general lighting will increase the degree of emphasis. Some of these effects are illustrated in Figure 2.2.

Figure 2.2 shows different display effects (see Table 2.1) related to the objective display illuminance ratio (DIR) for the same object against a medium grey background. The visual impact will be influenced by changing the contrast between the object and its background for the same DIR. Wall and shelf displays enable more control of contrast than free standing displays which are seen against other objects and surfaces in the general interior. Both the reflectance and the colour of objects and backgrounds can be used to increase or decrease the impact of the displays. Nevertheless, the DIR gives a useful guide to the order of difference that should be achieved between the general lighting and the accent lighting to give the required degree of emphasis.

Modelling of form, texture and surface finish related to the direction, or directions, of the display lighting and the direction of view can provide further visual impact. See section 1.6 and Figure 1.14 (page 16), Figure 1.15 (page 17) and Figure 1.17 (pages 18–19).

2.4.9   Glare

Information on glare formulations is given in sections 4.5.6 and 5.4. Specified values of limiting glare indices are provided in sections 2.6.1 (*a*) and 2.6.4 for individual task areas and applications.

2.5   Energy efficiency recommendations

2.5.1   Introduction

Lighting must provide a suitable visual environment within a particular space: sufficient and suitable lighting for the performance of a range of tasks, provision of a desired appearance etc. This objective should be achieved without waste of energy. However, it is important not to compromise the visual aspects of a lighting installation simply to reduce energy consumption. In most organisations the cost of lighting energy, although substantial, is only a small fraction of the total costs associated with the activity in

Figure 2.2(a) 'Subtle' with DIR of approximately 5:1

Figure 2.2(b) 'Moderate' with a DIR of 15:1

Figure 2.2(c) 'Strong' with DIR of 30:1

Figure 2.2(d) 'Dramatic' with a DIR of 50:1

Figure 2.2 Different display effects (see Table 2.1) related to the objective display illuminance ratio (DIR) for the same object against a medium grey background

the space. For example, the impact of poor visual conditions on work quality and productivity costs is likely to be many times greater than the lighting energy costs in an office, or in a factory (labour costs may typically be around 100 times greater than lighting energy costs). It is thus a false economy to save energy at the expense of human effectiveness.

Similarly, in a shop, the sales turnover resulting from correct display of merchandise will be very much greater than the energy costs for lighting. On the other hand, the profligate and unnecessary use of energy and the associated costs, both financial and environmental, should be avoided. The environmental impact of lighting is discussed in section 5.11.

The recommendations that follow provide guidance on energy efficiency for lighting installations. They assume that good design has been combined with the use of modern equipment. New lighting designs should normally meet these levels. The recommendations can also be used to gauge the efficiency of existing installations and to determine whether or not the existing installation needs remedial action to achieve acceptable energy efficiency.

During the life of this edition of the *Code* lighting energy efficiency may become subject to building regulations.

2.5.2   Power and time

The energy (kWh) used by a lighting installation depends on both the power (kW) and time (h). Energy efficiency can be achieved:

(*a*) by using the most efficient lighting equipment (see Part 3) to obtain the desired lighting solution, i.e. the electrical load (kW) is kept to a minimum while achieving the lighting design objectives

(*b*) by using effective controls so that the lighting is not in operation at times when it is not needed, i.e. the period of operation (h) is kept to a minimum.

The lighting designer can limit the electrical power loading and the use of energy, but it is the operator of the installation who will ultimately be responsible for achieving high energy efficiency in practice.

2.5.3   Energy efficient equipment

Information on the energy efficiency of lamps and luminaires is given in Part 3. While the lighting requirements for different spaces within a building can be met most appropriately using different lamps or luminaires, *an average initial circuit luminous efficacy of at least 65 lm/W for the fixed lighting equipment within the building should be achieved. Both emergency lighting systems and equipment which is not fixed, e.g. track-mounted luminaires, are excluded from this figure*. Thus it is possible to use equipment of lower energy efficiency (e.g. tungsten–halogen spotlights) in some areas combined with more energy efficient equipment (e.g. fluorescent lamps with high frequency electronic ballasts) in other areas. This recommendation can be used as a guideline at the design concept stage, but it does not take account of energy use.

In practice, much energy is wasted outside normal working hours, by lighting being left on when not required, although some lighting may be needed for cleaning and security. Override controls should provide full lighting in emergency conditions at night. Similarly, lighting may not be needed during working hours if there is sufficient daylight or if spaces in the building are vacant. Adequate lighting controls should be installed to allow the building occupants to use only that lighting which is actually needed at any particular time. The control system should be flexible enough to allow an appropriate level of lighting to be achieved and lighting which is not required to be switched off. This may be achieved by:

— localised switching, using switches provided throughout the space and not concentrated at the point of entry

— time switching, providing automatic switching of luminaires to a predetermined schedule

— automatic switching or dimming of lighting in relation to occupancy and daylight level measured by a photoelectric sensor.

Further details of such control systems are given in sections 3.4, 4.4.4 and 4.5.1.

The ultimate aim must be to achieve the desired lighting solution at the lowest practical energy use. It is possible that a higher installed load combined with a suitable control system to give low hours of use will result in lower energy consumption than an alternative installation with a lower power loading but poorer control. It is thus important to consider both aspects.

2.5.4 Installed power density per 100 lux

The installed power density per 100 lux is the power needed per square metre of floor area to achieve 100 lux on a horizontal reference plane, usually the horizontal working plane, with general lighting and is expressed in terms of $W/m^2/100$ lux. The ranges shown in Table 2.2 are appropriate for different interiors with 'normal' environmental conditions, lit by common types of lamps and luminaires when the recommended illuminance refers to the horizontal working plane. Greater energy efficiency is associated with lower values of installed power density per 100 lux.

As a lighting installation ages, the electrical load does not normally change significantly, but the light output of the installation deteriorates. The installed power density per 100 lux therefore increases. Calculations of installed power density per 100 lux for existing installations should be based upon the actual measured average illuminance (see section 5.3) produced by the installation rather than the illuminance for which the installation was originally designed.

The installed power density targets given in Table 2.2 do not take into account the energy savings achieved by controls. Power is the rate of flow of energy. To calculate energy consumed, power must be multiplied by time of use. Thus by multiplying the above power targets by the target period of use or occupation of a space (hours/year), the annual energy use target can be calculated. See sections 4.5.1.4 and 4.5.1.5 and Table 4.3 (page 152).

2.5.5 Status

The ranges of installed power density per 100 lux recommended are representative of good lighting practice. With careful design and the selection of lamps and luminaires with good maintenance characteristics (see sections 3.3.2, 3.5 and 4.5.2), it should be possible to achieve a suitable lighting installation at an installed power density per 100 lux within the range recommended.

Ideally, the actual installed power density per 100 lux will be towards, or even beyond, the low end of the recommended range. Conversely, there are situations where financial, lighting and architectural requirements justify values above the range recommended. In any case, achieving the target will depend not only on the design of the lighting installation, but also on the user ensuring that the maintenance programme allowed for in the design calculations is undertaken in practice.

2.5.6 Method of use

The ranges of installed power density per 100 lux appropriate for different application areas are given in Table 2.2. The ranges are classified according to application area, room surface reflectance, room index, luminaire maintenance categories and the light source type and wattage used. The values given in the table provide design targets, for the stated conditions, for energy efficiency related to maintained illuminance.

The influence of different lamp types on the installed power density can be clearly seen from the different ranges in Table 2.2. In general, the most efficient equipment, compatible with the lighting requirements of the space, should be used.

When considering the recommended ranges of installed power density per 100 lux the following points should be borne in mind.

(a) The ranges of installed power density per 100 lux have been derived from the luminaire and maintenance data given in Table 4.8 (page 156) and from an examination of current lighting practice using modern lighting equipment.

(b) The classification by application area is used because of the influence of the mounting heights likely to be available and hence the light sources and luminaires which can be used.

(c) The classification by room index is used because the proportions of the room influence the proportion of the luminous flux which reaches the working plane (see section 4.5.3). Where considerable obstruction to the lighting is likely to occur, e.g. from furniture, plant, screens, partitions, or structural elements, the range of installed power density per 100 lux may be increased considerably, i.e. the effective room index will be lower.

(d) A range of installed power density per 100 lux, rather than a single value, is necessary because the range of applications may require design maintained illuminance values from 150 to 750 lux. This will affect the choice of lamp wattage which, in turn, affects the circuit luminous efficacy. Table 2.2 does not necessarily include all the wattage ratings which are available for each lamp type.

(e) The target values also take account of the range of reflection factors shown for each application area, which are independent of environmental conditions. For interiors with a dirty environment it may be necessary to increase the target which assumes 'normal' environmental conditions. Guidance on the size of this increase, or decrease in the case of 'clean' areas, can be gauged by referring to Table 4.8 (page 156) which shows typical maintenance factors for clean, normal and dirty conditions.

(f) The ranges of installed power density per 100 lux apply to general lighting installations using a conventional layout. When the luminaire-to-wall spacing must be reduced to achieve a specified task-to-wall illuminance ratio, increased power densities per 100 lux are likely to result (see section 4.5.3.5(h)). The range of values shown cannot be applied to localised or local lighting systems, although these will achieve lower overall power densities (except for local display lighting which is also not allowed for in Table 2.2).

Table 2.2 Target ranges of installed power density per 100 lux maintained illuminance for general lighting installations in W/m²/100 lux (based on Table 4.8, page156)

Lamp type	Wattage range used to calculate target ranges	CIE colour rendering group	Luminaire maintenance categories (see Table 4.5, page 153, and section 3.3.2)	Working plane power density range (W/m²/100 lux) Room index		
				K=1	K=2.5	K=5
(a) High bay industrial — reflectance C,W,F = 50, 50, 20 to 30, 30, 10 ~~0·5 ,0·5 , 0·2 to 0·3 ,0·1~~						
Metal halide						
— clear or coated	250–400	2	B,C,E	2.6–4.5	2.1–3.6	2.0–3.4
High pressure mercury						
— coated	250–400	3	B,C,E	4.2–6.2	3.5–5.1	3.3–4.8
High pressure sodium						
— improved colour	250–400	3	B,C,E	2.4–3.6	2.0–2.9	1.9–2.8
— standard or high efficiency	250–1000	4	B,C,E	1.4–2.7	1.2–2.2	1.1–2.1
(b) Industrial — reflectance C,W,F = 70, 50, 20 to 30, 50, 20						
Fluorescent						
— triphosphor	32–100	1b	B,C,E	2.5–4.9	1.9–3.5	1.6–2.9
— halophosphate	32–100	2–3	B,C,E	3.2–6.3	2.4–4.5	2.1–3.7
Metal halide						
— clear or coated	150–400	2	B,C,E	2.9–6.8	2.3–4.4	2.1–3.9
High pressure mercury						
— coated	125–400	3	B,C,E	4.8–9.4	3.7–6.1	3.5–5.5
High pressure sodium						
— improved colour	150–400	3	B,C,E	2.7–5.5	2.1–3.5	2.0–3.2
— standard or high efficiency	100–400	4	B,C,E	1.8–4.7	1.3–3.0	1.3–2.7
(c) Commercial — reflectance C,W,F, = 70, 50, 20 to 50, 50, 20						
Fluorescent						
— triphosphor	32–100	1b	A,B,C,D,E	2.7–5.4	2.2–4.2	2.1–3.7
— halophosphate	32–100	2–3	A,B,C,D,E	3.4–7.0	2.8–5.4	2.6–4.8
— compact	36–55	1b	A,B,C,D,E	3.3–6.4	2.8–4.9	2.6–4.4
Metal halide						
— clear or coated	150–400	2	B,C	4.4–7.1	3.6–5.7	3.4–5.3
High pressure mercury						
— coated	125–400	3	B,C	6.6–9.9	5.4–7.9	5.1–7.3
High pressure sodium						
— improved colour	150–400	3	B,C	3.8–5.8	3.1–4.6	2.9–4.3
— standard or high efficiency	100–400	4	B,C	2.4–4.9	2.0–3.9	1.9–3.6

2.6   Additional lighting recommendations for specific types of interior and activity

2.6.1   Introduction

These recommendations provide the following:

(a) Quantitative guidance on the maintained illuminance and limiting glare index appropriate for a wide range of interiors and/or activities (see also section 2.4.2).

The maintained illuminance in the lighting schedule has been selected from the following Commission Internationale de l'Eclairage (CIE) scale: 20, 30, 50, 75, 100, 150, 200, 300, 500, 750, 1000, 1500, 2000 lux (see Table 2.3). With the introduction of maintained illuminance the installed load for an installation can be increased by typically 5–15% compared with a design based on service illuminance of the same value. Reducing the time between cleaning and maintenance is one way to counteract the effect (section 4.5.2.6), but when this is not possible and the increase in installed load is unacceptable, the flow chart can be used with intermediate steps of 250, 400, 600 and 900 lux (see Figure 2.3, page 43, and section 2.6.3.1 (*e*)).

The recommended limiting glare indices are based on formal assessments of actual installations and on accumulated experience of the degree of discomfort glare acceptable in different situations. The limits recommended have been selected from the following

Table 2.3 Examples of activities/interiors appropriate for each maintained illuminance

Standard maintained illuminance (lux)	Characteristics of activity/interior	Representative activities/interiors
50	Interiors used rarely with visual tasks confined to movement and casual seeing without perception of detail	Cable tunnels, indoor storage tanks, walkways
100	Interiors used occasionally with visual tasks confined to movement and casual seeing calling for only limited perception of detail	Corridors, changing rooms, bulk stores, auditoria
150	Interiors used occasionally or with visual tasks not requiring perception of detail but involving some risk to people, plant or product	Loading bays, medical stores, plant rooms
200	Interiors occupied for long periods, or for visual tasks requiring some perception of detail	Foyers and entrances, monitoring automatic processes, casting concrete, turbine halls, dining rooms
300†	Interiors occupied for long periods, or when visual tasks are moderately easy, i.e. large details >10 min arc and/or high contrast	Libraries, sports and assembly halls, teaching spaces, lecture theatres, packing
500†	Visual tasks moderately difficult, i.e. details to be seen are of moderate size (5–10 min arc) and may be of low contrast; also colour judgement may be required	General offices, engine assembly, painting and spraying, kitchens, laboratories, retail shops
750†	Visual tasks difficult, i.e. details to be seen are small (3–5 min arc) and of low contrast; also good colour judgements or the creation of a well lit, inviting interior may be required	Drawing offices, ceramic decoration, meat inspection, chain stores
1000†	Visual tasks very difficult, i.e. details to be seen are very small (2–3 min arc) and can be of very low contrast; also accurate colour judgements or the creation of a well lit, inviting interior may be required	General inspection, electronic assembly, gauge and tool rooms, retouching paintwork, cabinet making, supermarkets
1500†	Visual tasks extremely difficult, i.e. details to be seen extremely small (1–2 min arc) and of low contrast; optical aids and local lighting may be of advantage	Fine work and inspection, hand tailoring, precision assembly
2000†	Visual tasks exceptionally difficult, i.e. details to be seen exceptionally small (<1 min arc) with very low contrasts; optical aids and local lighting will be of advantage	Assembly of minute mechanisms, finished fabric inspection

† 1 minute of arc (min arc) is 1/60 of a degree. This is the angle of which the tangent is given by the dimension of the task detail to be seen divided by the viewing distance.

scale: 16, 19, 22, 25 and 28. A difference of three units is necessary for a significant change in discomfort glare sensation to occur.

(b) Qualitative advice on the aspects of the interior/activity which should influence the selection of lighting equipment and the design of the lighting installation.

(c) Notification of statutory and advisory documents relevant to each interior/activity. Those listed in the schedule are intended to be pertinent but may not be exhaustive. Much of the relevant legislation for a specific area will be contained in more general legislation such as the *Health and Safety at Work etc. Act 1974*[22]; the *Factories Act 1961*[23]; and the *Electricity at Work Act 1989*[24] together with a series of recent statutory instruments implementing various European Community (EC) directives (see section 5.10).

The recommendations contained in the schedule (section 2.6.4) are classified by application. If a specific interior/activity cannot be found in the schedule then appropriate recommendations can be obtained either by using an analogous interior/activity or by using the generic details given in Table 2.3.

The values of 'standard' maintained illuminance for general tasks, between 200 and 750 lux, found in the schedule should be converted to the 'design' maintained illuminance by referring to the flow chart, Figure 2.3 and the associated notes.

The modifying factors shown at the head of Figure 2.3 and explained in the notes, can only give a general indication of the increases or decreases in illuminance that may be justified. The designer must ultimately make a judgement based on the unique combination of conditions which apply to an individual project. At the initial design stage there is little point in selecting values other than those shown on the flow chart. At the detailed design stage (see section 4.5), however, the designer will need to decide whether the calculated illuminance for an actual installation is acceptable within the practical constraints of luminaire layout, through life performance and cost, energy use etc.

2.6.2   Lighting schedule explanatory notes

When considering the recommendations in the schedule (section 2.6.4) and the flow chart (section 2.6.3), the following points should be borne in mind:

(a) The design maintained illuminance is the minimum illuminance at which maintenance of the lighting installation must be carried out. This value is averaged over the relevant area, which may be a part or the whole of an interior or the area of each visual task, depending on the lighting approach adopted. For practical reasons the recommended illuminance is that achieved without the obstruction losses caused by the worker's body (see section 4.4.2).

(b) The recommended standard maintained illuminance assumes that the task or interior is representative of its type. For example, the maintained illuminance recommended for rough sawing in a woodwork shop assumes that the materials being handled, the age and ability of people doing the work (section 2.4.2), the duration of the work and the consequences of any mistakes are typical of woodwork shops in general.

(c) The design maintained illuminance is obtained by referring to the flow chart in Figure 2.3. The modifying factors allow for departures from the assumed typical conditions. These are:

— the visual demands of the task

— the duration of the work

— the consequences of any errors

— energy considerations.

For details, see section 2.6.3.1(a)–(e).

(d) Where more than one activity takes place in an interior and a general lighting approach is necessary, then the highest of the maintained illuminances recommended for the individual activities should be adopted.

(e) Where the recommendations refer to an activity rather than an interior in general, the maintained illuminance should be provided over a surface appropriate for that activity. This surface may be complex in shape but it is usually assumed to be a horizontal, vertical or possibly an inclined plane. The maintained illuminance need only be provided over the task area. The illumination of areas remote from the task area will then be determined by the type of lighting approach adopted (see sections 2.4.3 and 4.4.2). Particularly where the maintained illuminance is 750 lux or greater, careful consideration should be given to using local lighting or optical aids, e.g. magnifiers. Local rather than general lighting systems, covered in section 2.5, will usually provide the most economical, energy efficient solution where these high values of illuminance are recommended.

(f) Where the recommendations refer to an interior in general rather than an activity, the maintained illuminance should be provided over the core area (see section 2.4.3) unless otherwise stated in the notes accompanying the recommendations.

(g) For information on the factors affecting the accuracy of calculation and measurement of these recommended values and the practical tolerances that should be allowed for, see sections 4.7 and 5.3.

(h) The limiting glare index specifies the degree of discomfort glare which will be acceptable from a regular layout of lighting equipment; it is not applicable to local lighting installations (see section 4.5.6). The glare index will vary with viewing position and viewing direction. The recommended limiting glare index for each application should not be exceeded for any viewing position and viewing direction of practical importance. Where more than one activity takes place in an interior, the lowest recommended limiting index rating should be adopted.

(i) Emergency lighting requirements are not included in the schedule. Information on these requirements is given in section 4.5.7.

2.6.3 Design maintained illuminance flow chart (Figure 2.3)

The flow chart in Figure 2.3 should be used for all standard maintained illuminance recommendations from 200 lux to 750 lux for general activities and interiors in the lighting schedule. For recommendations of 150 lux or less, the modifying factors are not relevant, see Table 2.3. Where a 'standard' maintained illuminance of more than 750 lux is recommended, this always applies to a stated task for specific industries or activities where the modifying factors have usually been taken into account.

Due to the adoption of maintained illuminance, half-step values in the illuminance scale in Table 2.3 have been introduced into Figure 2.3. The use of these is explained in paragraph (e) below.

To use the chart, follow the horizontal path from the 'standard' maintained illuminance in the schedule until the answer to a question is 'yes'. If the 'yes' is strong, follow the solid arrow; if moderate, follow the dashed arrow.

2.6.3.1 Further explanatory notes

(a) The 'standard' maintained illuminance given in the schedule assumes the task is representative of its type (section 2.6.2 (b)). If the task is much more visually difficult than usual (e.g.

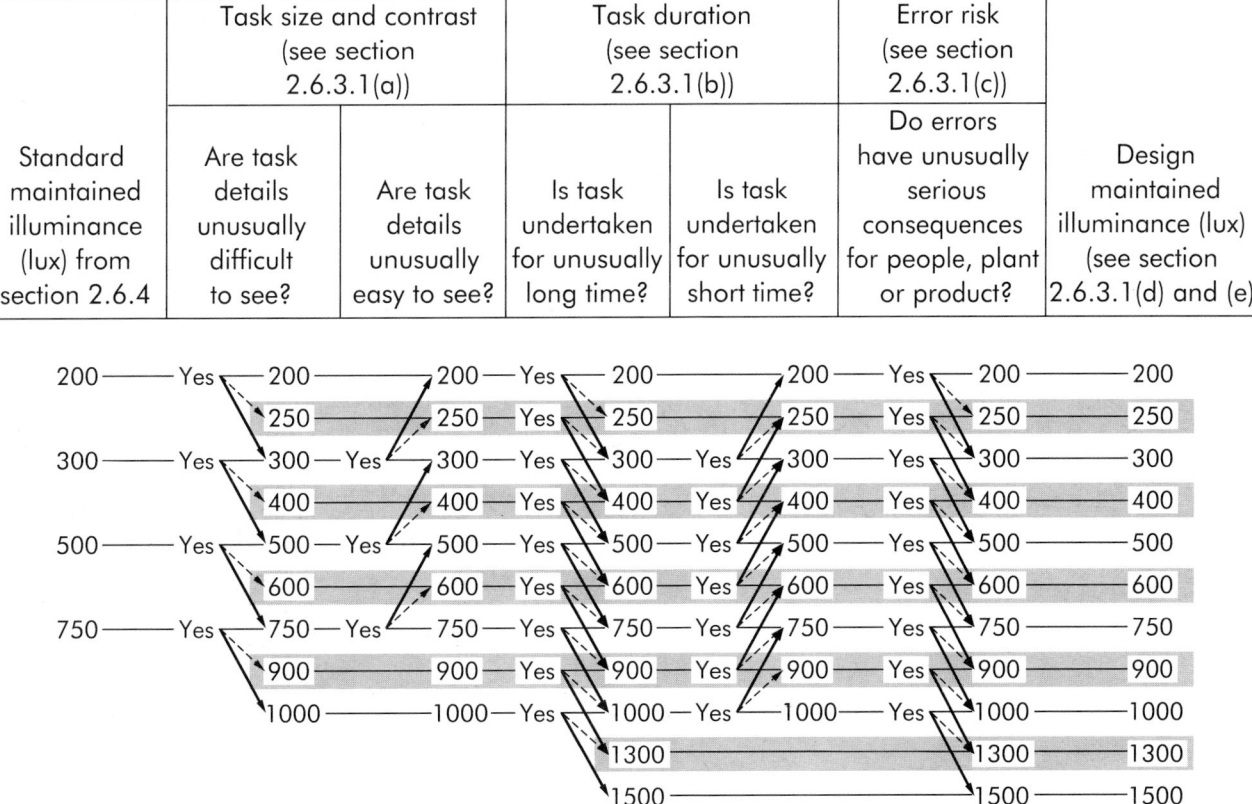

Figure 2.3 Design maintained illuminance flow chart (for explanatory notes see section 2.6.3 above)

smaller size, lower contrast), then an increase in the maintained illuminance is appropriate[17,18]. Reduced contrast may arise from the use of safety lenses or safety screens, since they reduce the transmission of light. Unless maintained in good condition, these devices also increase the scattered component of what light is transmitted. The need to increase illuminance to take account of the age or eyesight of the operator has been discussed in section 2.4.2.

Conversely, if the task detail is such that the task is easier to see than usual, e.g. larger size, higher contrast, a reduction in maintained illuminance can be made.

(b) The 'standard' maintained illuminance given in the schedule assumes that the task is to be undertaken over a conventional working period. If the work is to be undertaken continually for a much longer period than usual, the maintained illuminance should be increased in order to diminish the risk of visual fatigue. Conversely, if the work is to be carried out over a much shorter period than usual, the maintained illuminance may be reduced.

(c) The schedule assumes that the consequences of any errors are typical of the activity. However, if errors have unusually serious consequences for people, plant or product then an increase in illuminance may be appropriate.

(d) If the design maintained illuminance is more than two full steps (e.g. 300–750 lux) on the illuminance scale above the standard maintained illuminance, consideration should be given to whether changes in the task details or organisation of the work are more appropriate than substantial increases in the maintained illuminance.

(e) When an increase in the standard maintained illuminance is justified, the reduced energy loadings offered by local or localised systems (sections 4.4.2.2 and 4.4.2.3) should be considered. Also, the change from illuminance recommendations based on service to those based on maintained illuminance can result in increased energy loadings. The need to reduce this may justify the selection of a lower, intermediate (half-step) value. However, this should only be done when the requirements of visual performance and satisfaction are fully met at the reduced value. Alternatively, it may be equally valid to adopt the higher value to achieve improved visual performance and satisfaction.

2.6.4 Lighting schedule

The information in this schedule will be influenced by reference to the 'core recommendations' in sections 2.4, 2.5, 2.6.1 and 2.6.3.

Index

The alphabetical index enables individual items to be located in the schedule.

The activities/interiors listed in the schedule are grouped under seven main headings:

2.6.4.1   General building areas

Areas common to most buildings

Other relevant documents:

— CIBSE Lighting Guide LG1: *The industrial environment*[7]
— CIBSE Lighting Guide LG3: *Areas for visual display terminals*[25]
— CIBSE Lighting Guide LG6: *The outdoor environment*[26]
— CIBSE Lighting Guide LG7: *Lighting for offices*[27]
— *Recommended Practice for Lighting of Railway Premises, British Railways Board 1969*[28]
— *EC Workplace Directive 89/654/EEC*[29] (see also SI 3004[30])
— *Approved Code of Practice and Guidance L24* (HMSO)[31]
— *EC Use of Work Equipment Directive 89/655/EEC*[32] (see also SI 2932 [33])
— *Guidance on Regulations L22* (HMSO)[34]
— *EC Display Screen Directive 90/270/EEC*[35] (see also SI 2792[36])
— *Guidance on Regulations L26* (HMSO)[37].

General notes

The information in the following section will be influenced by reference to the 'core recommendations' in sections 2.4, 2.5 and 2.6.1 to 2.6.3.

	Standard maintained illuminance (lux)	Limiting glare index	Notes
Entrances			
Entrance halls, lobbies, waiting rooms	200	19	The lighting of vertical surfaces is important to the appearance of the space. Care should be taken with entrance areas to avoid a large difference in illuminance between inside and outside, by day or night.
Enquiry desks	500	19	Localised lighting may be appropriate.
Gatehouses	200	19	Flexible switching or dimming facilities and low surface reflectances may be desirable for security reasons.
Circulation areas			
Lifts	100	—	BS 5655[38] Part 1 specifies a minimum illuminance of 50 lux on the lift car floor.
Corridors, passageways, stairs	100	22	Stairs should be lit to provide a contrast between the treads and the risers. Avoid specular reflections on the treads. Safety will be enhanced by the use of coloured nosings which contrast with the finish of the treads and risers.
Escalators, 'travellators'(passenger conveyors):	150	—	Escalators should be lit to provide a contrast between the treads and the risers, below step lighting can be effective. For both escalators and travellators specular reflections on the treads should be avoided. Particular attention should be paid to entrances and exits. See Health and Safety Executive Guidance Note PM34 *Escalator Safety*[39].
—entrances and exits	200	—	
Atria:			
—general movement	50–200	22	Depending on building and the areas opening off the atrium.
—plant growth	500–3000	—	See reference 27 above.
Staff rooms			
Changing, locker and cleaner's rooms, cloakrooms, lavatories	100	—	Various sections of the *Factories Act 1961*[23] apply to lavatories.
Rest rooms	150	19	Lighting should be different in style from the work areas.

Staff restaurants, canteens, cafeterias, dining rooms, messrooms	200	22	The lighting should aim to provide a relaxed but interesting atmosphere. Various regulations made under the *Factories Act 1961* apply to canteens and messrooms.

Kitchens and food preparation

Serveries, vegetable preparation, washing-up areas	300	22	The *Food Safety Act 1990*[40] applies. Luminaires should be constructed so that no part of the luminaire can fall into the foodstuffs. The luminaires should be capable of being washed or hosed down in safety. Lamps suitable for operation at low temperatures will be necessary for some food storage areas. Lamps and luminaires suitable for hot humid conditions may be required for some other areas.
Food preparation and cooking	500	22	
Food stores, cellars	150	22	

Communications

Switchboard rooms	300	19	Avoid veiling reflections from controls. Too high an illuminance may reduce the visibility of signal lights. Supplementary local lighting may be desirable where directories are used.
Telephone apparatus room	150	25	
Telex room, post room	500	19	
Reprographic room	300	19	

Building services

Boiler houses:

—general	100	25	
—boiler front	150	—	
Control rooms	300	19	Localised lighting of the control display and the control desks may be appropriate. In all cases, care should be taken to avoid shadows and veiling reflections on instruments. Care is also required to avoid reflections on VDTs. Where a mainly self-luminous display is used the ability to dim the room lighting may be useful. Where a large mimic diagram containing detail which has to be seen from a distance is used, special lighting providing a minimum illuminance of 500 lux on the diagram is desirable. For maintenance purposes, an illuminance of at least 150 lux should be provided on the appropriate surface of the control panels.
Mechanical plant rooms	150	25	Supplementary portable lighting may be required for maintenance.
Electrical switch rooms	200	—	Additional local lighting of instruments and controls may be required.
Cable flats	50	—	
Store rooms	100	—	See Distribution and storage.

Car parks

—covered			Luminaires suitable for hazardous area lighting may be necessary. Higher values of illuminance are a deterrent to criminals and the choice of illuminance will depend upon achieving personal security and the degree of risk of theft and vandalism. See *BS 5489*[41] Part 9 .

Floors:

—low risk	50	—	Care is required in the positioning of luminaires to avoid glare to drivers and pedestrians.
—high risk	200	—	
Ramps and corners:			
—low risk	75	—	
—high risk	200	—	

Vehicle entrances and exits	100	—	The lighting of exits and entrances should provide a transition zone to avoid sudden changes in illuminance between inside and outside by day or night. Care should be taken to avoid glare to drivers and pedestrians.
Control booths	200	—	Local lighting may be appropriate.

Distribution and storage

Other relevant documents:

— CIBSE Lighting Guide: *Lighting in hostile and hazardous environments*[42]
— CIBSE Lighting Guide LG1: *The industrial environment* [7]
— *EC Workplace Directive 89/654/EEC*[29] (see also SI 3004[30])
— *Approved Code of Practice and Guidance L24* (HMSO)[31]
— *EC Use of Work Equipment Directive 89/655/EEC*[32] (see also SI 2932 [33])
— *Guidance on Regulations L22* (HMSO)[34]
— *EC Display Screen Directive 90/270/EEC*[35] (see also SI 2792[36])
— *Guidance on Regulations L26* (HMSO)[37].

General notes

The information in the following section will be influenced by reference to the 'core recommendations' in sections 2.4, 2.5 and 2.6.1–2.6.3.

In some storage areas, the materials being stored (e.g. chemicals, gases etc.) may produce a corrosive atmosphere or represent a fire or explosion hazard. Luminaires appropriate to these conditions will be required. In cold stores, special luminaires and circuitry may be necessary for some light sources to operate at low temperatures. Eye protection will be required for some activities.

	Standard maintained illuminance (lux)	Limiting glare index	Notes
Loading bays	150	—	Avoid glare to drivers of vehicles approaching the loading bay. Light and mark clearly the edge of the loading bay.
Work stores			
Unpacking, sorting	200	25	
Large item storage	100	25	Supplementary local lighting may be necessary if identification of items requires perception of detail. Selective switching may be appropriate.
Small item rack storage	300	25	Supplementary local lighting may be necessary if the identification of items is visually difficult. Considerable obstruction is likely. Selective switching may be appropriate.
Issue counter, records, storeman's desks	500	22	Local or localised lighting may be appropriate. Avoid reflections on display screens.
Warehouses and bulk stores			
Storage of goods where identification requires only limited perception of detail	100	25	Lighting should be designed to emphasise the features which enable the operator to identify the required item and its position.
Storage of goods where identification requires perception of detail	150	25	The lighting of vertical surfaces is important. Considerable obstruction is likely. If the area is continuously occupied, the maintained illuminance should be increased to 200 lux and to 300 lux where identification requires perception of detail. Avoid glare to forklift truck operators.
Automatic high bay rack stores:			
—gangway	20	—	Supplementary lighting may be required for maintenance.
—control station	200	—	Avoid glare to operator. Local lighting should be considered.

Packing and despatch	300	25

Cold stores
—general   300   —   Cold and wet conditions likely, see general notes. Care should be taken with the lighting of entrance and exit areas to avoid noticeable differences in illuminance, by day and by night.

General exterior areas

Other relevant documents:

— BS 5489: Road lighting[41]
— CIBSE Lighting Guide LG1: The industrial environment[7]
— CIBSE Lighting Guide: Shipbuilding and ship repair[43]
— CIBSE Lighting Guide: Lighting in hostile and hazardous environments[42]
— CIBSE Lighting Guide LG6: The outdoor environment[26]
— EC Use of Work Equipment Directive 89/655/EEC[32] (see also SI 2932 [33])
— Guidance on Regulations L22 (HMSO)[34]
— CIE Publication No 68 Guide to the lighting of exterior working areas[44]
— CIE Publication No 94 Guide to decorative floodlighting[45]
— ILE Guidance Notes for the reduction of light pollution (1992)[46].

General notes

The luminaires used outdoors must be protected against dust, weather and corrosion. Luminaires must be mounted in the planes in which they are intended by the manufacturer. In areas where the luminaires are subject to damage they must be of robust construction made from impact resistant materials and where unauthorised interference may take place they should have tamper proof fixings. Higher illuminance values should be used where there is a high risk of crime.

	Standard maintained illuminance (lux)	Limiting glare index	Notes
Car parks			Higher values of illuminance are a deterrent to criminals and the choice of illuminance will depend upon achieving personal security and the degree of risk of theft and vandalism. See BS 5489[41] Part 9.
—low risk	20	—	Avoid glare to road users.
—high risk	50	—	
Pedestrian precincts			
—low risk	20	—	Lighting equipment should harmonise with
—high risk	100	—	surround.
Covered pavement and steps	75	—	
Service areas	50	—	Avoid glare to road users.
Sales areas			
—low district brightness	50	—	Avoid glare to road users.
—high district brightness	200	—	
Floodlighting buildings and structures			
—low district brightness	30	—	These recommendations are based on concrete with reflection factor 0.8 and should be adjusted for other materials. See reference 26 above.
—high district brightness	100	—	
Storage areas	20	—	
Working areas	50–100	—	

Roadways on industrial and commercial sites

Other relevant documents:

— CIBSE Lighting Guide LG1: The industrial environment[7]
— CIBSE Lighting Guide LG6 :The outdoor environment[26]
— BS 5489: Road lighting[41] Part 3
— EC Use of Work Equipment Directive 89/655/EEC[32](see also SI2932[33])
— Guidance on Regulations L22 (HMSO)[34]
— ILE Guidance notes for the reduction of light pollution (1992)[46].

General notes

The lighting of public highways is outside the scope of this Code, the principles being well documented in BS 5489: Road lighting[41]. The approach adopted here is suitable for roadway, footway and footpath lighting within factories and industrial sites where the speed of vehicles is restricted to less than 30 mph and vehicles normally drive with dipped headlights during hours of darkness. If the roadway within a site should fall within the category of a major traffic route then its design should be in accordance with BS 5489, Part 2.

	Standard maintained illuminance (lux)	Limiting glare index	Notes
Road, footway or footpath	5–10	—	BS 5489 recognises three categories depending on usage and crime risk for which average illuminance steps of 10, 6 and 3.5 lux and minima of 5, 2.5 and 1.0 lux respectively are specified. Lanterns emitting less than 3500 lumens in the lower hemisphere are unlikely to cause glare. For lanterns emitting 3500 lumens or more in the lower hemisphere, the maximum luminous intensity/1000 lumens are 160 candelas/1000 lumens at 80° to the downward vertical and 80 candelas/1000 lumens at 90° to the downward vertical.

Security

Other relevant documents:

— CIBSE Lighting Guide LG1: The industrial environment[7]
— CIBSE Lighting Guide LG6: The outdoor environment[26]
— CIBSE Applications Manual AM4: Security engineering[47]
— ILE Guidance Notes for the reduction of light pollution (1992)[46].

General notes

The arrangement of luminaires should conceal the observer and reveal the intruder. Luminaires may be subjected to impact damage.

	Standard maintained illuminance (lux)	Limiting glare index	Notes
Area lighting	5–20	—	The greater the lighting of the adjacent area the higher the illuminance which should be used.
Perimeter lighting	1	—	Minimum vertical illuminance at the distance which detection is required.
Checkpoints	150	—	Flexible switching or dimming facilities and low surface reflectances may be desirable for security reasons.
Gatehouses	200	—	Flexible switching or dimming facilities and low surface reflectances may be desirable for security reasons.

2.6.4.2   Industrial areas and processes

Mechanical engineering

Other relevant documents:

— CIBSE Lighting Guide: *Lighting in hostile and hazardous environments*[42]
— CIBSE Lighting Guide *LG1: The industrial environment*[7]
— CIBSE Lighting Guide *LG3: Areas for visual display terminals*[25]
— *Protection against ultra-violet radiation in the workplace*, National Radiological Protection Board[48]
— *EC Workplace Directive 89/654/EEC*[29] (see also SI 3004[30])
— *Approved Code of Practice and Guidance L24* (HMSO)[31]
— *EC Use of Work Equipment Directive 89/655/EEC*[32] (see also SI 2932[33])
— *Guidance on Regulations L22* (HMSO)[34]
— *EC Display Screen Directive 90/270/EEC*[35] (see also SI 2792[36])
— *Guidance on Regulations L26* (HMSO)[37].

General notes

The information in the following section will be influenced by reference to the 'core recommendations' in sections 2.4, 2.5 and 2.6.1 to 2.6.3.

Robust, easily maintained luminaires are desirable. For many operations local lighting is preferred to provide directional effects on the workpiece. Where brass, copper or similarly coloured materials are used, care should be taken to ensure that high pressure sodium discharge lamps enable the task details to be adequately discriminated.

Some areas may represent corrosion or fire/explosion hazards. Luminaires appropriate to these conditions are necessary. Many machines and equipment are fitted with display screens, so care must be taken to avoid specular reflections. Eye protection will be required for some activities.

	Standard maintained illuminance (lux)	Limiting glare index	Notes
Structural steel fabrication			
General	300	28	
Marking-off	500	28	Local lighting may be appropriate.
Sheet metal works			
Pressing, punching, shearing, stamping, spinning, folding	500	22	
Benchwork, scribing, inspection	750	22	Care should be taken to avoid multiple shadows. Where scribing coatings are used, care should be taken to ensure that high pressure sodium discharge lamps allow the task to be adequately discriminated.
Machine and tool shops			
Rough bench and machine work	300	25	Some obstruction is likely. Care should be taken to minimise stroboscopic effects on rotating machinery. Supplementary local lighting on machines is desirable.
Medium bench and machine work	500	22	
Fine bench and machine work	750	22	
Gauge rooms	1000	19	Optical aids may be required.
Die sinking shops			
General	500	22	
Fine work	1500	—	Portable local lighting is desirable.
Welding and soldering shops			
Gas and arc welding, rough spot welding	300	28	Care is necessary to prevent exposure of eyes and skin to radiation. Welding screens will be used so considerable obstruction is likely. Portable lighting may be useful.
Medium soldering, brazing, spot welding	500	25	
Fine soldering, fine spot welding	1000	—	Local lighting is desirable.

Assembly shops

Rough work, e.g. frame and heavy machinery assembly	300	25	Considerable obstruction is likely. Portable local lighting may be useful. The lighting of vertical surfaces may be important.
Medium work, e.g. engine assembly, vehicle body assembly	500	22	Some obstruction likely.
Fine work, e.g. office machinery assembly	750	19	Local or localised lighting may be appropriate.
Very fine work, e.g. instrument assembly	1000	—	Local lighting and optical aids are desirable.
Minute work, e.g. watch making	1500	—	Local lighting and optical aids are desirable.

Inspection and testing shops

Coarse work, e.g. using go/no go gauges, inspection of large sub-assemblies	500	22	Local or localised lighting may be appropriate. Use of lamps of colour rendering groups 1A or 1B is recommended if colour judgements are important.
Medium work, e.g. inspection of painted surfaces	750	19	Local or localised lighting may be appropriate. Use of lamps of colour rendering groups 1A or 1B is recommended if colour judgements are important.
Fine work, e.g. using calibrated scales, inspection of precision mechanisms	1000	19	Local lighting and optical aids are desirable. Use of lamps of colour rendering groups 1A or 1B is recommended if colour judgements are important.
Very fine work, e.g. gauging and inspection of small intricate parts	1500	—	Local lighting and optical aids are desirable. Use of lamps of colour rendering groups 1A or 1B is recommended if colour judgements are important.
Minute work, e.g. inspection of very small instruments	2000	—	Local lighting and optical aids are desirable. Use of lamps of colour rendering groups 1A or 1B is recommended if colour judgements are important.

Paint shops and spray booths

			Local authority regulations may apply. Luminaires suitable for a hazardous environment are normally necessary. Eye protection will be required for some activities. Frequent maintenance will be required if luminaires are likely to be sprayed during painting operations. See also BS 5345[49].
Dipping, rough spraying	300	25	
Preparation, ordinary painting spraying and finishing	500	22	
Fine painting, spraying and finishing	750	22	Lamps of colour rendering groups 1A or 1B are desirable.
Inspection, retouching, matching	1000	22	Lamps of colour rendering groups 1A or 1B are desirable.

Plating shops

			Easily maintained luminaires suitable for a humid, corrosive atmosphere are desirable.
Vats and baths	300	25	
Buffing, polishing, burnishing	500	22	
Final buffing and polishing	750	22	
Inspection			See reference 7 above.

Electrical and electronic engineering

Other relevant documents:

— CIBSE Lighting Guide *LG1: The industrial environment*[7]
— CIBSE Lighting Guide *LG3: Areas for visual display terminals*[25]
— *EC Workplace Directive 89/654/EEC*[29] (see also SI 3004[30])
— *Approved Code of Practice and Guidance L24* (HMSO)[31]
— *EC Use of Work Equipment Directive 89/655/EEC*[32] (see also SI 2932 [33])
— *Guidance on Regulations L22* (HMSO)[34]
— *EC Display Screen Directive 90/270/EEC*[35] (see also SI 2792[36])
— *Guidance on Regulations L26* (HMSO)[37]
— *EC Electromagnetic Compatibility Directive 89/336/EEC*[50].

General notes

The information in the following section will be influenced by reference to the 'core recommendations' in sections 2.4, 2.5 and 2.6.1 to 2.6.3.

Where colour judgements are important, lamps of colour rendering groups 1A or 1B are desirable. Where copper, brass and similarly coloured materials are used, care should be taken to ensure that high pressure sodium discharge lamps enable task details to be adequately discriminated. Eye protection will be required for some activities. In clean areas luminaires must be constructed and fitted so that the room seal is unaffected and the flow of air unobstructed. In some areas designated special 'clean' luminaires are not required. In others rigorous cleaning methods including hosing down takes place requiring IP65 protected luminaires.

	Standard maintained illuminance (lux)	Limiting glare index	Notes
Electrical equipment manufacture			
Manufacture of cables and insulated wires, winding, varnishing and immersion of coils, assembly of large machines, simple assembly work	300	25	For large machines, some obstruction is likely. Portable local lighting may be needed.
Medium assembly, e.g. telephones, small motors	500	25	Local lighting may be appropriate.
Assembly of precision components, e.g. telecommunications equipment; adjustment, inspection and calibration	1000	—	Local lighting is desirable. Care is necessary to control specular reflections. Optical aids may be useful.
Assembly of high precision parts	1500	—	Local lighting is desirable. Care is necessary to control specular reflections. Optical aids may be useful.
Electronic equipment manufacture			
Printed circuit boards:			
—silk screening	500	—	Local lighting may be appropriate.
—hand insertion of components, soldering	750	—	Local lighting may be appropriate.
—inspection	1000	—	A large, low-luminance luminaire overhead ensures specular reflection conditions which are helpful for inspection of printed circuits. See reference 7 above.
Assembly of wiring harness, cleating harness, testing and calibration	750	—	Local lighting may be appropriate.
Chassis assembly	1000	—	Local lighting may be appropriate.
Inspection and testing:			
—soak test	200	25	
—safety and functional tests	300	25	Care should be taken to avoid veiling reflections from instrument displays.

Metal manufacture

Other relevant documents:

— CIBSE Lighting Guide: *Lighting in hostile and hazardous environments*[42]
— CIBSE Lighting Guide LG1: *The industrial environment*[7]
— CIBSE Lighting Guide LG3: *Areas for visual display terminals*[25]
— BS 6467: *Selection of apparatus for use in the presence of combustible dusts*[51]
— EC Workplace Directive 89/654/EEC[29] (see also SI 3004[30])
— Approved Code of Practice and Guidance L24 (HMSO)[31]
— EC Use of Work Equipment Directive 89/655/EEC[32] (see also SI 2932 [33])
— Guidance on Regulations L22 (HMSO)[34]
— EC Display Screen Directive 90/270/EEC[35] (see also SI 2792[36])
— Guidance on Regulations L26 (HMSO)[37].

General notes

The information in the following section will be influenced by reference to the 'core recommendations' in sections 2.4, 2.5 and 2.6.1 to 2.6.3.

Lamps and luminaires may be subject to severe fouling and vibration and a wide range of ambient temperatures. Corrosive conditions may be present in some locations. Dustproof (IP5X) or other luminaires with good maintenance properties are desirable, as is easy access to them. The accurate visual judgement of hot metal may be difficult under high pressure sodium discharge lamps. For some metals, dusts formed during production may represent an explosion hazard. Luminaires should be chosen appropriately. Eye protection will be required in some areas. Many machines and equipment use display screens, so care must be taken to avoid specular reflections.

	Standard maintained illuminance (lux)	Limiting glare index	Notes
Ironmaking			
Sinter plant:			
—plant floor	200	28	Supplementary lighting may be needed for maintenance work.
Mixer drum, fan house, screen houses, coolers, transfer stations	150	28	
Furnaces, cupolas:			
—general	150	28	
—control platforms	300	—	Local lighting may be appropriate.
—conveyor galleries, walkways	50	28	
Steelmaking			
Electric melting shops	200	28	Supplementary lighting may be needed for maintenance work.
Basic oxygen steel making plants:			
—general	150	28	
—converter floor, teeming bay	200	28	
—control platforms and pulpits	300	—	Local lighting may be appropriate.
—scrap bays	150	28	
Metal forming and treatment			
Ingot stripping, soaking pits, annealing and heat treatment bays, acid recovery plant	200	28	Supplementary lighting may be needed for maintenance work. Luminaires capable of withstanding corrosive atmospheres may be needed.
Pickling and cleaning bays, roughing mills, cold mills, finishing mills, tinning and galvanising lines, cut up and rewind lines			
—general	150	28	
—control platforms and pulpits	300	—	Local lighting may be appropriate.
Wire mills, product finishing steel inspection and treatment	300	28	
Plate/strip inspection	500	25	

Inspection of tinplate, stainless steel, etc.	—	—	Special lighting to reveal faults in the specular surface of the material will be required. See reference 7 above.

Foundries

Automatic plant:			
—without manual operation	50	28	Supplementary lighting may be needed for maintenance work.
—with occasional manual operation	150	28	
—with continuous manual operation	200	28	
Non-automatic plant:			
—charging floor, pouring, shaking out, cleaning, grinding, fettling	300	28	If blast cleaning is used the luminaires should be positioned away from the work area. Where metal castings are cleaned by means of abrasive wheels or bands, the dust produced may represent an explosion hazard; luminaires should be chosen appropriately.
Rough moulding, rough core making	300	28	Light distribution needs to be diffused and flexible to ensure good lighting of deep moulds. If coloured moulding sands are used, high pressure sodium discharge lamps may not be suitable.
Fine moulding, fine core making	500	25	
Inspection	500	—	See reference 7 above.

Forges

			Severe vibration is likely to occur.
General	300	25	
Inspection	500	—	See reference 7 above.
Control platforms and pulpits	300	19	Local lighting of the control display and the control desk may be appropriate. In all cases, care should be taken to avoid shadows and veiling reflections occurring on instruments. Care is also required to avoid reflections on VDTs.
Control rooms			See General building areas, section 2.6.4.1.

Plastics and rubber

Other relevant documents:

— CIBSE Lighting Guide: *Lighting in hostile and hazardous environments*[42]
— CIBSE Lighting Guide *LG1: The industrial environment*[7]
— *Protection against ultra-violet radiation in the workplace*, National Radiological Protection Board, 1977[48]
— *BS 5345: Code of practice for selection, installation and maintenance of electrical apparatus for use in potentially explosive atmospheres*[49]
— *BS 6467: Electrical apparatus with protection by enclosure for use in the presence of combustible dusts*[51]
— *EC Workplace Directive 89/654/EEC*[29] (see also SI 3004[30])
— *Approved Code of Practice and Guidance L24* (HMSO)[31]
— *EC Use of Work Equipment Directive 89/655/EEC*[32] (see also SI 2932 [33])
— *Guidance on Regulations L22* (HMSO)[34].

General notes

The information in the following section will be influenced by reference to the 'core recommendations' in sections 2.4, 2.5 and 2.6.1 to 2.6.3.

Some areas in plastic and rubber production may present a fire, explosion, or corrosion hazard. Luminaires appropriate to these conditions are necessary. Dirty conditions are likely in rubber processing factories. Dustproof (IP5X) or other luminaires with good maintenance properties are desirable for such applications. For both rubber and plastic processing high ambient temperatures may occur in some areas. Therefore, lamps and circuitry capable of operating in high temperatures are desirable in such areas. Eye protection will be required for some activities.

	Standard maintained illuminance (lux)	Limiting glare index	Notes
Plastic products			
Automatic plant:			
—without manual control	50	28	Supplementary lighting may be
—with occasional manual control	100	28	needed for maintenance work.
—with continuous manual control	300	28	
Control platforms	300	—	Local lighting may be appropriate.
Control rooms			See section 2.6.4.1 General building areas.
Non-automatic plant:			
—mixing, calendering, extrusion injection, compression and blow moulding, sheet fabrication	300	25	
—trimming, cutting, polishing, cementing	500	22	
—printing, inspection	1000	19	Use lamps of colour rendering groups 1A or 1B when colour judgements are important. When ultra-violet radiation is used to cure inks or lacquers, care is necessary to prevent exposure of eyes and skin (see section 5.9).
Rubber products			
Stock preparation, plasticising, milling	200	25	
Calendering, fabric, preparation, stock cutting	500	25	
Extruding, moulding, curing	500	22	
Inspection	1000	—	Use local lighting. See reference 7 above.

Leather industry

Other relevant documents:

— CIBSE Lighting Guide: *Lighting in hostile and hazardous environments*[42]
— CIBSE Lighting Guide *LG1: The industrial environment*[7]
— *EC Workplace Directive 89/654/EEC*[29] (see also SI 3004[30])
— *Approved Code of Practice and Guidance L24* (HMSO)[31]
— *EC Use of Work Equipment Directive 89/655/EEC*[32] (see also SI 2932 [33])
— *Guidance on Regulations L22* (HMSO)[34].

General notes

The information in the following section will be influenced by reference to the 'core recommendations' in sections 2.4, 2.5 and 2.6.1 to 2.6.3.

A highly corrosive humid atmosphere will exist in some areas of leather manufacture. Luminaires appropriate to these conditions are necessary.

	Standard maintained illuminance (lux)	Limiting glare index	Notes
Leather manufacture			
Cleaning, tanning and stretching, vats, cutting, fleshing, stuffing	300	25	
Finishing, scarfing	500	25	
Leather working			
General	300	25	
Pressing, glazing	500	22	
Cutting, splitting, scarfing, sewing	750	22	Directional lighting may be useful.
Grading, matching	1000	—	Use lamps of colour rendering group 1A. If glossy leathers are being examined, a large-area, low brightness luminaire should be used. See reference 7 above.

Textiles

Other relevant documents:

— CIBSE Lighting Guide: *Lighting in hostile and hazardous environments*[42]
— CIBSE Lighting Guide *LG1: The industrial environment*[7]
— *BS 950: Specification for artificial daylight for the assessment of colour*[21]
— *BS 6467: Electrical apparatus for use in the presence of combustible dusts*[51]
— *EC Workplace Directive 89/654/EEC*[29] (see also SI 3004[30])
— *Approved Code of Practice and Guidance L24* (HMSO)[31]
— *EC Use of Work Equipment Directive 89/655/EEC*[32] (see also SI 2932 [33])
— *Guidance on Regulations L22* (HMSO)[34]
— *EC Display Screen Directive 90/270/EEC*[35] (see also SI 2792[36])
— *Guidance on Regulations L26* (HMSO)[37].

General notes

The information in the following section will be influenced by reference to the 'core recommendations' in sections 2.4, 2.5 and 2.6.1 to 2.6.3.

Where accurate colour judgements are necessary lamps of colour rendering groups 1A or 1B are desirable. Dirty conditions are likely in many areas of fibre production. Dustproof (IP5X) luminaires are desirable.

	Standard maintained illuminance (lux)	Limiting glare index	Notes
Cotton			
Ginning, separators, dryers	200	28	Dust may cause explosive hazards.
Bale breaking, blowing, carding	300	25	
Roving, slubbing, spinning (ordinary counts), winding, reeling, combing, hackling, spreading, cabling	500	25	
Beaming, sizing, dressing and dyeing, doubling (fancy), spinning (fine counts)	500	25	
Healding (drawing-in)	1000	—	Local lighting required.
Weaving:			
—plain 'grey' cloth	750	19	
—patterned cloths, fine counts	1000	19	
Inspection	1500	16	See reference 7 above.
Synthetic or silk			
Soaking, fugitive tinting, conditioning or setting of twist	300	25	
Winding, twisting, rewinding, crimping, coning, quilting, sizing, beaming	500	25	
Spinning	500	22	
Flat bed knitting machines	500	22	
Healding (drawing-in)	1000	—	Local lighting required.
Weaving	1000	19	
Inspection	1500	16	See reference 7 above.
Woollen			
Scouring, carbonising, teasing, preparing, raising, brushing, pressing, back-washing, gilling, crabbing and blowing, blending, carding, combing (white), tentering, drying, cropping	300	25	
Spinning, roving, winding, beaming, combing (coloured), twisting	500	22	
Healding (drawing-in)	1000	—	Local lighting required.
Weaving:			
—heavy woollens	500	19	

	Standard maintained illuminance (lux)	Limiting glare index	
—medium worsteds, fine woollens	750	19	
—fine worsteds	1000	19	
Burling	1000	19	See reference 7 above.
Mending	1500	16	
Inspection (perching):			
—grey cloth	1000	19	Local lighting may be appropriate.
—final	3000	19	
Jute			
Weaving, spinning flax, cop winding, yarn calender	300	25	
Carpet manufacture			
Winding, beaming	300	25	
Setting pattern, tufting, cropping, trimming, fringing, latexing and latex drying	500	22	
Designing, weaving, mending	750	22	
Inspection:			
—general	1000	19	See reference 7 above.
Piece dyeing	750	—	

Clothing and footwear

Other relevant documents:

— CIBSE Lighting Guide: *Lighting in hostile and hazardous environments*[42]
— CIBSE Lighting Guide LG1: *The industrial environment*[7]
— *EC Workplace Directive 89/654/EEC*[29] (see also SI 3004[30])
— *Approved Code of Practice and Guidance L24 (HMSO)*[31]
— *EC Use of Work Equipment Directive 89/655/EEC*[32] (see also SI 2932[33])
— *Guidance on Regulations L22 (HMSO)*[34].

General notes

The information in the following section will be influenced by reference to the 'core recommendations' in sections 2.4, 2.5 and 2.6.1 to 2.6.3.

Wherever accurate colour judgements are required, lamps of colour rendering groups 1A or 1B should be used.

	Standard maintained illuminance (lux)	Limiting glare index	Notes
Clothing manufacture			
Preparation of cloth	300	22	Supplementary lighting will be needed for inspecting cloth. See reference 7 above.
Cutting	750	19	Hand and manually operated machines.
Matching	750	19	Use lamps of colour rendering group 1A.
Sewing	1000	19	Supplementary local lighting should be provided on the machines.
Pressing	500	22	
Inspection	1500	16	Use lamps of colour rendering groups 1A or 1B. See reference 7 above.
Hand tailoring	1500	—	Local lighting may be appropriate.
Hosiery and knitwear manufacture			
Flat bed knitting machines	500	22	
Circular knitting machines	750	22	Additional local lighting may be required.
Lockstitch and over-locking machines	1000	19	
Linking or running on	1000	19	
Mending, hand finishing	1500	—	Use local lighting.

Inspection	1500	—	Use local lighting with lamps of colour rendering groups 1A or 1B. See reference 7 above.
Glove manufacture			
Sorting and grading	750	19	Use lamps of colour rendering groups 1A or 1B.
Pressing, knitting, cutting	500	22	
Sewing	750	22	Supplementary local lighting should be provided on the machines.
Inspection	1500	—	Use local lighting with lamps of colour rendering groups 1A or 1B.
Hat manufacture			
Stiffening, braiding, refining, forming, sizing, pouncing, ironing	300	22	
Cleaning, flanging, finishing	500	22	
Sewing	750	22	Supplementary local lighting should be provided on the machines.
Inspection	1500	—	Use local lighting with lamps of colour rendering groups 1A or 1B. See reference 7 above.
Boot and shoe manufacture			
Leather and synthetic:			
—sorting and grading	1000	16	Use lamps of colour rendering groups 1A or 1B. Directional lighting may be useful.
—clicking, closing	1000	22	
—preparatory operations	1000	22	Local or localised lighting may be
—cutting tables and presses	1500	16	appropriate.
—bottom stock preparation, lasting, bottoming, finishing, show rooms	1000	19	
Rubber:			
—washing, compounding, coating, drying, varnishing, vulcanising, calendering, cutting	300	25	Drying may involve an explosion risk. Appropriate luminaires are necessary.
—lining, making and finishing	500	22	

Food, drink and tobacco

Other relevant documents:

— *The Food Hygiene (General) Regulations 1970*[52]
— *The Slaughterhouse (Hygiene) Regulations 1958*[53]
— CIBSE Lighting Guide: *Lighting in hostile and hazardous environments*[42]
— CIBSE Lighting Guide LG1: *The industrial environment*[7]
— BS 5345: *Selection of electrical apparatus for use in potentially explosive atmospheres*[49]
— BS 6467: *Selection of electrical apparatus for use in the presence of combustible dusts*[51]
— *EC Workplace Directive 89/654/EEC*[29] (see also SI 3004[30])
— *Approved Code of Practice and Guidance L24 (HMSO)*[31]
— *EC Use of Work Equipment Directive 89/655/EEC*[32] (see also SI 2932[33])
— *Guidance on Regulations L22 (HMSO)*[34]
— *EC Display Screen Directive 90/270/EEC*[35] (see also SI 2792[36])
— *Guidance on Regulations L26 (HMSO)*[37].

General notes

Recommendations in the following section will be influenced by reference to the 'core recommendations' in sections 2.4, 2.5 and 2.6.1 to 2.6.3.

Equipment requirements vary widely with the application. *The Food Safety Act 1990*[40] requires that there be no likelihood of any part of the luminaire or lamp falling into foodstuffs.Therefore in some locations any openable part of a luminaire should be hinged or made captive, and all fixings should be captive. Further, the lamps should be enclosed to ensure that accidental lamp breakage does not allow debris to fall into the product. Hosing down may be part of the cleaning procedure for some areas, so IPX5 luminaires are desirable. Some locations involve fire or explosion risks, so equipment suitable for use in hazardous areas is required. For some applications lamps and circuitry which operate efficiently at high or low temperatures and in humid atmospheres are necessary. Other areas will be wet or dusty. In all cases the chosen luminaire should be appropriate for the operating conditions. Many processes are monitored by display screens; care should be taken to avoid specular reflections.

	Standard maintained illuminance (lux)	Limiting glare index	Notes
Slaughterhouses/ abattoirs			Damp conditions may be present, hosing down may be part of the cleaning process. Luminaires should be chosen appropriately.
General	500	25	Statutory minimum illuminance = 20 lumen/ft^2 (215 lux, see reference 7).
Inspection	750	19	Statutory minimum illuminance = 50 lumen/ft^2 (540 lux see reference 7). Lamps of colour rendering group 1A are required.
Canning, preserving and freezing Grading and sorting of raw materials	750	22	The choice of light source is important if colour judgement is required, use lamps with colour rendering groups 1A or 1B.
Preparation	500	25	
Canned and bottled goods:			Obstruction is likely. Warm and humid conditions may be present. Supplementary lighting may be necessary for cleaning and maintenance.
—retorts	300	25	
—automatic processes	200	25	
Labelling and packaging	300	25	
Frozen foods:			
—process area	300	25	
—packaging and storage	300	25	For cold stores see Distribution and storage, section 2.6.4.1.
—dairies	300	—	
Bottling, brewing and distilling			Distilleries may contain areas which involve a fire and explosion hazard. Warm, humid conditions may be present in some areas. Luminaires should be chosen appropriately.
Keg washing and handling, bottle washing	200	28	
Keg/bottle inspection	300	25	Optical aids may be used for internal inspection, see reference 51 above.
Process areas	300	25	
Bottle filling	750	25	
Edible oils and fats processing			Areas containing a fire or explosion hazard may be present. Luminaires should be chosen appropriately.
Refining and blending	300	25	
Production	500	25	
Mills			Areas containing a dust explosion hazard may be present. Luminaires should be chosen appropriately. Dust deposition on luminaires may cause maintenance problems.
Milling, filtering and packing	300	25	
Bakeries General	300	22	
Hand decorating, icing	500	22	
Chocolate and confectionery manufacture General	300	25	
Automatic processes	200	25	Supplementary lighting may be necessary for cleaning and maintenance.

	Standard maintained illuminance (lux)	Limiting glare index	Notes
Hand decoration, inspection, wrapping and packing	500	22	If accurate colour judgements are required lamps of colour rendering groups 1A or B should be used.
Tobacco processing			
Material preparation, making and packing	500	22	
Hand processes	750	22	
Control rooms			See General building areas, section 2.6.4.1.

Timber and furniture

Other relevant documents:

— CIBSE Lighting Guide: *Lighting in hostile and hazardous environments*[42]
— CIBSE Lighting Guide LG1: *The industrial environment*[7]
— BS 5345: *Selection of electrical apparatus in potentially explosive atmospheres*[49]
— BS 6467: *Selection of electrical apparatus in the presence of combustible dusts*[51]
— EC Workplace Directive 89/654/EEC[29] (see also SI 3004[30])
— Approved Code of Practice and Guidance L24 (HMSO)[31]
— EC Use of Work Equipment Directive 89/655/EEC[32] (see also SI 2932[33])
— Guidance on Regulations L22 (HMSO)[34].

General notes

The recommendations in the following section will be influenced by reference to the 'core recommendations' in sections 2.4, 2.5 and 2.6.1 to 2.6.3.

Dusty conditions are likely anywhere where timber is machined. For these areas dust-tight (IP6X) luminaires are desirable. Luminaires should be cleaned regularly. Wherever rotating machinery is used care should be taken to minimise any stroboscopic effects produced by the lighting. Eye protection will be required in some areas.

	Standard maintained illuminance (lux)	Limiting glare index	Notes
Sawmills			
General	200	25	
Head saw	500	—	Local lighting may be appropriate.
Grading	750	—	Directional lighting may be useful.
Woodwork shops			
Rough sawing, bench work	300	22	
Sizing, planing, sanding medium machining and bench work	500	22	Dust from sanding may represent an explosion hazard; luminaires should be chosen appropriately.
Fine bench and machine work, fine sanding, finishing	750	22	Localised lighting may be appropriate. Dust may represent explosion hazard; luminaires should be chosen appropriately.
Furniture manufacture			
Raw materials stores	100	28	
Finished goods stores	150	25	
Wood matching and assembly, rough sawing, cutting	300	22	
Machining, sanding and assembly, polishing	500	22	The materials used in polishing may represent a fire hazard. Appropriate luminaires will be required.
Tool rooms	500	22	
Spray booths:	500	—	Local authority regulations may apply. Luminaires should be chosen appropriately.
—colour finishing	500	—	Eye protection will be required for some activities. Lamps of colour rendering groups 1A and 1B are desirable.

	Standard maintained illuminance (lux)	Limiting glare index	Notes
—clear finishing	300	—	Eye protection will be required for some activities. Lamps of colour rendering groups 1A or 1B are desirable.
Cabinet making:			
—veneer sorting and grading	1000	19	Use lamps of colour rendering groups 1A or 1B. Directional lighting may be useful.
—marquetry, pressing, patching and fitting	500	22	
Final inspection	750	—	See reference 7 above.
Upholstery manufacture			
Cloth inspection	1500	—	Use local lighting with lamps of colour rendering groups 1A or 1B. See reference 7 above.
Filling, covering	500	22	
Slipping, cutting, sewing	750	22	
Mattress making:			
—assembly	500	22	
—tape edging	1000	22	Local lighting may be appropriate.

Paper and printing

Other relevant documents:

— CIBSE Lighting Guide: *Lighting in hostile and hazardous environments*[42]
— CIBSE Lighting Guide LG1: *The industrial environment*[7]
— CIBSE Lighting Guide LG3: *Areas for visual display terminals*[25]
— *Lighting in Printing Works* (1980)[54], British Printing Industries Federation
— *Protection against ultra-violet radiation in the workplace* (1977)[48], National Radiological Protection Board
— *BS 950: Artificial daylight for the assessment of colour*[21]
— *BS 5345: Selection of electrical apparatus in potentially explosive atmospheres*[49]
— *EC Workplace Directive 89/654/EEC*[29] (see also SI 3004[30])
— *Approved Code of Practice and Guidance L24* (HMSO)[31]
— *EC Use of Work Equipment Directive 89/655/EEC*[32] (see also SI 2932[33])
— *Guidance on Regulations L22* (HMSO)[34]
— *EC Display Screen Directive 90/270/EEC*[35] (see also SI 2792[36])
— *Guidance on Regulations L26* (HMSO)[37].

General notes

The recommendations in the following section will be influenced by reference to the 'core recommendations' in sections 2.4, 2.5 and 2.6.1 to 2.6.3.

Damp and dirty conditions are likely in paper mills. Easily maintained, corrosion resistant luminaires are desirable for this application. If volatile inks are used in printing, a hazardous environment may be present in some areas. Luminaires should be chosen appropriately. In areas where accurate colour matching is required refer to *BS 950*[21].

	Standard maintained illuminance (lux)	Limiting glare index	Notes
Paper mills			
Pulp mills, preparation plants	300	25	
Paper and board making:			
—general	300	25	
—automatic processes	200	25	Supplementary lighting may be necessary for maintenance work.
—inspection, sorting	500	19	See reference 7 above.
Paper converting processes:			
—general	300	25	
—associated printing	500	22	When ultra-violet radiation is used for curing ink, special care is necessary to avoid exposure of eyes and skin (see section 5.9).
Printing works			
Type foundries:			
—matrix making, dressing type, hand and machine casting	300	25	

—fount assembly, sorting	750	22	
Composing rooms:			Large area, low-luminance luminaires are desirable.
—hand composing, imposition and distribution	750	19	
—hot metal (keyboard)	750	19	
—hot metal (casting)	300	22	
Photocomposing:			See reference 25 above.
—keyboard setting	500	19	
—paste-up	750	16	
Illuminated tables (general)	300	—	Where colour judgements are important use lamps of colour rendering groups 1A or 1B. Dimming may be required.
Proof presses	500	22	Where ultra-violet radiation is used for curing ink, special care is necessary to prevent exposure of eyes and skin (see section 5.9).
Proof reading	750	16	
Graphic reproduction:			
—general	500	22	
—precision proofing, retouching, etching	1000	—	Local lighting may be appropriate. *BS 950*[21] should be consulted where colour is important.
—colour reproduction and inspection	1500	—	
Printing machine room:			
—presses	500	22	When ultra-violet radiation is used for curing ink, special care is necessary to prevent exposure of eyes and skin (see section 5.9).
—pre-make ready	500	22	
—printed sheet inspection	1000	19	
Binding:			
—folding, pasting, punching, stitching	500	22	
—cutting, assembling, embossing	750	22	

Ceramics and glass

Other relevant documents:

— CIBSE Lighting Guide *LG1: The industrial environment*[7]
— *EC Workplace Directive 89/654/EEC*[29] (see also SI 3004[30])
— *Approved Code of Practice and Guidance L24* (HMSO)[31]
— *EC Use of Work Equipment Directive 89/655/EEC*[32] (see also SI 2932 [33])
— *Guidance on Regulations L22* (HMSO)[34]
— *EC Display Screen Directive 90/270/EEC*[35] (see also SI 2792[36])
— *Guidance on Regulations L26* (HMSO)[37].

General notes

The information in the following section will be influenced by reference to the 'core recommendation' in 2.4, 2.5 and 2.6.1 to 2.6.3.

Lamps and luminaires may be subject to severe fouling and high ambient temperatures in some areas. Dustproof (IP5X) or other luminaires with good maintenance properties are desirable in areas where raw materials are formed into the basic product. Eye protection will be required for some activities.

	Standard maintained illuminance (lux)	Limiting glare index	Notes
Concrete products			
Mixing, casting, cleaning	200	28	
Potteries			
Grinding, moulding, pressing, cleaning, trimming, glazing, firing	300	28	
Enamelling, colouring	750	16	Where good colour judgements are necessary lamps of colour rendering groups 1A or 1B are desirable.

Glass works

Furnace rooms, bending, annealing lehrs	150	28
Mixing rooms, forming, cutting, grinding, polishing, toughening	300	28	Supplementary local lighting may be appropriate. Care should be taken to avoid specular reflections in the work pieces.
Bevelling, decorative cutting, engraving, etching, silvering	500	22	Supplementary local lighting is necessary. Indirect background lighting is desirable to avoid specular reflections in the work pieces.
Inspection	500	—	See reference 7 above.

Chemicals

Other relevant documents:

— CIBSE Lighting Guide: *Lighting in hostile and hazardous environments*[42]
— CIBSE Lighting Guide *LG3: Areas for visual display terminals*[25]
— *Protection against ultra-violet radiation in the workplace*[48], The National Radiological Protection Board 1977
— *BS 5345: Selection of electrical apparatus for use in potentially explosive atmospheres*[49]
— *BS 6467: Selection of electrical apparatus for use in the presence of combustible dusts*[51]
— *EC Workplace Directive 89/654/EEC*[29] (see also SI 3004[30])
— *Approved Code of Practice and Guidance L24* (HMSO)[31]
— *EC Use of Work Equipment Directive 89/655/EEC*[32] (see also SI 2932[33])
— *Guidance on Regulations L22* (HMSO)[34]
— *EC Display Screen Directive 90/270/EEC*[35] (see also SI 2792[36])
— *Guidance on Regulations L26* (HMSO)[37].

General notes

The information in the following section will be influenced by reference to the 'core recommendations' in sections 2.4, 2.5 and 2.6.1 to 2.6.3.

Many activities in the chemical industry involve a risk of corrosion, fire or explosion. In areas where these risks exist, luminaires appropriate to the nature of the hazard are required. Steam or dust may be continually present in some areas and frequent maintenance may be required. Luminaires should be chosen appropriately. Where accurate colour judgements are needed, lamps of colour rendering groups 1A or 1B should be used. Eye protection will be required for some activities. In clean areas luminaires must be constructed and fitted so that the room seal is unaffected and the flow of air unobstructed. In some areas designated special 'clean' luminaires are not required. In others, rigorous cleaning methods, including hosing down, take place which require IP65 protected luminaires.

	Standard maintained illuminance (lux)	Limiting glare index	Notes
Petroleum, chemical and petrochemical works			
Exterior walkways, platforms, stairs and ladders	50	—	
Exterior pump and valve areas	100	—	
Pump and compressor houses	150	—	
Process plant with remote control	50	—	Supplementary local lighting may be needed for maintenance work.
Process plant:			
—requiring occasional manual intervention	100	—	
—permanently occupied work stations	200	—	
—control rooms			See General building areas, section 2.6.4.1.

Pharmaceuticals and fine chemicals manufacture

Pharmaceutical manufacture: —grinding, granulating, mixing, drying, tableting sterilising, washing, preparation of solutions, filling, capping, wrapping, hardening	500	22	Clean area technology will often apply. See General notes above.
Fine chemical manufacture: —exterior walkways, platforms, stairs and ladders	50	—	
—valves, instruments	100	—	
—process plant	100	25	Supplementary local lighting may be needed for maintenance work.
Fine chemical finishing	500	25	
Inspection	500	—	Local lighting may be applicable. Lamps of colour rendering groups 1A or 1B are desirable.

Soap manufacture

			Luminaires suitable for damp conditions may be required.
General area	300	25	
Automatic processes	200	25	
Control panels	300	—	Local lighting may be appropriate. Care should be taken to avoid veiling reflections from instrument displays.
Machines	300	25	

Paint works

General	300	25	If colour judgement is used on the production line, lamps of colour rendering groups 1A or 1B are desirable.
Automatic processes	200	25	
Control panels	300	—	Local lighting may be appropriate. Care should be taken to avoid veiling reflections from instrument displays.
Special batch mixing	750	22	For exact colour matching work lamps of colour rendering group 1A are necessary. BS 950[21] applies.
Colour matching	1000	19	For exact colour matching work lamps of colour rendering group 1A are necessary. BS 950[21] applies.

Agriculture and horticulture

Other relevant documents:

— CIBSE Lighting Guide: *Lighting in hostile and hazardous environments*[42]
— *Essentials of farm lighting*[55] (Electricity Association Technology Ltd)
— *Lighting for horticultural production*[56] (Electricity Association Technology Ltd)
— *BS 5502: Design of buildings and structures for agriculture*[57]
— *BS 6467: Electrical apparatus in the presence of combustible dusts*[51] Part 2
— *EC Workplace Directive 89/654/EEC*[29] (see also SI 3004[30])
— *Approved Code of Practice and Guidance L24* (HMSO)[31]
— *EC Use of Work Equipment Directive 89/655/EEC*[32] (see also SI 2932 [33])
— *Guidance on Regulations L22* (HMSO)[34].

General notes

The information in the following section will be influenced by reference to the 'core recommendations' in sections 2.4, 2.5 and 2.6.1 to 2.6.3.

Luminaires should be positioned where mechanical damage is unlikely and be capable of withstanding dirty corrosive conditions. In some farm buildings an explosive dust hazard may exist; in these circumstances special equipment will be required. In some areas, luminaires capable of being safely hosed down are needed (IPX5). Low voltage switching is desirable.

	Standard maintained illuminance (lux)	Limiting glare index	Notes
Inspection of farm produce			The choice of light source is important. Local lighting may be appropriate. Use of lamps with colour rendering groups 1A or 1B.
Where colour is important	500	25	
Other inspection tasks	300	25	Local lighting may be appropriate.
Farm workshops			Eye protection will be required for some activities. Supplementary local lighting will be necessary.
General	100	25	
Workbench or machine	300	25	Local or portable lighting may be appropriate.
Milking parlours	100	25	Luminaires suitable for being hosed down may be required in some areas.
Sick animal pens, calf nurseries	50	—	A lower illuminance is acceptable in the absence of the stockman.
Other farm and horticultural buildings			
Where adequate daylight is admitted	20	25	A 5% average daylight factor will give adequate daylight.
All other buildings	50	25	For a windowless building a maintained illuminance of 20 lux may be used provided the building is entered through a vestibule which excludes daylight and which has a maintained illuminance of 50 lux.
Growing areas			Refer to references 55 and 56 above.

Mines (surface buildings) and quarries

Other relevant documents:

— CIBSE Lighting Guide: *Lighting in hostile and hazardous environments*[42]
— CIBSE Lighting Guide LG1: *The industrial environment*[7]
— CIBSE Lighting Guide LG3: *Areas for visual display terminals*[25]
— CIBSE Lighting Guide LG6: *The outdoor environment*[26]
— *National Coal Board Underground Lighting Recommendations*[58]
— *National Coal Board Design Guide for Coal Preparation Plants*[59]
— BS 6467: *Electrical apparatus in the presence of combustible dusts*[51] Part 2
— EC Workplace Directive 89/654/EEC[29] (see also SI 3004[30])
— *Approved Code of Practice and Guidance L24* (HMSO)[31]
— EC Use of Work Equipment Directive 89/655/EEC[32] (see also SI 2932[33])
— *Guidance on Regulations L22* (HMSO)[34]
— EC Display Screen Directive 90/270/EEC[35] (see also SI 2792[36])
— *Guidance on Regulations L26* (HMSO)[37]
— ILE *Guidance Notes for the reduction of light pollution* (1992)[46].

General notes

The information in the following section will be influenced by reference to the 'core recommendations' in sections 2.4, 2.5 and 2.6.1 to 2.6.3.

Luminaires suitable for hazardous atmospheres will be required in some areas. Dirt and damp are likely to produce difficult maintenance conditions in some areas. Luminaires with good maintenance properties are desirable as is easy access to them. Luminaires may be hosed down, and damage due to impact and vibration, may occur.

	Standard maintained illuminance (lux)	Limiting glare index	Notes
Coal preparation plants			Severe fouling of luminaires likely, may be hosed down. IP65 luminaires may be required.
Working areas	300	—	
Picking belts	500	—	Local lighting may be appropriate.
Other areas	200	—	

	Standard maintained illuminance (lux)	Limiting glare index	Notes
Winding houses:			Lighting should give clear view from cab.
—general	150	25	
—motor room	300	—	
Lamp rooms:			
— main areas	150	28	
— repair sections	300	25	
Screens	200	—	
Kilns	200	—	
Weigh houses	150	—	Reflections in window must be avoided.
Fan houses	150	28	
Materials handling			
Conveyors and gantries	100	—	Luminaires should be positioned to light main access way and belt.
Transfer houses:			
— general	100	—	
— manned areas	150	—	
Silos and elevators	100	—	
Sampling towers	150	—	
Wagon loading	50	—	
Unloading points	50	—	
Tiplers	100	—	
Bagging plant	200	—	
Switch rooms			See General building areas, section 2.6.4.1.
Control rooms			See General building areas, section 2.6.4.1.
Workshops machine and tool shops			See Mechanical engineering, section 2.6.4.2.
Stores			See Distribution and storage, section 2.6.4.1.

Electricity generation, transmission and distribution

Other relevant documents:

— CIBSE Lighting Guide: *Lighting in hostile and hazardous environments*[42]
— CIBSE Lighting Guide LG1: *The industrial environment*[7]
— CIBSE Lighting Guide LG3: *Areas for visual display terminals*[25]
— CIBSE Lighting Guide LG6: *The outdoor environment*[26]
— *EC Workplace Directive 89/654/EEC*[29] (see also SI 3004[30])
— *Approved Code of Practice and Guidance L24 (HMSO)*[31]
— *EC Use of Work Equipment Directive 89/655/EEC*[32] (see also SI 2932 [33])
— *Guidance on Regulations L22 (HMSO)*[34]
— *EC Display Screen Directive 90/270/EEC*[35] (see also SI 2792[36])
— *Guidance on Regulations L26 (HMSO)*[37]
— *ILE Guidance Notes for the reduction of light pollution*[46].

General notes

The information in the following section will be influenced by the 'core recommendations' in sections 2.4, 2.5 and 2.6.1 to 2.6.3.

Robust luminaires are needed to withstand vibration in some areas. A damp, dirty and corrosive environment requiring appropriate luminaires will exist in some parts of the plant.

	Standard maintained illuminance (lux)	Limiting glare index	Notes
Electricity generating stations			
Boiler houses:			
—access platforms	50	—	
—burners and other working areas	100	—	
—boiler and turbine house basements (including feed pump bay)	100	—	

Turbine and gas turbine houses operating at floor level	200	25	Additional local lighting of instruments and inspection points may be required.
Ancilliary areas:			
—ash handling plants, settling pits	100	—	
—battery rooms, chargers and rectifiers	100	—	Corrosive and hazardous atmospheres possible.
Cable tunnels, cable basement circulating water culverts, screen chambers	50	—	
Outdoor transformer compounds	30	—	See reference 26 above.
Pump houses	200	—	
Relay and telecommunications rooms	300	—	
Storage tanks (indoor), operating areas and filling points of outdoor tanks	50	—	
Substation and switch rooms:			
—diesel generator rooms	150	—	
—high-voltage substations, indoor	100	—	
—high-voltage substations, outdoor	30	—	
—switch rooms (metal clad) and cubicle switchgear	200	—	
Precipitator:			
—basement areas	100	—	
—working platforms and gantries	100	—	
—transformers/rectifiers	200	—	
Precipitator top	100	—	
Water treatment			See 'Services', section 2.6.4.3 Water and sewage treatment works.

Control rooms

Localised lighting of the control display and the control desks may be appropriate.

Desks	300	19	In all cases, care should be taken to avoid shadows and veiling reflections occurring on instruments. Care is also required to avoid reflections on VDTs. Where a mainly self-luminous display is used the ability to dim the room lighting may be useful. Where a large mimic diagram containing detail which has to be seen from a considerable distance is used, special lighting providing a minimum illuminance of 500 lux on the diagram is desirable.
Vertical panels	500	—	
Rear of panels	100	—	For maintenance purposes, an illuminance of at least 150 lux should be provided on the appropriate surface of the control panels.

Coal handling plant

Conveyors over bunkers, conveyor houses, gantries, junction towers and unloading hoppers	100	—	Very dirty conditions possible, luminaires may be subject to hosing down.
Reclamation hoppers	50	—	
Storage areas (outdoor)	5	—	
Unloading areas (outdoor)	5	—	
Other areas where operators are in attendance	150	—	

Nuclear reactor plant

Gas circulation bays, reactor areas, boilers, platform, reactor charge and discharge faces	150	—	

Gas storage and distribution

Other relevant documents:

— CIBSE Lighting Guide: *Lighting in hostile and hazardous environments*[42]
— CIBSE Lighting Guide LG1: *The industrial environment*[7]
— CIBSE Lighting Guide LG3: *Areas for visual display terminals*[25]
— CIBSE Lighting Guide LG6: *The outdoor environment*[26]
— *EC Workplace Directive 89/654/EEC*[29] (see also SI 3004[30])
— *Approved Code of Practice and Guidance L24* (HMSO)[31]
— *EC Use of Work Equipment Directive 89/655/EEC*[32] (see also SI 2932 [33])
— *Guidance on Regulations L22* (HMSO)[34]
— *EC Display Screen Directive 90/270/EEC*[35] (see also SI 2792[36])
— *Guidance on Regulations L26* (HMSO)[37].

General notes

The information in the following section will be influenced by reference to the 'core recommendations' in sections 2.4, 2.5 and 2.6.1 to 2.6.3.

Luminaires certified as suitable for hazardous areas will be needed where explosive gas-air mixtures may arise.

	Standard maintained illuminance (lux)	Limiting glare index	Notes
Control rooms			See General building areas, section 2.6.4.1.
Relay and telecommunication			See General building areas, section 2.6.4.1.
Switchrooms			See General building areas, section 2.6.4.1.
Pump houses, water treatment plant house	200	—	
Standby generator rooms, compressor rooms	150	—	Additional local lighting of instruments and controls may be required.
Off-take/pressure reduction stations:			
—indoor	150	—	Additional local lighting of instruments and controls may be required.
—outdoor	30	—	
Storage tanks (indoor) and operating areas and filling points at outdoor tanks	50	—	

Building construction sites

Other relevant documents:

— CIBSE Lighting Guide: *Building and civil engineering sites* (1975)[60]
— CIBSE Lighting Guide LG1: *The industrial environment*[7]
— CIBSE Technical Memoranda TM12: *Emergency lighting*[61]
— *Construction (General Provisions) Regulations 1961*[62], Regulation 44
— *BS 7375: Code of practice for distribution of electricity on construction and building sites*[63]
— *BS 7671: 1992 Requirements for electrical installations (IEE Regulations for electrical installations 16th edition)*[64]
— *Guidance on Regulations L22* (HMSO)[34]
— *ILE Guidance Notes for the reduction of light pollution* (1992)[46]
— *EC Use of Work Equipment Directive (89/654/EEC)*[32](SI 2932[33]).

General notes

High pressure discharge lamps offer long life and resistance to failure due to vibration and shock but restrike delay may cause problems. Luminaires must be positioned to reduce risk of damage or electric shock. Equipment fixed within reach and portable lighting equipment should be operated at not more than 110 volts (V) (or 55 V to earth). Inside metal vessels such as boilers or wet surroundings, it is recommended that they be operated at 50 V or 25 V (maximum 25 V to earth).

For offices and workshops etc., refer to the appropriate section of the schedule.

	Standard maintained illuminance (lux)	Limiting glare index	Notes
Outdoor			
Site entrance	30	—	Horizontal at ground level. Avoid glare to road users.

Office and huts	20	—	Horizontal at ground level.
Site roads	5–10	—	On road surface.
Movement areas	20	—	Horizontal.
Cranes	100	—	On ground or on work being lifted, care must be taken to avoid glare to crane drivers.
Craft work	100	—	On task.
Indoor Walkways and access	20–50	—	On relevant surfaces higher value may be required depending on the degree of hazard.
General work areas	100	—	On task plane over whole working area. Illuminance may be reduced if task requires little perception of detail or is carried out for a short period.

2.6.4.3   Offices and shops

Commerce

Other relevant documents:

— CIBSE Lighting Guide LG3: Areas for visual display terminals[25]
— CIBSE Lighting Guide LG7: Lighting for offices[27]
— EC Workplace Directive 89/654/EEC[29] (see also SI 3004[30])
— Approved Code of Practice and Guidance L24 (HMSO)[31]
— EC Use of Work Equipment Directive 89/655/EEC[32] (see also SI 2932 [33])
— Guidance on Regulations L22 (HMSO)[34]
— EC Display Screen Directive 90/270/EEC[35] (see also SI 2792[36])
— Guidance on Regulations L26 (HMSO)[37].

General notes

The information in the following section will be influenced by reference to the 'core recommendations' in sections 2.4, 2.5 and 2.6.1 to 2.6.3.

Check that installations designed to meet the needs of visual display screen tasks also satisfy the task-to-wall and task-to-ceiling ratios recommended in section 2.4.4. See also sections 3.3.2.9–3.3.2.11. Where air conditioning or mechanical ventilation is required, air-handling luminaires may be appropriate. For information on the lighting of atria, refer to General building areas in the schedule and reference 27 above.

	Standard maintained illuminance (lux)	Limiting glare index	Notes
Offices General offices	500	19	Local lighting may be appropriate.
Computer work stations	300–500	19	See reference 25 above.
Conference rooms, executive offices	300–500	19	Dimming or switching to permit use of visual aids may be necessary.
Computer and data preparation rooms	500	19	See reference 25 above.
Filing rooms	300	19	Vertical surfaces may be especially important.
Drawing offices General	500	16	
Drawing boards	750	16	Local lighting may be appropriate.
Computer aided design and drafting	300–500	—	Special lighting is required, see reference 25 above.
Print rooms	300	19	
Banks and building societies Counter, office area	500	19	
Public area	300	19	

Retailing

Other relevant documents:

— CIBSE Lighting Guide *LG6: The outdoor environment*[26]
— *EC Workplace Directive 89/654/EEC*[29] (see also SI 3004[30])
— *Approved Code of Practice and Guidance L24* (HMSO)[31]
— *EC Use of Work Equipment Directive 89/655/EEC*[32] (see also SI 2932 [33])
— *Guidance on Regulations L22* (HMSO)[34]
— *EC Display Screen Directive 90/270/EEC*[35] (see also SI 2792[36])
— *Guidance on Regulations L26* (HMSO)[37].

General notes

The information in the following section will be influenced by reference to the 'core recommendations' in sections 2.4, 2.5 and 2.6.1 to 2.6.3.

The types of lighting equipment used will depend greatly on the approach adopted to displaying the merchandise. For some interiors, e.g. a supermarket, simple uniform lighting may be appropriate. For others, e.g. a jeweller's shop, localised lighting creating highlights in the merchandise is more suitable (see sections 1.6.3 and 2.4.8). The recommendations given below generally refer to uniform lighting conditions. Where good colour judgement is considered an advantage then lamps of colour rendering group 1B should be used, such lamps will also enhance the colourfulness of an interior.

	Standard maintained illuminance (lux)	Limiting glare index	Notes
Fashion and household stores			
Departmental store	500	19	Lighting of both the vertical and horizontal planes is important. Display and layout changes need to be considered. Accent lighting required (section 2.4.8).
Chain store	750	19	
Specialist retailer	500	19	
Food stores			
Hypermarket/superstore	1000	22	Lighting of vertical displays is required. Check-out conveyors: it is important that this level is achieved on conveyors. The use of visual display terminals should be considered in the design.
Supermarket	750	22	
Grocery/vegetable store	500	19	
Specialist store	500	19	
Retail catering outlets			
Food court	300	19	Point of sale lighting needs to be considered at design stage.
Fast food outlet	500	19	
Family restaurant	200	19	
Small retail outlets			
Newsagent	500	19	Lighting of both vertical and horizontal planes is important. Display and layout changes need to be considered. Accent lighting required (see section 2.4.8)
Stationer/bookshop	500	19	
Chemist/drug store	500	19	
Jeweller	500	19	
Petrol filling stations (external apron)			
General	30	—	Luminaires suitable for a hazardous area are appropriate. Illuminance depends on district brightness. Care should be taken to avoid glare to drivers and neighbouring residents.
Pump area (forecourt sales)	300–500	—	
Do-it-yourself			
Superstore	1000	22	Lighting of both the vertical and horizontal surfaces may be important in some instances.
Car accessory store	1000	22	
Electrical/furniture store	750	19	Lighting of both the vertical and horizontal surfaces may be important in some instances.
Hardware store	500	19	Lighting of both the vertical and horizontal surfaces may be important in some instances.
Garden centres:			
—indoors	500	22	High daylight factor desirable. Special light sources may be necessary in plant storage and sales areas. See General exterior sales areas, section 2.6.4.1.
—outdoors	50–200	—	

	Standard maintained illuminance (lux)	Limiting glare index	Notes
Showrooms	500–750	—	Supplementary display lighting required (see section 2.4.8)
Shopping precincts (exterior)	50–200	22	See reference 26 above. Dependent on ambience required and balance with shop window lighting and illuminated signs.
Covered arcades and malls	50–300	22	See reference 26 above. Dependent on ambience required and balance with shop window lighting and illuminated signs.

Services

Other relevant documents:

— CIBSE Lighting Guide: *Lighting in hostile and hazardous environments*[42]
— CIBSE Lighting Guide *LG1: The industrial environment*[7]
— CIBSE Lighting Guide *LG3: Areas for visual display terminals*[25]
— *EC Workplace Directive 89/654/EEC*[29] (see also SI 3004[30])
— *Approved Code of Practice and Guidance L24* (HMSO)[31]
— *EC Use of Work Equipment Directive 89/655/EEC*[32] (see also SI 2932[33])
— *Guidance on Regulations L22* (HMSO)[34]
— *EC Display Screen Directive 90/270/EEC*[35] (see also SI 2792[36])
— *Guidance on Regulations L26* (HMSO)[37].

General notes

The information in the following section will be influenced by reference to the 'core recommendations' in sections 2.4, 2.5 and 2.6.1 to 2.6.3.

The nature of the equipment used varies widely with the application. For garages and sewage treatment works easily maintained luminaires capable of operating where a fire or explosion hazard may exist are necessary in some areas. For laundries and sewage treatment works, luminaires capable of withstanding a corrosive damp atmosphere are necessary.

	Standard maintained illuminance (lux)	Limiting glare index	Notes
Garages			Hazardous area lighting will be required in many areas, e.g. petrol vehicle servicing pits, spray booths, pump service areas. Local authority bylaws may apply. Eye protection is required for some activities.
Interior parking areas	50	22	
General repair, servicing, washing, polishing	300	22	Luminaires in pits should be easily cleaned and suitable for hazardous areas. Supplementary local lighting will be necessary.
Workbench	500	19	Localised or local lighting may be appropriate.
Spray booths	500	19	See Mechanical engineering, section 2.6.4.2.
Car showrooms	500–750	—	Supplementary display lighting required.
Appliance servicing Workshop:			
—general	300	25	Supplementary portable local lighting is desirable.
—workbench	500	—	Localised lighting may be appropriate.
Counter	300	—	Localised lighting may be appropriate.
Stores			See Distribution and storage, section 2.6.4.1.
Laundries			Luminaires suitable for a warm, damp atmosphere are necessary.
Commercial laundries: — receiving, sorting, washing, drying, ironing, despatch, dry cleaning, bulk machine work	300	25	
— hand ironing, pressing, mending, spotting, inspection	500	25	
Launderettes	300	25	

Water and sewage treatment works

Walkways	50	—	Luminaires capable of withstanding damp, corrosive conditions will be required in some areas. Some areas may be hazardous.
Pump rooms, motor rooms, chemical treatment areas	200	28	
Sumps and cable flats	50	—	Submersible luminaires may be required.
Control rooms			See General building areas, section 2.6.4.1.
Outdoors (general)	20	—	
Sludge beds and sluices	50	—	

2.6.4.4   Public and education buildings

Places of public assembly

Other relevant documents:

— CIBSE Lighting Guide: *Libraries*[65]
— CIBSE Lighting Guide LG3: *Areas for visual display terminals*[25]
— CIBSE Lighting Guide LG5: *The visual environment in lecture, teaching and conference rooms*[66]
— CIBSE Lighting Guide: *Museums and art galleries*[67]
— *Lighting and wiring of churches*, Church of England Church Information Office[68]
— *BS CP 1007: Maintained lighting for cinemas*[69]
— *ABTT Theatres planning guidance for design and adaptation*, (Architectural Press)[70]
— *EC Workplace Directive 89/654/EEC*[29] (see also SI 3004[30])
— *Approved Code of Practice and Guidance L24* (HMSO)[31]
— *EC Use of Work Equipment Directive 89/655/EEC*[32] (see also SI 2932 [33])
— *Guidance on Regulations L22* (HMSO)[34]
— *EC Display Screen Directive 90/270/EEC*[35] (see also SI 2792[36])
— *Guidance on Regulations L26* (HMSO)[37].

General notes

The information in the following section will be influenced by reference to the 'core recommendations' in sections 2.4, 2.5 and 2.6.1 to 2.6.3.

The type of equipment used will vary widely with application depending on the importance attached to the appearance of the equipment and the desired display effects. For applications where materials sensitive to light are being used, e.g. in libraries, museums and art galleries, the thermal and ultra-violet emission of the lighting installation needs to be considered (see reference 67). For very quiet interiors, e.g. churches or libraries, care is need to minimise noise emission by the lighting installation. For sports areas, impact resistant luminaires may be desirable. For many applications some form of dimming or switching facility is desirable. Where colour is important use lamps with colour rendering groups 1A or 1B.

	Standard maintained illuminance (lux)	Limiting glare index	Notes
Assembly rooms			
Public rooms, village halls, church halls	300	19	These rooms are often used for many different functions, e.g. see section 2.6.4.7 Sports. The lighting should be flexible in the effects it can produce. Selective switching or dimming is desirable.
Concert halls, cinemas and theatres			
Foyers	200	—	
Booking offices	300	—	Local or localised lighting may be appropriate.
Auditoria	100–150	—	Dimming facilities will be necessary. Special lighting of the aisles may be desirable. The level of maintained emergency lighting and the luminance of signs must not adversely affect the primary use of the space.

Dressing rooms	300	—	Incandescent mirror lighting for make-up is required.
Projection rooms	150	—	Lighting should be provided on the working side of the projector. The lighting should not detract from the view into the auditorium. Dimming facilities are desirable.
Places of worship			It is desirable that the lighting should be sympathetic to the architecture and style of the interior, in addition it should focus attention on the important area from which the service is conducted and features of special regard. Any emphasis should not detract from the central focus.
Body of church	100–200	—	Depending on architecture and form of worship.
Pulpit, lectern	300	—	Use local lighting if required.
Choir stalls	200	—	Local lighting may be appropriate.
Religiously significant areas e.g. altars, communion tables etc.	300	—	Additional lighting to provide emphasis is desirable.
Chancel, sanctuary, platform	200	—	
Vestries	150	—	
Organ	300	—	Use local lighting for organist.
Libraries			See reference 65 above.
Lending library:			
—general	300	19	
—counters	500	—	Localised lighting may be appropriate.
—bookshelves	150	—	The illuminance should be provided on the vertical face at the bottom of the bookstack.
—reading rooms	300	19	
—reading tables	300	19	Local lighting may be appropriate. Supplementary lighting or optical aids for the partially sighted should be considered.
—catalogues (cards)	150	—	The illuminance should be provided on the plane of the cards.
—catalogues (microfiche readers/visual display terminals)	150	—	Care should be taken to avoid reflections on the screen, see reference 25 above.
Reference libraries			Care should be taken to minimise the noise emitted by the lighting installation.
—general	300	19	
—counters	500	—	Localised lighting may be appropriate.
—bookshelves	150	—	The illuminance should be provided on a vertical surface at the foot of the bookshelves.
—study tables, carrels	500	19	Local lighting may be appropriate, care should be taken to avoid veiling reflections.
—map room	500	19	Supplementary local lighting is desirable when using maps.
—display and exhibition areas: exhibits insensitive to light	300	—	
—display and exhibition areas: light-sensitive exhibits e.g. pictures, prints, rare books in archives	—	—	See reference 67 above.
Library workrooms			
Book repair and binding	500	19	
Catalogue and sorting	500	19	
Remote book stores	150	—	The illuminance should be provided on a vertical plane at the foot of the book stack. Switching arrangements should be considered.
Museums and art galleries			See reference 67 above.
Exhibits insensitive to light	300	—	The lighting will be mainly determined by the display requirements.

	Standard maintained illuminance (lux)	Limiting glare index	Notes
Light-sensitive exhibits, e.g. oil and tempera paints, undyed leather, bone, ivory, wood, etc.	200	—	This is a maximum illuminance to be provided on the principal plane of the exhibit from electric lighting and daylight. It is preferable to consider a maximum total exposure of 600 klux per year. Ultra-violet radiation should be limited to 75 µW/lm.
Extremely light sensitive exhibits, e.g. textiles, water colours, prints and drawings, skins, botanical specimens, etc.	50	—	This is a maximum illuminance to be provided on the principal plane of the exhibit from electric lighting and daylight. Switching and covering to limit exposure is desirable. It is preferable to consider a maximum total exposure of 150 klux/annum. Ultra violet radiation should be limited to 75 µW/lm. At these low lighting levels particular attention should be paid to adaptation effects.
Conservation studios and workshops	500	19	Supplementary local lighting is desirable for detailed work. Usually colour judgement is important, light sources of group 1A should be used. Careful control of illuminance by switching/dimming is desirable.

Education

Other relevant documents:

- Education (School Premises) Regs 1981 (73)
- CIBSE Lighting Guide: *Libraries* [65]
- CIBSE Lighting Guide *LG4: Sports*[71]
- CIBSE Lighting Guide *LG5: The visual environment in lecture, teaching and conference rooms*[66]
- *Guidelines for environmental design and fuel conservation in educational buildings*, Department of Education and Science, Architects and Building Branch, Design Note 17 (1981) (currently under review)[72]
- *EC Workplace Directive 89/654/EEC*[29] (see also SI 3004[30])
- *Approved Code of Practice and Guidance L24* (HMSO)[31]
- *EC Use of Work Equipment Directive 89/655/EEC*[32] (see also SI 2932 [33])
- *Guidance on Regulations L22* (HMSO)[34]
- *EC Display Screen Directive 90/270/EEC*[35] (see also SI 2792[36])
- *Guidance on Regulations L26* (HMSO)[37].

General notes

The information in the following section will be influenced by reference to the 'core recommendations' in sections 2.4, 2.5 and 2.6.1 to 2.6.3.

Education buildings are usually designed to be lit by daylight whenever and wherever possible. Lighting controls should ensure that the lighting can be easily adjusted to accommodate variation in daylight conditions. Special areas in educational buildings, e.g. in workshops, sports halls, laboratories etc., need luminaires appropriate to the conditions met in these places.

	Standard maintained illuminance (lux)	Limiting glare index	Notes
Assembly halls			
General	300	19	Switching or dimming systems which enable the hall to be used for theatrical or cinematic functions are desirable. See also reference 71 above.
Platform and stage	—	—	Special lighting to provide emphasis and to facilitate the use of the platform/stage is desirable. See reference 66 above.
Teaching spaces			
General	300	19	~~Reference 71 above, which contains~~ statutory requirements under the Education (School Premises) Regulations 1981[73], specifies: (a) a minimum illuminance of 150 lux at any point on the working plane no matter what the light source, (b) a maintained illuminance of not less than 300 lux where fluorescent lamps are used (c) where the lighting of a space is achieved by a combination of daylight and electric light an illuminance of not less

			than 350 lux will usually be necessary. Also the illuminance on the walls should be from 0.5 to 0.8 of the working plane illuminance. Care should be taken with the lighting of chalk boards to avoid veiling reflections and give uniformity. Facilities for switching and dimming are desirable where visual aids are to be used. Lamps of colour rendering group 1B are desirable.
Lecture theatres General	300	19	Switching or dimming facilities are desirable to allow for the use of visual aids; some light should be provided for the lecturer and for note taking.
Demonstration benches	500	—	Localised lighting may be appropriate.
Seminar rooms	500	19	Switching or dimming facilities are desirable to allow for the use of visual aids but some lighting should be provided for the lecturer and for note taking.
Art rooms	500	19	Lamps of colour rendering groups 1A or 1B should be used. Some form of flexible display lighting is desirable.
Needlework rooms	500	19	Supplementary local lighting is desirable.
Laboratories	500	19	If accurate colour judgements are required lamps of colour rendering groups 1A or 1B should be used. In some laboratories there will be fire or chemical hazards. A corrosive atmosphere may also be present. Appropriate luminaires are required. Eye protection will be required for some activities.
Libraries	300	19	See reference 65 above.
Music rooms	300	19	Care should be taken to minimise the noise emitted by the lighting system.
Sports halls	300	—	See reference 71 above. Impact resistant luminaires may be required. See section 2.6.4.7 for specific sports activities.
Workshops	300	19	See the appropriate industrial process in section 2.6.4.2. Supplementary local lighting may be desirable. Eye protection will be required for some activities.

Transport buildings

Other relevant documents:

— CIBSE Lighting Guide LG1: The industrial environment[7]
— CIBSE Lighting Guide LG3: Areas for visual display terminals[25]
— CIBSE Lighting Guide LG6: The outdoor environment[26]
— EC Workplace Directive 89/654/EEC[29] (see also SI 3004[30])
— Approved Code of Practice and Guidance L24 (HMSO)[31]
— EC Use of Work Equipment Directive 89/655/EEC[32] (see also SI 2932[33])
— Guidance on Regulations L22 (HMSO)[34]
— EC Display Screen Directive 90/270/EEC[35] (see also SI 2792[36])
— Guidance on Regulations L26 (HMSO)[37].

General notes

The information in the following section will be influenced by reference to the 'core recommendations' in sections 2.4, 2.5 and 2.6.1 to 2.6.3.

Some areas in transport facilities are open to the weather. Weatherproof luminaires (IPX4) are desirable for these areas.

	Standard maintained illuminance (lux)	Limiting glare index	Notes
Ticket counters, check-in desks and information desks	500	—	Localised lighting may be appropriate. Care should be taken to avoid reflections in visual display terminals.
Departure lounges and other areas	200	19	The lighting should create a relaxed atmosphere.
Baggage reclaim points and counters (public)	200	22	Localised lighting to provide higher illuminance may be appropriate.
Baggage and parcel handling (staff)	200	22	
Customs and immigration halls	500	22	Localised lighting may be appropriate.
Concourse	200	22	The lighting of vertical surfaces is important to the appearance of the concourse. Care should be taken with the lighting of information boards.
Platforms: —covered —open	50 10	— —	Care should be taken to light and mark clearly the edge of the platform.
Loading areas	150	—	

2.6.4.5 Hospitals and health care buildings

Other relevant documents:

— CIBSE Lighting Guide LG2: Hospitals and health care buildings[74]
— CIBSE Lighting Guide LG3: Areas for visual display terminals[25]
— BS 4533: Section 102.55: 1986: Specification for luminaires for hospitals and health care buildings[75]
— Department of Health and Social Security Hospital Technical Memorandum No. 6[76]
— BS 4533: Section 103.2: 1986: Specification for photometric characteristics of luminaires for hospitals and health care buildings[77]
— Medical Research Council Memorandum 43: Special requirements of light sources for clinical purposes[78]
— EC Workplace Directive 89/654/EEC[29] (see also SI 3004[30])
— Approved Code of Practice and Guidance L24 (HMSO)[31]
— EC Use of Work Equipment Directive 89/655/EEC[32] (see also SI 2932[33])
— Guidance on Regulations L22 (HMSO)[34]
— EC Display Screen Directive 90/270/EEC[35] (see also SI 2792[36])
— Guidance on Regulations L26 (HMSO)[37]
— EC Electromagnetic Compatibility Directive 89/336/EEC[50].

General notes

The information in the following section will be influenced by reference to the 'core recommendations' in sections 2.4, 2.5 and 2.6.1 to 2.6.3.

In clinical areas lamps should have approved chromaticity and colour rendering properties. Luminaires used in hospitals and health care buildings must meet high standards of safety and hygiene appropriate to the areas in which they are used. Lamps and control gear should be silent in operation in patient areas. Radio interference can cause problems and gear should be suppressed to reduce radio frequency interference below the limit required by BS 4533 Part 103.2[77]. In some areas earthing, including an earthed front screen to luminaires is required. In clean areas luminaires must be constructed and fitted so that the room seal is unaffected and the flow of air unobstructed. In some areas designated 'clean' special luminaires are not required. In others rigorous cleaning methods including hosing down takes place requiring IP65 protected luminaires.

	Standard maintained illuminance (lux)	Limiting glare index	Notes
Accident and emergency			Clinical quality colour rendering lamps required.
Duty crew room	300	—	
Dressings (medical) area	200–300	—	
Plaster theatre: —general —local	400 15 000–30 000	— —	Minor operating luminaire required.

Resuscitation:			
—general	400	—	
—local	15 000	—	Minor operating luminaire required.
Blood bank	200–300	—	
Chiropody:			
—general	300	—	
—local	1000	—	Examination luminaire required.
Consulting rooms	300	—	
Corridors			Transversely mounted luminaires are not recommended.
General	150	—	Illuminance measured on floor.
Hospital street	150	—	Illuminance measured on floor.
Ward corridors open to daylight:			
—day	150–200	—	Illuminance measured on floor.
—night	3–5	—	Illuminance measured on floor, normal uniformity does not apply.
Ward corridors screened from bed:			
—day	150	—	Illuminance measured on floor.
—night	5–10	—	Illuminance measured on floor, normal uniformity does not apply.
Day room	100–200	—	Domestic style luminaires preferred.
Dentistry			
Operations:			
—general	300	—	
—mouth	8 000–22 000	—	Dental inspection luminaire required.
Treatment:			
—general	400–500	—	
—mouth	1000	—	Examination luminaire required.
Examination rooms:			
—general	300	—	
—local	1000	—	Examination luminaire required.
			Where VDTs are used see reference 25 above.
Laboratories			
Dental	500	19	
Pathology:			
—bench	300	19	Special luminaires may be required for tuberculosis.
—local	500	—	
Pharmacy	300	19	
Dispensary	300	—	
Maternity			
Delivery:			
—general	150–400	—	
—local	1000	—	Examination luminaire required.
Mortuary			
Post-mortem room:			
—general	300–400	—	Luminaires may be hosed down.
—local	1000	—	Examination luminaire required.
Operating and treatment areas			Clinical quality colour rendering lamps required in clean areas, special totally enclosed luminaires required. Avoid glare to patients.
Operating room:			
—general	400–500	—	
—cavity	10 000–50 000	—	Operating luminaire required.
Endoscopy	400	—	
Anaesthesia room:			
—general	200–400	—	

—local	1000	—	Examination luminaire required.
Minor treatment:			
—general	300	—	
—local	1000	—	
Major treatment:			
—general	400	—	Treat similarly to operating rooms.
—local	15 000–30 000	—	Operating luminaires required.
Recovery room	300	—	
Scrub-up room	300	—	
Viewing	150	—	Avoid reflections in view window.
Ophthalmology			
General	50–300	—	
Vision chart	300	—	Local luminaire required.
Chair	1000	—	Local luminaire required.
Utility areas			
Bathroom and shower	100–300	—	Luminaires must be suitable for damp and humid situations.
Changing room	100–150	—	
Cloak room	150	—	
Dark room	50	—	Special lighting using dark room equipment required.
Clean and dirty utility rooms	150	—	
Laundry	300	—	Luminaires may be subject to damp high humidity and high temperatures.
Stores	100	—	
Wards			Clinical quality colour rendering lamps required, luminaires approved for use in wards should be used.
Circulation:			
—day	100	—	
—night	3–5	—	Normal uniformity does not apply.
Bed head	30–50	—	Local luminaires required.
Reading	150	—	Local luminaires required.
Intensive care and observation	400	—	Whole bed area.
Baby care unit:			
—day	50–100	—	
—local	1000	—	Examination luminaire required.
—night	3–5	—	Normal uniformity does not apply.
Watch:			Dimmed bed head lights may be used.
—night (adult)	0.1	—	
—night (children)	1	—	
—night (mentally ill)	1–5	—	
—night (mother and baby)	5–10	—	
—night (intensive care)	5–10	—	
Nurses' station:			See reference 74 above.
—day	300	—	
—night	30–200	—	Light sources should be shielded from patient view.
X-ray			
Couch	20–100	—	Dimmable lighting may be required.
General	300	—	Two-way switching from control desk and door may be required.

2.6.4.6   **Residential buildings**

General notes

The information in the following section will be influenced by reference to the 'core recommendations' in sections 2.4, 2.5 and 2.6.1 to 2.6.3.

This section covers lighting for residential accommodation in hotels as well as that provided for students, nurses, staff, handicapped and elderly people. Particularly in the case of accommodation for the elderly and partially sighted, the recommended values of illuminance should be considered as general amenity levels which will need to be substantially increased in hazardous areas such as stairs and kitchens. For reading and other visually difficult tasks individuals may require optical aids, such as magnifiers and local lighting, to meet their particular needs. Private dwellings are not specifically covered by this section. Lighting plays a part in determining the social atmosphere. Light sources should have colour rendering of group 1B, colour temperature should be 4000 K or below. Compact fluorescent lamps are appropriate for many applications reducing lighting loads and extending lamp replacement periods. Lighting energy management systems based on the occupancy and available daylight should be considered for public and commercial areas.

	Standard maintained illuminance (lux)	Limiting glare index	Notes
Institutional accommodation			Uniform lighting in small spaces is unlikely to be appropriate.
Flats/bedsits			
Entrance lobbies	200	—	
Lounges	150	—	Supplementary wall/table lighting to create appropriate atmosphere.
Kitchens	150–300	—	Avoid shadows on work surfaces and sink.
Bedrooms	100	—	Two-way switching desirable. Additional local lighting at table and bedhead.
Bathrooms	150	—	Additional shaver light at mirror position.
Toilets	100	—	
Communal areas			
Main entrances	200	19	Possibly supplemented by wall/picture lighting.
Corridors	20–100	19	Low level late night lighting with override facility.
Staircases	100	—	Luminaires to provide contrast between treads and risers. Safety will be enhanced by the use of coloured nosings which contrast with the finish of the treads and risers.
Lounges	100–300	19	Multiple switching levels desirable. Use wall/picture lights to create a pleasing atmosphere.
Television lounges	50	—	

Quiet/rest rooms	100	—	
Dining rooms	150	—	
Laundries	300	—	
Stores	100	—	
Treatment rooms	300	—	Medical inspection lamp at couch position.
Libraries	300	—	See Public buildings, section 2.6.4.4.
Hotels (public and staff areas)			
Entrance halls	100	—	The lighting of vertical surfaces is important to the appearance of the space.
Reception, cashiers' and porters' desks	300	—	Localised lighting may be appropriate.
Bars, coffee bars, dining rooms, grill rooms, restaurants, lounges	50–200	—	The lighting should be designed to create an appropriate atmosphere. Switching and dimming controls can provide flexibility of the lighting effects. Local lighting to provide emphasis may be appropriate in some areas, e.g. cash desks, bar counters. Separate lighting may be necessary for cleaning.
Cloakrooms, baggage rooms	100	—	
Commercial food preparation, stores, cellars, lifts and corridors	—	—	See General building areas, section 2.6.4.1.
Guest accommodation:			
—bedrooms/lounges	50–100	—	Particularly when lower level of general lighting is possible, supplementary local lighting to 100 lux at the bedhead, desk and mirror is desirable. Two-way switching from bedhead is required.
—bathrooms	150	—	Supplementary local lighting near the mirror is desirable.
Kitchens	150–300	—	Use lamps of colour rendering group 1B and colour temperature less than 4000 K.

2.6.4.7   **Sports and recreation facilities**

Other relevant documents:

— CIBSE Lighting Guide *LG4: Sports*[71]
— Sports Council: *Handbook of sports and recreational building design*[79]
— Sports Council: *Lighting in small multi-purpose sports halls*[80]
— Sports Council: *Energy data sheets*[81]
— Sports Council: *Data sheets*[82]
— CIE Publication No. 62 *Lighting for swimming pools* (1984)[83]
— CIE Publication No. 67 *Guide to the photometric specifications and management of sports lighting installations* (1986)[84]
— CIE Publication No. 83 *Guide to the lighting of sports events for CTV and film systems* (1989)[85]
— ILE *Guidance Notes for the reduction of light pollution* (1992)[46].

General notes

Sports not listed here may be found in the 'other relevant documents'. The illuminance values are based on reference 71. In some cases, these do not follow the steps shown in Table 2.3 (page 40). Colour is important in most sports and colour rendering properties of lamps must be considered. Stroboscopic effects are noticeable in sports where a fast moving object is used and steps to minimise this must be taken. For many sports it is necessary to minimise glare to players and spectators looking upwards. Impact to equipment can cause breakages and falling objects are a danger to players and spectators. It is essential that lighting equipment is capable of withstanding and absorbing impact and shock and is securely fixed. If the largest proportion of players are elderly, increase illuminance levels by 50%.

	Standard maintained illuminance (lux)	Limiting glare index	Notes
Archery ranges (recreational/club)			
Target	100	—	Vertical.
Shooting zone	50	—	Horizontal.
Ground between shooting zone and target	25	—	Horizontal.
Badminton			Horizontal on court.
Recreational	300	—	
Supervised training practice	400	—	
Club and county	400	—	
National and international	500	—	
Bowls (indoor)			Horizontal on court.
Recreational and practice	300	—	
Club and county	400	—	
National and international	500	—	
Boxing			Horizontal on floor of ring. Vertical illuminance should be as high possibly within the limitations of controlling glare.
Supervised training and club	500	—	
Regional	750	—	
National	1000	—	
International and special events	2000	—	
Cricket (indoor)			Horizontal across pitch. The luminaires should be screened from angle of view of all players. The walls should also have a reflectance of 0.4–0.6 to provide good contrast with the ball.
Recreational	400	—	
Supervised training	400	—	
Club and county	500	—	
Cycle racing (indoor)			Horizontal on track.
Training	300	—	
Club	500	—	
National and international	750	—	
Equestrian sports (indoor)			Horizontal on ground.
Schooling (supervised practice and training):			
—show jumping	400	—	
—dressage	300	—	
Competition:			
—show jumping	700	—	
—dressage	500	—	
Five-a-side football (indoor)			Horizontal on ground.
Recreational	300	—	
Supervised training practice	300	—	
Club and county	400	—	
National and international	500	—	
Handball			Horizontal on court.
Recreational	300	—	
Supervised training practice	300	—	
Club	400	—	
County and national	500	—	

International	750	—	
Hockey (indoor)			Horizontal at floor level.
Recreational	300	—	
Supervised training practice	300	—	
Club	400	—	
County and national	500	—	
International	750	—	
Ice rinks			On rink surface.
Ice hockey and figure skating:			
—training	200	—	
—competition	750	—	
Ice skating (recreational)	100	—	
Lawn tennis (indoor)			Horizontal on court.
Recreational	300	—	
Practice and club	400	—	
County	500	—	
National and international	750	—	
Lawn tennis (outdoor)			See reference 71 above for the detailed requirements laid down by the Lawn Tennis Association.
Recreational	200	—	
Club	300	—	
County	400	—	
National/international	500	—	
Martial arts			Horizontal at floor/mat level.
Supervised training and practice	300	—	
Club	400	—	
National	500	—	
Netball			Horizontal on court.
Recreational and supervised training and practice	300	—	
Club and county	400	—	
National and international	500	—	
Shooting (indoor)			
All levels of competition:			
—target position	1000	—	Vertical.
—shooting position	300	—	Horizontal.
Snooker/billiards			Horizontal on table.
Recreational and club	750	—	Suitable illumination is normally provided by a purpose made canopy containing several light sources. General lighting should be provided to the surrounding areas.
International	1000	—	
Squash			Horizontal on floor.
Recreational and supervised training and practice	300	—	See reference 71 above for recommended values of wall illuminance.
Club and county	400	—	
National	500	—	
International	750	—	
Swimming (indoors)			Horizontal at pool surface level.
Recreational	200	—	
Training, club and county	300	—	
National	500	—	

International	1000	—	
Table tennis			Horizontal on table.
Recreational	200	—	
Training, club and county	300	—	
National	500	—	
International	750	—	
Volleyball			Horizontal on court.
Recreational and training	300	—	
Club	400	—	
County and national	500	—	
International	750	—	
Weight training			Horizontal at floor level.
Supervised training	400	—	
Multi-purpose facilities			Use illuminance values to meet the most exacting sports requirements if these are greater than those listed below. Horizontal.
Indoor sports halls:			
—recreational	300	—	
—club and county	400–500	—	
—national and international	500–750	—	
—televised	1000–2000	—	Vertical/normal to camera.
Indoor arenas:			Horizontal.
—maintenance of arena	100	—	
—general lighting and training	300	—	
—competition	500	—	
—spectator-viewed events	900	—	
—televised	1000–2000	—	Vertical/normal to camera.

Part 3

Equipment

3.1 Introduction

The aims of this part of the *Code* are:

(*a*) to provide an outline of the properties of the main types of lighting equipment currently used for interior lighting

(*b*) to give details of appropriate maintenance procedures.

It must be emphasised that the information given is only sufficient to demonstrate the differences between broad classes of equipment and that rapid developments are taking place with all lighting equipment.

Note: for design work, up-to-date, accurate information on light sources, luminaires and control systems should be obtained from manufacturers.

3.2 Light sources

A frequently updated source of information on lamp types is the Lighting Industry Federation *Lamp guide*[86].

3.2.1 Types of light source

The seven principal types of related lamp are shown in Table 3.1.

Within each group there is a range of lamps available which differ in construction, wattage, luminous efficacy, colour properties, cost etc. Associated with most lamps is a set of prefix code letters to facilitate identification. Table 3.2 shows the prefix letters for the main variants in each lamp type. The prefix letters are usually accompanied by the lamp rating in watts (W) and, if necessary, by details of lamp length, colour, cap and operating position.

Table 3.1 Principal lamp types and their relationship

Section number	Lamp type	Lamp group	
3.2.4.1	Filament (GLS and tungsten–halogen)	Incandescent	
3.2.4.2	Fluorescent (tubular and compact) (induction HF excitation)†	Low pressure	Discharge
3.2.4.3	Low pressure sodium		
3.2.4.4	High pressure sodium§	High pressure (HID)¶	
3.2.4.5	High pressure mercury		
3.2.4.6	High pressure metal halide		

† Fluorescent lamps incorporate a low pressure discharge, but the majority of the light output is from phosphors on the inside of the glass.

¶ High pressure discharge lamps are sometimes known as high intensity discharge (HID) lamps.

§ The pressure of high pressure sodium lamps can be below 1 atmosphere, but they are so-called to distinguish them from low pressure sodium lamps.

Table 3.2   Lamp prefix code letters. Note: The groups shown against each description only indicate a general similarity of function. The individual lamps are not necessarily interchangeable either electrically or photometrically. Manufacturers' data should be consulted.

Lamp type	Description
Filament lamps	
GLS	General lighting service
TH	Tungsten–halogen
PAR	Parabolic aluminised reflector filament lamp with an internal reflector coating, followed by lamp nominal diameter in eighths of an inch
PAR-E	PAR lamp with reduced wattage and increased optical efficiency, followed by lamp nominal diameter in eighths of an inch
R	(Previously ISL with nominal diameter in eighths of an inch) blown glass with an internal reflector coating, nominal diameter in mm
K	Linear and tubular tungsten–halogen
M	General display and miscellaneous mains and ELV filament lamps
Tubular fluorescent lamps	
MCF	Lamp for switch start circuit (also used for tubular fluorescent lamps in general)
MCFE	Lamp for starterless circuit, silicone coat (also suitable for switch start operation)
MCFA	Lamp for starterless circuit with earth strip (also suitable for switch start operation)
MCFR	As MCF with internal reflector
T5, L	16 mm (5/8 inch) nominal diameter
T8, TLD, L	26 mm (1 inch) nominal diameter
T12, TL, L	38 mm (1 1/2 inch) nominal diameter
Compact fluorescent lamps	
SL, SLD, SLR, Globalux	Lamps which incorporate starter and ballast
PLEC, PLET, SLDE, Dulux EL	Lamps which incorporate electronic control gear
PLS-2P, PLC-2P, 2D-2P, 4L-2P, Dulux S, Dulux D, Biax S, Double Biax	2-pin lamps with internal starter, requiring an external ballast
PLS-4P, PLC-4P, PLL, 2L, 2D-4P, 4L-4P, Dulux F, Dulux L, Dulux SE, Dulux DE, Biax SE, Double Biax	4-pin lamps which require an external ballast and starter or with an electronic ballast
Induction lamps	
QL	A high frequency electromagnetic induction lamp with a metal or ferrite core and a fluorescent coating on the inside of the outer envelope
Low pressure sodium lamps	
SLI	Linear arc tube, double-ended
SOX	U-shaped arc tube, single-ended
SOX-E	SOX with increased efficacy
High pressure sodium lamps	
SON, SON-E, NAV-E, LU-D	Diffuse ellipsoidal outer bulb, single-ended
SON-I	SON with internal starting device
SON-EXTRA	Twin arc tube, single-ended
SON-T, NAV-T, LU-T	Clear tubular outer bulb, single-ended
SON-T COMFORT	SON-T with improved colour rendering
NAV-DSX-T	SON-T with improved colour rendering, no mercury
SON-TD, SON-L, NAV-TS, LU-TD	Clear tubular outer bulb, double-ended
SON-R, NAV-R	SON with internal reflector
SON-H, NAV-T, LU-H	SON for use on mercury control gear
SON-DL, SON COMFORT, NAV-DL, LU-DX, LU-CL	SON with improved colour rendering
SON-S, SON PLUS, NAV Super, LU-XL	SON with increased efficacy
SON-ST, SON-T PLUS, NAV-T Super	SON-T with increased efficacy
SDW-T, LU95	'White' SON, tubular outer bulb, single-ended

Table 3.2 (continued)

Lamp type	Description
/E\	For use with external starting device
/I\	Contains internal starting device

High pressure mercury lamps

MB, HQ	High pressure mercury with outer bulb
MBF, HQL, HPL-N, HR-DX, HAX	High pressure mercury with phosphor coated outer bulb
MBFR, HQLR, HPL-R	MBF with internal reflector
HPL COMFORT, HQL-DL, HWDX, HR-WDX	MBF with improved colour rendering and efficacy

High pressure mercury blended lamps

MBTF, HWL, ML, HMLI	Combination of MBF lamp and filament acting as a ballast
MBTFR, HWLR, MLR	MBTF with internal reflector

Metal halide lamps

MBI, HQI, HPI, MVR, MXR, HgMI	Clear or diffuse outer bulb, single-ended
MBIF, MVR-C, MBID	MBI with phosphor coated outer bulb
MBIL, HQI-TS	Linear arc tube, double-ended
MBI-T, HPI-T, HQI-T	Clear tubular outer bulb, single-ended
MHD	Compact, double-ended
MHN-T, HQI-T, MVR	Tubular outer bulb, single-ended
MHN-TD, NDL, HQI-TS, MQI/N	Double-ended tubular, low wattage (cool appearance)
MHW-TD, HQI-TS, WDL, MQI/W	Double-ended tubular, low wattage (warm appearance)
CSI, CID	Compact source sometimes with internal reflector

Operating positions

/U	Universal (not usually marked)
/V	Vertical
/H or /HOR	Horizontal
/BD or /VBD	Base down
/BDH	Base down to horizontal
/BU or /VBU	Base up
/BUH	Base up to horizontal
/BUS	Base up, with internal starting device

3.2.2 Lamp characteristics

The characteristics of the lamp types are described in section 3.2.4 where information is given in terms of construction, operation, minimum starting temperatures and colour properties along with some typical applications. The range of luminous efficacies is shown in Figure 3.4 (page 102)and an indication of life and lumen maintenance in Table 3.4 (page 101) and Figures 3.1 and 3.2 (page 91).

3.2.2.1 Construction

Each basic lamp type can have a number of variations in construction. These variations can involve its shape, the number and type of caps it has, the presence of a fluorescent or diffusing coating on an outer envelope, the chemical composition of any fluorescent coating and the provision of a reflector coating inside the lamp.

3.2.2.2 Operation

The operating details given are concerned with such matters as run-up time, re-starting time, operating positions, and susceptibility to environmental conditions. Run-up times and re-starting times are important because most of the discharge lamps do not produce their maximum light output immediately after being switched on. Usually several minutes are required before the maximum light output is achieved. Further, unless special circuits are used, high pressure discharge lamps will not immediately re-start after an interruption of supply. Usually a period of several minutes is necessary for the lamp to cool before it will re-start. These factors limit the suitability of some lamp types for rapid switching and dimming. Also, not all lamp types can operate in all positions and luminous efficacy is affected by the orientation in some cases. Some lamp types are sensitive to external environmental factors such as ambient temperature and vibration.

3.2.2.3 Luminous efficacy

The luminous efficacies indicated in Figure 3.4 (page 102) are expressed in lumens per lamp watt (lm/lamp W) i.e. excluding gear losses. The lumen output of each discharge lamp type used in the calculation of luminous efficacy is the 'initial' (100-hour) lumen value. Figure 3.4 also shows luminous efficacies for the wattage range of different lamp types. For circuit efficacy see section 3.2.3.

3.2.2.4 Lamp life and lumen (luminous flux) maintenance (see also sections 4.5.2.2 and 4.5.2.3)

Lamp life and lumen depreciation values in lamp data sheets refer to groups of lamps, rather than to individual lamps, measured under standard test conditions, and not to service conditions. For standard test conditions there are two meanings of 'lamp life':

(a) For filament lamps (and blended lamps) — the time at which 50% of a large sample batch have failed (see Figure 3.1).

(b) For fluorescent lamps and other discharge lamps — the time at which the light output (or efficacy) of a large sample batch has fallen to a stated percentage of the 100-hour value (see Figure 3.2).

Under service conditions, the group life, (a) and (b), is usually less than under test conditions, because of factors such as voltage variations, switching frequency, vibration, ambient temperature and ballast design. The service life and lumen maintenance of an individual lamp cannot be predicted.

The life of an installation of lamps is usually determined by the point at which the maintained illuminance is reached, although the lamps may go on 'working' beyond this point. (In exceptional cases a change in the colour of the lamp with time may dictate the point of replacement.) In calculating the maintained illuminance a maintenance regime will have been specified or assumed and part of this will be the economic life of the lamps. This can be defined as the point in time at which it is cheaper to replace the lamps than to continue to operate them (section 5.1).

While it is easy to calculate the cost of replacement, i.e. lamp purchase plus labour plus disturbance or 'down' time, it is not so easy to calculate the 'wasted' costs of the old lamps. This must include consideration of electricity cost, the lumen depreciation of the lamps and the increasing frequency and cost of spot replacements as the lamps fail (see section 3.5.2).

The 'guaranteed' life of a group of lamps is a matter for commercial agreement.

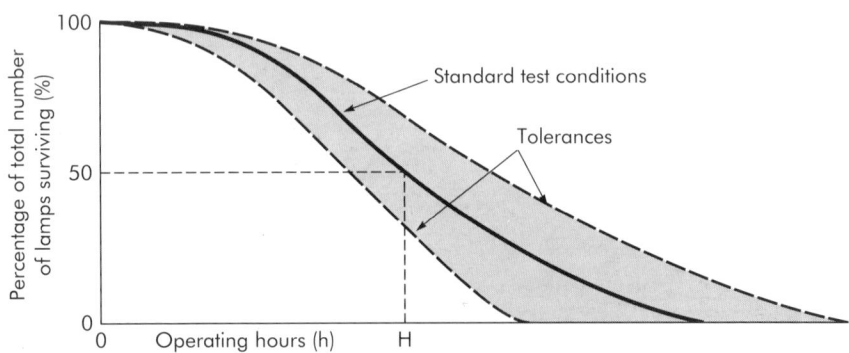

Figure 3.1 Typical lamp survival curve with tolerances

For standard test conditions, the average life of a batch of lamps is 'H' hours to 50% survival. Average survival curves with tolerances, under standard test conditions, should be available from manufacturers together with the information showing the effect of voltage deviations and switching frequency where appropriate. The survival characteristics depend on lamp type and the rating and construction within a type. Under service conditions, survival may be better or worse (see section 4.5.2.3).

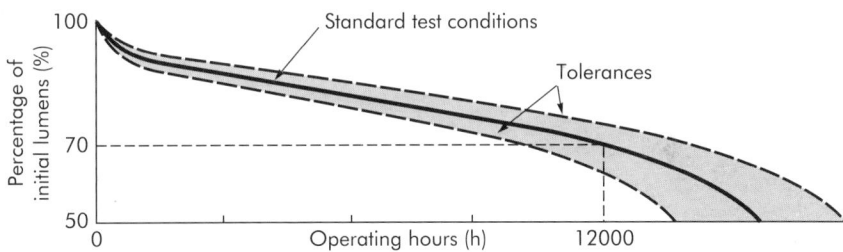

Figure 3.2 Typical lamp lumen maintenance curve with tolerances

The lamp shown here has an overall maintenance rate, under standard test conditions, of 2.5% per 1000 h, i.e. 70% maintenance at 12 000 h. Average lumen maintenance curves with tolerances, under standard test conditions, should be available from manufacturers. Lumen maintenance characteristics depend on lamp type and rating, circuit and construction within a type. For service conditions, see section 4.5.2.2.

3.2.2.5 Colour properties

Different lamp types have different colour properties. Furthermore, for some lamp types these colour properties can be changed by using fluorescent coatings or arc tube dosing of different chemical composition. The colour properties of lamps are characterised by their correlated colour temperature (CCT) class and colour rendering group (CRG) in Table 1.1 (page 23). See also section 3.2.4 and Table 3.3 (page 96). For some types of high pressure discharge lamps, colour correction is possible with electronic control gear.

3.2.3 Control gear

The control gear which is associated with discharge lamps has three functions:

(*a*) starting the lamp

(*b*) controlling the lamp current after starting

(*c*) correcting the power factor (if necessary).

Control gear consumes energy and, for a given lamp type, some circuits consume more than others. The efficacy of a lamp circuit as a whole depends on the total power taken by the lamp and the control gear. It is also necessary to consider the power factor of the circuit in order to ensure correct cable ratings and to minimise certain electricity charges.

The current ratings of cables, fuses and switchgear must be related to the total running current of the circuit, although allowance may be necessary with some types for increased current during the run-up period of the lamp. Harmonic phase currents appear in the neutral of a four-wire, three-phase system. Current ratings of neutral conductors should be the same as that of phase conductors. Manufacturers can supply information about the losses, power factor and harmonic currents of their control gear. It is important to follow manufacturers guidance on circuit data for the selection of MCBs (peak starting current and duration values of the ballasts) and for earth leakage circuit breakers (leakage current values of the ballast). For insulation resistance testing all electronic devices must be isolated so that they are not damaged by the test voltage.

All electrical installations should comply with the current edition, and amendments, of the *Regulations for Electrical Installations*[87], published by the Institution of Electrical Engineers (also published as *BS 7671*[64]).

The lamp and associated control gear constitute an integrated unit for producing light. Lamps from different manufacturers may not operate on the same control gear even when they are nominally of the same type. Whenever any change is proposed in either lamp or control gear, care should be taken to ensure that the proposed combination is compatible electrically, physically and photometrically.

Special types of control gear are necessary if dimming or rapid re-starting of some types of discharge lamp is required.

The life of control gear is sensitive to ambient temperature. The control gear used should have an appropriate temperature rating (t_a) for the situation. If this temperature is exceeded the insulating material may deteriorate rapidly.

Key to Figure 3.3

1 General lighting service lamp
2 Low voltage tungsten–halogen, single-ended lamp
3 Low voltage tungsten–halogen reflector lamps
4 Low voltage tungsten–halogen dichroic reflector lamp
5 Mains voltage tungsten–halogen, single-ended lamps with either diffuse envelope or reflector
6 Mains voltage tungsten–halogen, linear, double-ended lamp
7 Triphosphor 26 mm diameter fluorescent lamp
8 Multi-band 26 mm diameter fluorescent lamp
9 Low wattage compact fluorescent lamps with integral electronic ballast
10 Low wattage compact fluorescent lamp with integral wire-wound ballast
11 Low wattage compact fluorescent lamps with 4-pin cap for use with separate ballast
12 High wattage compact fluorescent lamps with 4-pin cap for use with separate ballast
13 High pressure sodium single-ended lamp
14 High pressure sodium, improved colour rendering, single-ended lamp
15 High pressure sodium, good colour rendering, single-ended lamp
16 High wattage metal halide, single-ended lamp
17 Low wattage metal halide, single-ended lamps with either diffuse envelope or bare arc tube
18 Low wattage metal halide, double-ended lamp
19 High pressure mercury, colour-corrected, single-ended lamp
20 Low pressure sodium, single-ended lamp

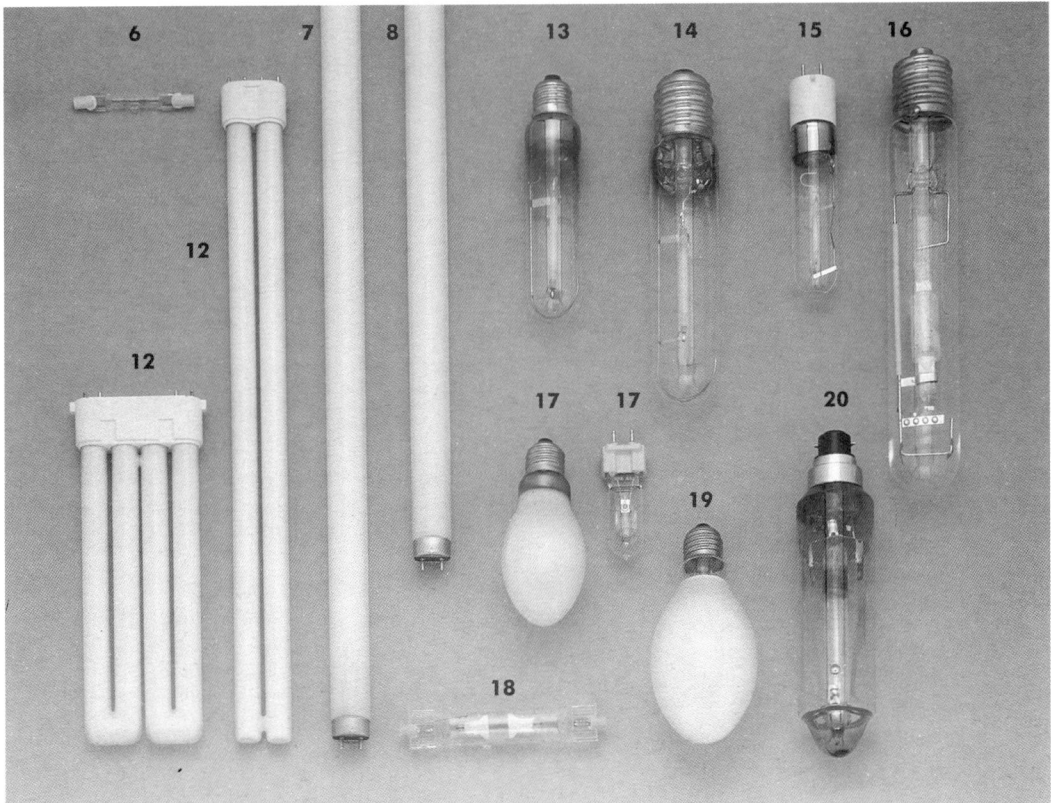

Figure 3.3   Photographs of a range of lamps, illustrating the relative lamp sizes not shown by the line drawings in this section

3.2.4   Principal lamp type characteristics

Relative sizes of most types of lamp are shown in Figure 3.3 (page 93).

3.2.4.1   Filament lamps

Light is produced by an incandescent filament sealed in a glass bulb, usually containing an inert gas filling.

GLS and reflector

There are many types of filament lamp. The most common types are known as general lighting service (GLS) and decorative (e.g. candle lamps). Their finish (i.e. clear, diffuse or coloured) is often a significant factor in their application.

Reflector lamps, blown bulb, PAR and crown-silvered lamps have a bulb with an internal reflector coating.

Replacements should normally be of the same type as originally used. Crown-silvered lamps are intended to be used in conjunction with a metal reflector as part of the luminaire.

The advantages of the filament lamp are: low initial cost, simple operation, ease of dimming, good colour rendering and lumen maintenance. The disadvantages are: low efficacy and relatively short life with increased life only being obtained at the cost of a substantial reduction in efficacy. Life is, therefore, very sensitive to voltage fluctuations and also to vibration.

Filament lamps are mainly used for domestic and display lighting.

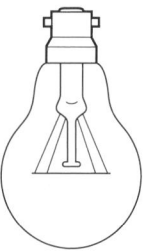   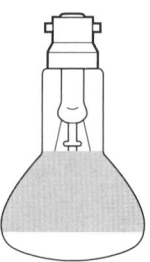

Operating position	Any
Control gear	No
Starting	Prompt
Restarting	Prompt
Dimmable	Yes
Colour temperature (K)	2700 (approximately)
Colour rendering group See Table 3.4 (page 101) and Figure 3.4 (page 102)	1A
IEC standard	IEC 64

Tungsten–halogen

These are filament lamps with a halogen added to the gas filling which prevents evaporated tungsten blackening the bulb and thus ensures excellent lumen maintenance. Tungsten–halogen lamps have an increased efficacy and/or extended life compared with standard filament lamps. The bulb is much smaller, and made of quartz or hard glass. When re-lamping, quartz bulbs should be wiped clean of finger marks before switching on.

Mains voltage lamps (e.g. for floodlights) are usually linear with contacts at each end. Single-ended lamps have applications as for GLS lamps.

ELV (extra low voltage) lamps are more compact than their mains voltage counterparts and the small filament size improves the optical efficiency of integral or external reflectors.

ELV reflector lamps make possible compact luminaires for display lighting. A range of beam intensities and widths is available for lamps of the same size. On mains supplies ELV lamps are operated via a transformer. ELV lamps are also used for projectors and vehicle headlamps.

Life for all types is sensitive to voltage variations and vibration. Guidance on UV limits for bare quartz types is provided by manufacturers (see also section 5.9). The dichroic reflector, used with ELV types, transmits heat so that suitable lampholder and luminaire designs are required.

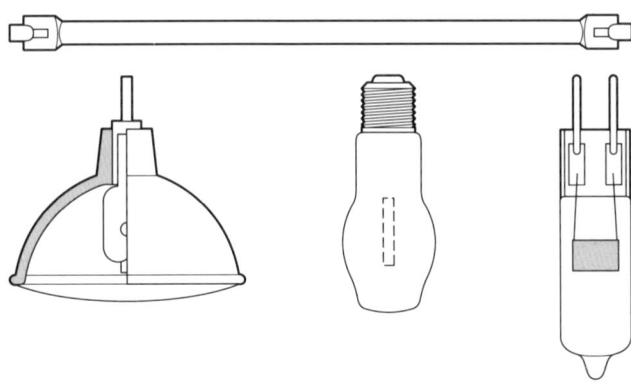

Operating position	Horizontal for double-ended, any for single-ended
Control gear	Transformer for ELV lamps
Starting	Prompt
Restarting	Prompt
Dimmable	Yes
Colour temperature (K)	3000 (approximately)
Colour rendering group	1A
See Table 3.4 (page 101) and Figure 3.4 (page 102)	
IEC standard	IEC 357

3.2.4.2 Fluorescent lamps

Fluorescent lamps have a tubular glass envelope. The light output comes from phosphors which convert energy from a low pressure mercury discharge. The spectral light distribution is 'tailored' by the mix of phosphors. A wide range of 'white' triphosphor, multiband and halophosphate phosphors plus special colours (e.g. for use in photocopiers) is available. 'White' lamps are differentiated by colour appearance or correlated colour temperature and colour rendering group (see Table 3.3 and Table 1.1, page 23).

The main advantages are high efficacy, long life and relatively low cost. However, the efficiency of fluorescent lamps is affected by the ambient temperature in which they operate. Maximum output is achieved at an optimum lamp wall temperature (usually around

Table 3.3   Proprietary names of fluorescent lamps grouped by colour rendering group (CRG) and correlated colour temperature (CCT). Colour rendering index values are also cited for each CRG.

CCT (K)	CRG: 1A (CRI): (90–100)	1B (80–90)	2 (60–80)	3 (40–60)
Warm (<3300)	Colour 93 Lumilux de Luxe 32 Polylux Deluxe 930	Colour 82 and 83 Energy saver 183 Lumilux 31 and 41 Polylux 827 and 830	Deluxe Warm white	Colour 29 Warm white 29 and 30
Intermediate (3300–5300)	Chroma 50 Colour 94 Deluxe Natural 36 Lumilux de Luxe 22 Polylux Deluxe 940 and 950	Colour 84 Energy Saver 84 Lumilux 21 and 26 Kolor-Rite 38 Polylux 835 and 840	Colour 33 Cool white 20 and 33 Natural 25 Universal white 25	Colour 35 White 23 and 35
Cold (>5300)	Artificial daylight Biolux Colour 95 and 96 Colour matching Lumilux de Luxe 12 Northlight 55	Colour 85 and 86 Lumilux 11 Polylux 860	Daylight 54	

40°C) which is measured at a defined position depending on the lamp type. Enclosed and unventilated interior luminaires tend to operate at higher temperatures, while low ambient temperatures in exterior or cold store applications can result in lamp wall temperatures below the optimum value. Both conditions can substantially reduce lamp efficacy unless lamp manufacturers' guidance is followed when designing luminaires.

Tubular fluorescent lamps

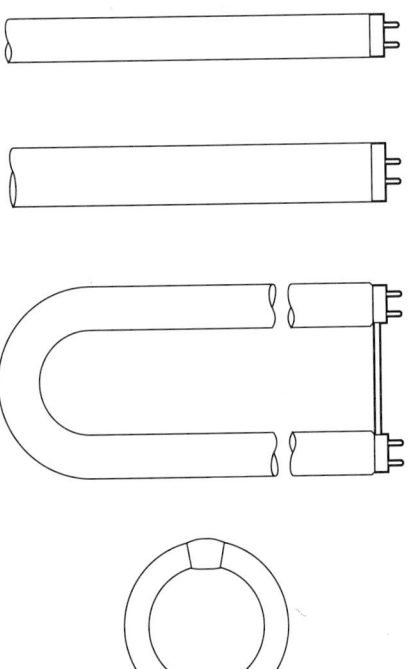

The principal lamp lengths for lighting installations range from 600 mm to 2400 mm. The early lamps were argon-filled, with a diameter of 38 mm, and are still available for starterless circuits. The modern range of krypton-filled triphosphor lamps, with a diameter of 26 mm (lamps of 100 W have 38 mm diameters) are the preferred choice for switch start circuits, for suitable electronic start circuits, and may also be used for operation on high frequency ballasts. They offer optimum efficiency and increased light output ratio (LOR) for many luminaires. Alternatively, halophosphate phosphors provide a lower initial cost but less efficient solution with reduced colour rendering index (CRI). Argon-filled, 26 mm-diameter lamps are used with some high frequency ballasts.

Other 26 mm-diameter lamps are available, amongst which are lamps for UV applications and a range of miniature fluorescent lamps (4 W–13 W) with 16 mm diameters. There are also other shapes e.g. circular, U-bend.

Note: 'Cold cathode' lamps have long thin tubing often formed into shapes for signs. In some types gas fillings other than mercury vapour, provide certain colours and do not have a fluorescent coating. Apart from shaping, the main advantage is long life (30 000 h), but the efficacy is lower (circa 50 lm/W) and high voltage control gear is required.

Operating position	Any
Control gear	Yes
Starting	Prompt
Restarting	Prompt
Colour temperature (K)	See Table 3.3
Colour rendering group	See Table 3.3
Minimum starting temperature	+ 5°C for quick-start circuits
	−15°C HF circuits
	−10°C other circuits
	−30°C special luminaire (low temperature)
See Table 3.4 (page 101) and Figure 3.4 (page 102)	
IEC standard	IEC 81

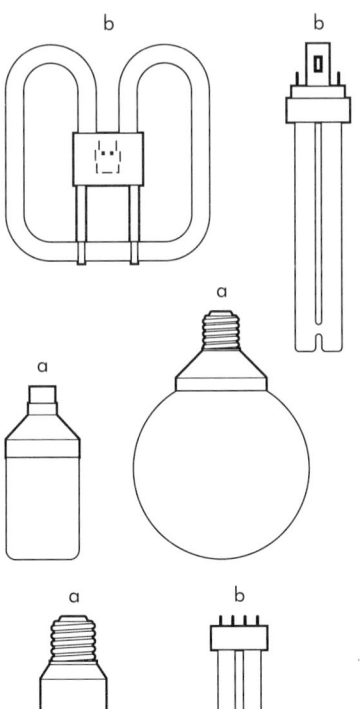

Compact fluorescent lamps

For a given light output, compact fluorescent lamps have small dimensions compared with linear fluorescent lamps. Compact size is achieved by folding the discharge path. Power consumption is between one quarter and one fifth that of GLS filament lamps of similar light output, and lives, on average, five to eight times longer. The main application is as an alternative to filament lamps and lower ratings of discharge lamps for lamp wattages below 25 W. Above 25 W they provide a more compact alternative to linear fluorescent lamps. Particular note should be taken of the manufacturers' guidance when these lamps are used in air handling luminaires.

Compact fluorescent lamps fall into two categories (see also Table 3.2):

(a) (a in figure on the left) replacements for GLS lamps; these lamps can be connected direct to the mains supply (category b lamps only with a suitable adaptor)

(b) (b in figure on the left) lamps for new luminaires; these lamps make possible the design of small luminaires using low-cost materials.

Operating position	Any†
Control gear	Yes
Starting	Prompt
Restarting	Prompt
Colour temperature (K)	2700–6500
Colour rendering group	1B
Minimum starting temperature	−20°C HF circuits
	0°C for other circuits
See Table 3.4 (page 101) and Figure 3.4 (page 102)	
IEC standard	IEC 901

† Position can affect the operating temperature and efficacy, refer to manufacturers' data.

Induction lamps

These lamps are based on the low-pressure gas discharge of normal fluorescent lamps, but an induction coil, located in the centre of the bulb, excites a gas discharge in the electrode-less fluorescent bulb. The light output comes from the phosphor. The induction coil is

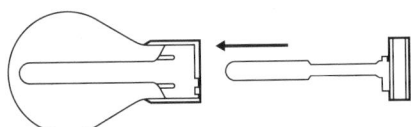

operated from a high frequency generator attached to the lamp by a power coupler, either operating within a frequency band of 2.2–3.0 MHz for self-oscillating circuits or, using crystal control at 13.56 MHz. Special luminaires are required to prevent electromagnetic interference by controlling the HF emissions from the lamp.

The main advantages are the exceptionally long lamp life, e.g. 60 000 hours and practically maintenance free operation together with no flicker or stroboscopic effect. Presently, 85 W lamps with different colour temperatures are available.

In the future it is possible that the induction principle could be applied to high pressure discharge sources.

Operating position	Any
Control gear	Yes
Starting	Prompt
Restarting	Prompt
Colour temperature (K)	3000–4000
Colour rendering group	1B
Minimum starting temperature	–20°C

3.2.4.3   Low pressure sodium lamps

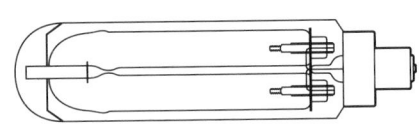

These lamps consist of a U-tube containing the discharge with an outer thermal jacket. There is also a linear double-ended version.

The arc produces light only in the yellow part of the spectrum. This is close to the maximum sensitivity of the human eye and the efficacy is the highest of all lamp types but the 'monochromatic' light provides no colour rendering. These lamps are mainly used for exterior applications such as road and security lighting.

SOX-E (high efficacy) lamps operate in SOX circuits, but SOX lamps do not operate in SOX-E circuits.

Operating position	Usually horizontal
Control gear	Yes
Starting	8–12 min run-up
Restarting	Up to 55 W: prompt
	90 W and above: 10 min
Colour temperature (K)	—
Colour rendering group	—
Minimum starting temperature	–20°C
See Table 3.4 (page 101) and Figure 3.4 (page 102)	
IEC standard	IEC 192

3.2.4.4   High pressure sodium lamps

These lamps have a ceramic arc tube with a clear or diffusing outer envelope. The sodium and mercury amalgam discharge operates at a higher pressure than in SOX lamps. This increases the colour temperature and improves colour rendering.

HPS lamps are used for road lighting especially in city centres, for floodlighting and industrial interior lighting. They also have some commercial applications, e.g. for sports halls and public concourses.

There are also versions for exterior and industrial applications which have a significant increase in light output and lumen maintenance, with no reduction in life. A range of 'plug-in' high pressure sodium lamps is also available. These are designed to replace high pressure mercury lamps on ballasts which comply with specifications. Small changes may be required; reference should be made to the technical literature of lamp manufacturers.

Deluxe versions with improved colour rendering operate at increased pressures in the discharge but the gain in colour is at the expense of life and efficacy. Some versions use no mercury and can be operated at two different colour temperatures. Low wattage lamps with a white colour appearance, and a colour temperature of around 2500 K, and good colour rendering have been designed for display lighting.

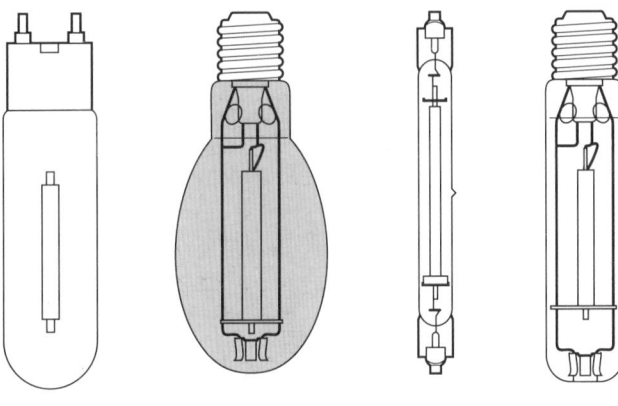

Operating position	Any
Control gear	Yes
Starting	1.5–6 min run-up
Restarting	>1 min (1000 W: 3 min)
Colour temperature (K)	2000–3000
Colour rendering group	1B-4
Minimum starting temperature	–40°C
See Table 3.4 (page 101) and Figure 3.4 (page 102)	
IEC standard	IEC 662

3.2.4.5 High pressure mercury lamps

The high pressure mercury discharge operates in a quartz arc tube enclosed in an outer ellipsoidal bulb with an internal phosphor coating which improves the colour rendering. Reflector versions of these lamps are also available.

Mercury lamps are used for road lighting, industrial lighting and for some commercial applications. Deluxe versions, with improved colour rendering, have a special phosphor coating.

Mercury blended lamps (MBT) combine a mercury-arc tube and a tungsten filament in the same envelope. The filament is connected in series and acts as a ballast. It also adds a warm colour component to the light. The envelope has a fluorescent coating. Although there is a run-up period for the mercury discharge, the light from the filament is immediate. The overall efficacy is low but the lamps can be used as long-life replacements for filament lamps.

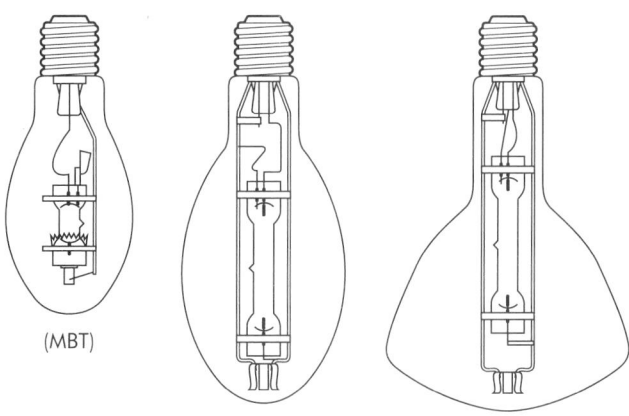

Operating position	Any (usually cap-up for MBT)
Control gear	Yes (except MBT)
Starting	2–5 min run-up
Restarting	4–7 min
Colour temperature (K)	3300–4000
Colour rendering group	3
Minimum starting temperature	–20°C
See Table 3.4 (page 101) and Figure 3.4 (page 102)	
IEC standard	*IEC 188*

3.2.4.6 Metal halide lamps

The high pressure mercury discharge with other metallic elements, introduced in the form of halides, operates in a quartz arc tube. Some lamps have an outer envelope, which may have a fluorescent coating.

According to the mix of elements, there is a wide range of efficacy, colour appearance and colour rendering.

No standard specifications exist and lamps of different makes may not be interchangeable, either photometrically or electrically. Compatibility between lamps and control gear should always be checked with the individual manufacturers.

Guidance on uv limits for bare arc tube types is provided by manufacturers (see also section 5.9). When re-lamping, quartz bulbs should be wiped clean of finger marks before switching on.

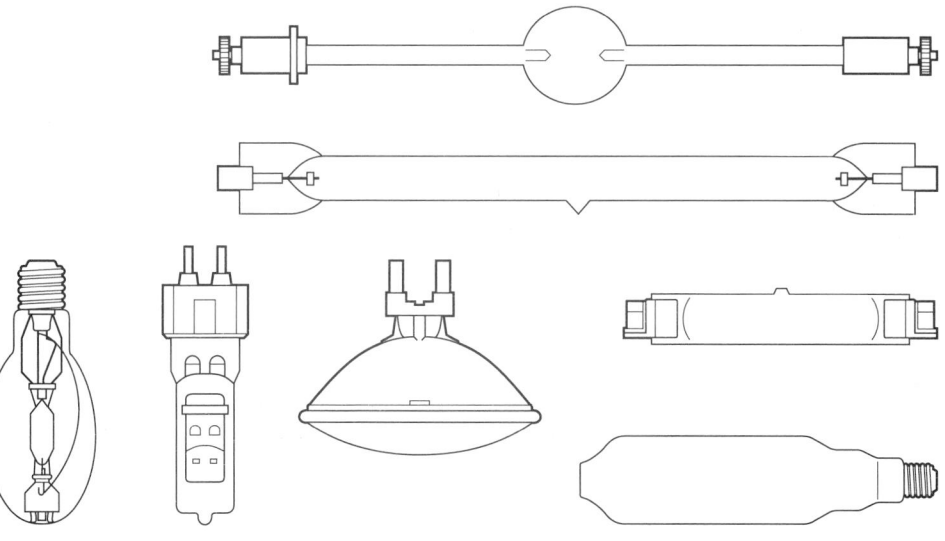

Metal halide lamps are mainly used in commercial interiors, industry and floodlighting, as well as for colour TV lighting in stadia and studios. Lower ratings are used for display lighting.

Operating position	Horizontal for double-ended, any for single- ended†
Control gear	Yes
Starting	1–2 min run-up
Restarting	5–15 min
Colour temperature (K)	3000–6000
Colour rendering group	1A-2
Minimum starting temperature	–20°C
See Table 3.4 (page 101) and Figure 3.4 (page 102)	
IEC standard	IEC 1167

† Orientation can affect efficacy and optical performance.

Table 3.4   Generic lamp life and lumen maintenance characteristics†. Note: these data should not be used for lighting design. Consult manufacturer for information on specific lamp types and operating conditions.

Lamp type	Standard average life to 50% survival (h)	Hours to 70% lumen maintenance (h)
Filament GLS	1000	—
Filament tungsten–halogen	2000	—
Filament tungsten–halogen (ELV)	4000	—
Fluorescent tubular (26 mm)		
—multi- and triphosphor	6000–12 000	12 000–24 000
—(HF operation)	7500–15 000	15 000–30 000
—(halophosphate)	6000–12 000	12 000–24 000
Fluorescent tubular (38 mm)		
—halophosphate	5000–10 000	10 000–24 000
Fluorescent compact	8000–10 000§	10 000–14 000§
Induction (fluorescent)	60 000 (to 80% survival)	60 000
Low pressure sodium	11 500–23 000	15 000–30 000
High pressure sodium	14 000–28 000	13 500–27 000
High pressure sodium		
—Plus	15 000–30 000	16 500–31 000
—Deluxe	14 000–28 000	14 000–28 000
—'White'	10 000 (6000)¶	>90% at 6000
High pressure mercury		
—fluorescent	14 000–28 000	14 000–28 000
—blended	6000–12 000	6500–13 000
Metal halide		
—fluorescent	5600–13 000	6000–12 000
—MBI-T, HPI-T	6500–13 000	6500–13 000

† Where a range of values is given, these values represent measurements on controlled test conditions, e.g. voltage, ambient temperature switching cycle, and circuit parameters. Practical values would tend to be in the lower limits of the ranges.
§ Dependent on wattage.
¶ Dependent on colour quality.

Figure 3.4(a) and (b) Graphs showing the relationship between initial lamp luminous efficacy (excluding circuit losses) and the lamp lumen 'package' over the commonly available wattage range for each lamp type. For clarity fluorescent lamps are shown separately in Figure 3.4(b). The most commonly used lumen package ranges from 2000 to 10 000 lm. Lamps below 2000 lm tend to be used for domestic, display and local lighting applications. Lamps above 10 000 lm tend to be used for heavy industrial and exterior lighting.

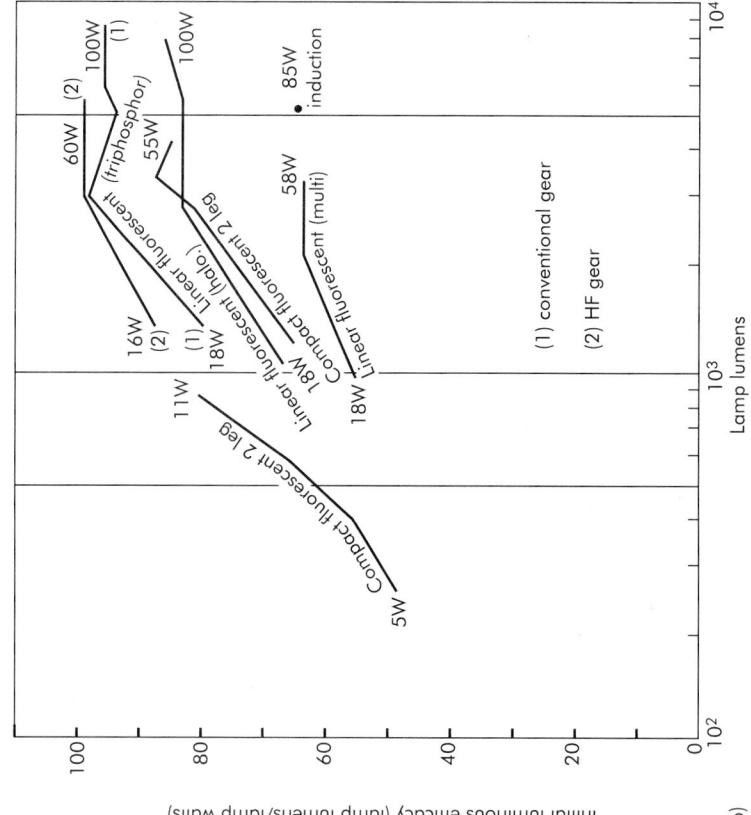

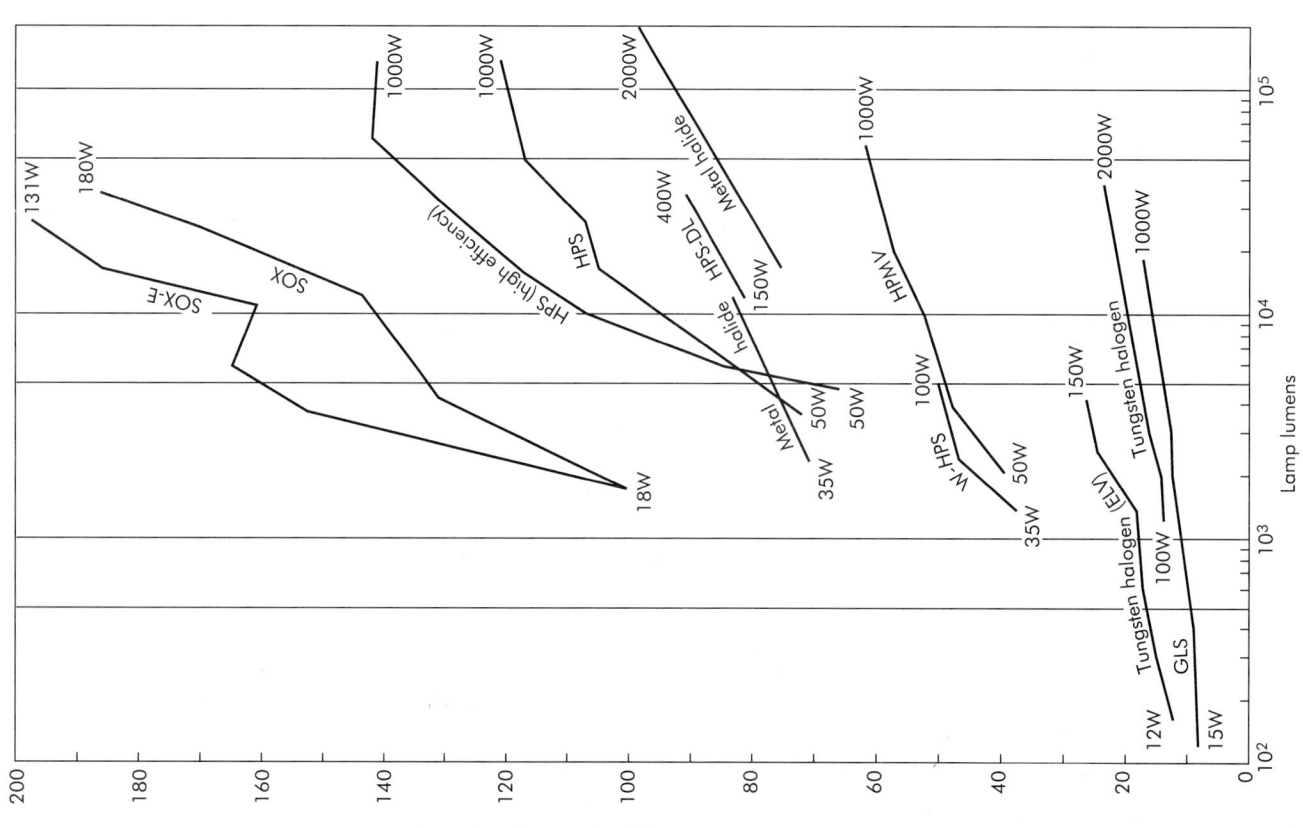

3.3 Luminaires

3.3.1 Luminaire standards and markings

Luminaires can take many different forms, but all have to provide support, protection and electrical connection to the lamp. In addition luminaires have to be safe during installation and operation and be able to withstand the conditions in the operating environments. The standard which covers most luminaires in the UK is *BS 4533: Luminaires*[88]. The equivalent European standard is *EN60 598-1:1989*[89] which, in turn, is based on *IEC 598*[90]. Both apply to luminaires containing tungsten filament, tubular fluorescent and other discharge lamps running on supply voltages not exceeding 1 kV and cover the electrical, mechanical and thermal aspects of safety.

Luminaires are classified according to the type of protection against electric shock, the degree of protection against ingress of dust or moisture and according to the material of the surface to which the luminaire can be fixed.

Table 3.5 lists the luminaire classes according to the type of protection against electric shock. Class 0 luminaires are not permitted in the UK by reason of the *Low Voltage Electrical Equipment (Safety) Regulations* (1989)[91], the *Electricity (Factories Act) Special Regulations 1944*[92] and the *Electricity at Work Act 1989*[24].

The degree of protection the luminaire provides against the ingress of dust and moisture is classified according to the Ingress Protection (IP) System. This system, as detailed in *IEC 529*[93] (*BS 5490*[94]) and based on *IEC 598*[90] (*BS 4533*[88]), describes a luminaire by a two-digit number, e.g. IP54. The first digit classifies the degree of protection against the ingress of solid foreign bodies,

Table 3.5 Classification of luminaires according to the type of protection provided against electric shock (from *BS 4533*[84]/*EN60 598*[85,86])

Class	Type of protection	Symbol used to mark luminaires
0†	A luminaire in which protection against electric shock relies upon basic insulation; this implies that there are no means for the connection of accessible conductive parts, if any, to the protective conductor in the fixed wiring of the installation, reliance in the event of a failure of the basic insulation being placed on the environment.	No symbol
I	A luminaire in which protection against electric shock does not rely on basic insulation only, but which includes an additional safety precaution in such a way that means are provided for the connection of accessible conductive parts to the protective (earthing) conductor in the fixed wiring of the installation in such a way that the accessible conductive parts cannot become live in the event of a failure of the basic insulation.	No symbol
II	A luminaire in which protection against electric shock does not rely on basic insulation only, but in which additional safety precautions such as double insulation or reinforced insulation are provided, there being no provision for protective earthing or reliance upon installation conditions.	▢
III	A luminaire in which protection against electric shock relies upon supply at safety extra low voltage (SELV) and in which voltages higher than SELV are not generated. The SELV is defined as a voltage which does not exceed 50 V AC, RMS between conductors or between any conductor and earth in a circuit which is isolated from the supply mains by means such as a safety isolating transformer or converter with separate windings.	◇III◇

† Class 0 luminaires are not permitted in the UK

Table 3.6   The degrees of protection against the ingress of solid bodies (first characteristic numeral) and moisture (second characteristic numeral) in the Ingress Protection (IP) system of luminaire classification

First characteristic numeral	Degree of protection and short description	Details of solid objects which will be 'excluded' from luminaire
0	Non-protected	No special protection.
1	Protected against solid objects greater than 50 mm	A large surface of the body, such as a hand, (but no protection against deliberate access); solid objects exceeding 50 mm in diameter.
2	Protected against solid objects greater than 12 mm	Fingers or similar objects not exceeding 80 mm in length; solid objects exceeding 12 mm in diameter.
3	Protected against solid objects greater than 2.5 mm	Tools, wires etc., of diameter or thickness greater than 2.5 mm; solid objects exceeding 2.5 mm in diameter.
4	Protected against solid objects greater than 1.0 mm	Wires or strips of thickness greater than 1.0 mm; solid objects exceeding 1.0 mm in diameter.
5	Dust-protected	Ingress of dust is not totally prevented but dust does not enter in sufficient quantity to interfere with the satisfactory operation of the equipment.
6	Dust-tight	No ingress of dust.

Second characteristic numeral	Degree of protection and short description	Details of the type of protection from moisture provided by the luminaire
0	Non-protected	No special protection.
1	Protected against dripping water	Dripping water (vertically falling drops) shall have no harmful effect.
2	Protected against dripping water when tilted up to 15°	Vertically dripping water shall have no harmful effect when the luminaire is tilted at any angle up to 15° from its normal position.
3	Protected against spraying water	Water falling as spray at an angle up to 60° from the vertical shall have no harmful effect.
4	Protected against splashing water	Water splashed against the enclosure from any direction shall have no harmful effect.
5	Protected against water jets	Water projected by a nozzle against the enclosure from any direction shall have no harmful effect.
6	Protected against heavy seas	Water from heavy seas or water projected in powerful jets shall not enter the luminaire in harmful quantities.
7	Protected against the effects of immersion	Ingress of water in a harmful quantity shall not be possible when the luminaire is immersed in water under defined conditions of pressure and time.
8	Protected against submersion	The equipment is suitable for continuous submersion in water under conditions which shall be specified by the manufacturer.

from fingers and tools to fine dust. The second digit classifies the degree of protection against the ingress of moisture. Table 3.6 lists the classes of these two digits. Table 3.7 lists the IP numbers which correspond to some commonly used descriptions of luminaire types and the symbols which may be used to mark the luminaires in addition to the IP number. Sometimes a third digit is used which refers to a French standard *UTE C20 0 10*[95] for impact testing.

Table 3.8 lists the classification of luminaires according to the material of the supporting surface for which the luminaire is designed.

Table 3.7 Ingress Protection (IP) numbers corresponding to some commonly used descriptions of luminaire types and the symbols which may be used to mark a luminaire in addition to the IP number

Commonly used description of luminaire type	IP number†	Symbol which may be used in addition to the IP classification number	
Ordinary	IP20§	No symbol	
Drip-proof	IPX1	▲	(one drop)
Rain-proof	IPX3	▢	(one drop in square)
Splash-proof	IPX4	△	(one drop in triangle)
Jet-proof	IPX5	△△	(two triangles with one drop in each)
Watertight (immersible)	IPX7	▲▲	(two drops)
Pressure-/watertight (submersible)	IPX8	▲▲--m	(two drops followed by an indication of the maximum depth of submersion in metres)
Proof against 1 mm diameter probe	IP4X	No symbol	
Dust-proof	IP5X	▨	(mesh without frame)
Dust-tight	IP6X	◈	(mesh with frame)

† Where X is used in an IP number in this *Code*, it indicates a missing character numeral. However, on any luminaire, both appropriate characteristic numerals should be marked.

§ Marking of IP20 on ordinary luminaires is not required. In this context an ordinary luminaire is one without special protection against dirt or moisture.

Table 3.8 Classification of luminaires according to the material of the supporting surface for which the luminaire is designed from *BS 4533*[88]/*EN60 598*[89, 90]

Description of class	Symbol used to mark luminaires
Luminaires suitable for direct mounting only on non-combustible surfaces	No symbol, but a warning notice is required
Luminaires with or without built-in ballast or transformers, suitable for direct mounting on normally flammable surfaces	▽F
Recessed luminaires suitable for mounting in or on a normally flammable surface, but with the indicated distance (mm) to normally flammable objects to be maintained (conditional F mark)	▽F/75
Recessed luminaires suitable for mounting in or on a normally flammable surface where thermal insulating material may cover the luminaire (insulated ceiling F mark)	▽F
Thermally protected ballast. The dots are replaced by the maximum case temperature (°C) (up to 130°C) when the cut-out opens the circuit	▽P or ▽...

Figure 3.5 Symbol warning against using 'cool beam' lamp in luminaire

Figure 3.6 Symbol for earthing termination

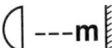

Figure 3.7 Symbol for minimum distance from lighted objects

Figure 3.8 Symbol for rough service luminaire

Figure 3.9 Symbol for bowl mirror (crown-silvered) lamp

Figure 3.10 High voltage warning symbol

The following information should be distinctly and durably marked on the luminaire in a position where it can be seen during maintenance, if necessary after the removal of covers or similar components. In addition to this information all details which are necessary to ensure proper installation, use and maintenance should be provided on the luminaire, on control gear components or in the manufacturer's instructions provided with the luminaire.

(a) Mark of origin.

(b) Rated voltage(s) in volts (luminaires for tungsten filament lamps are only marked if the rated voltage is different from 250 V).

(c) Rated maximum ambient temperature if other than 25 °C (t_a ... °C).

(d) Symbol of class II or class III luminaire, where applicable (see Table 3.5).

(e) Ingress protection (IP) number, where applicable (see Tables 3.6 and 3.7).

(f) Maker's model number or type reference.

(g) Rated wattage of the lamp(s) in watts. Where the lamp wattage alone is insufficient, the number of lamps and the type should also be given. Luminaires for tungsten filament lamps should be marked with the maximum rated wattage and number of lamps.

(h) Symbols for luminaires with or without built-in ballasts or transformer suitable for direct-mounting on normally flammable surfaces, if applicable (see Table 3.8).

(i) Information concerning special lamps, if applicable, e.g. high pressure sodium lamps requiring an external or internal ignitor or starting device (see Table 3.2).

(j) Symbol for luminaires using lamps of similar shape to 'cool beam' lamps where the use of a 'cool beam' lamp might impair safety, if applicable (see Figure 3.5).

(k) Terminations to be clearly marked to identify which termination should be connected to the live side of the supply, where necessary for safety or to ensure satisfactory operation. Earthing terminations should be clearly indicated (see Figure 3.6).

(l) Symbols for the minimum distance from lighted objects, for spotlights and the like, where applicable (see Figure 3.7).

(m) Symbol, if applicable, for rough service luminaires (see Figure 3.8).

(n) Symbol, if applicable, for luminaires which are designed for use with bowl mirror (crown-silvered) lamps (see Figure 3.9).

(o) Luminaires incorporating a glass safety shield should be marked 'Replace any cracked safety shield'.

(p) For luminaires with remote gear, the range of lamps for which the luminaire is designed should be shown.

(q) For luminaires housing double-ended high pressure discharge lamps, with an ignitor producing a high starting voltage under specified measurement conditions, should carry the warning symbol so that it is visible during replacement of the lamp (see Figure 3.10).

There is also the general requirement that written instructions relating to safety shall be in a language which is acceptable to the country in which the equipment is to be installed.

BS 4533[88]/*EN 60 598*[89,90] apply to most luminaires intended for use in neutral or hostile environments, including luminaires with type of protection 'N' (non-sparking). Many of the luminaires intended for use in hazardous environments, i.e. environments in which there is a risk of fire or explosion, are not included. For such applications there are different requirements so different standards and certification procedures apply. Detailed guidance on this topic can be found in the *CIBSE Lighting Guide: Lighting for hostile and hazardous environments*[42].

3.3.1.1   Quality systems and approval marks

As part of *BS 4533*[88], BSI Safety Mark, and Kitemark licenses for lamps, starters, ballasts, lamp holders and luminaires indicate compliance with the relevant BSI/EN product standards. In addition, a manufacturer may be accredited by recognised national accreditation authorities to *BS 5750*[96], which is identical to the *ISO 9000*[97] and *EN 29000*[98] series of quality assurance system standards. These approvals can cover design, development, manufacture, distribution and sales operations to ensure that customers receive reliable and consistent products and services.

The ENEC mark (see Figure 3.11) is a new European harmonised safety mark for luminaires. The mark shows that the product has been tested and approved to the harmonised European standard *EN 60 598*[86] including the most onerous national deviation. In the UK this being the supply voltages of 240 V. The mark came into use in 1993.

For the UK, the BSI operates Safety Mark (see Figure 3.12) and Kitemark schemes (to *BS 4533* and *BS 5750)* and a Registered Firm scheme to *BS 5750*. The Safety Mark is only a guarantee of electrical, mechanical and thermal safety and not necessarily of performance in other respects. The BSI Kitemark scheme is a certificate of conformity with tests and quality control.

For the BSI Safety Mark, manufacturers have three options:

(*a*) To mark with the BSI Safety Mark: this is a guarantee endorsed by the Department of Prices and Consumer Protection and supported by an independent testing authority. The Mark guarantees product compliance with *BS 4533* and that the manufacturer is accredited to *BS 5750*.

(*b*) To mark the product *BS 4533*: this indicates that the manufacturer or importer claims compliance with *BS 4533* in all respects. The claim of safety is valid, but might not be supported by quality assurance systems.

(*c*) Self-certification: the manufacturer claims without reference to any specification that the luminaire is safe within the meaning of the regulations. If the claim is unsupported by independent evidence it will be more difficult to substantiate in law.

The BSI Kitemark (the official term is the 'BSI Certification Trade Mark'), see Figure 3.13, can be used only by those manufacturers granted a license under the certification mark scheme operated by the BSI. The presence of the Kitemark on, or in relation to, a product is an assurance that the product has been produced under

Figure 3.11   ENEC mark

Figure 3.12   BSI Safety Mark

Figure 3.13   BSI Kitemark

accreditation to *BS 5750*. The Kitemark may not necessarily cover safety, unless the appropriate British Standard includes these necessary requirements. The BSI Kitemark must be shown with the relevant British Standard number.

A manufacturer may also apply for Registered Firm status. This is used by the registered firm only in advertising, correspondence and promotional material to show that it has been independently assessed and complies with *BS 5750*. It must always be used in conjunction with the company's name and have the certificate of registration number adjacent to it. It must be used only in connection with those goods or services listed on the appendix to the Certification of Registration.

3.3.2 Luminaire characteristics

Although meeting the requirements of *BS 4533*[88]/*EN 60 598*[89,90] is a common factor in luminaire design, it does not limit the variety of luminaires that is available. Luminaires vary in their construction, mounting position, distribution of light, maintenance characteristics, the efficiency with which they provide light on the working plane, the extent to which they are likely to cause discomfort glare and the manner in which they light an interior. The most commonly occurring types of luminaire used for general, localised, display and emergency lighting and their typical performance characteristics are described in this section. This section is only intended to give a general overview of the types of equipment available. For detailed design purposes, performance data from the manufacturer should be used.

Over 70 typical luminaires are divided into 21 groups with similar characteristics. For each group, line drawings illustrate the common variants with the following information:

— Notes for each group: the text gives a description of the typical lighting and efficiency characteristics. General guidance is also given on the degrees of glare control achieved by each group as well as the illuminance ratios (covered in sections 2.4.4 and 2.4.5) which influence the lit appearance of the interior (see also section 4.4.3.2).

— Luminaire typical maintenance characteristics: the maintenance category A–F shown beside each line drawing refers to those given in Tables 4.5 and 4.8. In the associated notes, for some groups, an indication is given of how the typical maintenance category can change for different versions of the same basic type of luminaire.

— Mounting position: luminaires can be recessed into the ceiling (R), surface-mounted on the ceiling (S), pendant-mounted from the ceiling (P), floor standing, or furniture or wall-mounted (F). Some luminaires can be mounted in more than one mode.

— Typical polar curve shape: the polar curve shape is a schematic illustration of the luminous intensity distribution of the luminaire. This characterises the way in which the luminaire controls the light from the lamp. For linear luminaires two curves, representing transverse (T) and axial (A) luminous intensity distributions, are shown. For symmetrical luminaires a curve (T) representing the average luminous intensity distribution is given.

— Typical maximum spacing-to-height ratio (SHR): when designing a uniform lighting installation using the lumen method of calculation, this indicates the limit on the spacing between the luminaire centres. The maximum spacing that is allowable is determined by the luminous intensity distribution of the luminaire and its mounting height above the reference working plane. Therefore, the spacing allowable for each luminaire type is expressed as a ratio of the spacing to the mounting height. These data are calculated to provide a mid-point ratio of greater than 0.7. For a regular array of luminaires where there are no significant obstructions this has been shown, empirically, to provide uniformity over the task area of better than 0.8. For more details on the spacing-to-height ratio, see section 4.5.3.4.

There are many forms of luminaire other than those displayed and within each group of luminaires considerable variation exists. For accurate information, the manufacturers should always be consulted. Photometric data supplied by manufacturers should have been obtained from photometric measurements according to *BS 5225*[99] and calculated according to CIBSE *TM5*[100].

3.3.2.1 Bare batten luminaires

These luminaires are basic and inexpensive. They emit light efficiently but do not control its direction, so that all room surfaces are illuminated. System efficiency depends strongly on the reflectances of room surfaces (particularly ceiling reflectances) and therefore high reflectance finishes should be used. There is no control of glare and therefore the luminaire is only suitable for applications where higher glare ratings are acceptable or in small rooms. Surface reflectance will strongly affect the glare rating and, once again, light finishes, particularly for the ceiling, are important. Modelling is soft/flat.

A feature of the batten luminaire is that attachments can be used to obtain light control. The spine of the luminaire above the lamp reflects some of the light, reducing the upward light and increasing the downward light. Twin lamp versions are available with either close or widely space lamps. The closely spaced versions have lamps which are below the luminaire body giving a similar performance to the single lamp version, whereas with widely spaced lamps beyond the luminaire body, far more light is directed upwards. When most attachments are added to either type some difference in upward light, due to lamp spacing, will remain.

Luminaire	Main-tenance category	Mount-ing	Polar curve T A	SHR
Batten	A	SP		1·75
Batten	A	SP		1·75
Batten	A	SP		1·75
Batten	A	SP		1·75

Luminaire	Maintenance category	Mounting	Polar curve T A	SHR
Slim opal diffuser	D	SP		1·75
Slim opal diffuser	D	SP		1·75
Wide twin opal diffuser	D	SP		1·75

3.3.2.2 Battens with opal diffusers

These luminaires are batten luminaires with an opal diffuser attachment. The opal diffuser does not significantly alter the light distribution of the bare batten luminaire but reduces its overall brightness and improves its appearance. Efficiency is less than the bare batten version but the glare rating will be reduced. Depending upon the room size and reflectance this type of luminaire may be suitable for applications with a limiting glare rating of 19. The illuminance ratios which are achieved will be similar to those of a bare batten: namely, the room surfaces will be well illuminated and the modelling will tend to be flat. This type usually has an open top and must therefore be regularly cleaned to maintain system efficiency.

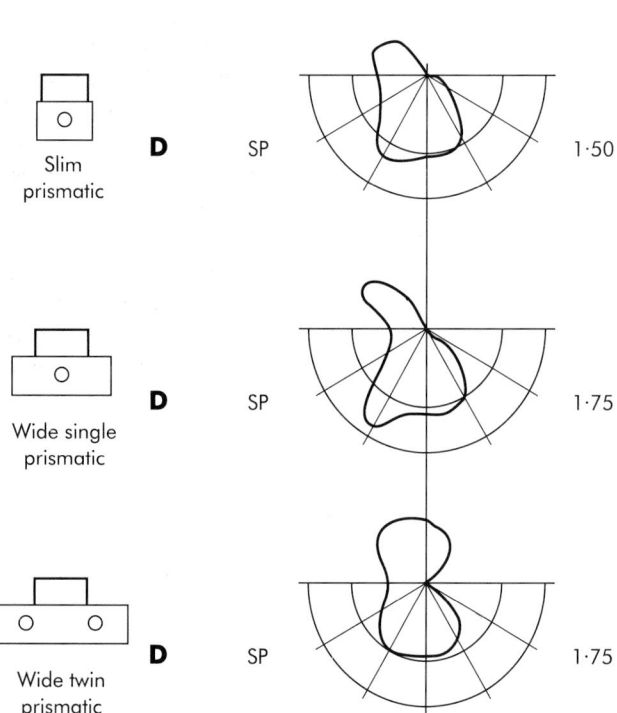

Luminaire	Maintenance category	Mounting	Polar curve T A	SHR
Slim prismatic	D	SP		1·50
Wide single prismatic	D	SP		1·75
Wide twin prismatic	D	SP		1·75

3.3.2.3 Battens with prismatic controllers

These luminaires are commonly used for office lighting. Clear plastic with prisms is used to control and redirect the light. Light output is reduced at angles which would cause glare and directed downwards. Therefore, although the controller absorbs some light the utilisation factor with the prismatic controller, for the same light output ratio, is better than that with the opal attachments (section 3.3.2.2). The glare control of these luminaires is designed to make them satisfactory for most office applications requiring a limiting glare rating of 19. This glare rating will be exceeded if room reflectances are low, especially if the room index is high. The wall-to-task and ceiling-to-task illuminance ratios will be reduced compared to those for a bare batten luminaire and modelling will be slightly stronger. Because the controller is not sealed and uses prisms, the build-up of dirt will reduce efficiency and alter the light control if it is not regularly cleaned.

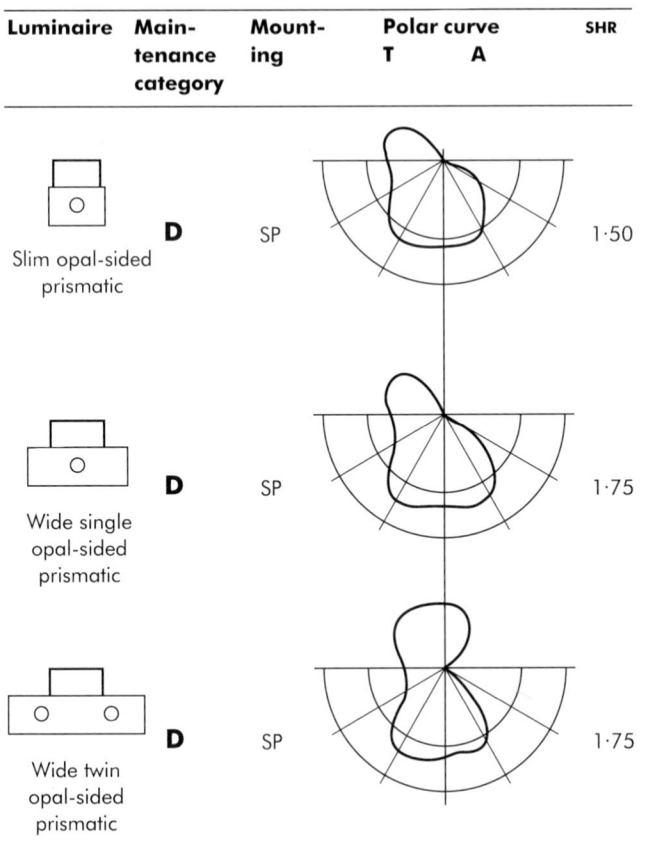

Luminaire	Main-tenance category	Mount-ing	Polar curve T A	SHR
Slim opal-sided prismatic	D	SP		1·50
Wide single opal-sided prismatic	D	SP		1·75
Wide twin opal-sided prismatic	D	SP		1·75

Luminaire	Main-tenance category	Mount-ing	Polar curve T A	SHR
VDT specular reflector	B	SP		1·00
VDT specular reflector	B	SP		1·00

3.3.2.4   Batten with opal side and prismatic base

These luminaires have almost identical properties to those described in section 3.3.2.3. The sides comprise opal plastic rather than clear prisms. This can improve the appearance of the luminaire with a slight reduction in light output.

The glare control of these luminaires is designed to make them satisfactory for most office applications requiring a limiting glare rating of 19. This glare rating will be exceeded if room reflectances are low, especially if the room index is high. The wall-to-task and ceiling-to-task illuminance ratios will be reduced compared to that of a bare batten luminaire. Modelling will be slightly stronger. Because the base controller uses prisms, the build-up of dirt will reduce efficiency and alter the light control if not regularly cleaned.

3.3.2.5   Batten with VDT reflector

This type of attachment is designed to replace existing diffusers when visual display terminals (VDTs) are introduced into an office. VDT reflector attachments are designed to control the light output at angles which would produce reflections on VDT screens. Designs vary considerably in their ability to provide sufficient cut-off for VDT use. Generally these devices achieve CIBSE Lighting Guide *LG3*[25] category 2 light control (see section 3.3.2.9). The addition of the VDT reflector attachment dramatically reduces the efficiency of the luminaire. The glare rating will be very low and suitable for VDT applications. The illuminance ratios will be low with strong modelling. There is likely to be a sharp cut-off line on the walls of the room which may look gloomy and dull unless the floor cavity reflectance is high.

Luminaire	Main-tenance category	Mount-ing	Polar curve T A	SHR
Slotted white trough reflector	B	SP		1·75
Slotted white trough reflector	B	SP		1·50
Specular reflector (racking)	C	SP		0·75
Specular reflector (racking)	C	SP		1·00
Angled reflector	B	SP		N/A

3.3.2.6   Batten with industrial reflector

Metal reflectors are used on batten luminaires to improve their performance in industrial and similar applications. The commonly occurring types are shown (opposite).

White-painted metal reflectors are used to direct light downwards onto the working plane. This is useful in any application where the ceiling cavity reflectance is low and as a result the performance of a bare batten luminaire would be inadequate. This can occur when luminaires are suspended from the ceiling or the ceiling finish is dark (often the case in industry). The system efficiency of such luminaires is normally very high. The reflector gives good glare control (cut-off) in the transverse direction and meets the glare limits for most industrial situations. Slots in the top of the reflector permit a small amount of upward light which prevents the ceiling from being too dark and helps slightly to reduce glare. Wall-to-task and ceiling-to-task illuminance ratios will be low. Modelling will be medium.

Alternatively, specular aluminium reflectors are designed for use in warehouses and other applications where a more concentrated distribution is required to illuminate narrow aisles without waste. Comments about the lighting performance are similar to those for the industrial white reflector units, except that, where they are to be used for general lighting, the illuminance ratios would be lower and the modelling stronger.

A variant of this type of luminaire uses an asymmetrical reflector with either white or specular finish. It can be appropriate for local lighting (e.g. chalkboards) or localised lighting of the sides of areas where there is overhead obstruction (e.g. car production lines). For these applications the usual lumen method of design is not valid (see section 5.13).

Luminaire	Main-tenance category	Mount-ing	Polar curve T A	SHR
Single opal	See notes **E**	SP		1·50
Twin opal	**E**	SP		1·50
Single prismatic	**E**	SP		1·50
Twin prismatic	**E**	SP		1·50
Single opal sides prismatic base	**E**	SP		1·50
Twin opal sides prismatic base	**E**	SP		1·50

3.3.2.7   Surface modular luminaires

Surface modular luminaires are surface-mounted or occasionally suspended, and have a neat appearance. They are available with opal, prismatic or opal-sided prismatic base attachments similar to those described in sections 3.3.2.2, 3.3.2.3 and 3.3.2.4 respectively. They have comparable efficiencies although, without careful design, overheating can reduce fluorescent lamp light output. It is possible to achieve a good seal between the diffuser and the luminaire body which results in a type E maintenance characteristic, otherwise category D would apply.

With opal diffusers the ratio of the upward light to downward light will be determined by the area of the opal sides to the area of the base. These luminaires provide moderate efficiency and the glare rating may be better than 19 if the room reflectances are high. The wall-to-task illuminance ratios will be medium and the ceiling-to-task illuminance ratios will be low. Modelling will tend to be soft/flat.

Prismatic versions of these luminaires provide better light control and an attractive appearance. The efficiency is better than the opal version. They are normally designed to give a limiting glare rating of 19 or better when the room reflectances are medium to high. The wall-to-task illuminance ratios are medium and the ceiling-to-task illuminance ratios will be low. Modelling will tend to be soft/flat.

The opal-sided prismatic base attachments provide similar performance to the prismatic versions, but the opal sides provide an alternative appearance.

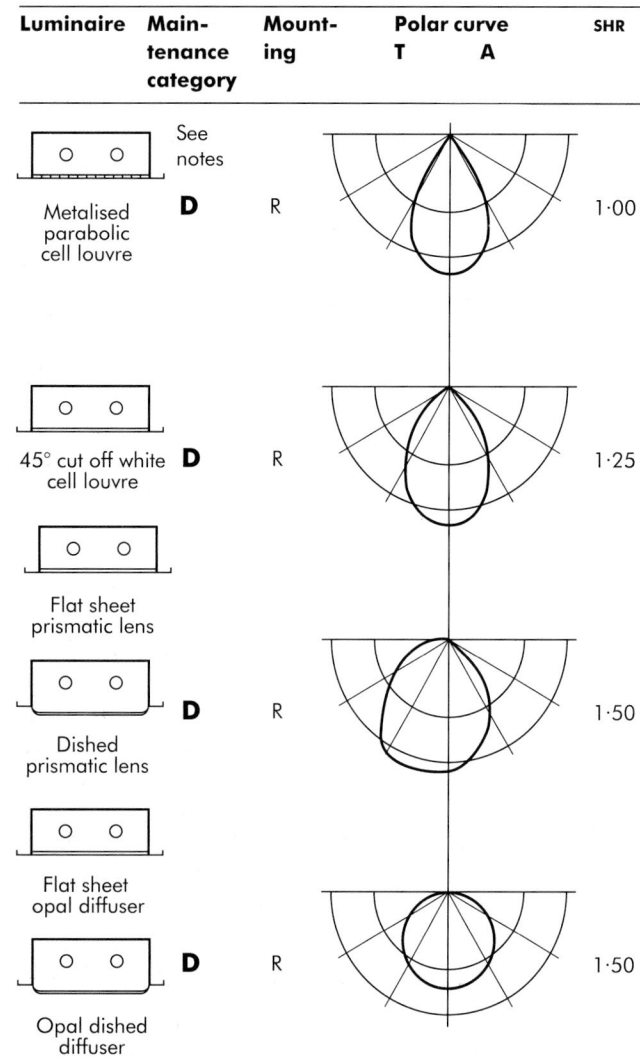

Luminaire	Main-tenance category	Mount-ing	Polar curve T A	SHR
Metalised parabolic cell louvre	See notes **D**	R		1·00
45° cut off white cell louvre	**D**	R		1·25
Flat sheet prismatic lens				
Dished prismatic lens	**D**	R		1·50
Flat sheet opal diffuser				
Opal dished diffuser	**D**	R		1·50

3.3.2.8 Recessed modular luminaires

Recessed modular luminaires are available with specular louvres, white louvres, flat or dished, prismatic or opal panels. Taking them in the above sequence, the downward flux distribution becomes wider and the glare and the efficiency increases.

As with all recessed luminaires, the ceiling-to-task illuminance ratio is low. The wall-to-task ratio is also low. Floor cavity reflectance has a significant effect on the lit appearance of the space, but generally modelling is strong. These effects become less marked if the various attachments are taken in the same sequence as above.

Prismatic panels providing an asymmetrical distribution in the transverse plane are also available. For these the lumen method is not valid.

Where opal or prismatic panels close the mouth of the luminaire body, reduced ventilation can decrease the light output of the fluorescent lamps. All types are available in air handling versions which exhaust air through the fitting. With correct design and suitable air flow rates, the efficiency of the lamps can be optimised with maintenance category B. For typical non-air handling versions the maintenance category D applies.

Luminaire	Main-tenance category	Mount-ing	Polar curve T A	SHR
Aluminium reflector with transverse blades VDT category 1	See notes C	RSP		1·00
Aluminium reflector with transverse blades VDT category 2	C	RSP		1·50
Aluminium batwing reflector with transverse blades VDT category 3	C	RSP		1·75

3.3.2.9 Modular VDT luminaires

Modular VDT luminaires may be surface-mounted or recessed. They use reflector optics in various forms to achieve suitable lighting for VDT use. In this and the following group of luminaires (section 3.3.2.10) the variety of reflector design enables a wide choice of intensity distributions to be offered. The designer is advised to examine a range of manufacturers' data before settling on a design solution.

As detailed in CIBSE Lighting Guide *LG3*[25], category 1 is for the most demanding (and least common) tasks, category 3 is for the least demanding tasks.

Category 1 is significantly less efficient than category 3. For each category the luminaire has a limiting angle, above which the luminance of the luminaire must not exceed 200 cd/m^2 (category 1: 55°, category 2: 65°, category 3: 75°).

Recessed luminaires with slotted tops for ventilation and air handling give a maintenance category B. For unslotted recessed and surface-mounted units, category C applies.

All three luminaires provide glare control, with category 1 giving the tightest control. All three produce low wall-to-task and ceiling-to-task illuminance ratios and strong modelling.

When luminaires are mounted parallel to a wall, a cut-off 'shadow' may be cast. The lower the reflector category number the greater will be the dark area. This may need correcting by:

(*a*) mounting the luminaires closer to the wall; this will reduce the utilisation factor (UF)[100]

(*b*) increasing the reflectances of the floor cavity to increase the inter-reflected light, or

(*c*) installing additional wall-washing luminaires.

The *Display Screen Directive*[35] stipulates that the lighting of room surfaces must achieve an acceptable balance (see sections 2.4.5, 4.4.3.3, 4.5.3 and 5.13). The use of these luminaires without adequate attention to room surface reflectances and illuminances will not meet the intentions of the Directive and may cause problems.

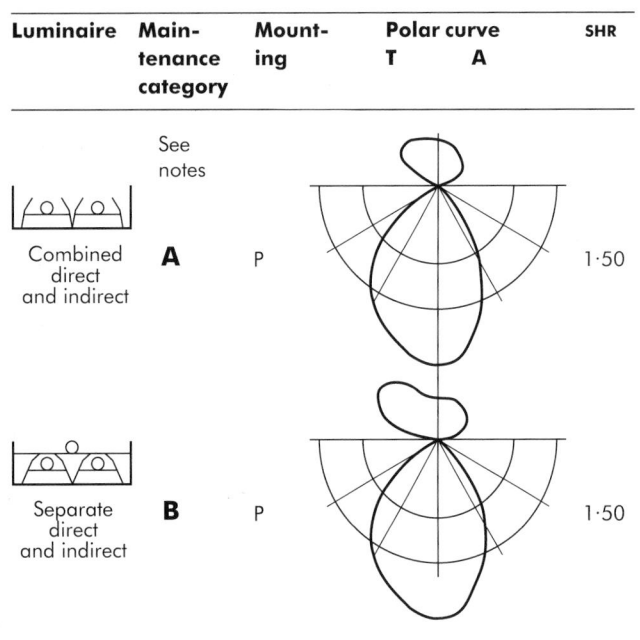

Luminaire	Main-tenance category	Mount-ing	Polar curve T A	SHR
Combined direct and indirect	A	P		1·50
Separate direct and indirect	B	P		1·50

Luminaire	Main-tenance category	Mount-ing	Polar curve T , A	SHR
Symmetrical	F	F		N/A
Asymmetrical	F	F		N/A
Decorative	F	F		N/A

3.3.2.10 Combined direct and indirect VDT luminaires

These luminaires combine direct illumination from a suitable reflector system with indirect or uplighting from the same or additional light sources.

The luminaires can be free standing, like uplighters, or, more commonly, suspended. In some designs the same lamps provide both the upward and downward components and in others separate lamps are used. When the latter type is fitted with controllable output ballasts this permits greater control over the balance between the lighting of the task and the room surfaces.

A range of maintenance categories can apply, partly because these luminaires provide separate direct and indirect lighting components and may be designed as open or fully sealed with free air flow or no ventilation.

3.3.2.11 Uplighters

Uplighters direct all the light from high pressure discharge or fluorescent lamps into the ceiling cavity. They can achieve high system efficiency, subject to ceiling reflectance, have excellent glare control and, subject to limits on the ceiling luminance (see sections 2.4.5 and 5.14), meet all the requirements for use in VDT areas and can be used for category 1, 2 or 3 task areas (see section 3.3.2.9).

The performance is dictated by the reflector design, and therefore a range of uplighters exists with significantly different outward appearances but similar performance. Units are designed to be floor standing or for mounting on walls or incorporation into furniture. Symmetrical reflectors are designed to evenly light as large an area of ceiling as possible. In offices, they are usually located at the workstations and as such provide localised rather than a general lighting system.

Asymmetric reflectors are used for wall- or column-mounted uplighters to direct light onto the ceiling rather than the mounting surface.

Wall-to-task ratios are medium and ceiling-to-task ratios are high. Modelling can be weak or medium, depending on room reflectances.

Uplighters with tungsten–halogen lamps are designed to be aesthetically attractive, decorative units and are not usually suitable for VDT/office use.

Luminaire	Main-tenance category	Mount-ing	Polar curve T A	SHR
Industrial clear patterned	E	SP		1·75
Industrial clear patterned	E	SP		1·50

3.3.2.12 Proof fluorescent luminaires

These luminaires provide suitable ingress protection for hostile environments (see Table 3.6). The light distribution is similar to single and closely spaced twin lamp batten luminaires (see section 3.3.2.1) with poor glare control, similar illuminance ratios and weak modelling.

Some units are available with reflector attachments which modify the distribution generally, as described in section 3.3.2.6.

As the lamps are enclosed in either a clear or lightly stippled, sealed plastic cover or sleeve, the LOR (light output ratio) is lower than that for bare batten luminaires, but the maintenance characteristics are improved. However, the external surfaces will need to be regularly cleaned to maintain system efficiency and the body and accessories must be of corrosion-resistant materials.

Luminaire	Main-tenance category	Mount-ing	Polar curve T A	SHR
High bay concentrating reflector	See notes **B**	P		0·75
High bay medium spread reflector	**B**	P		1·25
High bay wide spread reflector	**B**	P		1·50
High bay prismatic glass reflector	**B**	P		1·75
High bay batwing reflector	**B**	P		1·75
Reflector lamp with skirt	**B**	P		1·25

3.3.2.13 High bay luminaires

These luminaires have aluminium, plastic or glass reflectors to concentrate the light from high intensity discharge lamps from 250 W to 1000 W. They are normally used at mounting heights of 5 m and above and are suitable for a wide range of commercial and industrial interiors. The types available differ only in the degree of light dispersion and, hence, the spacing-to-height ratio recommended. All have good maintenance characteristics; with open-mouth and slotted-top reflectors the scouring action of convection currents tends to keep the lamp and reflector surfaces free of heavy deposition of dirt and dust resulting in a maintenance category of B. For particularly dirty interiors, or to give complete protection from very occasional lamp breakages (e.g. in food manufacture), clear visors are available giving totally sealed units with a maintenance category of E. For unventilated open-base units the maintenance category would be C. Unlike tubular fluorescent lamps, high intensity discharge sources are not temperature dependent and therefore enclosure results in only reduced output due to transmission losses in the visor material. Alternatively, there is a type of reflector lamp unit which uses a 'skirt' for glare control. The performance is therefore dictated by the lamp.

In all cases the luminaires are efficient, provide good glare control for industrial use, give low to medium illuminance ratios, dependent on the intensity distribution and floor cavity reflectance, and tend to provide strong modelling.

Compared to fluorescent lighting, high intensity discharge fittings produce crisp, harsh shadows with little 'fill-in'. For this reason, luminaires should not be used close to their maximum SHR (spacing-to-height ratio) but should be spaced to allow cross-over of the distributions to lessen shadows and obstruction losses. A second problem is that a single lamp failure can result in a substantial reduction in local illuminance. Again, under-spacing can be used to avoid this.

With certain distributions, under-spacing may give uniformity problems (see section 4.5.3.4).

The problems of access to high-mounted luminaires and the long life of discharge lamps means that planned maintenance is usually adopted.

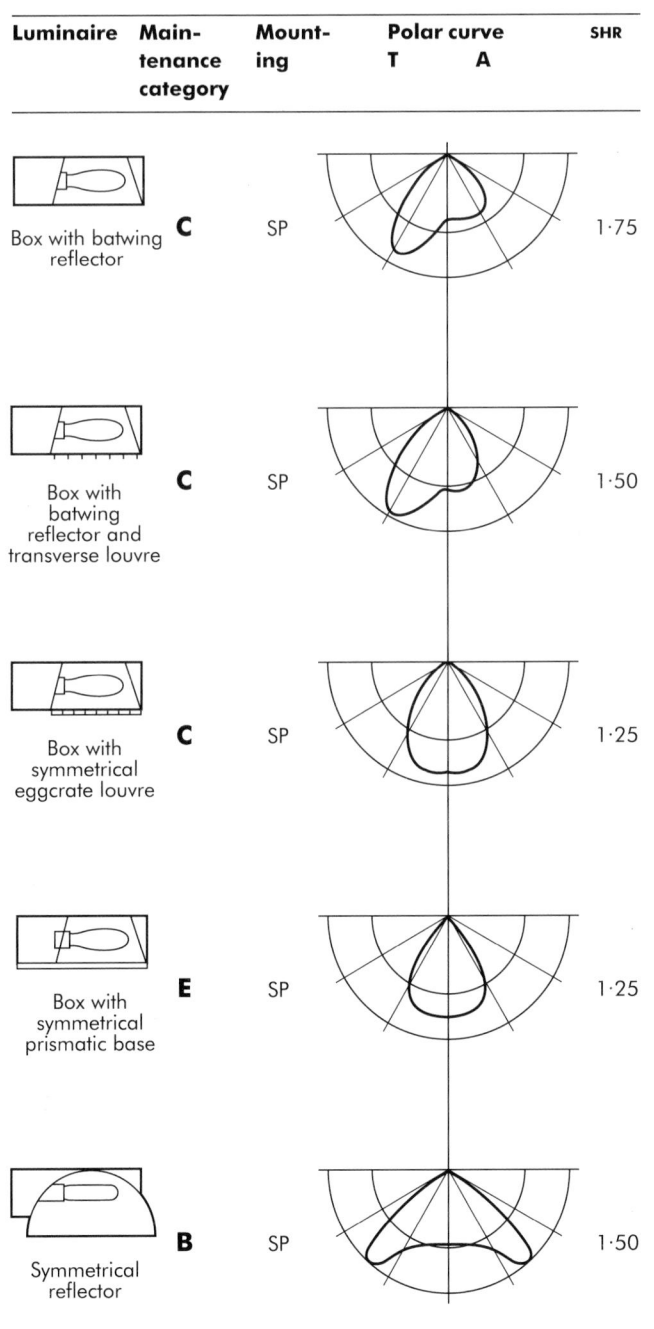

Luminaire	Maintenance category	Mounting	Polar curve T A	SHR
Box with batwing reflector	C	SP		1·75
Box with batwing reflector and transverse louvre	C	SP		1·50
Box with symmetrical eggcrate louvre	C	SP		1·25
Box with symmetrical prismatic base	E	SP		1·25
Symmetrical reflector	B	SP		1·50

3.3.2.14 Low bay luminaires

These luminaires use high intensity discharge lamps of 150 W to 400 W and are more dispersive than their 'high bay' counterparts, permitting them to be used at lower heights of usually 3 m to 5 m. Efficiency is good. Illuminance ratios are low and modelling is strong. Baffles and egg-crate louvres are used to improve glare control in one or both directions, but otherwise the glare control is suitable for factory or warehouse lighting. Sealed units with clear visors are also available.

The 'box'-shaped luminaires with a trough reflectors normally have wider distributions in the transverse direction. Symmetrical reflector and prismatic versions give radial distributions. The comments in section 3.3.2.13 concerning layout, uniformity and lamp failures are also generally applicable.

Luminaire	Main-tenance category	Mount-ing	Polar curve T	SHR
Narrow beam with Par 38 lamp or tungsten-halogen lamp	B	RSP		0·25
Medium beam reflector lamp	B	RSP		0·50
GLS lamp plus reflector	B	RSP		1·25
Compact fluorescent lamp plus reflector	B	RSP		1·25

3.3.2.15 Downlighters

Downlighters come in a range of forms and their performances may be dictated by the beam of the reflector lamp or by a separate optical system. Designed originally for filament lamps the compact fluorescent versions provide much higher system efficiencies when used with suitable reflectors giving medium to wide beam angles.

The illuminance ratios will be low and modelling strong. Downlighters are often selected according to their ability to create a 'patch' of light on the floor as a visual effect. In these cases the aim is not to produce general lighting with its associated uniformity. The range of beam angles is large and is similar to that for display lighting luminaires (see section 3.3.2.17).

Luminaire	Main-tenance category	Mount-ing	Polar curve T	SHR
Opal cylinder	E	SP		1·75
Opal bowl	E	SP		1·50
Opal sphere	E	SP		1·75

3.3.2.16 General diffusing compact luminaires

These luminaires come in a range of styles and forms. Designed originally for filament lamps, the compact fluorescent versions provide much higher system efficiency. These luminaires rarely provide more than 2000 lamp lumens per point and as such are chosen either to provide amenity lighting in small areas such as toilets or for lower illuminance applications where the compact appearance of the luminaire or a smaller source is preferred to linear lamp luminaires.

The ratio of vertical to horizontal luminous area will strongly influence their performance. Three basic shapes are shown. Those that use a flat prismatic panel, louvres etc. can be compared to similar forms of control described in section 3.3.2.8.

Luminaire	Main-tenance category	Mount-ing	Polar curve T	SHR
Low voltage TH spot	N/A	SP		N/A
Mains crown-silvered spot	N/A	SP		N/A
Mains PAR spot	N/A	SP		N/A
'Eyeball' spot	N/A	SP		N/A
Main linear TH, HID of CFL flood	N/A	SP		N/A
Fibre optics	N/A	SP		N/A

3.3.2.17 Display lighting luminaires

The distinguishing feature of this range of luminaires is that they are adjustable. For this reason, the lumen method of design cannot be used and the lighting effects they produce cannot be described in terms of wall-to-task or ceiling-to-task illuminance ratios or glare characteristics, as the final result depends on their layout and, more importantly, their aiming.

Like downlighters, they were designed originally for mains voltage filament lamps, but low voltage single-ended tungsten–halogen, mains voltage linear tungsten–halogen, compact fluorescent and high pressure discharge lamps are now generally available to provide much higher system efficiency.

Reflector lamps or separate optical systems are used to provide an extensive range of distributions from very narrow to wide spots as well as asymmetric floodlighting distributions. The luminaires range in design from those which are intended to be small and unobtrusive to those which provide an architectural feature within a space. They can be suspended, surface-mounted or recessed into ceilings, wall- or floor-mounted, free standing or designed for use with track systems.

Display lighting is usually intended to provide local emphasis or accent lighting to general lighting, but these luminaires can also be used to provide localised or even general lighting of an area.

Fibre optic systems can also be used for display and accent lighting. A typical system consists of a harness of separate fibre optics with tail-end projectors, brought together into a common end at a light box containing the light source and optical system. Tungsten–halogen light boxes can produce, from a single 20° tail end, approximately 1000 lux at 0.5 m or, with the metal halide lamp, an illuminance of about 5000 lux at the same distance. Although capital cost is double that of conventional low voltage systems, they are ideal for short range applications requiring cool, safe lighting without UV and where space is at a premium.

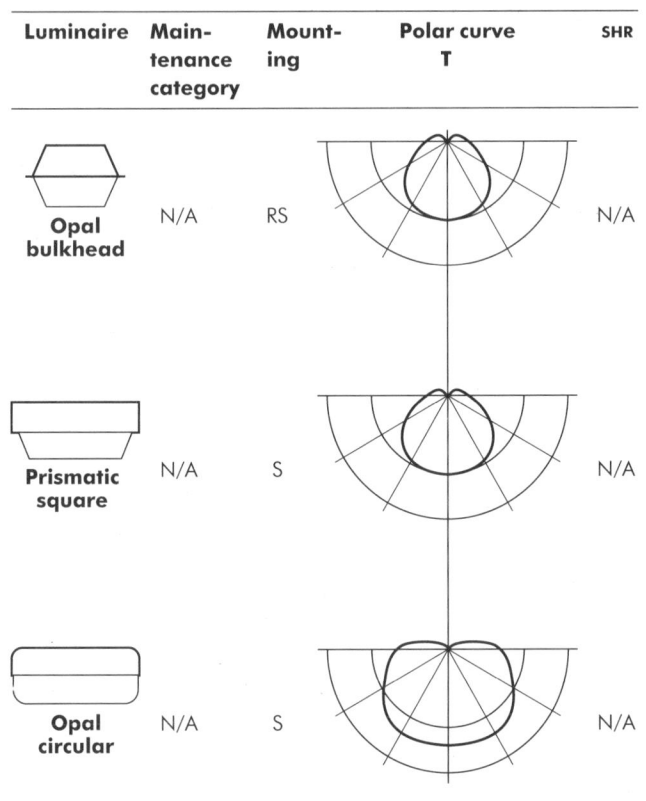

Luminaire	Main-tenance category	Mount-ing	Polar curve T	SHR
Opal bulkhead	N/A	RS		N/A
Prismatic square	N/A	S		N/A
Opal circular	N/A	S		N/A

3.3.2.18 Emergency/escape self-contained luminaires

Self-contained emergency lighting units come in a variety of shapes and sizes. Their purpose is to illuminate an escape route for safe movement to an exit. The majority of types contain a small fluorescent lamp, a set of rechargeable batteries and a combined inverter and electronic ballast capable of operating the lamp at reduced output from the batteries.

In normal operation (mains on), the control gear does not operate the lamp but charges the batteries.

In the event of a supply interruption, the circuit switches over to battery operation and the lamp comes on.

Escape lighting levels are low and the system must normally provide light for a duration of up to three hours. For these reasons, the light source is a miniature or compact fluorescent lamp which is under-run to extend battery life.

In order to achieve good uniformity with wide spacing, these luminaires normally have a significant area of vertical surface capable of emitting light at high angles. Recessed luminaires are available but are less common because of their more restricted distribution (see section 4.5.7).

Most luminaires are 'non-maintained', that is, the lamp is normally off and only comes on during an interruption of the supply. With the introduction of decorative luminaires for compact fluorescent lamps, 'maintained' luminaires are becoming more common. In these, the lamps operate normally from the mains when the supply is available and switch over to battery operation during an interruption of the supply. One advantage is that the same luminaires may be used throughout, with some providing escape lighting in the event of power supply interruption. Another advantage of self-contained luminaires is that they do not require special wiring to the luminaire capable of withstanding fire.

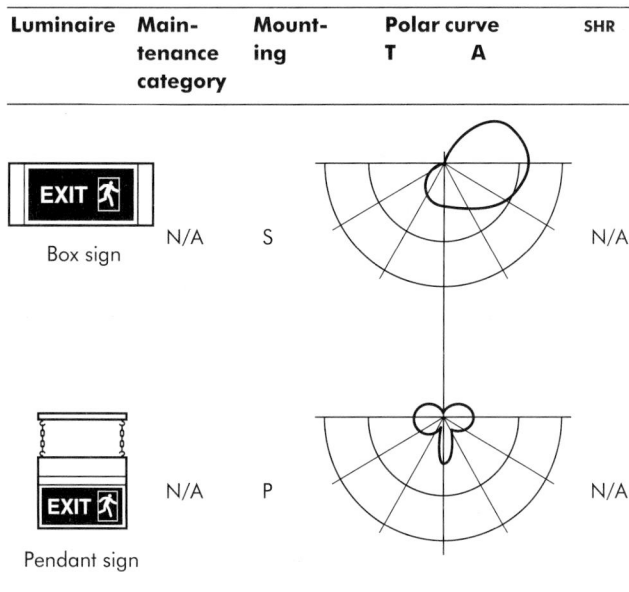

Luminaire	Main-tenance category	Mount-ing	Polar curve T A	SHR
Box sign	N/A	S		N/A
Pendant sign	N/A	P		N/A

Luminaire	Main-tenance category	Mount-ing	Polar curve T A	SHR
Opal bowl	N/A	S		N/A
Prismatic square	N/A	S		N/A
Opal circular	N/A	S		N/A

3.3.2.19 Emergency/escape self-contained signs

Sign luminaires are similar to conventional self-contained luminaires. Their purpose is to display an emergency sign in order to direct people towards the correct escape route and exit. For this reason they normally exhibit a large illuminated vertical surface area capable of displaying the appropriate sign. They can operate in a 'non-maintained', 'maintained' or 'sustained' mode.

In the non-maintained mode the lamp only operates in the event of a supply interruption. In maintained luminaires the lamp operates from the mains and then switches to battery supply in the event of supply interruption. In sustained luminaires, the result is identical, but two separate lamps are used: one on the mains and the other during a supply interruption. One important point is that such luminaires should have an even and high surface luminance in order to ensure that the signs remain legible in smoke-filled rooms.

3.3.2.20 Emergency/escape slave luminaires

The alternative to self-contained luminaires is to use an emergency supply. This may be extra low voltage from a battery room or battery cubicle or it may be a mains supply from a safety source.

In both cases the wiring needs to be fire-resisting. The luminaires are similar to those for self-contained systems, except that no battery is required and the circuit is less complex. At one time luminaires with tungsten lamps were common, but these have given way to fluorescent luminaires. Where the emergency supply is at mains voltage, conventional luminaires are often used.

3.3.2.21 Emergency/escape long lamp inverters

In many situations it is not desirable to include separate self-contained luminaires in the project. For this reason long lamp inverter units with battery packs may be built into conventional luminaires. The luminaires may be of any fluorescent type. They operate normally from the mains, but also charge an internal set of batteries. Upon supply interruption one of the lamps is operated at reduced output from the battery pack and inverter unit. The optical performance of the escape luminaire is dictated by the performance of the host luminaire. It is also important to note that such a luminaire will need to have an unswitched mains supply for the emergency unit. This system, with lamps built into the general lighting luminaires, is often used in preference to additional, small escape lighting units.

3.4   Control systems (see also section 4.4.4)

3.4.1   Function of control systems

Control systems are an inherent part of any lighting installation. They can take many forms, varying from a simple wall switch to being a part of a sophisticated microprocessor-controlled, building management system. Whatever the method used, the aim of a control system is always to ensure that the lighting is only operating when it is required, and that when it is, it is operating in the required state. Control systems vary the light output of the installation, either by switching or by controlling the output of the lamps and so reducing energy use (see section 4.5.1.3).

3.4.2   Switching (see also section 4.5.1.4)

In principle, all light sources can be switched but the light output that is immediately available on switch-on and the interval necessary between switch-off and switch-on varies with lamp type (see section 3.2.4). Switching can be achieved by a number of different methods. The simplest is the manual switch. Remote switches which use an infra-red transmitter and a receiver in the luminaire are also available. Both forms of switching directly involve the user. Alternatively, lamps can be controlled by time switches or in response to the availability of daylight or the occupation of the interior. Photocells are used to sense the level of daylight available in an interior, whilst sensors of noise level, movement or body heat have all been used to detect the presence of people in an interior.

One particular aspect of manual switching which has limited its flexibility in the past has been the difficulty of switching individual or small groups of luminaires without excessive wiring costs. Recent developments have made it possible to send switching signals by low voltage wiring or by introducing high frequency pulses onto the mains supply wiring. However, luminaires that switch on and off for no obvious reason are distracting and can be counter-productive in terms of staff satisfaction. High frequency electronic ballasts for fluorescent lamps allow individual luminaires to respond in several different ways, e.g. dimming or switching in response to available daylight and occupancy. Such systems provide greater flexibility in the way the lighting installation can be unobtrusively controlled either centrally or by individuals at their workstations.

3.4.3   Dimming/regulation (also section 4.5.1.5)

Not all discharge lamps can be dimmed and those that can, such as tubular fluorescent lamps, need special control gear. Dimming reduces the energy consumed by the lamp, not necessarily in proportion to the light output, and can cause changes in colour. Dimmers can be controlled manually or automatically, for example, in response to daylight availability. The electronic ballast developments, mentioned in relation to switching, can also provide dimming or regulation.

Current lighting practice favours the use of high frequency systems where individual ballasts are capable of controlling or regulating lamps' output up or down to suit changing work patterns and visual needs. This obviates the need for centralised control systems. The choice and design of energy management lighting control is covered in more detail in section 4.4.4.

3.4.4 Dimming for lighting effects

There are many areas within both commercial and non-commercial buildings, such as entrance foyers, board or meeting rooms, auditoria, restaurants, museums and display areas, where accent or display lighting is used to make a statement, convey an image, command attention or emphasise the architectural form rather than simply provide task lighting. The introduction of a dimming system provides two major advantages for this type of lighting scheme. Firstly, the ability to control the intensity of individual circuits. This makes it possible to change the atmosphere or mood of the space, adding interest with dramatic or subtle variation. These balanced lighting scenes or 'presets' may be memorised by the control systems so that they can be recalled from simple push-button controls positioned within the area.

The second advantage is being able to make maximum use of the space. If the lighting of a room is designed to serve a single activity, then it may be unsuitable for other purposes. The introduction of a dimming system will enable the user to modify the lighting to match varying demands such as audio-visual presentations, banquets and conferences.

Dimmer control systems should be 'user friendly'. These can range from simple manual control for a single circuit, push-button control of several circuits recalling pre-programmed lighting scenes to sophisticated multi-circuit, programmed systems with timed automatic lighting changes and cross-fades.

3.5 Maintenance of lighting installation

3.5.1 Introduction

It is essential for a lighting installation to be properly maintained. Lamps which have failed or which are flickering not only fail in their function, but convey the impression that nobody cares. Maintenance of all lighting, including emergency and standby installations, keeps the performance of the system within the design limits and promotes safety and the efficient use of energy.

The change to recommendations in terms of maintained illuminance in this edition (sections 2.6.1, 2.6.3 and 4.5.2) means that the designer must obtain a decision from the client on the maintenance policy to be implemented throughout the life of the installation. If this cannot be achieved, the designer must clearly state the assumed maintenance programme used to calculate and justify the value of initial illuminance. In turn this will influence the electrical load and therefore the electricity cost (section 4.5.1) which is the major cost element in the operation of the system. It will also influence the capital cost and it is important to maintain this asset to ensure an adequate return from the investment (see section 5.1). Maintenance includes replacement of failed or deteriorated lamps (see section 3.2.2.4) and control gear, the cleaning of luminaires and cleaning and redecoration of room surfaces at suitable intervals.

Figure 4.13 (page 161) shows the changes in the illuminance produced over time by an installation of tubular fluorescent lamps, with various combinations of lamp replacement and luminaire cleaning intervals.

3.5.2 Lamp replacement

There are two factors which need to be considered when determining the timing of lamp replacement: the change in light output and the probability of lamp failure. The relative weight given to these two factors depends on the lamp type. Mains and low voltage tungsten filament and tungsten–halogen lamps usually fail before the decline in light output becomes significant. Therefore the replacement time for these lamps is determined by the probability of lamp failure alone. All the other light sources, conventionally used in interiors, show a significant reduction in light output before a large proportion fail. Therefore, for these lamps, both the decline in light output and the probability of lamp failure are important in determining the lamp replacement time (see section 3.2.2.4 and Table 3.4, page 101 and Table 4.4, page 153). Frequently it is desirable to replace such lamps even though they are still operating electrically, simply because the light output has fallen to an uneconomic level.

For the majority of installations the most sensible procedure is to replace all the lamps at planned intervals. This procedure, which is known as group replacement, has visual, electrical and financial advantages over the alternative of 'spot replacement' e.g. replacing individual lamps as they fail. Visually, group replacement ensures that the installation maintains a uniform appearance. Electrically, group replacement reduces the risk of damage to the control gear caused by the faulty operation of lamps nearing the end of life. Financially, by arranging that the lamp replacement is associated with luminaire cleaning and doing it at a time when it will cause the minimum of disturbance to the activities in the interior, the cost of maintenance can be minimised. Group replacement is an appropriate procedure for routine maintenance and its frequency will have a direct bearing on the installed electrical load (see section 4.5.2). However, in any large installation, a few lamps can be expected to fail prematurely. These lamps should be replaced promptly on an individual basis.

As light source development proceeds there is a temptation to replace one light source with another which is superficially similar but of higher luminous efficacy. However, it is essential to establish that the replacement light source and the existing control gear are compatible physically, electrically and photometrically. Before replacing any discharge light source with another of a different type, or the same type but from a different manufacturer, advice on compatibility should be sought.

The timing and nature of lamp replacement are usually a matter of economic and managerial judgement and may well be determined by factors other than those directly related to the lighting. When designing for maintained illuminance the proposed lamp replacement procedure must be considered at the initial design stage of the installation.

3.5.3 Luminaire cleaning interval

The rate at which dirt is deposited on and in a luminaire depends on the amount and composition of the dirt in the atmosphere, and on the type of luminaire. Over the same period and in the same location, dust-proof (IP5X) and dust-tight (IP6X) luminaires and open reflectors with slots in the top will collect less dirt than louvred luminaires with closed tops, or luminaires with unsealed diffusers (see Tables 4.5, page 153 and 4.6, page 154).

For particularly dirty atmospheres or where access is difficult, the best choice would be dust-proof or dust-tight luminaires, ventilated luminaires which are designed to use air currents to keep them clean, or lamps with internal reflectors. Even the most protected luminaires, e.g. dust-tight luminaires, will collect dirt on their external surfaces. Therefore even these luminaires will need cleaning regularly.

The appropriate cleaning interval for luminaires and the lamps they contain is a basic design decision. The factors that need to be considered are the cost and convenience of cleaning at a particular time and the illuminance at that time in relation to the design maintained illuminance. As a general guide, luminaires should be cleaned at least once a year but for some locations this will not be sufficient. In section 4.5.2.6, on the calculation of maintenance factor, representative luminaire light output depreciation data are given in Table 4.6 (page 154) for different luminaire types and atmospheric conditions. To design to specified values of maintained illuminance it is essential to establish suitable cleaning intervals for the installation. Wherever possible, this should be based on manufacturers' data rather than the generic tables included in Part 4 of this *Code*. It is usually advantageous to co-ordinate luminaire cleaning with lamp replacement.

3.5.4 Room cleaning interval

All room surfaces should be cleaned and redecorated regularly if a dirty appearance and light loss is to be avoided. Regular cleaning is particularly important where light reflected from the room surfaces makes an important contribution to the lighting of the interior, e.g. where daylight from the side windows is used or where the electric lighting installation has a high indirect component (see Table 4.7, page 155).

3.5.5 Design aspects

The maintenance requirements for a lighting installation must be considered at the design stage. Three aspects are particularly important:

— The maintenance factor to be used in the calculation of the number of lamps and luminaires needed to provide the maintained illuminance: the closer the maintenance factor is to unity, the smaller the number of lamps and luminaires which will be needed, but this demands a commitment to regular and frequent maintenance. Unless this commitment is fulfilled the installation will not meet the maintained illuminance levels during its life.

— Practical access and handling: good maintenance will only occur if access to the lighting installation is safe and easy, and the lighting equipment is simple to handle.

— Equipment selection: the dirtier the operating environment, the more important it is to select equipment which is resistant to dirt deposition.

3.5.6   Practical aspects

A wide range of different materials are used in luminaires. Table 3.9 summarises the most suitable cleaning methods for use with these different materials. Additionally, equipment manufacturers provide useful information on the most appropriate cleaning methods, or guidance can be obtained from specialist cleaning product suppliers.

Different lighting installations call for varying levels of skill from the people carrying out the maintenance. However, working with electricity and safe access to luminaires, together with the appropriate disposal of waste lamps and materials, determines that even for the simplest of lighting maintenance tasks, experienced and skilled operators should be used. For example, operatives should have received specialist and certificated training to satisfy health and safety legislation.

Similarly, there are obligations under the *Electricity at Work Act 1989*[24] when working on electrical equipment (see also references 101 and 102). Where control systems form a part of the installation, the maintenance operator will need to understand the operation of the system and the consequences of any alterations made.

Table 3.9   Suitable cleaning methods for lighting maintenance

Materials	Cleaning methods
Anodised aluminium louvres/reflectors	Surfaces should be cleaned with a non-abrasive cloth or sponge using a neutral detergent in warm water which does not leave a residue and then allow to air dry. Ultrasonic cleaning techniques.. Severe staining or contamination should be removed first by metal polish.
Stainless steel	Surfaces should be cleaned with a non-abrasive cloth or sponge using a neutral detergent in warm water and the surface dried with a clean cloth, following the grain of brushed finishes where applicable. Surface lustre may be restored by applying an oil-based cleaning compound with a cloth, wiping off all surplus.
Galvanised steel, natural aluminium	Surfaces should be cleaned with a neutral-based detergent and wiped dry.
Enamel paint finish, polyester powder coat	Surfaces should be cleaned with a non-abrasive cloth or sponge using a neutral detergent in warm water and the surface dried with a clean cloth. Solvent-based cleaners should not be used.
Glass	Surfaces should be cleaned with a non-abrasive cloth or sponge using a neutral detergent in warm water that does not leave a residue, then wiped and allowed to air dry.
Acrylic, polycarbonate, glass-polyester, reinforced plastic	Remove loose dirt and dust with a vacuum cleaner. Surfaces should be cleaned with a non-abrasive cloth or sponge using a neutral-based detergent which does not leave a residue, then rinsed and wiped dry with warm water containing an anti-static solution. Solvent-based cleaners should not be used under any circumstances. Ultrasonic cleaning techniques..

3.5.7   Waste disposal of lighting products

Consideration should be given to the disposal of waste material such as redundant lamps and gear. Guidance on waste disposal is available from the Lighting Industry Federation[101]. This is regularly updated in line with changes in legislation and industry practice[22,102,103]. It advises on treatment of intact products, broken products and accidental breakage of lamps (see also section 5.11).

Part 4

Lighting design

4.1 Introduction

The flow diagram in Figure 4.1 presents a design approach, based on reasonable practice, to applying the principles, recommendations and technology described elsewhere in the *Code*. With experience, the lighting designer will develop this to arrive at individual design solutions. This reference to 'the lighting designer' should not be read to imply that the design process can be carried out in isolation. All successful lighting is the result of close collaboration and interaction within the building design team, to interpret the client's brief. The purpose of this section, however, is to concentrate on the lighting designer's responsibility and contribution to the total design process.

4.2 Objectives

The first stage in planning is to establish the lighting design objectives which guide the decisions in all the other stages of the design process. It is a matter of deciding for what, and for whom, the lighting is intended, rather than referring at this stage to the lighting schedule. These objectives can be considered in three parts.

4.2.1 Safety

The lighting installation must be electrically and mechanically safe and must allow the occupants to use the space safely. These are not

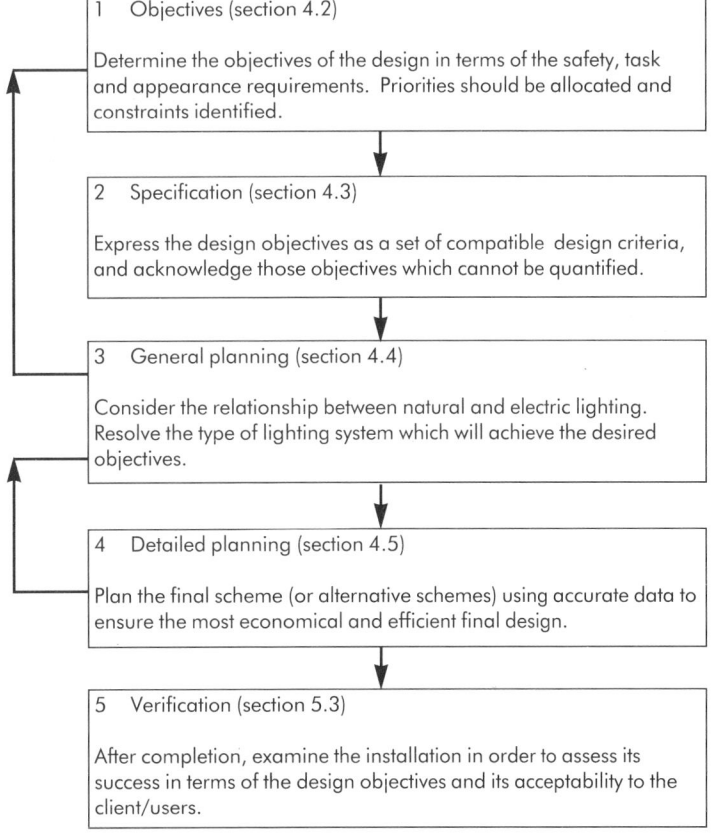

Figure 4.1 Lighting design flow diagram

only primary objectives but also statutory obligations. It is, therefore, necessary to identify any hazards present and the need for emergency lighting (see section 4.5.7).

4.2.2 Visual tasks

The type of work which takes place in the interior will define the nature and variety of the visual tasks. An analysis of the visual tasks (there is rarely just one) in terms of size, contrast, duration and need for colour discrimination is essential to establish the quantity and quality of the lighting required to achieve satisfactory visual conditions.

In a 'general' office, for example, at one extreme the task may be to answer the telephone (a simple visual task). At the other extreme the occupants may have to transcribe text, hand-written in pencil, using VDTs. This presents a complex set of visual tasks. In addition to establishing the nature of the tasks it is also necessary to identify the positions and planes on which the tasks lie. This information is essential if lighting matched to the tasks is to be provided.

4.2.3 Appearance and character

It is necessary to establish what mood or atmosphere is to be created. This is not just for prestige offices, places of entertainment, and the like, but should be considered in all designs, even where it will be given less importance than other factors.

4.2.4 Priorities and constraints

The above objectives will not have equal weight. Some will be 'essential' while others can only be 'desirable'. The evaluation will depend upon the priorities and constraints set by the client or the application.

Often the most obvious constraint is financial. Everyone wants to spend the minimum possible, but different owners will spend according to their own valuation of the final result. This will temper and modify the importance of the various design objectives, but should be opposed if solely financial consideration suppresses any of the essential requirements of the design solutions.

Both capital expenditure and running costs should be considered to achieve the most economical scheme. This does not always happen because a second system of budget control applies to the running cost. This is an unsatisfactory approach and should, if possible, be resisted. Capital and running costs should be taken together to establish the lowest overall investment (see section 5.1).

Other constraints which may affect the design objectives are:

— energy consumption

— hazardous or onerous environmental considerations (which may limit the range of acceptable luminaires)

— physical problems affecting the installation of equipment

— access for maintenance.

These constraints must be recognised when setting the objectives of the design.

4.3 Specification

The designer must always take due note of statutory instruments that affect lighting conditions. These are referred to as appropriate throughout this *Code* and listed in section 6.3 (bibliography) and section 6.4 (references). Most of these demand that lighting shall be both sufficient and suitable. 'Sufficiency' is normally related to the quantity of illumination (illuminance) on the tasks and for safe movement, whilst 'suitability' covers discomfort and disability glare, colour, veiling reflections, shadows, and so on. Legislation is concerned with what is essential, and is generally less onerous than the recommendations in this *Code*, which are concerned with good practice. Lighting designers have a responsibility to ensure that lighting is not liable to cause injury to the health of occupants (see section 5.9). Bad lighting can contribute towards accidents or result in inadequate working conditions.

The lighting objectives now need to be expressed in a suitable form. Although many can be expressed in physical terms, suitable design techniques may not exist or may be too cumbersome. For example, obstruction losses (section 4.5.4) and contrast rendering factors (section 5.5) are two quantities that are difficult to calculate and predict accurately. Not all design objectives can be expressed as measurable quantities. For example, the need to make an environment appear 'prestigious', 'efficient' or 'vibrant' cannot be quantified. This does not mean that these objectives should be ignored, but experience and judgement may have to replace calculation.

A full specification can be established by reference to Part 2 of this *Code* and by taking the design objectives into account.

4.4 General planning

The remaining stage of design is to translate the design specification into the best possible solution, to meet the original objectives. The specification is, therefore, only a stepping stone; if it proves difficult to plan an installation which meets the design specification it may be necessary to reassess the original objectives.

At the general planning stage, as distinct from detailed planning (see section 4.5), the designer aims to establish whether the original objectives are viable, and to resolve what type of design can be employed to satisfy these objectives. The first stage in the general planning of a lighting installation is to consider the interior to be lit, its proportions, its contents, and the daylight available.

4.4.1 Daylight

The use of daylighting and electric lighting together can both contribute towards the efficient use of primary energy and increase the satisfaction of users. The specification of daylight requirements is covered in *BS 8206* Part 2[1] and the design of windows is described in the CIBSE Applications Manual: *Window design*[2].

The energy saving from daylight use can be estimated from the average daylight factor using the method given in reference 104. The analysis of energy use is described in section 2.5, while information on control systems for electric lighting used in conjunction with daylight is provided in sections 3.4 and 4.4.4.

When working on an existing building or when the window design of a new building has already been fixed, the designer should take the following steps:

— Check whether any form of shading devices or blinds will be required to control sunlight penetration.

— Analyse the extent to which daylight will provide general room lighting or task lighting.

— Design the electric light for daylight hours and for night.

— Select control equipment to ensure efficient use of electric lighting.

4.4.1.1 Initial appraisal of daylight quantity

The extent of daylight penetration can be assessed initially with the following guidelines.

(a) If the sky is not directly visible from a point in an interior, the level of daylight at that point will be small. The 'no-sky line' (the boundary of the region in the room from which no sky can be seen) gives an indication of the area beyond which daylight may not contribute to general room lighting. Windows can, however, still be important in providing an external view from parts of a room distant from the window walls.

(b) In areas of a room adjacent to a side window, the region in which daylight might contribute significantly towards task lighting extends back from the window for a distance of about twice the height of the window head above the working plane (provided that there are not large external obstructions, that there is clear glazing, and that the sill is not significantly higher than the working plane).

4.4.1.2 Daylight to enhance the general brightness of the room

The use of daylight for general room lighting is described in sections 1.2 and 2.3. The extent to which existing windows may give a daylit appearance and also provide the necessary overall brightness of the room can be found by calculating the average daylight factor. This value can then be compared with the criteria given in section 2.3.1.

The average daylight factor may be calculated as follows:

$$D = \frac{TA_w\theta}{A(1-R^2)}$$

where T is the diffuse light transmittance of the glazing, including the effects of dirt, blinds, curtains, and any other obstructions or coverings; A_w is the net glazed area of the window (m^2); θ is the angle subtended by the visible sky ($°$) (it is measured in a vertical plane normal to the glass, from the window reference point, as illustrated in Figures 4.2(a) and (b); A is the total area of the interior surfaces: ceiling, walls, windows, floor (m^2); R is the area-weighted average reflectance of these interior surfaces (in initial calculations for rooms with white ceilings and mid-reflectance walls, this may be taken as 0.5).

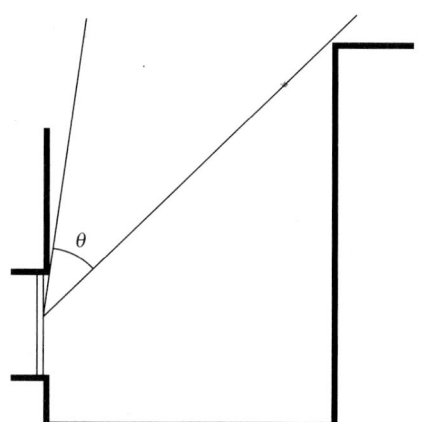

Figure 4.2(a) θ is the angle subtended in a vertical plane normal to the window, by sky visible from the centre of the window

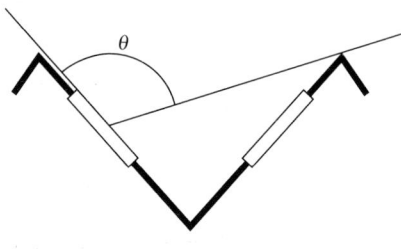

Figure 4.2(b) θ is the angle subtended in a vertical plane normal to the rooflight, by sky visible from the centre of a rooflight

The equation should not be applied where external obstructions cannot be represented by a single angle of elevation, such as where a window faces into a courtyard. Alternative calculation methods are available for complex cases[105,106].

If all windows in a room have the same transmittance and face the same angle of obstruction, the average daylight factor may be found at once by letting A_w be the total glazed area. Otherwise the average daylight factor should be found for each window separately, and the results summed.

4.4.1.3 Daylight for task illumination

The daylight illuminance at a point in a room may be estimated with this equation:

$$E_{in} = E_h f_o D$$

where E_h is the external unobstructed horizontal illuminance in lux (see Figures 4.3 and 4.4); f_o is a window orientation factor. This allows for the effects of window orientation (see Table 4.1); D is the daylight factor at the point in the room, expressed as a fraction (i.e. the percentage value divided by 100).

Methods for calculating the point daylight factor are given in section 5.12 and in reference 2.

Table 4.1 Diffuse orientation factors for a 0900 h–1700 h working day

Orientation	Orientation factor(f_o)
North	0.97
East	1.15
South	1.55
West	1.21
Horizontal rooflight	1.00

The factors for other orientations may be obtained by interpolation. The factors given may be applied with reasonable

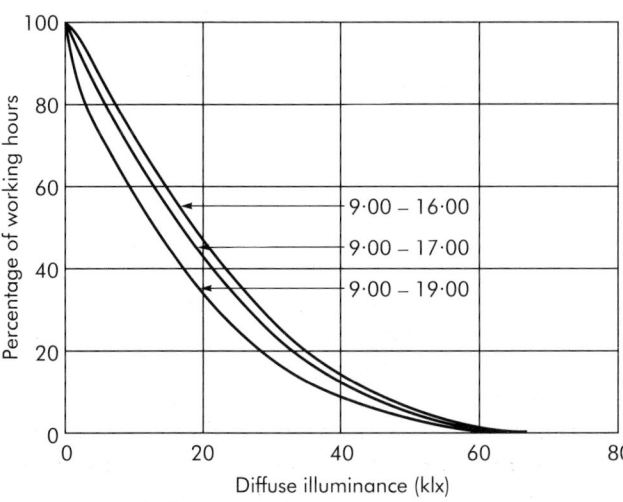

Figure 4.3 Diffused illuminance (E_h) availability for London

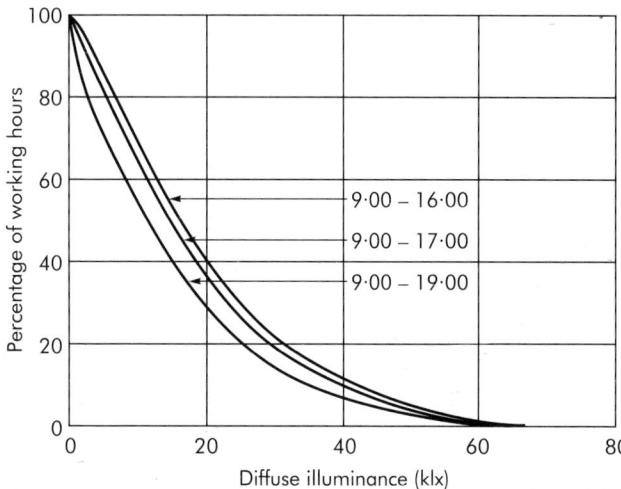

Figure 4.4 Diffused illuminance (E_h) availability for Edinburgh

accuracy for working days finishing at 1600 h or 1800 h in Figures 4.3 and 4.4.

Figures 4.3 and 4.4 give the availability of daylight in London and Edinburgh for various lengths of the working day. The graph for London should be applied to sites in southern and midland England; the Edinburgh graph should be applied to sites in Scotland and northern England, and Northern Ireland. Further information about daylight availability is given in reference 107.

Example

An illuminance of 500 lux is required on a desk for a 0900 h to 1700 h working day. The daylight factor at the desk, from an east-facing window, is 0.015 or 1.5%. The building is in south-east England.

The orientation factor is 1.15. The external illuminance required to give 500 lux on the desk is $500/(1.15 \times 0.015) = 28\,986$ lux, approximately 29 klux. From Figure 4.3 it can be seen that this level is achieved for 28% of working hours.

4.4.2   Choice of electric lighting systems

4.4.2.1   General lighting

Lighting systems which provide an approximately uniform illuminance over the whole working plane are called general lighting systems (see Figure 4.5(a)). The luminaires are normally arranged in a regular layout. The appearance of the installation is usually tidy but may be rather bland. General lighting is simple to plan using the lumen method (see section 4.5.3) and requires no co-ordination with task locations. The greatest advantage of such systems is that they permit flexibility of task location.

If the installation design assumes an empty space between ceiling and working plane, it may be difficult to achieve the recommended uniformity if the area actually contains substantial obstruction or is divided into several small areas. If the degree of obstruction over the working plane is high, or if partitioning is installed, it will probably be necessary to increase the number of luminaires. This will have significant energy and economic implications especially if a larger number of lower wattage luminaires are required.

The major disadvantage of general lighting systems is that energy may be wasted illuminating the whole area to the level needed for the most critical tasks. Energy could be saved by providing the necessary illuminance over only the task areas and using a lower ambient level for circulation and other non-critical tasks.

4.4.2.2   Localised lighting

Localised lighting systems (see Figure 4.5(b)) employ an arrangement of luminaires designed to provide the required maintained illuminance on work areas together with a lower illuminance for the other areas. The average illuminance on the other areas should not be less than one-third of the average illuminance over the work areas (see sections 2.4.3 and 2.4.4).

The lighting layout must be co-ordinated with the task positions and orientation. The system can be inflexible and information on plant and furniture layout is essential at the design stage. Changes in the work layout can seriously impair a localised

Figure 4.5(a)   A general lighting system employs a regular array of luminaires to provide a uniform illuminance across the working plane.

Figure 4.5(b)   A localised lighting system uses luminaires located adjacent to the work stations to provide the required task illuminance. The necessary ambient illuminance in the surrounding areas is provided by additional luminaires if required.

Figure 4.5(c)   A local lighting system employs a general lighting scheme to provide the ambient illuminance for the main area with additional luminaires, located at the workstations, to provide the necessary task illuminance.

system, although uplighters and other easily re-locatable systems or energy management controls (see section 4.4.4) can overcome these problems.

Localised systems normally consume less energy than general lighting systems unless a high proportion of the area is occupied by work stations. This should be confirmed by calculations. Maintenance of localised systems can be more critical than general lighting systems.

4.4.2.3   Local lighting

Local lighting provides illumination only over the small area occupied by the task and its immediate surroundings (Figure 4.5(c)). A general lighting system must be installed to provide sufficient ambient illumination for circulation and non-critical tasks. This is then supplemented by the local lighting system to achieve the necessary design maintained illuminance over the task areas. The general surround average illuminance should not be less than one-third of the average task illuminance (see sections 2.4.3 and 2.4.4).

Local lighting can be a very efficient method for providing adequate task illumination, particularly where high illuminances are necessary or flexible directional lighting is required. Local lighting is frequently provided by luminaires mounted at the work place in offices and factories.

Local lighting must be positioned to minimise shadows, veiling reflections and glare. Although local luminaires allow efficient utilisation of emitted light, the lower wattage lamp circuits will be less efficient and the luminaires can be expensive. Most local lighting systems are accessible and often adjustable. This increases wear and tear and hence maintenance costs, but the system provides individual control which is often favoured by those working in the area.

Both local and localised lighting offer scope for switch control of individual luminaires which can be off when not required, but sufficient ambient illumination must be provided at all relevant times.

4.4.3   Choice of lamp and luminaire

The choice of lamp will affect the range of luminaires available, and vice versa. Therefore, one cannot be considered without reference to the other. One method of design is to follow a procedure which does not start with identifying a single lamp and luminaire combination but rather rejects those combinations which are unsatisfactory. In this manner, whatever remains will be acceptable and a final choice can be made by comparison. With such an approach, if all available choices are eliminated, this probably indicates that one or more of the objectives are unrealistic. Finally, all of the unrejected luminaire and lamp combinations are acceptable, so that the most efficient, economical and architecturally acceptable scheme can be selected.

4.4.3.1   Selection of lamp characteristics

The designer should compile a list of suitable lamps by rejecting those which do not satisfy the design objectives. For general guidance see section 3.2. However, up-to-date manufacturers' data should be used for final selections.

The run-up times of all but low pressure fluorescent discharge lamps are unsatisfactory for applications requiring instant illumination when switched on unless auxiliary tungsten or fluorescent lamps are provided.

Lamps must have colour rendering properties suited to their intended use. Good colour rendering may be required in order to achieve better discrimination between colours where this is part of the visual task. Alternatively, good colour rendering may be required to achieve a particular appearance or degree of comfort (e.g. merchandising, offices, or leisure activities).

The choice of colour appearance can be used by the designer to create an appropriate 'atmosphere'. For example, 'warm' colour appearance might be selected for informal situations, where a 'cold' appearance could be associated with formality[19,20,108]. This is an entirely subjective judgement, but adjacent areas should not be lit with sources of significantly different apparent colour unless a special effect is required.

The life and lumen maintenance characteristics of the lamps must be considered to arrive at a practicable and economic maintenance schedule.

Where moving machinery is used, care should be taken to avoid stroboscopic effects. All lamps operating on an alternating current exhibit some degree of cyclic variation of light output. It is most significant with discharge lamps which do not employ a phosphor coating. The problem can normally be reduced or eliminated by having alternate rows of luminaires on different phases of the supply and ensuring that critical areas receive illumination in roughly equal proportion from each phase. Alternatively, some lamps may be operated from high frequency electronic ballasts, or illumination from local luminaires (with acceptable lamps that do not cause stroboscopic problems) can be used to swamp the general illumination.

One other factor which may be a limitation on the use of certain lamp or circuit types is minimum starting temperature (see section 3.2.4). Particularly in the case of linear fluorescent lamps, this is also influenced by the luminaire design.

When selecting a range of suitable lamps, the designer must consider the types of luminaires which are available and the degree of light control and light output required. Accurate light control is more difficult with large area sources than with small area sources, however the latter will have a higher luminance (for the same output) and are potentially more glaring.

Standardisation of a limited selection of lamp types and sizes without compromising visual requirements for a particular site or company can simplify maintenance and stocking.

4.4.3.2   Selection of luminaire characteristics

In addition to being safe, luminaires may have to withstand a variety of physical conditions, such as vibration, moisture, dust, ambient temperature or vandalism. Also, the external appearance of the luminaire, its fixing and location must be in sympathy with the architectural style of the interior. General guidance on the characteristics of luminaires can be obtained from section 3.3.

Safety is assured by using equipment meeting *BS 4533*[88] (shown by the British Standard Safety Mark) or by obtaining written assurances from a manufacturer using systems operated in accordance with *BS 5750*[96]. When a luminaire carries the British Standard Safety Mark it means that the IP rating is applied to an already arduously tested luminaire (see section 3.3.1).

Luminaire reliability and life will have a direct impact on the economics of the scheme. The ease with which luminaires can be installed and maintained (see section 3.5) will also affect the overall economics and convenience of the scheme. For example, luminaires which can be unplugged and detached, or which have removable gear, can simplify maintenance by allowing remote servicing.

Not only must the luminaire withstand the ambient conditions, it may have to operate in a hazardous area, such as a refinery, mine or similar environment. In this event, special equipment is required to satisfy the safety regulations. This subject is covered by the CIBSE Lighting Guide: *Lighting in hostile and hazardous environments*[42].

The light distribution of the luminaire influences the distribution of luminance and the directional effects that will be achieved. The illuminance ratios are described in sections 3.3.2 and 4.4.3.3 for a regular array of a given luminaire, and can be calculated by the methods given in CIBSE *TM5*[100].

The utilisation factor (UF) for a luminaire is a measure of the efficiency with which light from the lamp is used for illuminating the working plane (see section 4.5.3.1).

For a given interior and set of environmental conditions the lamp, circuit and luminaire performance will influence the installed power of the lighting system. The power density (W/m^2/100 lux) of alternative solutions should be compared with the target ranges given in section 2.5 and Table 2.2 (page 39). Nevertheless, the system of the lowest installed load will not necessarily achieve the lowest energy use if a greater degree of energy management control can be achieved with one type of lamp rather than another (see section 4.4.4).

In addition to the practical performance of the luminaire consideration must be given to its appearance. This can range from the totally discrete, such as a fully recessed, low brightness downlighter to a highly decorative chandelier. The choice of luminaire style and degree of design expression will be strongly influenced by architectural and interior design considerations. Skill and care are required in the selection or specification of luminaires which satisfy aesthetic criteria whilst performing efficiently and safely.

4.4.3.3   Illuminance ratio (IR) charts

Illuminance ratio (IR) charts were published in CIBSE (IES) *TR15*[109]. They enable the designer to examine the effects of room index, surface reflectances, luminaire direct ratio (DR) and flux fraction ratio (FFR) upon illuminance ratios and the directional aspects of lighting.

They were presented in pairs for different combinations of ceiling, wall and floor reflectance and for different room indices. The reflectances are given the symbols *L*, *M* and *D* to signify, light, medium and dark reflectances respectively; see Table 4.2.

Table 4.2   Reflectances for room surfaces

	L	M	D
Ceiling cavity	0.70	0.50	0.30
Walls	0.50	0.30	0.10
Floor cavity	0.30	0.20	0.10

Figure 4.6 shows a typical pair of charts. The charts are identical for each room index except for the loci plotted on them. In each case the horizontal axis represents the direct ratio (DR) of the installation and the vertical axis is the flux fraction ratio (FFR) of the installation. Luminaires can therefore be plotted onto the charts according to their FFR and DR. The direct ratio is calculated from the distribution factor, for the working plane or floor (DF$_F$), of the luminaire for an appropriate room index (RI) and the downward light output ratio (DLOR) of the luminaire.

$$DR = \frac{DF_F}{DLOR}$$

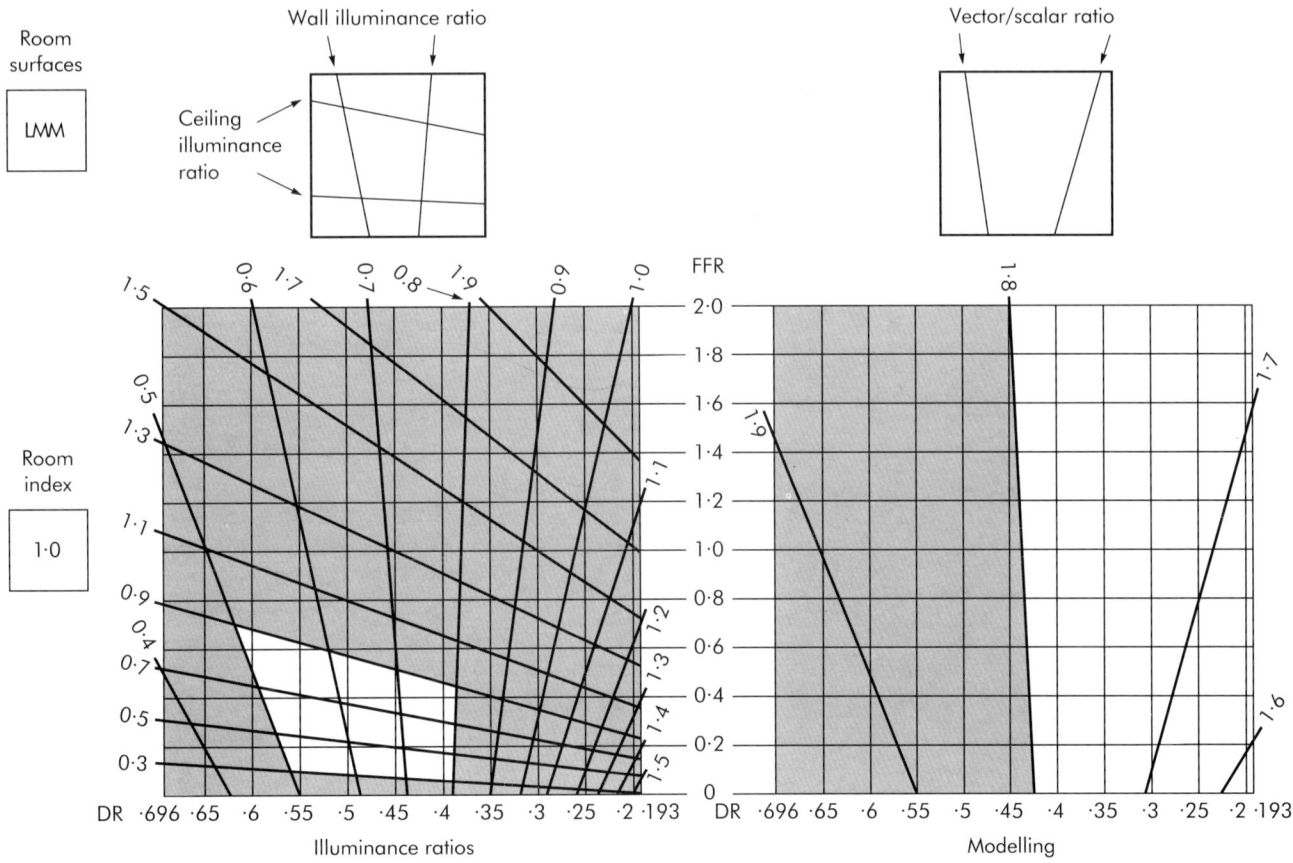

Figure 4.6   A typical illuminance ratio (IR) chart

The value of DF_F is the same as the utilisation factor (UF) of the chosen luminaire at zero reflectance. Figure 4.8 shows a typical table of utilisation factors.

Note: The charts in *TR15* were based on the British Zonal method (BZ) numbers and Figure 4.6 has been re-plotted for direct ratios. Figure 4.9 can be used to produce overlays for use with the IR charts in the last edition of *TR15*[109].

Loci of constant illuminance ratio are plotted on the left-hand chart and loci of constant average vector/scalar ratio are plotted on the right-hand chart (see sections 5.3.3.6 and 5.2.3).

The charts may be used in two ways. Luminaires can be plotted onto the charts to determine the illuminance ratios and average vector/scalar ratios that will be achieved by a regular array of such luminaires. Alternatively, at the general planning stage, the charts may be used to identify the range of reflectances and luminaires which can achieve the desired conditions. The range of acceptable luminaires can be identified by DR and FFR. The process of selection will be aided if the positions of luminaires are marked onto the charts or a transparent overlay.

Acceptable ranges of illuminance ratios and vector/scalar ratios are shown as unshaded (safe) areas on the charts. These values are not sacrosanct and there are reasons why a designer may wish to deviate from them. Bright walls can make a room seem larger and

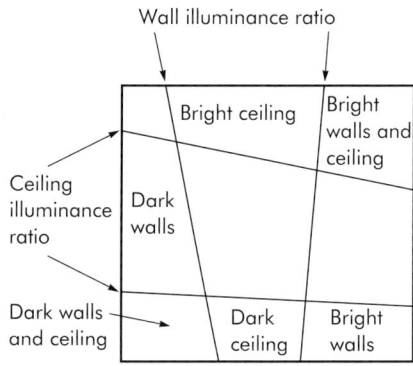

Figure 4.7 The effect of illuminance ratios upon room appearance

more spacious. Dark walls can make it seem small and possibly cramped or intimate. Bright ceilings and dark walls may give the impression of formality and tension, whilst the reverse (bright walls and dark ceiling) may create an informal and relaxed or sociable atmosphere. These are not hard and fast rules, but are supported by experimentation. Figure 4.7 shows these tendencies mapped onto a typical IR chart.

It is often impossible to simultaneously achieve the desired illuminance ratios and vector/scalar ratios without changes in reflectance, and even then it may still be impossible. Wall-washers may be employed to increase the wall-to-task illuminance ratio. The IR charts illustrate that for most cases a proportion of upward light from the luminaire is desirable to achieve acceptable ceiling-to-task illuminance ratios.

Using the photometric data for the category 3 luminaire in Figure 4.8: DLOR = 0.64, DF_F (room index $K = 1.0$) = 0.43, therefore DR = 0.67. As the ULOR = 0%, the FFR = 0.

By plotting these values on Figure 4.6, which applies to reflectances LMM and $K = 1.0$, both the illuminance ratios and vector/scalar ratio are outside the 'safe area'. From Figure 4.7 it can be seen that an installation of this luminaire in a small room would produce dark walls and ceilings.

By referring to the diagrams for other reflectances and room sizes in *TR15*[109], it will be found, for example, that this luminaire falls within the illuminance ratio and vector/scalar ratio 'safe areas'

Figure 4.8 Typical presentation of utilisation factor table and associated performance data for a twin lamp unventilated VDT luminaire

Nadir intensity†	302 cd/1000 lm
CIE flux code[100]	68 99 100 100 64
SHR_{max} (square)	1.36
$SHR_{max\,tr}$ (continuous rows)	1.75
ULOR†	0.00
DLOR†	0.64
LOR†	0.64
CIBSE *LG3*[25] category	3

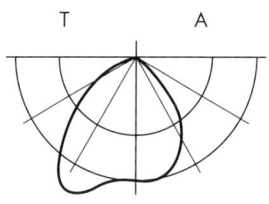

†Correction factors

	36 W	58 W	32 W	50 W
Length factor	1.00	1.00	1.00	1.00
HF factor	—	—	1.01	1.01

Utilisation factors UF_F for SHR_{nom} of 1.25

Room reflectances			Room index (K)								
C	W	F	0.75	1.00	1.25	1.50	2.00	2.50	3.00	4.00	5.00
70	50	20	0.45	0.51	0.56	0.58	0.62	0.64	0.66	0.68	0.69
	30		0.41	0.48	0.52	0.55	0.59	0.62	0.64	0.66	0.68
	10		0.38	0.45	0.49	0.53	0.57	0.60	0.62	0.65	0.66
50	50	20	0.44	0.50	0.54	0.57	0.60	0.62	0.64	0.65	0.67
	30		0.40	0.47	0.51	0.54	0.58	0.60	0.62	0.64	0.65
	10		0.38	0.44	0.49	0.52	0.56	0.58	0.60	0.63	0.64
30	50	20	0.43	0.49	0.53	0.55	0.58	0.60	0.62	0.63	0.64
	30		0.40	0.46	0.50	0.53	0.56	0.59	0.60	0.62	0.63
	10		0.37	0.44	0.48	0.51	0.55	0.57	0.59	0.61	0.62
0	0	0	0.36	0.43	0.47	0.49	0.53	0.55	0.56	0.58	0.59

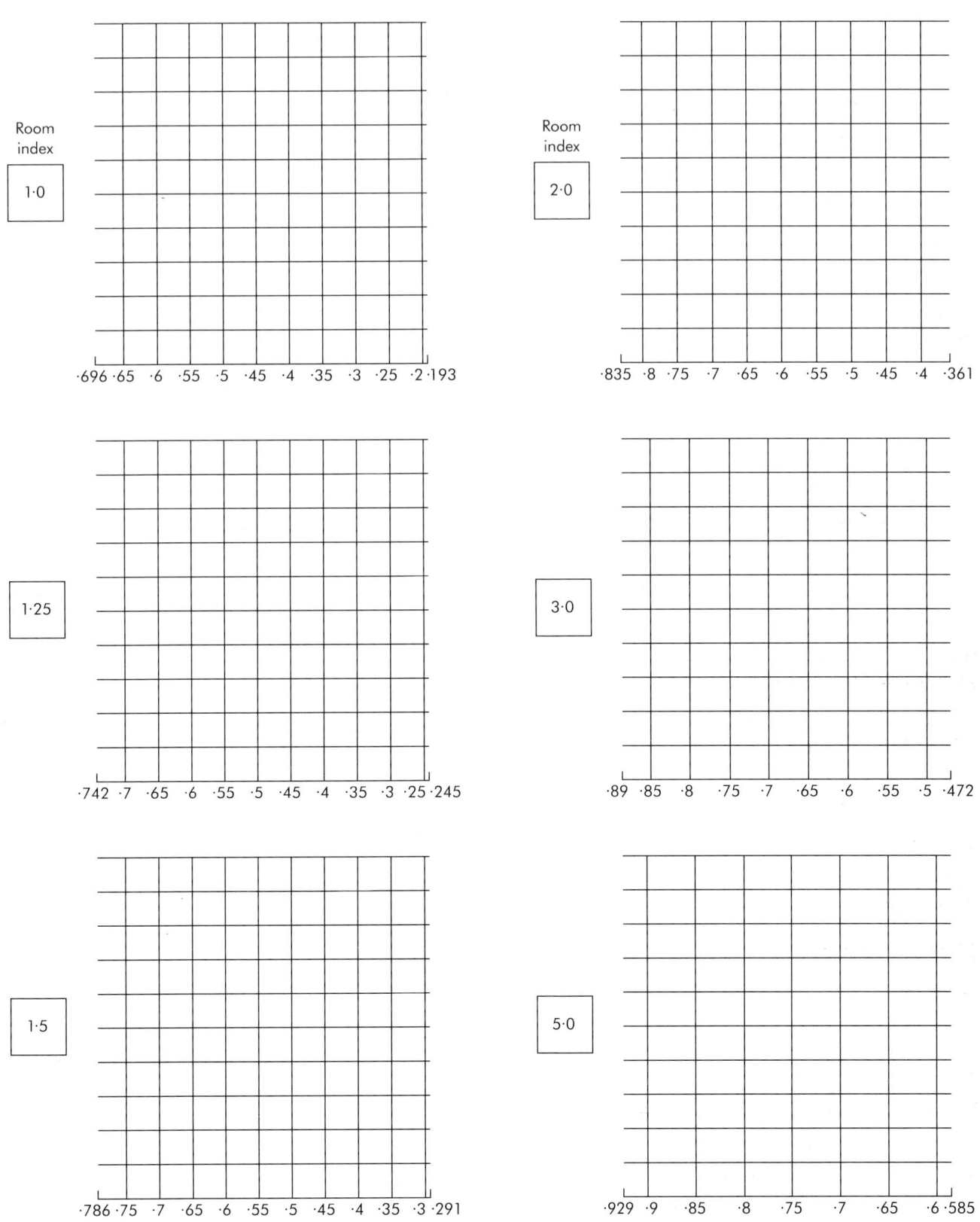

Figure 4.9 IR chart grids for six room indices from *TR15*[109] re-plotted to direct ratios. This figure can be used to produce overlays for use with the illuminance ratio diagrams in *TR15*.

for $K = 1.5$ to 2.0 with reflectances LLL and for $K = 3.0$ for reflectances LLM and LML. This exercise also confirms that a luminaire with a FFR of 0.1 (rather than 0) would bring the results within the 'safe areas' when the room index is between 2.0 and 3.0 and reflectances are either 'light' or 'medium'. However, the purpose of the diagrams is to guide the designer in the choice that can be made and not to represent a 'go/no go' situation.

4.4.4   Energy management

A lighting system must be designed and managed to achieve good control of energy use. This is important during the working day and outside working hours.

4.4.4.1   Choice of controls

The factors which influence the specification of controls include occupancy, occupancy pattern, available daylight, type of lighting (i.e. can it be dimmed?), the desired level of control sophistication and, of course, costs.

The cost of a control system installation should be compared with the cost of a traditional hard-wire installation, and the difference related to the projected energy savings. Especially with new buildings, the cost difference may be very small. For existing installations there may be constraints on selection of controls where the existing wiring gives little scope for alteration or change. The use of mains-borne signalling may reduce these constraints and allow a central system to be installed without disturbing existing wiring but it is essential to ensure compatibility with other electrical and signalling circuits. Simple reset switches may also be installed without significantly affecting existing wiring.

Alternatively, the use of self-contained luminaires, each with its own sensor, may be a more practical and economic solution than centralised control. For this it has to be accepted that certain refinements of centralised control cannot be achieved.

The following control elements can be considered.

Daylight linking

One or more of the lighting rows adjacent to the windows (section 4.4.1.1(*b*)) may be linked to either external or internal photocells to monitor daylight and adjust the electric lighting accordingly, either by switching or dimming.

Constant illuminance

Designing for maintained illuminance means that initially, when lamps are new and luminaires and room surfaces are clean, the illuminance will be substantially higher than the design level. How much higher will depend on the characteristics of the installation and the maintenance programme which the user intends to follow.

High frequency fluorescent lamp systems, which can be regulated, can be linked to photocells which will hold the lighting at the design maintained illuminance value.

As the system ages, the controls will automatically increase the power to the lamp. Eventually, the system will operate at full load in order to produce the maintained illuminance. This is the time at which maintenance should be carried out.

The same control system can also cover change of use. If the function of an area changes, requiring a lower task illuminance, the system can be adjusted to control the lighting to the revised level.

Occupancy

Lighting linked to occupancy, or more appropriately occupancy pattern, can show considerable savings in energy usage.

An example of occupancy detection is where lighting between warehouse aisles is switched by a detector sensing the approach of a fork-lift truck. A predetermined time delay should be built into the control system to avoid excessive switching which can shorten lamp life.

This form of control can be applied to a wider range of lamp types as long as the run-up and re-strike characteristics (see section 3.2) are taken into account.

Automatic control

This can take a number of forms.

A timer control system may switch the whole lighting installation on and off at predetermined times, or it may be programmed to send signals at certain times during the day (e.g. lunch time) which switch off selected luminaires. If daylight is sufficient, or lights go out over unoccupied areas, it is unlikely that these will be switched on again until needed. This type of system can be used for providing reduced lighting levels early in the morning and before the majority of staff arrive, or in the evening to cover cleaning or security operations. Local manual override switching is essential with this, and all other automatic controls. Security requirements may also demand a general override control to cover emergency conditions at night.

Occupancy detectors are used to detect the presence of people and to control the lighting accordingly. These can rely upon acoustic, infra-red, microwave, or other methods of detection. A time lag must normally be built into the system to prevent premature switch-offs or excessive switching.

Depending upon the size of area and number of occupants, it is desirable to provide a degree of individual control which enables personal choice of lighting conditions. In cellular offices, this could be from a combination of high frequency ballasts controlled by a potentiometer or suitable infra-red transmitter, which can be used to select or raise and lower the lighting levels. In larger offices, local controls should not noticeably affect the lighting conditions in, and viewing conditions from, adjoining areas (see sections 4.4.2.2 and 4.4.2.3).

Management control systems can address every luminaire in order to programme the appropriate lighting in individual areas. The main advantage to this system is that office alterations can be made and the lighting simply adjusted via the computer to suit the new layout. Combined with local override control, changes can be made without the need for expensive relocation of luminaires and alteration to switching arrangements.

It is possible to interface between a building energy management system (BEMS) and a lighting energy management system

(LEMS) in order to provide certain control commands from the BEMS to the lighting. It is not generally cost-effective to use the BEMS to provide discrete localised lighting control to individual luminaires, but rather to achieve load shedding or zone switching.

Maintenance control

Through the LEMS it is possible to check the status of the primary and emergency lighting. The system may be programmed to automatically provide the check at prescribed times, the status of each luminaire being checked and recorded.

4.4.4.2 Human factors

Control systems which are obtrusive (see section 4.5.1.5) are counter-productive and may even be sabotaged by the staff. For this reason, dimmer systems are often preferred. Photocells and other sensing circuitry must incorporate a delay to prevent sporadic and disruptive switch-offs, while responding immediately when a switch-on is called for.

Any control system must ensure that acceptable lighting conditions are always provided for the occupants. Safety and visual effectiveness and comfort must take priority over energy saving.

The Lighting Industry Federation publishes an Applications Guide which deals with this subject matter in further detail[110].

4.5 Detailed planning

When the overall design has been resolved in general terms, detailed calculations are required to determine such things as the number of luminaires, the glare index, the final cost and so on. When the design has been completed a check should be made to see how well the original objectives have been met. If this shows that the design is unsatisfactory in some regard, the only course of action is to revise the design until a suitable solution is found. This iterative procedure is a normal part of the design process.

The main calculations which may have to be carried out during the design process are detailed in the following sections.

4.5.1 Costs and energy use

The most powerful constraints on any design are financial: namely, how much will the scheme cost to install and operate.

Initially it is necessary to establish realistic economic and energy budgets commensurate with the design objectives. At all stages of the design, capital costs and running costs must be scrutinised and controlled. The economics and energy use of the lighting system must be considered within the total building energy use.

4.5.1.1 Financial evaluation

The methods of financial assessment employed by the designer must be acceptable to the client. This can cause difficulties because grants, tax benefits, tariffs, accounting methods and other factors can vary.

Comparisons are often made with an existing scheme or an alternative design. If the comparison is to be meaningful, the schemes must be designed to equitable standards. The principles of several methods of financial evaluation are discussed in section 5.1.

4.5.1.2 Energy and tariffs

Although certain large electricity users are able to negotiate a price with an electricity supplier the majority of consumers will use one of the tariffs published by the regional electricity companies (RECs). The most common commercial and industrial payment systems fall into two categories: quarterly and monthly.

Quarterly tariffs are applicable to most domestic, commercial and small industrial customers. They are relatively simple in structure, comprising a standing charge and one or more unit rates. As an alternative to the standard tariffs, customers may opt for a day/night tariff with different day and night rates but a higher standing charge.

Monthly tariffs are more complex and are generally for large supplies. The most widespread is the maximum demand (MD) tariff which typically comprises a standing charge, an availability charge linked to the capacity of the supply required, maximum demand charges in the winter months and one or two unit rates. Also available is a seasonal time of day (STOD) tariff which may have up to six rates but no MD charges. The RECs will offer advice on the most appropriate tariff for specific applications.

Control of the lighting load profile by switching or dimming, so that unnecessary lighting is not used, will reduce the units consumed. Maximum demand often occurs in the middle of the day when daylight is available and MD charges can be reduced if it is possible to shed lighting load at such times (see sections 4.5.1.4 and 4.5.1.5). Conversely, it is often possible to add all-night security lighting without increasing the daytime maximum demand, incurring only the appropriate unit cost.

4.5.1.3 Energy use

Designers should ensure that their designs do not waste energy. However, the most important consideration about energy consumption is usually financial. Few users are willing to invest extra money to achieve energy savings unless the savings offer a reasonable rate of return on that investment.

If the design objectives call for particular conditions to be created then they should be provided. If they are not provided, then although the design may use less energy it will not be effective and cannot, therefore, be regarded as satisfactory.

Section 2.5 of this *Code* gives ranges of installed power densities appropriate for various applications. These effectively set limits to the installed load but other means are required to control energy use and improve operational efficiency.

The load factor for a lighting installation, during a specified period of time, is the ratio of the energy actually consumed to the energy that would have been consumed had the full connected load been operated throughout the specified period. Thus if 25% of the lights in an installation are switched off on average throughout the working day, the load factor will be 0.75. For many installations the load factor will be determined by the ability of the lighting control system to switch the lighting in response to daylight availability. To compare the effectiveness of alternative control systems, the designer will need to estimate the probable annual use of electric lighting under each system.

4.5.1.4 Conventional switching

Field studies of switching behaviour have shown that, with traditional switching arrangements, electric lighting is usually either all switched on or all switched off. The act of switching is almost entirely confined to the beginning and end of a period of occupation; people may switch lighting on when entering a room but seldom turn it off until they all leave. The year-round probability that an occupant will switch lights on when entering a room depends on the time of day, orientation of the windows and the minimum orientation-weighted daylight factor on the working area (see Figure 4.10). Daylight factor calculations are covered in sections 4.4.1 and 5.12. When these are to be used with Figure 4.10 the following orientation weighting factors should be included:

— North-facing windows: 0.77

— East-facing windows: 1.04

— South-facing windows: 1.2

— West-facing windows: 1.00.

For example, if the minimum orientation-weighted daylight factor is 0.6% and work starts at 0900 h, Figure 4.10 shows a 56%

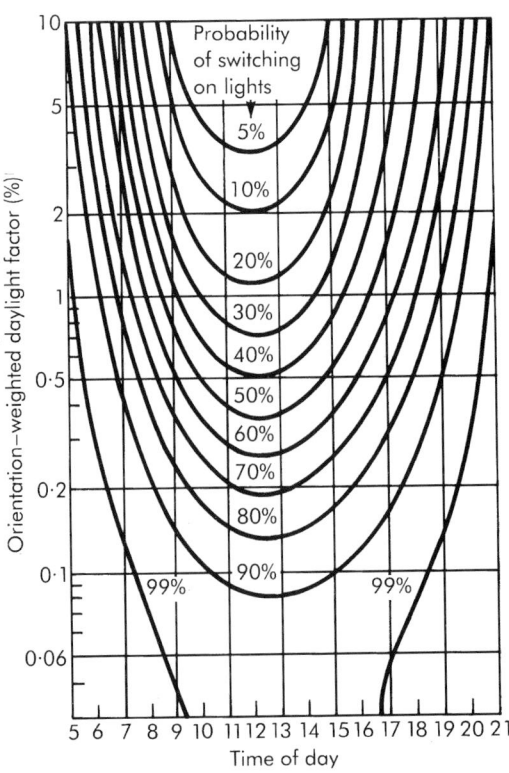

Figure 4.10   Probability of luminaires being switched on[111]

probability of switching. If the room is continually occupied, even through the lunch hour, we may conclude that this same figure — 56% — is the probability that the lights will be on at any moment during the working day. Thus for a lighting installation with a load of 3 kW, and a working year consisting of 260 days, each of 8 hours, the total annual energy consumption would be:

$$260 \times (8 \times 0.56) \times 3 = 3494 \text{ kWh}$$

In rooms which empty for lunch, the lighting may be switched off by the last person to leave. Here it would be reasonable to treat the periods before and after lunch separately. In the example cited above, if lunch ends at 1330 h, the probability of lights being switched on after lunch is taken as 37%, during lunch as 0% and during the morning as 56%, as before. Thus if morning is assumed to be 4 hours and afternoon 3 hours, with a 1-hour lunch period, the total annual energy consumption will be:

$$260 \times [(4 \times 0.56) + (3 \times 0.37)] \times 3 = 2613 \text{ kWh}$$

This represents a saving of 881 kWh per year compared with the installation without lunch time switch-off.

If luminaires are logically zoned with respect to the natural lighting with convenient pull-cord switches for the occupants to use, each zone can be treated as a separate room. The probability of switching would differ from zone to zone, depending on the minimum orientation-weighted daylight factor in each zone. Figure 4.10 would still be applicable but the minimum orientation-weighted daylight factor, and consequent energy savings, must be estimated separately for each zone.

A room occupied intermittently can be treated similarly but some assumption must be made about the periods when the space will be empty.

4.5.1.5   Photo-electric control

On/off switching

Photo-electric controls will normally be zoned to take full advantage of daylight. Figure 4.11 shows the percentage of a normal working year during which the luminaires would be off, as a function of the orientation-weighted daylight factor (see Table 4.1) and of the illuminance at which the luminaires are switched; the 'trigger' illuminance. These curves assume that 'on' and 'off' switching will occur at the same illuminance. Where this is not the case, where the luminaires are switched off at an illuminance appreciably greater than that at which they are switched on, the mean of the two illuminances should be taken as the 'trigger' illuminance for Figure 4.11.

Dimming 'top-up'

Estimation of energy saving from continuous dimming is complicated by the fact that the lamp circuit luminous efficacy generally decreases as a lamp is dimmed. For a well designed tubular fluorescent dimming circuit, the cathode heaters consume some 12% of

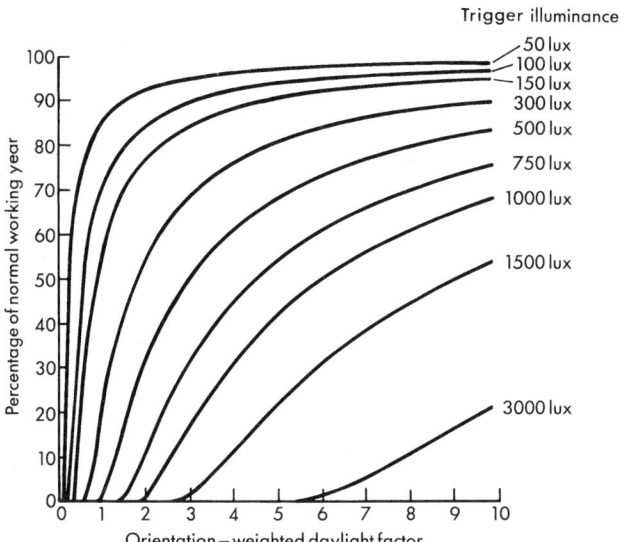

Figure 4.11   Percentage of normal working year during which luminaires will be switched off

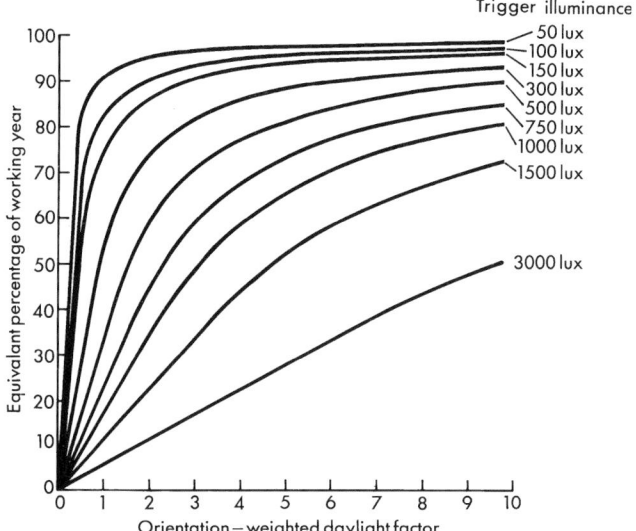

Figure 4.12   Percentage of normal working year during which luminaires would have to be switched off in order to ensure the same energy saving as dimming (top-up control)

the nominal power consumption and the remaining wattage is roughly proportional to the light output.

Figure 4.12 has been constructed on this basis. It shows the percentage of a normal working year during which the luminaires would have to be switched off in order to ensure the energy saving obtainable by continuous photo-electric dimming. It applies to dimmer systems which can control down to 10% output or less.

Dimmer systems can also be designed to operate at less than 100% output when the installation is new so that the maintained illuminance is achieved as a constant value (sections 4.4.4.1 and 4.5.2) through life. For example, if the maintenance factor (MF) is 0.5 then, when new, the luminaire will operate at 50% output (i.e. bringing the initial illuminance of 1000 lux down to the design maintained illuminance of 500 lux) then increasing power as the light losses increase. This approach will lead to valuable energy savings even before daylight is taken into account. Over lamp life, the percentage energy saving S_m (relative to an undimmed, fully lit installation) is of the order of:

$$S_m = \frac{1 - MF}{2} \times 100\%$$

The effect of the maintenance factor is to reduce the dimming range. In the example above, the effective dimming range with new lamps would be from 50% down to, say, 10% (e.g. from a maintained illuminance of 500 lux down to 100 lux). At the end of the effective lamp life, i.e. when the circuit is at full power, the dimming range will have increased to 100%–10%. In the example this would be 500–50 lux.

If the switching is to be relatively unnoticeable to the occupants, the proportion of the electric lighting should not be more than 20% of the total task illuminance. The use of dimming to compensate for the maintenance factor does not, therefore, affect the choice of trigger illuminance which, in the above example, would be set at not less than 500 lux.

4.5.2 Maintained illuminance (see also section 3.5)

Maintained illuminance (E_m) is defined as the average illuminance over the reference surface at the time maintenance has to be carried out by replacing lamps and/or cleaning the equipment and room surfaces.

Although the change in the basis of lighting design from *service* illuminance to *maintained* illuminance is very likely to be internationally agreed, this edition of the *Code* has been published before the CIE and CEN (Technical Committee TC/169) complete their full approval procedures. This *Code*, therefore, anticipates the final decision which contains one potentially confusing change of definition for 'maintenance factor'.

Previously, in the UK, the maintenance factor only took account of losses due to dirt collecting on the lamps, luminaires and room surfaces, it did not include lamp lumen maintenance and lamp failure losses.

The new definition of maintenance factor is 'the ratio of maintained illuminance to initial illuminance', i.e. taking account of all losses including lamp lumen maintenance.

In the 1984 CIBSE *Code for interior lighting*, Appendix 7.5, this was referred to as the 'light loss factor'. It should also be noted that the definition given in the 1987 edition of the *IEC/CIE International lighting vocabulary*[112] is also changed by this decision. It follows from this that to continue using the uniquely British term 'lighting design lumens' (LDL) is deprecated. As part of the harmonisation with European and international practice LDL have no relevance to the calculation of maintained illuminance.

4.5.2.1 Determination of maintenance factor

The maintenance factor (MF) is a multiple of factors:

$$MF = LLMF \times LSF \times LMF \times RSMF$$

where LLMF is the lamp lumen maintenance factor; LSF is the lamp survival factor (used only if spot-replacement of lamps is not carried out); LMF is the luminaire maintenance factor; RSMF is the room surface maintenance factor.

4.5.2.2 Lamp lumen (luminous flux) maintenance factor (LLMF) (see also sections 3.2.2.4 and 3.5.2)

The lumen output from all lamp types reduces with time of operation. The rate of fall-off varies for different lamp types and it is essential to consult manufacturers' data. From such data it is possible to obtain the lamp lumen maintenance factor for a specific number of hours of operation. The lamp lumen maintenance factor is therefore the proportion of the initial light output that is produced after a specified time and, where the rate of fall-off is regular, may be quoted as a percentage reduction per thousand hours of operation.

Manufacturers' data will normally be based on British Standards test procedures which specify the ambient temperature in which the lamp will be tested, with a regulated voltage applied to the lamp and, if appropriate, a reference set of control gear. If any of the aspects of the proposed design are unusual, e.g. high ambient temperature, vibration, switching cycle, operating attitude etc., the manufacturer should be made aware of the conditions and will advise if they affect the life and/or light output of the lamp.

4.5.2.3 Lamp survival factor (LSF) (see also sections 3.2.2.4 and 3.5.2)

As with lamp lumen maintenance factor it is essential to consult manufacturers' data. These will give the percentage of lamp failures for a specific number of hours operation and is only applicable where group lamp replacement, without spot replacement, is to be carried out. These data will also be based on assumptions such as switching cycle, supply voltage and control gear. Manufacturers should be made aware of these aspects and should advise if these will affect the lamp life or lamp survival. Typical lumen maintenance and lamp survival data are given in Table 4.4[113].

4.5.2.4 Luminaire maintenance factor (LMF) (see also section 3.5.3)

Dirt deposited on or in the luminaire will cause a reduction in light output from the luminaire. The rate at which dirt is deposited depends on the construction of the luminaire and on the extent to which dirt is present in the atmosphere, which in turn is related to the nature of the dirt generated in the specific environment. Table 4.6[113] shows typical changes in light output from a luminaire caused by dirt deposition, for a number of luminaire and

Table 4.3 Typical annual lamp operating hours (to be used in the absence of specific data)

Activity/ type of shift	Period of occupancy		Lights switched off when daylight is adequate (daylight link)	Lamp operation (hours)
	Days in use	Hours/day		
Industrial				
Continuous	365	24	None	8760
process/ control	365	24	Operated†	7300
Double shift/	310	16	None	4960
six-day week	310	16	Operated†	3720
Single shift/	310	10	None	3100
six-day week	310	10	Operated†	1760
Single shift/	258	10	None	2580
five-day week	258	10	Operated†	1550
Retail				
Six-day week	356 *(310)*	10	None§	3560 *(3100)*
Offices				
Five-day week	258	10	None	2580
	258	10	Operated†	1550

†   It is assumed that during daytime, adequate daylight is available for about half the working year. Penetration of daylight across a space varies. The switching of dimming control will need to be arranged accordingly. Near windows, the 'off' period can be much longer than for inner areas.
§   Additional trading days and special events will increase hours.

Table 4.4   Lamp lumen maintenance factor (LLMF) and lamp survival factor (LSF) (based on reference 113). Note: example only; use manufacturers' data.

		Operation time (1 000 h)															
		0.1	0.5	1.0	1.5	2.0	4.0	6.0	8.0	10.0	12.0	14.0	16.0	18.0	20.0	22.0	24.0
Fluorescent multi- and triphosphor	LLMF	1.00	0.98	0.96	0.95	0.94	0.91	0.87	0.86	0.85	0.84	0.83	0.81	—	—	—	—
	LSF	1.00	1.00	1.00	1.00	1.00	1.00	0.99	0.95	0.85	0.75	0.64	0.50	—	—	—	—
Fluorescent halophosphate	LLMF	1.00	0.97	0.94	0.91	0.89	0.83	0.80	0.78	0.76	0.74	0.72	0.70	—	—	—	—
	LSF	1.00	1.00	1.00	1.00	1.00	1.00	0.99	0.95	0.85	0.75	0.64	0.50	—	—	—	—
Mercury	LLMF	1.00	0.99	0.97	0.95	0.93	0.87	0.80	0.76	0.72	0.68	0.64	0.61	0.58	0.55	0.53	0.52
	LSF	1.00	1.00	1.00	1.00	0.99	0.98	0.97	0.95	0.92	0.88	0.84	0.80	0.75	0.68	0.59	0.50
Metal halide	LLMF	1.00	0.96	0.93	0.90	0.87	0.78	0.72	0.69	0.66	0.63	0.60	0.56	0.52	—	—	—
	LSF	1.00	1.00	0.97	0.96	0.95	0.93	0.91	0.87	0.83	0.77	0.70	0.60	0.50	—	—	—
High pressure sodium	LLMF	1.00	1.00	0.98	0.97	0.96	0.93	0.91	0.89	0.88	0.87	0.86	0.85	0.83	0.82	0.81	0.80
	LSF	1.00	1.00	1.00	1.00	0.99	0.98	0.96	0.94	0.92	0.89	0.85	0.80	0.75	0.69	0.60	0.50
High pressure sodium, improved colour	LLMF	1.00	0.99	0.97	0.95	0.94	0.89	0.84	0.81	0.79	0.78	—	—	—	—	—	—
	LSF	1.00	1.00	1.00	0.99	0.98	0.96	0.90	0.79	0.65	0.50	—	—	—	—	—	—

Table 4.5   Approximate cleaning intervals for luminaires used in various environments† (based on reference 113)

Maintenance category§	Typical luminaire type	Cleaning intervals and environment¶								
		1 year			2 years			3 years		
		C	N	D	C	N	D	C	N	D
A	Bare lamp batten	—	—	★	—	★	—	★	—	—
B	Open top reflector (ventilated self-cleaning)	—	—	★	—	★	—	★	—	—
C	Closed top reflector (unventilated)	—	★	—	★	—	—	—	—	—
D	Enclosed (IP2X)	—	★	—	★	—	—	—	—	—
E	Dustproof (IP5X)	—	—	—	—	—	★	★	★	—
F	Indirect uplighter	★	★	—	—	—	—	—	—	—

† The selection is based on a LMF of around 0.8. See Table 4.6.
§ For guidance as to under which maintenance category (**A–F**) individual luminaires fall, refer to section 3.3.2.
¶ Cleanliness classes for typical places of work:
  Clean (C): clean rooms, computer centres, electronic assembly, hospitals.
  Normal (N): offices, shops, schools, laboratories, restaurants, warehouses, assembly workshops.
  Dirty (D): steelworks, chemical works foundries, welding, polishing and woodwork areas.
  There may be cases, particularly in certain industrial processes where the environment is exceedingly dirty, that are outside the scope of the above classification.

Table 4.6   **Luminaire maintenance factor (LMF) (based on reference 113, see also references 114–122). Note: example only; use manufacturers' data if available†.**

Elapsed time between cleanings (years)	0.5			1.0			1.5		
Environment§/ luminaire type (see section 3.3.2 and Table 4.5)	C	N	D	C	N	D	C	N	D
A	0.95	0.92	0.88	0.93	0.89	0.83	0.91	0.87	0.80
B	0.95	0.91	0.88	0.90	0.86	0.83	0.87	0.83	0.79
C	0.93	0.89	0.83	0.89	0.81	0.72	0.84	0.74	0.64
D	0.92	0.87	0.83	0.88	0.82	0.77	0.85	0.79	0.73
E	0.96	0.93	0.91	0.94	0.90	0.86	0.92	0.88	0.83
F	0.92	0.89	0.85	0.86	0.81	0.74	0.81	0.73	0.65

Table 4.6   **(continued)**

Elapsed time between cleanings (years)	2.0			2.5			3.0		
Environment§/ luminaire type (see section 3.3.2 and Table 4.5)	C	N	D	C	N	D	C	N	D
A	0.89	0.84	0.78	0.87	0.82	0.75	0.85	0.79	0.73
B	0.84	0.80	0.75	0.82	0.76	0.71	0.79	0.74	0.68
C	0.80	0.69	0.59	0.77	0.64	0.54	0.74	0.61	0.52
D	0.83	0.77	0.71	0.81	0.75	0.68	0.79	0.73	0.65
E	0.91	0.86	0.81	0.90	0.85	0.80	0.90	0.84	0.79
F	0.77	0.66	0.57	0.73	0.60	0.51	0.70	0.55	0.45

†   As the concept of LMF is relatively new, research and work on procedures for manufacturers to produce luminaire maintenance factors for specific products are not yet complete. Until this information is available the values shown in Table 4.6 can be used for design purposes.

§   See ¶ under Table 4.5.

environment categories. The luminaire maintenance categories are defined in Table 4.5, covering a range of luminaire types from bare battens to indirect uplighters. These maintenance categories are also included in the information given in section 3.3.2. Three cleanliness classes (clean, normal and dirty) are used. Typical examples of work places associated with these classes are given in the notes for Table 4.5.

Non-recoverable losses due to discoloration of plastic attachments should also be allowed for.

4.5.2.5   Room surface maintenance factor (RSMF)

Changes in room surface reflectance caused by dirt deposition will cause changes in the illuminance produced by the lighting installation. The magnitude of these changes is governed by the extent of dirt deposition and the importance of inter-reflection to the illuminance produced. Inter-reflection is closely related to the distribution of light from the luminaire and the room index (K). For luminaires which have a strongly downward distribution, i.e.

direct luminaires, inter-reflection has little effect on the illuminance produced on the horizontal working plane. Conversely, indirect lighting is completely dependent on inter-reflections. Most luminaires lie somewhere between these extremes so most lighting installations are dependent to some extent on inter-reflection.

Table 4.7 shows the typical changes in the illuminance from an installation that occur with time due to dirt deposition on the room surfaces for clean, normal and dirty conditions in small, medium or large rooms lit by direct, semi-direct and indirect luminaires. From Table 4.7[113] it is possible to select a room surface maintenance factor appropriate to the circumstances. The room surface maintenance factor is the proportion of the initial inter-reflected component of illuminance after the specified time.

Table 4.7   Room surface maintenance factor (RSMF) (based on reference 113)

Elapsed time between cleanings (years)		0.5			1.0			1.5		
Environment†		C	N	D	C	N	D	C	N	D
Room size K	Luminaire flux distribution									
Small K=0.7	Direct	0.97	0.96	0.95	0.97	0.94	0.93	0.96	0.94	0.92
	Direct/indirect	0.94	0.88	0.84	0.90	0.86	0.82	0.89	0.83	0.80
	Indirect	0.90	0.84	0.80	0.85	0.78	0.73	0.83	0.75	0.69
Medium/large K=2.5/5.0	Direct	0.98	0.97	0.96	0.98	0.96	0.95	0.97	0.96	0.95
	Direct/indirect	0.95	0.90	0.86	0.92	0.88	0.85	0.90	0.86	0.83
	Indirect	0.92	0.87	0.83	0.88	0.82	0.77	0.86	0.79	0.74

Table 4.7   (continued)

Elapsed time between cleanings (years)		2.0			2.5			3.0		
Environment†		C	N	D	C	N	D	C	N	D
Room size K	Luminaire flux distribution									
Small K=0.7	Direct	0.95	0.93	0.90	0.94	0.92	0.89	0.94	0.92	0.88
	Direct/indirect	0.87	0.82	0.78	0.85	0.80	0.75	0.84	0.79	0.74
	Indirect	0.81	0.73	0.66	0.77	0.70	0.62	0.75	0.68	0.59
Medium/large K=2.5/5.0	Direct	0.96	0.95	0.94	0.96	0.95	0.94	0.96	0.95	0.94
	Direct/indirect	0.89	0.85	0.81	0.87	0.84	0.79	0.86	0.82	0.78
	Indirect	0.84	0.77	0.70	0.81	0.74	0.67	0.78	0.72	0.64

† See ¶ under Table 4.5

4.5.2.6 Maintenance factor calculation

The following example is a 'lumen method' calculation to find the necessary number of luminaires needed to provide a predetermined average illuminance level within an unobstructed space. The average illuminance level calculated is the 'maintained illuminance' (E_m) with the 'light loss factor' being replaced by the 'new' maintenance factor (MF).

The example considers a general office space where the cleanliness and atmospheric conditions are assumed to be 'normal', and the design brief requires a maintained illuminance of 500 lux.

Table 4.8 Typical maintenance factors (based on reference 113). Example only: this table should not be used for design purposes.

Lamp type		TF(tri)			TF(halo)			HPM		
Environment†		C	N	D	C	N	D	C	N	D
Luminaire type (See Table 4.5)	Luminaire flux distribution (see Table 4.7)									
A	Direct/ indirect	0.69	0.63	0.56	0.62	0.56	0.50	0.59	0.54	0.48
B	Direct	0.74	0.70	0.67	0.67	0.63	0.60	0.64	0.60	0.58
C	Direct	0.74	0.66	0.58	0.66	0.59	0.52	0.63	0.57	0.50
D	Direct	0.73	0.67	0.62	0.65	0.60	0.56	0.62	0.58	0.54
E	Direct	0.77	0.74	0.70	0.69	0.66	0.62	0.67	0.63	0.60
F	Indirect	0.58	0.50	0.41	0.52	0.45	0.36	0.50	0.43	0.35

Table 4.8 (continued)

Lamp type		MH(F)			HPS			HPSDL		
Environment†		C	N	D	C	N	D	C	N	D
Luminaire type (See Table 4.5)	Luminaire flux distribution (see Table 4.7)									
A	Direct/ indirect	0.58	0.53	0.47	0.69	0.63	0.56	0.67	0.61	0.54
B	Direct	0.62	0.59	0.56	0.74	0.70	0.67	0.73	0.69	0.66
C	Direct	0.62	0.55	0.48	0.74	0.66	0.58	0.72	0.65	0.57
D	Direct	0.61	0.56	0.52	0.73	0.67	0.62	0.71	0.64	0.61
E	Direct	0.65	0.62	0.58	0.77	0.74	0.70	0.76	0.72	0.68
F	Indirect	0.48	0.42	0.34	0.58	0.50	0.41	0.56	0.49	0.40

† See ¶ under Table 4.5.
Notes: Table 4.8 is based on the following assumptions:
(a) Failed lamps are spot-replaced.
(b) Re-lamping intervals :
    High pressure sodium lamps (HPS): 15 000 h
    High pressure sodium improved colour (HPSDL): 6000 h
    High pressure mercury lamps (HPM): 9000 h
    Metal halide lamps (MH): 6000 h
    Tubular fluorescent lamps (TF): 9000 h.
(c) Cleaning intervals :
    Lamps/ luminaires: 1 year
    Room surfaces: 3 years.
(d) Room index (K): 2.5(medium).

Example

Room dimensions are as follows:

— Length: 17.6 m

— Width: 8.0 m

— Height: 3.0 m.

The luminaire mounting height above working plane is 2.2 m and the room index (K) = 2.5. Room surface reflectances are as follows:

— Ceiling: 70%

— Walls: 50%

— Floor: 20%.

Where the text refers to the 'CIE report', this relates to the *CIE Publication number 97*[113]. Tables 4.4 to 4.8 are based on this report.

(*a*)   Step 1: Selection of luminaire and lamp

The luminaire is a 1200 mm recessed unventilated twin lamp luminaire with cross-louvres and polished reflectors giving a controlled light distribution suitable for areas where VDTs are in general use (see Figure 4.8, page 142); maintenance category C (see Table 4.5) applies.

The lamps are 1200 mm, 36 W triphosphor linear fluorescent lamps with a colour rendering index (R_a) 85 and providing initial lumens of 3440 lm.

(*b*)   Step 2: Determine group replacement interval of lamps

Assuming an occupancy period of a single-shift five-day week with 10-hour luminaire operation and no form of daylight linkage control means that, from Table 4.3, the lamps will operate for a period of 2580 h per year.

Calculations can be based on various group lamp replacement periods. In this example two years (5160 h), three years (7740 h) and four years (10 320 h) are considered. The notes to Table 4.8 show 9000 h as the typical re-lamping interval for tubular fluorescent lamps.

(*c*)   Step 3: Obtain lamp lumen maintenance factor and lamp survival

factor from manufacturers' data

An example of typical data is shown in Table 4.4. The factors in Table 4.9 are obtained from this table for a fluorescent triphosphor lamp after operation of 5000, 8000 and 10 000 hours:

Table 4.9   Lamp lumen maintenance factor and lamp survival factor for fluorescent triphosphor lamp after stated periods of operation (values obtained from Table 4.4)

Correction factor	Period of operation		
	5000 h	**8000 h**	**10 000 h**
LLMF	0.89	0.86	0.85
LSF	1.00	0.95†	0.85†

†   If spot lamp replacement procedure is followed then LSF = 1

(d)   Step 4: Determine cleaning interval of luminaires (Table 4.5) and
            room surfaces

            Since cleanliness is 'normal' in this example, the following
            cleaning cycles would be adopted:

            — Luminaires: one-year cleaning cycle

            — Room surfaces: two-year cleaning cycle.

(e)   Step 5: Obtain luminaire maintenance factor (LMF) (Table 4.6)

            LMF is obtained from Table 4.6, depending upon cleaning
            interval, luminaire type and environment.

            LMF = 0.81

(f)   Step 6: Obtain room surface maintenance factor (RSMF) (Table 4.7)

            RSMF is obtained from the table, depending upon cleaning
            interval, room index ($K = 2.5$), luminaire distribution and
            environment.

            RSMF = 0.95

(g)   Step 7: Calculation of maintenance factor (MF)

            The maintenance factor can be calculated from the following
            equation:

            $MF = LLMF \times LSF \times LMF \times RSMF$

            Substituting the values:

            For re-lamping every two years:

            $MF = 0.89 \times 1.00 \times 0.81 \times 0.95 = 0.69$

            For re-lamping every three years:

            $MF = 0.86 \times 0.95 \times 0.81 \times 0.95 = 0.63$

            For re-lamping every four years:

            $MF = 0.85 \times 0.85 \times 0.81 \times 0.95 = 0.56$

(h)   Step 8: Calculation of number of luminaires N

            $$N = \frac{E_{\mathrm{m}} \times A}{F \times n \times MF \times UF}$$

            (see section 4.5.3.5(f)), where $E_{\mathrm{m}} = 500$ lux; $A = 140.8$ m^2; $F =$
            3440 lumens; $n = 2$ lamps; UF $= 0.64$ (see Figure 4.8, page 142);
            MF $= 0.69$ (two-yearly re-lamping).

            Therefore:

            $$N = \frac{500 \times 140.8}{3440 \times 2 \times 0.64 \times 0.69}$$

Thus $N = 23.17$ luminaires (25.38 luminaires for three-yearly re-lamping).

An array of 6×4 luminaires would provide the required maintained illuminance with acceptable uniformity.

The actual illuminance being:

$$E_m = \frac{3440 \times 2 \times 24 \times 0.64 \times 0.69}{140.8}$$

$E_m = 517$ lux (472 lux for three-yearly re-lamping)

By comparing the results for the two- and three-yearly lamp replacement the practical design decision would probably be to opt for the longer period particularly as spot-replacement of three lamps in the final year would give a maintained illuminance of at least 497 lux. It is very unlikely that the additional equipment, installation and energy costs of installing an array of 7×4 luminaires would ever be considered economically justifiable to achieve a calculated value of 552 lux after three years.

When a four-year re-lamping interval is considered the MF = 0.56 results in the need for 28.55 luminaires. In this case a 7×4 array would have to be used giving a 17% increase in equipment and energy costs.

$$E_m = \frac{3440 \times 2 \times 28 \times 0.64 \times 0.56}{140.8} = 490 \text{ lux}$$

Spot lamp replacement would result in at least 570 lux after four years.

The initial illuminance of the 6×4 array would be 750 lux compared with 875 lux for the 7×4 layout. As this is 75% above the design maintained illuminance it is possible that this could lead to complaints of over-lighting when the installation is new.

In calculating the illuminance achieved when using spot lamp replacement, it has been assumed that the lumen output of the replacement lamp is similar to that of the lamps which have been operating since the installation was new. When new lamps are used to replace early failure this is not strictly true, but it is unnecessary and impractical to take account of this effect in the calculation of average illuminance. The random changes in local uniformity are also unlikely to be significant.

Table 4.8 shows some typical maintenance factors for stated maintenance procedures, lighting equipment and site conditions. It has been included to show some of the data used to arrive at the installed power densities in section 2.5 and Table 2.2. Table 4.8 must not be used for design purposes; the worked examples show that the maintenance factor for the cleaning and re-lamping programmes considered, ranged from 0.56 to 0.69. The relevant data in Tables 4.4, 4.6 and 4.7 should be used to investigate the effects of alternative maintenance regimes on the initial, through life performance and costs of an installation.

4.5.2.7 Use of maintenance factor

The maintenance factor can be used in the lumen method of illuminance calculation to estimate what the illuminance produced by the installation will be at any particular stage in its life[113,123].

By calculating the maintenance factor for different times and taking into account the proposed maintenance schedule, it is possible to predict the pattern of illuminance that will be produced by the installation over time (Figure 4.13). This pattern can be used to assess the suitability of any proposed maintenance schedule and to determine whether the installation is likely to meet the design maintained illuminance over an acceptable period of time. Table 4.3 shows typical annual lamp operating hours taking account of the hours per day and days per year that the space is occupied and whether or not LEMS is used. This is given as guidance only and the designer should make every effort to obtain the most accurate data possible for each specific project.

4.5.3 Average illuminance (lumen method)

The value of design maintained illuminance for an activity or interior is found by referring to the lighting schedule (section 2.6.4) and the design maintained illuminance flow chart (Figure 2.3, page 43). When this is to be achieved by designing a general lighting installation (section 4.4.2.1), the number of luminaires required to achieve the average illuminance can be calculated by means of utilisation factors.

4.5.3.1 Utilisation factors

The utilisation factor UF_S of an installation is the ratio of the total flux received by the reference surface S to the total lamp flux of the installation.

The average illuminance E_S over the reference surface S can therefore be calculated from the 'lumen method' formula:

$$E_S = \frac{F \times n \times N \times MF \times UF_S}{A_S}$$

where F is the initial bare lamp luminous flux (lumens); n is the number of lamps per luminaire; N is the number of luminaires; MF is the maintenance factor (see section 4.5.2); UF_S is the utilisation factor for the reference surface S; A_S is the area of the reference surface S(m^2).

The formula can be re-arranged to permit the calculation of the number of luminaires required to achieve a chosen illuminance (see section 4.5.3.5(f)).

Utilisation factors can be determined for any surface or layout of luminaires, but in practice, are only calculated for general lighting systems with regular arrays of luminaires and for the three main room surfaces, the ceiling cavity, the walls, and the floor cavity or horizontal reference plane, (see Figure 4.14). Utilisation factors for these surfaces are designated UF_C, UF_W and UF_F respectively. The method for calculating utilisation factors for these surfaces is given in CIBSE *TM5*[100].

Although utilisation factors can be calculated by the lighting designer, most manufacturers publish utilisation factors for

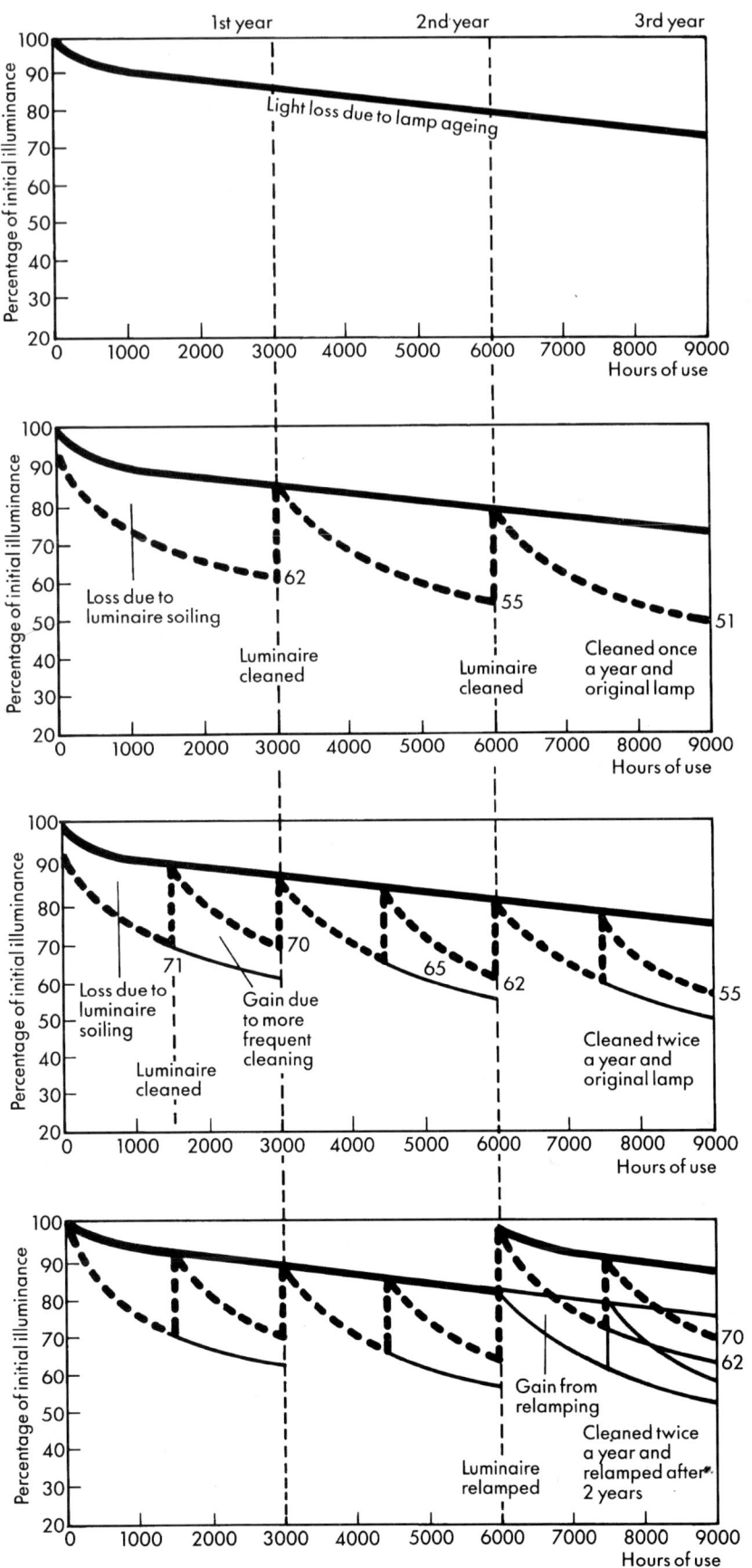

Figure 4.13 Changes in illumination with times for different maintenance schedules

standard conditions for their luminaires. CIBSE *TM5* defines a standard method of presentation and states the assumptions on which the tabulated values are based. Figure 4.8 (page 142) is an example of the standard presentation (see also section 4.5.3.4). *It should be noted that the calculation of UF as described above assumes an empty room. Absorption of light by room contents such as furniture and equipment may reduce the achieved illuminance on the working plane*[124,125].

4.5.3.2 Room index (K)

To use utilisation factor tables it is necessary to have values of the room index (K) and the reflectance values of the main room surfaces.

The room index is a measure of the proportions of the room (see Figure 4.14).

For rectangular rooms the room index is:

$$K = \frac{L \times W}{(L + W)h_{\mathrm{m}}}$$

where L = the length of the room; W is the width of the room; h_{m} is the height of the luminaire plane above the horizontal reference plane.

Results may be rounded to the nearest value in the utilisation factor table.

If the room is re-entrant in shape (e.g. L-shaped) then it must be divided into two or more non re-entrant sections which are treated separately.

When large areas are subdivided by screens, partitions, structural elements, furniture or machinery which project about the working plane it is usually advisable to calculate K for the smaller enclosed areas (see sections 2.4.3 and 4.5.4).

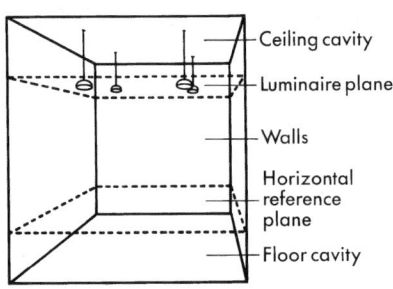

Figure 4.14 Ceiling cavity, walls and floor cavity

4.5.3.3 Effective reflectance

In order to use utilisation factor tables correctly the effective reflectances of the ceiling cavity, walls and floor cavity must be calculated.

For the ceiling cavity and floor cavity the cavity indices $\mathrm{CI_C}$ and $\mathrm{CI_F}$ must be calculated. The cavity index (CI), which is similar in concept to the room index, is given by the following (see Figure 4.15):

$$\mathrm{CI} = \frac{\text{Mouth area of cavity} + \text{Base area of cavity}}{\text{Wall area of cavity}}$$

For rectangular rooms:

$$\mathrm{CI_C} \text{ or } \mathrm{CI_F} = \frac{LW}{(L + W)h} = \frac{K \times h_{\mathrm{m}}}{h}$$

where h is the depth of the cavity.

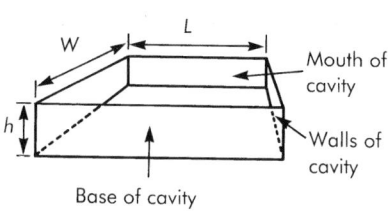

Figure 4.15 Calculation of cavity index

The effective reflectance RE_X of the cavity X can then be determined from Table 4.10 or from the simplified, but less accurate, formula:

$$RE_X = \frac{CI_X \times RA_X}{CI_X + 2(1 - RA_X)}$$

where RA_X is the average area weighted reflectance of the cavity X, and CI_X is the cavity index of the cavity X.

The average reflectance R_X of a series of surfaces S_1 to S_n with reflectances R_{Sn} and areas to A_1 to A_n respectively given by:

$$RA_X = \frac{\sum_{y=1}^{n} R(Sy)A(y)}{\sum_{y=1}^{n} A(y)}$$

It should be noted that in order to calculate the effective reflectances, it is not necessary to know the colours of the surfaces, only the value of reflectance (see Table 5.8, pages 215–216 and Table 5.9, page 217).

4.5.3.4 Maximum spacing-to-height ratio (SHR_{max})

The maximum spacing between the centres of luminaires divided by the mounting height above the horizontal reference plane should not exceed SHR_{max} if uniformity of illuminance is to be acceptable for general lighting. The maximum spacing-to-height ratio (SHR_{max}) for the luminaire can be obtained using the method described in CIBSE *TM5*[97]. The utilisation factor table is calculated for the nominal spacing-to-height ratio (SHR_{nom}). This is the SHR in the series 0.5, 0.75, 1.0 etc. which is not greater than SHR_{max}. For linear luminaires with conventional distributions, the maximum spacing-to-height ratio SHR_{max} can be supplemented by the maximum transverse spacing-to-height ratio ($SHR_{max\ tr}$) for continuous lines of luminaires.

The axial spacing-to-height ratio (SHR_{ax}) should not exceed SHR_{max} and the transverse spacing-to-height ratio SHR_{tr} should not exceed the maximum transverse spacing-to-height ratio $SHR_{max\ tr}$. In addition, the product of SHR_{ax} and SHR_{tr} should not exceed $(SHR_{max})^2$. Thus:

$$SHR_{ax}\ SHR_{tr} \leq (SHR_{max})^2$$

and
$$SHR_{ax} \leq SHR_{max}$$
and
$$SHR_{tr} \leq SHR_{max\ tr}$$

For some luminaires, notably those with a rapid rate of change in their intensity distributions, extra spacing-to-height ratio information may be given. This can be provided in the form of a graph showing acceptable combinations of axial and transverse spacing. Figure 4.16 is an example of this. The line indicates the range of spacing-to-height ratios which will achieve acceptable uniformity across the task area (i.e. mid-area ratio greater than 0.7).

Table 4.10 The effective reflectance of cavities. To use this table it is necessary to know the reflectance of the surfaces forming the cavity and the geometry of the cavity.

Reflectance of cavity		Cavity index									
Wall	Base	1	2	3	4	5	6	7	8	9	10
0.1	0.1	0.037	0.056	0.067	0.073	0.078	0.081	0.083	0.085	0.087	0.088
	0.2	0.056	0.098	0.122	0.137	0.148	0.155	0.161	0.165	0.168	0.171
	0.3	0.075	0.140	0.178	0.201	0.218	0.229	0.238	0.245	0.250	0.255
	0.4	0.094	0.182	0.234	0.266	0.288	0.303	0.315	0.325	0.332	0.338
	0.5	0.113	0.224	0.289	0.330	0.358	0.378	0.393	0.404	0.414	0.422
	0.6	0.132	0.267	0.345	0.395	0.428	0.452	0.470	0.484	0.496	0.505
	0.7	0.151	0.309	0.401	0.459	0.498	0.527	0.548	0.565	0.578	0.589
	0.8	0.171	0.352	0.458	0.524	0.569	0.601	0.626	0.645	0.660	0.673
0.2	0.1	0.058	0.073	0.080	0.084	0.087	0.089	0.090	0.092	0.092	0.093
	0.2	0.079	0.117	0.137	0.150	0.158	0.164	0.169	0.172	0.175	0.177
	0.3	0.100	0.161	0.195	0.216	0.230	0.240	0.247	0.253	0.258	0.262
	0.4	0.121	0.206	0.253	0.282	0.301	0.316	0.326	0.334	0.341	0.346
	0.5	0.142	0.250	0.311	0.348	0.373	0.391	0.405	0.416	0.424	0.431
	0.6	0.163	0.296	0.369	0.415	0.446	0.468	0.484	0.497	0.507	0.516
	0.7	0.185	0.341	0.428	0.482	0.518	0.544	0.563	0.579	0.591	0.601
	0.8	0.207	0.386	0.487	0.549	0.591	0.620	0.643	0.660	0.674	0.686
0.3	0.1	0.082	0.091	0.094	0.095	0.096	0.097	0.098	0.098	0.098	0.098
	0.2	0.105	0.137	0.153	0.163	0.169	0.174	0.177	0.180	0.182	0.184
	0.3	0.128	0.184	0.213	0.231	0.242	0.251	0.257	0.262	0.266	0.269
	0.4	0.151	0.231	0.273	0.299	0.316	0.328	0.337	0.344	0.350	0.355
	0.5	0.175	0.278	0.334	0.367	0.390	0.406	0.418	0.427	0.434	0.440
	0.6	0.199	0.326	0.395	0.436	0.464	0.484	0.498	0.510	0.519	0.526
	0.7	0.223	0.375	0.456	0.506	0.539	0.562	0.579	0.593	0.604	0.613
	0.8	0.248	0.424	0.518	0.575	0.613	0.641	0.661	0.676	0.689	0.699
0.4	0.1	0.107	0.109	0.108	0.107	0.106	0.105	0.105	0.104	0.104	0.104
	0.2	0.133	0.158	0.170	0.176	0.181	0.184	0.186	0.187	0.189	0.190
	0.3	0.159	0.208	0.232	0.246	0.255	0.262	0.267	0.271	0.274	0.276
	0.4	0.185	0.258	0.295	0.316	0.331	0.341	0.349	0.354	0.359	0.363
	0.5	0.211	0.308	0.358	0.387	0.407	0.420	0.431	0.439	0.445	0.450
	0.6	0.239	0.360	0.422	0.459	0.483	0.500	0.513	0.523	0.531	0.537
	0.7	0.266	0.412	0.486	0.531	0.560	0.581	0.596	0.608	0.617	0.625
	0.8	0.294	0.464	0.552	0.603	0.637	0.661	0.679	0.693	0.704	0.713

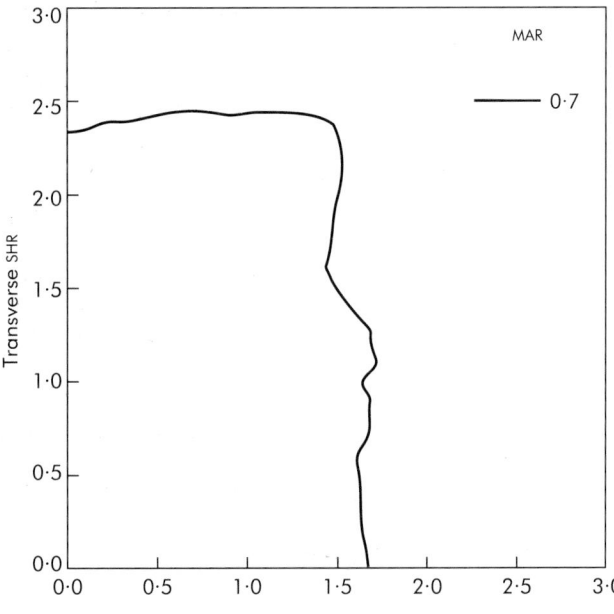

Figure 4.16 Combination of transverse and axial spacing-to-height ratios producing acceptable uniformity (batwing luminaire)

Table 4.10   (continued)

Reflectance of cavity		Cavity index									
Wall	Base	1	2	3	4	5	6	7	8	9	10
0.5	0.1	0.136	0.129	0.123	0.119	0.116	0.114	0.112	0.111	0.110	0.109
	0.2	0.164	0.181	0.187	0.190	0.192	0.194	0.195	0.195	0.196	0.196
	0.3	0.193	0.233	0.252	0.262	0.269	0.274	0.277	0.280	0.282	0.284
	0.4	0.233	0.287	0.317	0.335	0.346	0.354	0.360	0.365	0.369	0.372
	0.5	0.253	0.341	0.383	0.408	0.424	0.436	0.444	0.450	0.456	0.460
	0.6	0.284	0.396	0.450	0.482	0.503	0.517	0.528	0.537	0.543	0.548
	0.7	0.316	0.452	0.518	0.557	0.582	0.600	0.613	0.623	0.631	0.637
	0.8	0.348	0.509	0.587	0.633	0.662	0.683	0.698	0.710	0.719	0.727
0.6	0.1	0.168	0.151	0.139	0.131	0.126	0.123	0.120	0.118	0.116	0.115
	0.2	0.200	0.205	0.205	0.205	0.204	0.204	0.204	0.203	0.203	0.203
	0.3	0.232	0.261	0.273	0.279	0.283	0.286	0.288	0.289	0.290	0.291
	0.4	0.266	0.318	0.341	0.354	0.362	0.368	0.372	0.376	0.378	0.380
	0.5	0.301	0.376	0.410	0.430	0.443	0.451	0.458	0.463	0.467	0.470
	0.6	0.336	0.435	0.481	0.507	0.524	0.535	0.544	0.550	0.556	0.560
	0.7	0.373	0.496	0.552	0.585	0.605	0.620	0.630	0.639	0.645	0.650
	0.8	0.411	0.557	0.625	0.663	0.688	0.705	0.718	0.727	0.735	0.741
0.7	0.1	0.204	0.173	0.155	0.144	0.137	0.132	0.128	0.125	0.122	0.120
	0.2	0.240	0.231	0.224	0.220	0.217	0.215	0.213	0.211	0.210	0.210
	0.3	0.277	0.291	0.295	0.296	0.297	0.298	0.298	0.299	0.299	0.299
	0.4	0.315	0.352	0.366	0.374	0.379	0.382	0.385	0.387	0.388	0.389
	0.5	0.355	0.414	0.439	0.453	0.461	0.468	0.472	0.475	0.478	0.480
	0.6	0.397	0.478	0.513	0.533	0.545	0.554	0.560	0.565	0.568	0.571
	0.7	0.440	0.543	0.589	0.614	0.630	0.641	0.649	0.655	0.660	0.663
	0.8	0.485	0.611	0.666	0.696	0.715	0.728	0.738	0.745	0.751	0.756
0.8	0.1	0.245	0.198	0.173	0.158	0.148	0.141	0.136	0.132	0.129	0.126
	0.2	0.285	0.260	0.245	0.236	0.230	0.225	0.222	0.220	0.218	0.216
	0.3	0.328	0.323	0.318	0.315	0.312	0.311	0.309	0.308	0.308	0.307
	0.4	0.373	0.388	0.393	0.395	0.396	0.397	0.398	0.398	0.398	0.399
	0.5	0.419	0.456	0.469	0.477	0.481	0.484	0.487	0.488	0.490	0.491
	0.6	0.468	0.525	0.548	0.560	0.567	0.573	0.576	0.579	0.582	0.583
	0.7	0.519	0.596	0.627	0.644	0.655	0.662	0.667	0.671	0.674	0.677
	0.8	0.573	0.670	0.709	0.730	0.743	0.752	0.759	0.764	0.768	0.771

The mid-area is defined for a 4 × 4 array of luminaires as the rectangular (or square) area on the horizontal plane with corners directly below the centres of the four central luminaires. The mid-area ratio (MAR) is the ratio of the minimum direct illuminance to the maximum direct illuminance calculated over the mid-area. This is obtained by calculating the direct illuminance at every point on a regular 9 × 9 grid with the corner points of the grid at the corners of the area, i.e. one under the centre of each of the four luminaires. This is the general method described in *TM5* and is now preferred to the simpler mid-point ratio (MPR) method which is also included in *TM5*.

These spacing rules are provided as a guide for general design work and give approximate advice. Where computer programs are available, these can be used to check that correct uniformity has been achieved over task areas.

The SHR data and the majority of lighting programs take no account of obstructions or obstruction losses, nor do they take account of shadows or modelling. *Designers should not design installations close to their maximum spacing without considering the implications of doing so in terms of shadows, modelling, obstructions and the effect of lamp failures or local switching.*

4.5.3.5   Calculation procedure

The following procedure gives guidance on the sequence of calculations to be performed when calculating the number of luminaires necessary to obtain a chosen average illuminance on the horizontal reference plane by the lumen method.

(a) Calculate the room index K, the floor cavity index CI_F and the ceiling cavity index CF_C (see sections 4.5.3.2. and 4.5.3.3).

(b) Calculate the effective reflectances of the ceiling cavity, walls and floor cavity. Remember to include the effect of desks or machines in the latter (see section 4.5.3.3).

(c) Determine the utilisation factor value from the manufacturer's data for the luminaire, using the room index and effective reflectances calculated as above. See Table 5.24 (page 252) for correction factors for R_F other than 20%.

(d) Apply any correction factors, given in the utilisation factor table for lamp type or mounting position, to the utilisation factor UF value.

(e) Determine the maintenance factor (see section 4.5.2.6).

(f) Insert the appropriate variables into the lumen method formula to obtain the number of luminaires required:

$$N = \frac{E_F \times A_F}{F \times n \times MF \times UF_F}$$

where E_F is the average illuminance to be provided on the working plane (lux); A_F is the area of the working plane (m^2); F is the initial bare lamp luminous flux (lumens); n is the number of lamps per luminaires; MF is the maintenance factor; UF_F is the utilisation factor for the plane; F refers to horizontal reference plane.

(g) Determine a suitable layout.

(h) Check that the geometric mean spacing-to-height ratio of the layout is within the range of the nominal spacing-to-height ratio (SHR_{nom}) for which the utilisation factor table is based, i.e.

$$\sqrt{(SHR_{ax} \times SHR_{tr})} = SHR_{nom} \pm 0.5$$

If this is not the case, the UF can be recalculated for the actual spacing using the method given in *TM5*[100]. Corrections are also given for luminaire-to-wall spacing other than half of the spacing between luminaires.

(i) Check that the proposed layout does not exceed the maximum spacing-to-height ratios (see section 4.5.3.4).

(j) Calculate the illuminance that will be achieved by the final layout (see section 4.5.3.1).

4.5.4   Specification and interpretation of illuminance variation

It is possible to describe illuminance variation as a series of values or as some form of graphical representation (plot) of a magnitude of

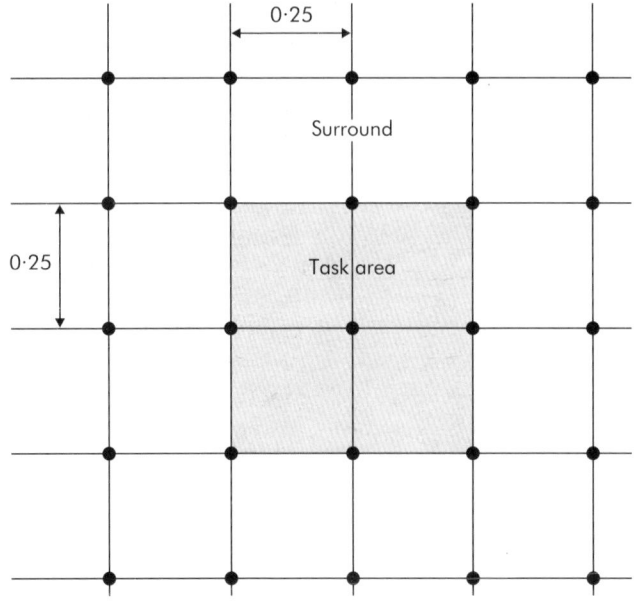

Figure 4.17 Grid for calculation and measurement of uniformity for a task area and surround

variation over a surface. The main methods used in this *Code* are 'uniformity' which is concerned with illuminance conditions on the task and immediate surround, and 'diversity' which expresses changes in illuminance across a larger space. Values of both may be calculated or measured from a grid of discrete illuminance values over a surface (see Figures 4.17 and 5.1, page 195).

The illuminance conditions on the task area locations across the working plane may be represented by a grid of points over the task and immediate surround. If a number of task areas exist, the uniformity must be determined for each and the worst taken as the limiting value of uniformity for the installation. The concept of uniformity thus does not apply to the whole working plane but to a series of defined task areas on the working plane. In the calculation of illuminance diversity, grid points within 0.5 m of walls or large fixed obstructions are ignored. This is because planar illuminances will, under normal circumstances, fall around the room perimeter and near large obstructions such as partitions or large structural columns that project above the working plane. Calculation or measurement of illuminance in these positions will therefore have little practical value and particular care should be taken in interpretation of computer-generated illuminance grids to make sure that the grid values chosen for assessment of illuminance variation are not at the very edge of rooms or adjacent to obstructions. See section 2.4.3.

4.5.4.1 Calculation of illuminance variation

No design method is available which will enable the various recommendations relating to illuminance uniformity or diversity to be optimised within a particular proposed design solution.

Widespread use is now made of computer programs that are capable of undertaking analysis in considerable detail of illuminance conditions in proposed installations. Most programs are capable of calculating illuminance on a grid of points across a working plane and in some cases other room surfaces and illuminance variation quantities are commonly generated as part of the output of such programs.

The purpose of this section is to explain how to calculate the different variation criteria to confirm that the design objectives have been met. To calculate diversity, illuminance values should be calculated on a grid of points located symmetrically over the core area of the working plane. For installations with ceiling heights of up to 5 m lit by a regular array of ceiling-mounted luminaires the grid of points should normally be at a spacing of 1 m. For other types of installation the grid size may vary. In larger interiors lit by luminaires with a smooth medium to wide intensity distribution and those with a mounting height greater than 5 m, the calculation grid size may be increased, in this case the total number of calculation points being determined by reference to Table 5.7 (page 194). On the other hand, a calculation grid size of less than 1 m may be necessary for installations where abrupt variations in working plane illuminance may occur, for example those using luminaires with bat-wing or narrow distribution. Care must be taken to ensure that the luminaire and calculation grids do not coincide and this may also necessitate a small change in the size of the calculation grid. The calculated illuminance value at each point must be made up of both illuminance arriving directly from light sources and illuminance received at the point after reflection from room surfaces (section 4.5.5.4). *The illuminance diversity is calculated from the maximum and minimum illuminance at any point on the grid over the core area of the working plane ignoring calculation points within 0.5 m of obstructions (see section 2.4.3).*

The calculation procedure for uniformity differs slightly depending upon whether or not the size and position of the task areas on the working plane are known. If task location can be identified, then the illuminance calculation should be on a 0.25 m² grid over the task and immediate surround for a typical workstation. If the task locations are unknown and may be at any position on the working plane, a suitable number of grid points used for the illuminance diversity assessment are chosen. These should, at least, include the points of minimum and maximum illuminance over the coarse grid. In this case, the task area may be assumed to be a 0.5 m square with one corner coinciding with the coarse grid point. The illuminance is then calculated on 9 points of a 0.25 m grid (see Figure 4.17). In most cases, it is not essential to include the inter-reflected component in the illuminance calculations over this small area. Task uniformity is assessed using the area-weighted arithmetic average of the points within the individual task areas and the minimum point illuminance value within each area. The lowest value of task uniformity calculated for the various potential or actual locations is taken as representative of the whole installation (see section 2.4.3).

Any discrete set of grid points (measured or calculated) cannot necessarily capture the minimum or maximum values over an area, and under some circumstances abrupt variations in rate of change can be missed by a grid. The representation of illuminance using a grid is therefore an approximation and is only as good as the choice of location and size of the grid. Hence the recommendation that two grids be used: a series of fine grids over task areas, and a coarse grid across the core area of the working plane (see Figures 4.17 and 5.1, page 195).

4.5.5 Illuminance at a point

In order to check illuminance variation for general lighting it is necessary to calculate the illuminance at all points of interest. This is also true when local or localised lighting systems are employed or when unusual layouts or luminaires with unconventional light distributions are used. In these cases, the calculation of average illuminance can be inadequate or meaningless.

These calculations can be done in one or more of three ways:

(a) Calculations by hand from basic photometric data

(b) calculation from pre-calculated aids such as isolux diagrams

(c) calculation using a computer program.

In all these cases the effect of the maintenance factor should also be included.

The first method involves the greatest amount of work and is only suitable for a few points. However, it can provide a useful quick check to see if more detailed calculations are necessary.

Isolux diagrams (Figure 4.18), if available for the particular set of circumstances, offer a faster method of carrying out the same calculations. For local and localised lighting systems they can provide considerable guidance on the correct location of luminaires. Isolux diagrams must normally be produced for the mounting height, scale and lumen output required. If this is not done then isolux diagrams can still be used but considerable correction is necessary.

Where a computer is available with suitable programs, illuminance values can be easily calculated. Although some limited design

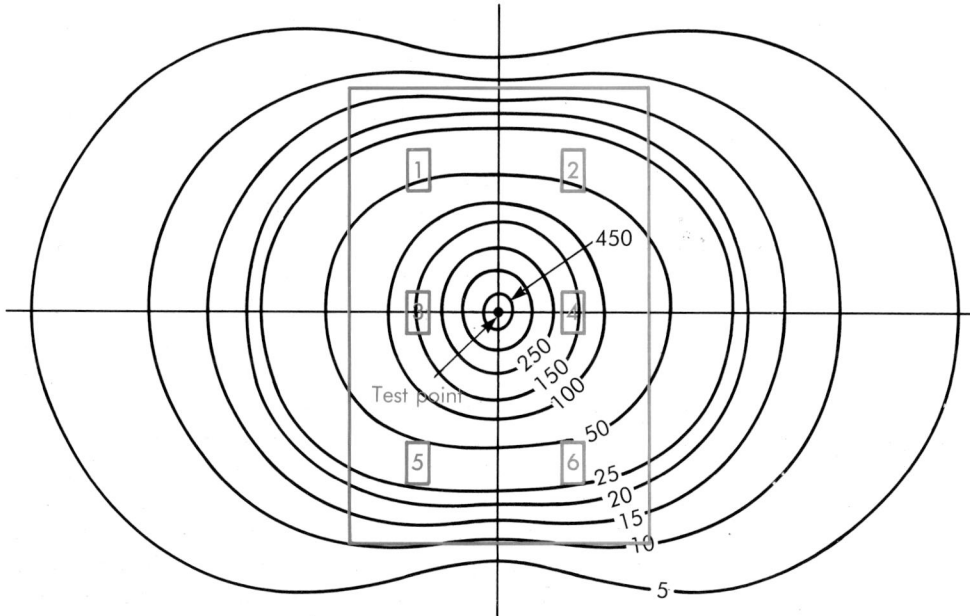

Figure 4.18 Use of isolux diagram to obtain total direct illuminance. By placing the central point of the isolux diagram over a given point on a plan of the room to the same scale, the illuminance at that point can be calculated. In the example, the contributions from luminaires 1 to 6 are 40, 40, 160, 160, 35 and 35 lux respectively. Thus the total illuminance is 470 lux.

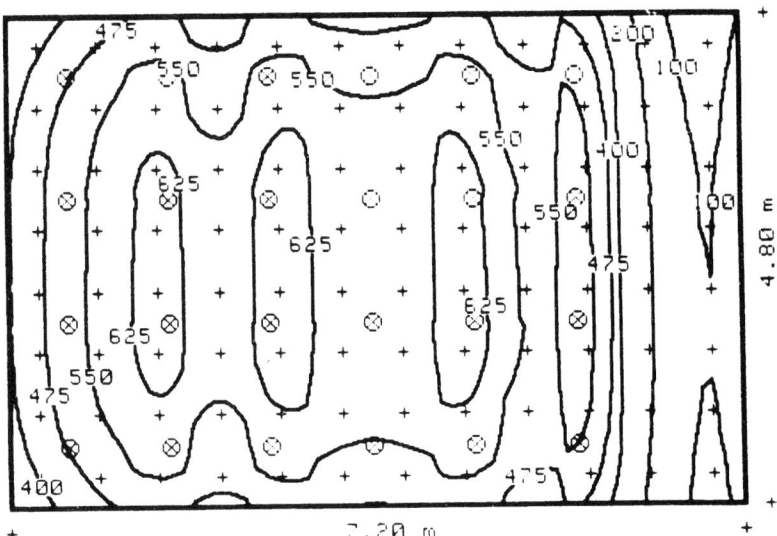

Figure 4.19 Isolux diagram of illuminance in an interior as drawn by a computer

programs do exist, most programs simulate the illuminance pattern produced by a chosen layout of luminaires. *Before using a computer program the designer should be aware of the assumptions contained within the program and ensure that the data used are appropriate to the equipment and the situation.*

At the planning stage it is often easier to analyse the illuminance plots for individual luminaires or a group of luminaires to assist in the selection of the best layout. When the complete layout has been established it can then be simulated on the computer.

The form of output is important. If the information is insufficiently detailed (see section 4.5.4.1) then important features may be overlooked. More commonly, too much detail becomes too complex to interpret.

Graphic methods such as isolux diagrams are easy to understand, and are preferable to tabulated data (Figure 4.19). However, they require more sophisticated software and hardware than conventional printouts.

The direct illuminance at a point can be calculated by the inverse square law. However, this only applies when the source is small compared with the distance between it and the point of illumination. When this is not the case, the calculation must be modified. Sources can be considered to be one of three basic types: point sources, line sources or area sources.

4.5.5.1 Point sources

A luminaire can be considered as a point source if its largest dimension is less than one fifth of the distance from it to the point being illuminated.

For a point source, the direct illuminance at a point can be found by applying the inverse square and cosine laws (see section 5.13.2 for formulae).

4.5.5.2   Line sources

A luminaire is only designated as a point source or a line source because of its distance from the point of illumination. Thus a 1.8 m batten will behave like a line source for points up to 9 m away, but at greater distances the errors in the inverse square law calculation become acceptable and the luminaire can be treated as a point source.

When a luminaire cannot be considered as a point source it can be regarded as a line source, providing that its width is less than one fifth of the distance from its centre to the point being illuminated. For most situations, fluorescent luminaires fall into this category. To perform calculations on line sources it is necessary to have some method of integrating the effect of the length of the luminaires. One such method is the 'aspect factor method'.

Aspect factors are derived from the axial luminous intensity distribution of the luminaire and, when used in the correct formula, make allowance for the effect of the length of the luminaire. Aspect factors can be published for almost all fluorescent luminaires, and must be used with the transverse luminous intensity distribution curves. For some low brightness reflector luminaires where the axial distribution varies with θ, inaccuracies may be introduced at high angles.

Two sets of aspect factors are provided. The parallel plane aspect factors are for calculating the direct illuminance on surfaces parallel to the axis of the luminaires, such as the floor, working plane or side walls. The other set of aspect factors, the perpendicular plane aspect factors are for calculating the direct illuminances on surfaces normal (i.e. at right angles) to the axis of the luminaire, such as the end walls (see section 5.13.3 for formulae).

Surfaces which are neither parallel nor perpendicular to the axis of the luminaire (such as an angled drawing board) can be dealt with by a combination of the two types of aspect factor (see section 5.13.3).

4.5.5.3   Area sources

When both the width and length of a luminaire are greater than one fifth of the distance from its centre to the point of illumination, then the source should be considered as an area source.

Area source calculations are by far the most complicated of the three types. There is no simple equivalent of the inverse square law or aspect factor calculation for area sources. Indeed, for many situations the formulae have not been solved. For this reason, the fact that area source calculations are not often required, only the simple case of a uniform area source is considered in this *Code* (see section 5.13.4).

4.5.5.4   Inter-reflected light at a point

The preceding methods of calculating illuminance at a point deal only with the calculation of direct illuminance and do not allow for inter-reflected light.

Inter-reflected light can be dealt with in one of four ways:

(*a*) Calculate the inter-reflected illuminance at the point and add it to the calculated direct illuminance. To do this, first calculate the final illuminances of the walls, floor and ceiling (using transfer factors, see CIBSE *TM5*[100]). Then treat each of these room surfaces as if it were an area source of intensity distribution *I(R)*:

$$I(R) = I \cos \theta$$

where $I = ER/\pi$; E being the illuminance of the surface, R being the reflectance, and θ being the angle from the normal to the surface.

The calculations involved are lengthy, and only really suited to a computer. The results are also somewhat artificial, since local changes in reflectance can significantly affect the amount of inter-reflected light.

(b) Ignore the inter-reflected light and assume that it will be a bonus, increasing the final illuminance. In other words, calculate the worst case. This is a more practical approach, but may not be adequate for some situations.

(c) Ignore the inter-reflected light at the point, but calculate the average illuminance on the horizontal reference plane (by the lumen method) for the actual reflectances and for a black room (zero reflectances). The difference gives a good indication of the average value of inter-reflected illuminance over the working plane. In many cases this can be added as a constant to the direct illuminance calculated for each point to give an acceptable approximation.

This relatively simple calculation can also be applied to planes other than the horizontal if the appropriate utilisation factors are available.

(d) Calculate the average indirect illuminance E_{ind} by the formula:

$$E_{ind} = \frac{F \; \text{DLOR}}{A_F} \times \frac{(\text{DR RE}_F) + [(1 - \text{DR})\text{RE}_W] + (\text{FFR RE}_C)\text{MF}}{2 + \dfrac{2}{K}(1 - \text{RE}_W) - \text{RE}_C - \text{RE}_F}$$

where F is the installed bare lamp luminous flux (lumens); DLOR is the downward light output ratio; A_F is the area of floor (m^2); DR is the direct ratio of installation; FFR is the flux fraction ratio of installation; K is the room index; RE$_F$, RE$_C$ and RE$_W$ are the effective reflectances of the floor cavity, ceiling cavity and walls respectively; MF is the maintenance factor (if relevant).

As in (c), this indirect illuminance is assumed to be uniformly distributed over all the room surfaces. It may therefore be added to the direct illuminance calculated at each individual point. This method is recommended when programmable calculators are to be used. It has the merit that it can also be used to show the effect of inter-reflected light on wall and ceiling illuminance ratios.

4.5.6 Glare index

The CIBSE glare index system for the evaluation of discomfort glare is described in CIBSE *TM10*[126].

There are two methods of calculation:

(a) The calculation of glare index for the actual installation using the basic formula (see section 5.4.2).

Table 4.11 Typical uncorrected glare index table

		____	____	____	Glare indices	____	____	____	____	____
Ceiling reflectance		0.70	0.70	0.50	0.50	0.30	0.70	0.70	0.50	0.50	0.30
Wall reflectance		0.50	0.30	0.50	0.30	0.30	0.50	0.30	0.50	0.30	0.30
Floor reflectance		0.20	0.20	0.20	0.20	0.20	0.20	0.20	0.20	0.20	0.20
Room dimension		Viewed cross-wise					Viewed end-wise				
x	y										
2H	2H	7.0	8.4	8.0	9.5	10.8	6.8	8.2	7.8	9.2	10.5
	3H	8.9	10.2	10.0	11.3	12.6	8.6	9.8	9.6	10.9	12.2
	4H	9.9	11.1	10.9	12.2	13.5	9.4	10.6	10.4	11.7	13.0
	6H	11.0	12.1	12.0	13.2	14.5	10.3	11.4	11.3	12.5	13.8
	8H	11.6	12.6	12.6	13.7	16.1	10.7	11.8	11.7	12.9	14.2
	12H	12.2	13.2	13.2	14.3	16.7	11.1	12.1	12.1	13.2	14.6
4H	2H	7.7	8.9	8.7	10.0	11.3	7.5	8.7	8.5	9.3	11.1
	3H	10.0	11.0	11.0	12.1	13.5	9.6	10.6	10.9	11.7	13.1
	4H	11.2	12.1	12.2	13.2	14.6	10.6	11.6	11.7	12.7	14.1
	6H	12.5	13.4	13.6	14.5	15.9	11.8	12.6	12.3	13.7	15.1
	8H	13.3	14.0	14.4	15.2	16.6	12.3	13.1	13.4	14.2	15.7
	12H	14.0	14.3	15.1	15.9	17.3	12.8	13.5	13.9	14.7	16.1
8H	4H	11.8	12.5	12.9	13.7	15.2	11.4	12.2	12.5	13.3	14.7
	6H	13.5	14.2	14.6	15.3	16.8	12.8	13.5	13.9	14.6	16.1
	8H	14.4	15.0	15.5	16.1	17.6	13.5	14.1	14.6	15.2	16.7
	12H	15.4	16.0	16.6	17.1	18.6	14.2	14.8	15.4	15.9	17.4
12H	4H	12.0	12.7	13.1	13.8	15.3	11.6	12.3	12.7	13.5	14.9
	6H	13.7	14.3	14.9	15.5	17.0	13.1	13.7	14.3	14.9	16.4
	8H	14.8	15.3	16.0	16.5	18.0	14.0	14.5	15.1	15.7	17.2
	12H	15.7	16.2	16.8	17.3	18.8	14.6	15.0	15.7	16.2	17.7

(b) The calculation of glare index from tables based on photometric data for the luminaire (published by the manufacturer), in the form of an uncorrected glare index with correction factors.

The first method requires the use of a suitable computer and program and the availability of detailed photometric data. The advantages to be gained from the use of a program are that any layout of luminaires seen from any viewing position can be considered. These advantages are seldom sufficient to justify the expense of developing or buying the software. The second method is sufficiently accurate for most purposes and is easy to use. Table 4.11 shows an uncorrected glare index table for a luminaire. It is calculated from the glare index formula discussed in section 5.4.2.

The table is based upon a number of assumptions. These are:

(a) the luminaires are at a spacing-to-height ratio of 1.0

(b) the luminaires are at a height of 2.0 m above eye level

(c) the total light output of the lamps in the luminaire is 1000 lumens

(d) the observer is located at the mid-point of a wall, with a horizontal line of sight towards the centre of the opposite wall

(e) the eye level is taken as 1.2 m above floor level.

Correction terms can be applied to the uncorrected glare index to allow for changes in mounting height and lamp output per luminaire. At the present time there is no correction for other spacing-to-height ratios.

Uncorrected glare indices are tabulated according to room dimensions and reflectances. Figure 4.20 shows the method of

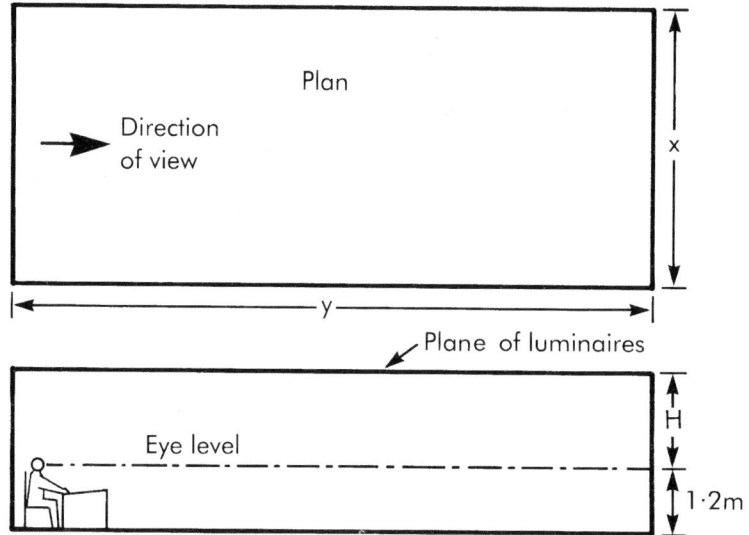

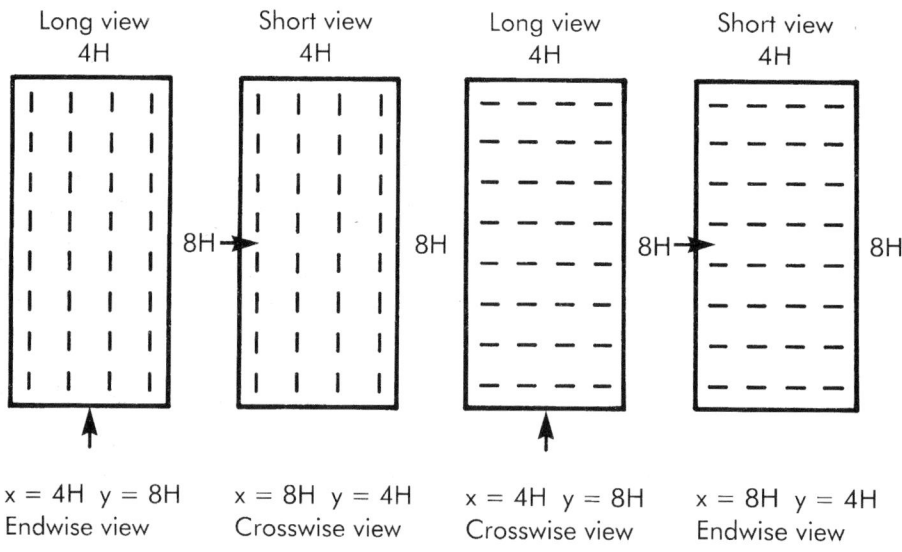

x = 4H y = 8H   x = 8H y = 4H   x = 4H y = 8H   x = 8H y = 4H
Endwise view   Crosswise view   Crosswise view   Endwise view

Figure 4.20 Method of specifying room dimensions in accordance with the direction of view for glare index calculations

specifying the room dimensions. The y dimension is always parallel to the line of sight and the x dimension is perpendicular to the line of sight. They are both expressed as multiples of the mounting height above eye level.

The worst glare condition will occur for viewing from the centre of either the long wall or the short wall. The tables permit either to be calculated by interchanging x and y.

One view of the room will show the ends of luminaires (end-wise view) and the other view will show the sides (cross-wise view). The two halves of the table cater for this.

When the glare index has been found (interpolation may be needed) it must be corrected for:

(*a*) mounting height above 1.2 m eye level if this differs from 2 m

(b) total lamp luminous flux per luminaire if this differs from 1000 lm

(c) extra correction terms if the published uncorrected glare index table covers a variety of luminaire sizes or lamp types.

These correction terms are added (or subtracted) from the initial glare index to give the final glare index of the installation.

The height correction term and the total luminous flux correction term can be calculated as follows:

Height correction term = $4 \log_{10} H - 1.2$ where H is the height above eye level (m).

Total lamp luminous flux per luminaire correction term

$$= 6 \log_{10} (n F) - 18$$

where F is the luminous flux per lamp (lumens) and n is the number of lamps per luminaire.

4.5.7 Emergency lighting

Emergency lighting is provided for use when the main lighting fails for whatever reason. There are two types: escape lighting and standby lighting.

Escape lighting

The *Fire Precautions Act 1971*[127] and the *Health and Safety at Work etc. Act of 1974*[22] make it obligatory to provide adequate means of escape in all places of work and public resort. Emergency lighting is generally considered to be an essential part of this requirement. *BS 5266 Code of practice for the emergency lighting of premises*[128], lays down minimum standards for the design, implementation and certification of emergency lighting installations.

Escape lighting is provided to ensure the safe and effective evacuation of the building. It must:

(a) indicate clearly and unambiguously the escape routes

(b) illuminate the escape routes to allow safe movement towards and out of the exits

(c) ensure that fire alarm call points and fire equipment provided along the escape route can be readily located.

See sections 3.3.2.18–3.3.2.21 for more information on emergency and escape luminaires.

Standby lighting

It may not be possible, or in some cases desirable, to evacuate some building areas immediately in the event of an emergency or power failure. This may be because life would be put at risk, as in a hospital operating theatre, or in some chemical plants where safe shut-down procedures must be used. In shops and offices, for instance, it may be advisable to determine the nature of the emergency before deciding upon evacuation. To evacuate a large store for a simple interruption of the public supply is to risk panic and the loss of stock by opportunist thieves. In these circumstances, standby lighting is required to allow appropriate actions to take place or activities to continue. The level of standby lighting will depend upon the nature of the activities, their duration and the associated risk, and can range from 50% to 100% of the maintained illuminance according to circumstances.

Standby lighting can be regarded as a special form of conventional lighting and dealt with accordingly. Escape lighting requires different treatment.

4.5.7.1   Escape lighting requirements

BS 5266[128] is part of the *Building Regulations* and is therefore a legal requirement. It also acquires legal status by being adopted as part of the local by-laws. Although most enforcing authorities quote *BS 5266*, many modify the conditions. For example, they may insist on a higher illuminance or a longer duration. In addition to any legal requirement, many organisations have their own more onerous standards. Therefore, the designer must thoroughly investigate all standards that may apply to the building[129,130].

For certain applications such as cinemas, theatres, lecture rooms and photographic darkrooms, the level of maintained emergency lighting and the luminance of signs must not adversely affect the primary use of the area.

Note: During the life of this *Code*, harmonised European emergency lighting standards being worked on in CEN/TC/169 and CENELEC 62(8) are likely to come into force. This may change some of the design values and equipment requirements quoted below.

4.5.7.2   Marking the route

All exits and emergency exits must have exit or emergency exit signs. Where direct sight of an exit is not possible, or there could be doubt as to the direction, then additional signs are required. These signs should comply with *BS 5499*[131].

4.5.7.3   Illuminating the route

BS 5266 requires that the minimum direct illuminance (i.e. excluding inter-reflections), measured at floor level, along the centre line of a clearly defined escape route should be 0.2 lux, and 50% of the route width for escape routes up to 2 m wide should be lit to a minimum of 0.1 lux. These criteria are sufficient for most interiors but for large open areas and auditoria, where many people may be assembled, other criteria are required and *BS 5266* should be consulted.

4.5.7.4   Other important factors

Speed of operation

The emergency lighting must be provided within 5 s of the failure of the main lighting system. If the occupants are familiar with the building, this time can be increased to 15 s at the discretion of the enforcing authority.

Glare

The emergency lighting luminaires should not cause problems of disability glare. Luminaires should be mounted at least 2 m above floor level to avoid glare but not be too high or they may become obscured by smoke.

Exits and changes of direction

Luminaires should be located near each exit door and emergency exit door and at points where it is necessary to emphasise the position of potential hazards, such as changes of direction, staircases, changes of floor level and so on.

Fire equipment

Fire fighting equipment and fire alarm call points along the escape route must be adequately illuminated at all reasonable times.

Lifts and escalators

Although lifts must not be used in the event of an emergency they should be illuminated. Emergency lighting is required in each lift car in which people can travel. Escalators must be illuminated to the same standard as the escape route to prevent accidents.

Special areas

Emergency lighting luminaires are required in all control rooms and plant rooms. In toilets, lobbies and closets exceeding 8 m^2, or if less than 8 m^2 without borrowed light, escape lighting should be provided as if it were part of an escape route.

4.5.7.5 Systems and calculations

The design aspects of conventional emergency lighting systems are discussed in detail in CIBSE *TM12*[61].

A proposed alternative system is to provide way-finding information (low-mounted luminous guidance and signage) along the escape route, rather than relying on general illumination. Such systems are currently under consideration for inclusion in the British Standard.

4.5.7.6 Maintenance and testing

The regular maintenance of emergency lighting equipment is essential to its correct operation. Generators will require periodic servicing of the prime mover, central batteries will require electrolyte checks, sealed batteries will need checking for loss of capacity and the luminaires will require checking for correct operation and light output.

A maintenance and testing schedule should be prepared based on the recommendations of the equipment manufacturers and the requirements of *BS 5266* and the appropriate enforcing authority.

4.5.7.7 Planning sequence

When planning an emergency lighting system the following sequence will help.

(*a*) Define the exits and emergency exits.

(*b*) Mark the escape routes.

(c) Identify any problem areas, e.g. areas that will contain people unfamiliar with the building, plant rooms, escalators, fire alarm call points, fire equipment etc.

(d) Mark the location of exit signs. These can be self-illuminated or illuminated by emergency lighting units nearby (see *BS 5499*[131]). Mark these on the plan.

(e) Where direction signs are required, mark these and provide necessary lighting.

(f) Identify the areas of the escape route illuminated by the lighting needed for signs.

(g) Add extra luminaires to complete the lighting of the escape route, paying attention to stairs and other hazards. Remember to allow for shadows caused by obstructions or bends in the route.

(h) Add extra luminaires to satisfy the problem areas identified in item (c) of this sequence. Make sure that lighting outside the building is also adequate for safe evacuation.

(i) Prepare a schedule for the regular maintenance and testing of all equipment and ensure that the building owners and operators are familiar with its requirements.

4.6   Design checklist

4.6.1   Checklist

The designer should check systematically that all the factors relevant to the design of the lighting installation have been taken into account. In the following checklist the headings indicate the areas to be considered and the most commonly occurring questions. In any specific situation there may be other questions which need to be considered.

4.6.1.1   Objectives

— Safety requirements: What hazards need to be seen clearly, what form of emergency lighting is needed, is a stroboscopic effect likely?

— Task requirements: Where are the tasks to be performed in the interior, what planes do they occupy? What aspects of lighting are important to the performance of these tasks? Are optical aids necessary?

— Appearance: What impression is the lighting required to create?

4.6.1.2   Constraints

— Statutory: Are there any statutory requirements which are relevant to the lighting installation?

— Financial: What is the budget available, and what is the relative importance of capital and running costs including maintenance?

— Physical: Is a hostile or hazardous environment present? Are high or low ambient temperatures likely to occur? Is noise from control gear likely to be a problem? Are mounting positions restricted, and is there a limit on luminaire size?

— Historical: Is the choice of equipment restricted by the need to make the installation compatible with existing installations?

4.6.1.3 Specification

— Source of recommendations: What is the source of the lighting recommendations used? How authoritative is this source?

— Form of recommendations: Have all the relevant lighting variables been considered, e.g. design maintained illuminance, uniformity, illuminance ratios, surface reflectances and colours, light source colour, colour rendering group, limiting glare index, veiling reflections?

— Qualitative requirements: Have the aspects of the design which cannot be quantified been carefully considered?

4.6.1.4 General planning

— Daylight and electric lighting: What is the relationship between these forms of lighting? Is it possible or desirable to provide a control system to match the electric lighting to the daylight available?

— Protection from solar glare and heat gain: Are the windows designed to limit the effects of solar glare and heat gain on the occupants of the building? Do the window walls have suitable reflectances?

— Choice of electric lighting system: Is general, localised or local lighting for task or display most appropriate for the situation? Does obstruction make some form of local lighting necessary?

— Choice of lamp and luminaire: Does the light source have the required lumen output, luminous efficacy, colour properties, lumen maintenance, life, run-up and re-strike properties? Is the proposed lamp and luminaire package suitable for the application? Is air handling heat recovery appropriate? Will the luminaire be safe in the environmental conditions? Will it withstand the environmental conditions? Does it have suitable maintenance characteristic and mounting facilities? Does it conform to *BS 4533*[88]/*EN60 598-1*[89] or other appropriate standard? Does the luminaire have an appropriate appearance and will it enable the desired effect to be created? Are reliable photometric data available?

— Maintenance: Has a maintenance schedule been agreed? Has a realistic maintenance factor been estimated based on the agreed schedule or, if not, have the assumptions used to derive the maintenance factor been clearly recorded? Is the equipment resistant to dirt deposition? Can the equipment be easily maintained, is the equipment easily accessible, and will replacement parts be readily available?

— Control systems: Are control systems for matching the operation of the lighting to the availability of daylight and the pattern of occupancy appropriate? Is a dimming facility desirable?

Have manual switches or local override facilities been provided, are they easily accessible and is their relationship to the lighting installation understandable?

— Interactions: How will the lighting installation influence other building services? Is it worth recovering the heat produced by the lamps? If so, have the air flow rates been checked in relation to the operating efficacy of the lamps?

4.6.1.5 Detailed planning

— Layout: Is the layout of the installation consistent with the objectives and the physical constraints? Has allowance been made for the effects of obstruction by building structure, other services, machinery and furniture? Has the possibility of undesirable high luminance reflections from specular surfaces been considered? Does the layout conform to the spacing-to-height ratio criteria?

— Mounting and electrical supply: How are the luminaires to be fixed to the building? What system of electricity supply is to be used? Does the electrical installation comply with the latest edition (with any amendments) of the *IEE Regulations for Electrical Installations*[67,87]?

— Calculations: Have the design maintained illuminance and variation been calculated for appropriate planes? Has an acceptable maintenance programme been specified? Have the most suitable calculation methods been used? Has the glare rating been calculated? Have up-to-date and accurate lamp and luminaire through-life photometric data been used?

— Verification: Does the proposed installation meet the specification of lighting conditions? Is it within the financial budget? Is the power density within the recommended range? Does the installation fulfil the design objectives?

4.7   Statement of assumptions

When submitting a design proposal to clients, it will usually be necessary to supply information on the following topics:

(a) the design specification, i.e. the type of lighting system, the design maintained illuminance, illuminance variation, the maintenance programme, the glare index, the lamp colour properties, the wall-to-task illuminance ratio, the ceiling-to-task illuminance ratio, and other criteria as applicable

(b) the equipment to be used, e.g. lamps, luminaires, control systems

(c) the layout of the equipment

(d) the costs, in an appropriate form

(e) the lighting conditions which will be achieved if the maintenance programme is implemented

(f) the calculation and measurement tolerances (see section 5.3.4) that apply to these values

(g) the power density and operating efficacy of the installation (*h*) all assumptions made in the design.

The level at which each of these topics is covered is a matter of commercial judgement. Ambiguity in the information supplied to the client should be avoided, particularly regarding the lighting conditions which will be achieved, the maintenance requirements and the assumptions made in the design. If the client is to compare design proposals on an equitable basis, ideally it is the client, or the client's consultant, who should specify the major design criteria and the assumptions to be made. In any case it is essential that the assumptions made in the design are stated by the designer for each aspect of the lighting conditions. Table 4.12 lists the assumptions that are usually involved in the estimation of the lighting conditions achieved by a general lighting installation. If localised lighting is being proposed, it will also be necessary to state the areas to which each illuminance applies and to give details for each area separately. If local lighting is being proposed, it will be necessary to give details of the general surround illuminance and the task illuminance, the latter being divided into the contributions from the local luminaire and from the general surround lighting. Special situations may involve additional assumptions, in which case these too should be stated.

Table 4.12 Assumptions to be made explicit when describing the lighting conditions that will be produced by a proposed general lighting installation (these assumptions may be made by the designer or by the client and given to the designer in the form of a specification)

Lighting condition	Assumptions that need to be stated
Initial illuminance	Room index, effective reflectance of ceiling cavity, walls and floor cavity used in establishing the utilisation factor; the initial luminous flux of the lamp used. Supply voltage, ambient temperature, obstruction losses etc.
Illuminance at a specified time	As for initial illuminance, plus the elapsed time for which the illuminance is given, and maintenance factor (see below).
Glare index	Calculation method and viewing position.
Wall-to-task illuminance ratio	As for initial and maintained illuminance.
Ceiling-to-task illuminance ratio	As for initial and maintained illuminance.
Vector/scalar ratio	As for initial and maintained illuminance.
Maintenance factor	Elapsed time for which maintenance factor is given, environmental conditions, lamp lumen maintenance factor, lamp survival factor and hours of operation of lamps, the luminaire maintenance factor and luminaire cleaning schedule, room surface maintenance factor and room cleaning and painting schedule.
Power density	As maintenance factor.
Operating efficacy	Maximum hours of use and hours of equivalent full installation use assumed in the calculation of load factor.

Part 5

Appendices

5.1   Financial appraisals

5.1.1   Introduction

It is desirable that life cycle costing, that is the consideration of all costs entailed in the lighting installation throughout its anticipated life, should be used when comparing proposals.

In attempting to put schemes in some order of merit there are two types of measures that may be applied.

Some lighting schemes will be designed to satisfy criteria that are not easily quantified. To compare such installations financially it is necessary to use appraisal methods that do not require a 'return' or income to set against the cost. Such methods include 'present value' (PV) which enables schemes to be placed in order of cost.

A more objective assessment is possible where schemes satisfy criteria that are easily quantified or are so precisely defined that the schemes are constrained to be more equal. Although the PV method is appropriate in determining a ranking, it may be possible to apply other methods which require some form of return.

The simplest example is where a new proposal is compared with an existing scheme. Here, it is usually the savings in energy and operating cost of the new installation which are used to justify the initial cost of the new equipment.

Suitable methods include 'simple payback', 'discounted cash flow' (DCF), 'net present value' (NPV) and 'internal rate of return' (IRR).

5.1.1.1   Initial costs

The initial costs of an installation should include all those costs that are incurred in getting the scheme installed and operating. These include:

— design: fees, site surveys, drawings

— luminaires: metalwork, optical system, control gear, lamps

— installation: wiring, fixing, switching, fusing

— controls: photocells, time switches, presence detection, energy management systems etc.

— builder's work: any alterations or additions that may be necessary to accommodate the lighting

— commissioning: checking and adjusting controls, testing circuits, measuring illuminances etc.

— making good: rectification of any faults not covered by guarantee.

It is all too easy to overlook some items of cost which could influence decisions. For example, using recessed modular luminaires could result in an additional cost if the ceiling aperture requires a special trim, or a saving if the ceiling tiles have been costed as a gross area and an area, equal to that of the luminaires, is not supplied. Free standing uplights will not require 'fixing' but may require up-rating of the electrical distribution system.

Other costs may be identified in relation to individual circumstances and it is important to ensure that all likely costs are considered when making comparisons.

5.1.1.2 Owning and operating

The annual cost of owning a lighting installation may include progressive payments of the initial purchase price, together with any interest, and will include operating costs which can, within a short time, far outweigh the initial purchase cost of a lighting installation and are usually made up of the following:

— energy: the cost of electricity to operate the installation and any control system

— re-lamping: cost of replacing lamps at the end of their economic lives

— cleaning: the cost of regular cleaning of lamps and luminaires to maintain the light output at the design level

— servicing: the cost of the labour for spot lamp replacement and the cost (initial and labour) of replacing any component failing or reaching the end of its economic life.

The energy costs of an installation will depend not only on the installed load but the hours and level at which it is operated. With a control system that responds to available daylight, time of day or occupancy levels, this may be difficult to determine without operating experience and an intelligent forecast must be made (see section 4.5.1). This will not automatically be the same for each installation.

It may also be necessary to consult the electricity supply company with regard to an appropriate tariff, as power factor, maximum demand, time of day or year and total units consumed may all affect the cost and can differ between installations (see section 4.5.1.2).

Annual lamp costs are usually shown as a proportion of their purchase price which is multiplied by the estimated annual operating hours and divided by the rated life. This may, however, require some modification. To minimise labour costs it is customary to coincide re-lamping with cleaning. Should the rated end of life not coincide with a cleaning operation it may be considered desirable either to change the lamp early and sacrifice some life or to change it late with the possible risk of failure or a depreciation in the task illuminance. Whichever is decided, the effective life should be used in place of rated life when calculating the annual cost. (The illuminance may also need to be recalculated, see section 4.5.2.6.)

The cost of cleaning should be carefully considered as it is all too easy to dismiss the cleaning of lamps and luminaires as a non-specialist job capable of being performed by the 'odd job' man. While this may occasionally be true, many luminaires require special cleaning materials and methods and are best dealt with by companies with experience in this field (see section 3.5 and Table 3.9, page 129).

The ideal cleaning interval will have been calculated but may need some adjustment (see section 4.5.2.6), to suit particular circumstances, such as a factory annual shutdown, stock-taking or other event which could facilitate the operation.

Lighting maintenance could include the cost of replacement prismatic panels as they age, ballast failures (usually towards the end of the life of the installation), reflector surfaces subject to corrosive deterioration, and so on.

All these costs need to be calculated, preferably on a year-by-year basis, but alternatively as an average annual figure, so that they can be inserted at the appropriate points in the financial assessment.

5.1.1.3 Benefits

Many financial assessments require an 'income' to set against expenditure so that a judgement can be made. The simplest example is that of a refurbishment where the expenditure of £x on new equipment results in an annual energy saving of £y, giving a payback period of x/y years.

Income may not, however, be so readily apparent and there may be other areas of return that should be considered. For instance, an assembly task may have a reject rate of 3%. The manufacturer may be aware that one third of the rejects are due to the intrinsic difficulty of the task. The other two thirds are attributed to various causes of which visual difficulty is one. Improving the lighting conditions could remove this difficulty with a consequent reduction in rejects. The savings due to this reduction should be considered as income and used to justify the cost of the improvement.

Such assessments can be used to examine the merits of various levels of lighting improvement, providing that some estimate of the consequent benefit can be made.

Apart from a reduction in errors and rejects, the following items may be applicable:

— increased productivity

— reduced absenteeism

— reduced crime (e.g. theft)

— improved safety

— improved staff recruitment

— improved morale

— improved amenity

— improved company image.

This list is not exhaustive and additional benefits will occur in relation to specific activities and organisations.

These benefits may not have an obvious direct financial return and some estimation may be necessary. The actual hours of absenteeism that are paid for can be costed, as can the value of lost production, but any 'knock-on' effect in other departments may not be so readily determined.

5.1.2 Appraisal methods

Engineers have tended to limit their financial involvement to calculating the simple payback period resulting from an investment. This may still be used as a first approximation but is not sufficiently refined to satisfy the financiers who may have several investment opportunities to appraise.

More refined methods that are accepted as suitable for comparisons are present value (PV), net present value (NPV), internal rate of return (IRR) etc. Which of these methods is preferred will depend on the accountancy practices of the investor but some comments on the factors in the calculation may be useful.

5.1.2.1 Life-cycle costing

It makes good sense to look not only at the initial costs of an installation, but also at its total cost throughout its anticipated, or required, life. A 100 W filament lamp may cost only a few pence, but if used for 4 000 h per year, will require changing every 1000 h and consume 400 units of electricity, plus labour costs. A compact 25 W fluorescent lamp will give around the same amount of light and cost many times more than the filament lamp. But it will last two or more years and consume only 100 units in the 4 000 hours, with a quarter of the labour costs.

Individuals will have their own expectation of installation life, but it is suggested that life-cycle costings should be based on the short term (five years) for the rapid change market, e.g. fashion retailers, the medium term (10 years) for the average user and the long term (20 years) for those situations where change is infrequent. Alternatively, developments in lighting equipment and techniques can be very rapid and may make the earlier replacement of an installation viable.

5.1.2.2 Interest rates

Fluctuations in interest rates are common and any attempt to forecast future rates is unlikely to be successful. To demonstrate the effect that interest rates can have on rankings, however, in the examples, Tables 5.4 to 5.6, three rates have been applied, namely 15% and then 10% and 20%, and it is suggested that, whatever interest rates may apply in the future, including rates a few percentage points either side of the norm would be prudent.

5.1.3 Examples

5.1.3.1 Simple financial appraisal

In assessing the value of any investment, two or more financial comparisons may be needed to give a comprehensive view. A liquidity index (payback), a growth index (net present value) or an earnings rate (yield) may each help to present a balanced picture.

Tables 5.1 to 5.3 show cost comparisons between colour-corrected mercury (HPM) lamps and two ratings of high pressure sodium (HPS) lamps as replacements for an existing filament (GLS) lamp installation.

It should be noted that the costs and quantities shown are for illustrative purposes only and do not necessarily represent real prices or numbers.

Table 5.1 deals with the initial purchase of equipment and the quantities of luminaires costed should be chosen to provide closely similar visual conditions. There is an opportunity here to bring out differences in the ease of installation and switching of individual types of luminaire.

Table 5.2 deals with the energy cost, considering total circuit consumption and power factor together with electricity cost. The example uses only a single unit price but this could be expanded to consider seasonal time of day (STOD) tariffs, maximum demand and fuel variation charges (section 4.5.1.2). The effect of the control system on hours of use can be shown (see sections 4.5.1.4 and 4.5.1.5, and Table 4.3, page 152).

Many large users of electricity will be metered in kVA rather than kW to take account of power factor. The electricity account will give full details of the current charges.

Table 5.1   Cost comparison: initial purchase costs

	Lamp type and wattage (W)			
	GLS	HPM	HPS	HPS
	1000	400	400	250
Number of luminaires	126	105	48	84
Cost of luminaires including gear (each) (£)		85	120	110
Cost of lamps (each) (£)	8	23	32	25
Cost of installation (each) (£)		50	60	55
Cost of switching, etc. (each) (£)		15	20	15
Total initial cost (£)		18 165	11 136	17 220

Table 5.2   Cost comparison: energy costs

	Lamp type and wattage (W)			
	GLS	HPM	HPS	HPS
	1000	400	400	250
Number of luminaires	126	105	48	84
Consumption (W)	1000	424	431	275
Power factor	1.0	0.85	0.85	0.9
Cost per kVAh(£)	0.07	0.07	0.07	0.07
Operating hours (h/year)	3000†	3000†	2700§	2500¶
Total energy cost (£)	26 460	10 999	4600	4491

Notes:
†   This assumes lighting is manually controlled with no set regime.
§   This assumes lighting is time switch controlled to coincide with working hours.
¶   This assumes lighting is controlled by an energy management system to optimise energy consumption.

Table 5.3   Cost comparison: operational costs

	Lamp type and wattage (W)			
	GLS	HPM	HPS	HPS
	1000	400	400	250
Number of luminaires	126	105	48	84
Cost of replacement lamp (£)	8	23	32	25
Cost of cleaning luminaire (£)	2.5	2.5	2.5	2.5
Cleaning period (years)	0.33	0.5	0.5	0.5
Maintenance cost (£/year)	4009	1491	752	1120
Total operating costs (£) from Tables 5.2 and 5.3	**30 469**	**12 490**	**5352**	**5611**

Table 5.3 considers the other operational costs, again presenting an opportunity to consider individual luminaire and lamp characteristics in life, soiling rate, ease of cleaning etc.

5.1.3.2 Comparisons

Traditionally, the engineer would look at the savings offered by the proposed alternatives and relate this to the capital required to arrive at a simple payback period.

5.1.3.3 Discounted cash flow (DCF)

An improvement to the simple payback calculation is to consider the discounted value of the annual savings. Money today is worth more than money in the future because it can be invested now to produce a greater sum in the future. If £100 were invested at a real rate of return of 10%, it would be worth £110 in one year's time. Put another way, £110 in one year's time is worth £100 today if discounted at 10%.

By discounting future savings by the rate of return expected on an investment it is possible to calculate what those savings are worth today. Tables are available[132] that give discount factors for single years, and cumulative factors for multiple years.

The factor for single year discounting is obtained from:

$$f = \frac{1}{(1 + \text{INT})^n}$$

where f is the discount factor, INT is the interest rate, and n is the number of years.

As an example, the factor for the third year at 10% would be:

$$\frac{1}{(1 + 0.1)^3} = 0.751$$

This calculation is often available as a financial function in spreadsheet programs, calculating the number of periods needed to reduce the present value of an investment to zero at a return per period for a given rate of interest.

The cumulative discount factor c over n years is given by:

$$c = \frac{[1 - (1 + \text{INT})^{-n}]}{\text{INT}}$$

5.1.3.4 Present value (PV)

The present value of money is calculated by discounting it at a rate of interest equivalent to the rate at which it could be invested.

$$\text{PV} = \text{Annual savings} \times c$$

The net present value (NPV) of an investment is the present value of the income (savings) that the investment will generate, less the capital cost of the investment.

$$\text{NPV} = \text{PV} - \text{Capital investment}$$

An investment of £10 000 which will show savings of £1000 per year over the existing system and have a life of 10 years will, if discounted at 10%, have the following values:

$$\text{PV} = £1000 \times 61446$$
$$= £6144.60$$

and

$$\text{NPV} = £6144.60 - £10\,000$$
$$= -£3855.40$$

As a generalisation, any investment that produced a negative NPV would not be considered viable. However, PV can be used in two ways. One would be to evaluate the worth of future income. In

Table 5.4   Example internal rate of return (IRR) calculation for interest rate of 15% and term of 5 years

| | Lamp type and wattage (W) | | |
| | HPM | HPS | HPS |
	400	400	250
Simple payback versus GLS (years)	1.01	0.44	0.69
Discounted cash flow (DCF) payback (years)	1.18	0.49	0.79
Present value (PV) (£)	60 269	84 196	83 326
Net present value (NPV) (£)	42 104	73 060	66 106
Internal rate of return (IRR) (%)	99	226	144

Table 5.5   Example internal rate of return (IRR) calculation for interest rate of 10% and term of 5 years

| | Lamp type and wattage (W) | | |
| | HPM | HPS | HPS |
	400	400	250
Simple payback versus GLS (years)	1.01	0.44	0.69
Discounted cash flow (DCF) payback (years)	1.12	0.48	0.75
Present value (PV) (£)	68 155	95 213	94 229
Net present value (NPV) (£)	49 990	84 077	77 009
Internal rate of return (IRR) (%)	99	226	144

Table 5.6   Example internal rate of return (IRR) calculation for interest rate of 20% and term of 5 years

| | Lamp type and wattage (W) | | |
| | HPM | HPS | HPS |
	400	400	250
Simple payback versus GLS (years)	1.01	0.44	0.69
Discounted cash flow (DCF) payback (years)	1.24	0.51	0.82
Present value (PV) (£)	53 768	75 115	74 339
Net present value (NPV) (£)	35 603	63 979	57 119
Internal rate of return (IRR) %	99	226	144

this case the higher the PV the more valuable the income. The other would be to evaluate future expenditure, i.e. the investment with the lower PV represents the better buy.

The term NPV is sometimes used to refer to the sum of the PVs. This often leads to confusion and it should be established whether income or expenditure is being considered and whether the capital investment has been included.

5.1.3.5   Internal rate of return (IRR)

IRR is that rate of interest which, when used to discount the cash flows associated with an investment project, reduces its net present value to zero. This is usually calculated by 'guessing' an interest rate and then refining that guess. Computers use an iterative technique requiring the initial investment and the cash flows together with a first guess at an interest rate.

Returning to the examples in Tables 5.1 to 5.3, Tables 5.4 to 5.6 provide example calculations of IRR.

It will be seen from the comparisons in Tables 5.4 to 5.6 that only DCF, PV and NPV are influenced by interest rates. The users should select those most appropriate to their needs.

5.2   Alternative calculations of illuminance

5.2.1   Introduction

The maintained illuminances recommended in this *Code* are to be provided on a plane appropriate for the application. This plane may be horizontal, vertical or inclined. However, there will be some applications for which:

(*a*) there are a large number of different planes which all have to be lit adequately by the same lighting installation

(*b*) the planes of interest are not defined for the lighting designer or are likely to change rapidly with time

(*c*) there are no obviously important planes.

In any of these circumstances the usual procedure is to assume the important plane is horizontal and design to provide the design maintained illuminance on this horizontal plane. For most cases this will give a satisfactory result because the inter-reflection of light in the space ensures that the illuminance of vertical and inclined planes is a reasonable proportion of the illuminance on the horizontal plane. This can be greater than 0.4 when the wall-to-task illuminance ratios suggested in Figure 2.1 (page 30) are met. However, where the inter-reflected proportion of the luminous flux in the interior is low, then this assumption is no longer valid. The inter-reflected component can be low because there is considerable obstruction within the space, because the room surface reflectances are low, or because the luminous intensity distribution of the luminaire is strongly directional, usually vertically downward. In these circumstances the designer can use one of three approaches to check that the installation proposed will give a satisfactory illuminance on planes other than the horizontal. These approaches are:

(*a*) calculate the illuminances on appropriate vertical planes

(b) calculate the mean scalar illuminance

(c) calculate the mean cylindrical illuminance.

5.2.2 Vertical illuminance

For all installations, the illuminance on a specific vertical surface can be calculated using a point-by-point method (see section 5.13), but for a regular array of symmetrical luminaires a simpler method is available. The average wall-to-task illuminance ratio due to a regular array of symmetrical luminances is virtually independent of the room index and depends principally on the luminaire and on surface reflectances. This means that the average illuminance on vertical surfaces should be approximately the same as the average wall illuminance.

This is found from the expression:

Average wall illuminance = average horizontal illuminance × wall-to-task illuminance ratio

The average horizontal illuminance is normally found by the lumen method; the wall-to-task illuminance ratio can be calculated by the methods given in CIBSE TM5[100]. See also section 4.4.3.3.

5.2.3 Scalar illuminance

The scalar illuminance is the average illuminance over the surface of a very small sphere at a point[133].

The mean scalar illuminance (i.e. the mean value of the scalar illuminance averaged over a horizontal reference plane) can be calculated by deriving the scalar utilisation factor by the method given in CIBSE TM5[100].

As a scalar illuminance is entirely independent of the direction from which the light is incident, it is a very appropriate measure for use in interiors where there are no obviously important planes. A hotel lobby is an example of such an interior. *For a satisfactory appearance, the mean scalar illuminance should be at least 40% of the illuminance on the horizontal plane. Methods of measuring scalar illuminance in the field are discussed in section 5.3.3.4.*

5.2.4 Mean cylindrical illuminance

The mean cylindrical illuminance is the average illuminance over the surface of a very small cylinder at a point, the axis of the cylinder being vertical[134]. It is related approximately to the mean scalar illuminance and the illuminance on a horizontal plane by the equation:

$$\overline{E}_c = 1.5\overline{E}_s - 0.25E_h(1 + \text{RE}_F)$$

where $\overline{E}_c$ is the average mean cylindrical illuminance (i.e. the mean cylindrical illuminance averaged over a horizontal reference plane); $\overline{E}_s$ is the mean scalar illuminance (i.e. the mean value of the scalar illuminance averaged over a horizontal reference plane); E_h is the illuminance on the horizontal reference plane; RE_F is the floor cavity reflectance.

The mean cylindrical illuminance is most sensitive to the illuminance on vertical planes and is insensitive to illuminance on horizontal planes. Therefore it can be used where vertical or near vertical planes are likely to be important. This is the situation in much of industry[135]. *For a satisfactory installation mean cylindrical illuminance should be at least 0.4 of the horizontal illuminance.* Methods whereby mean cylindrical illuminance can be measured in the field are discussed in section 5.3.3.5.

5.3 Verification of lighting installation performance

5.3.1 Aims of field appraisal and measurements

After an installation has been completed it is instructive for the designer to undertake an appraisal. In addition to the subjective assessment made by the designer, a completed appraisal should involve:

— a photometric survey of the initial lighting conditions achieved by the installation

— a discussion with the clients centred on their assessment

— a discussion with the users of the installation to discover their reactions.

The results of the photometric survey can be compared with the quantitative elements of the specification. Hence, the extent to which the installation meets the specification can be verified. The discussion with the clients and the users of the installation should reveal the extent to which the installation meets their expectations and requirements, although it may tell the designer more about the limitations of the original design objectives and specification than of the design itself. The justification for undertaking an appraisal is reassurance and education. Field measurements of lighting can also be part of a validation process or for identifying the causes of complaints about the lighting.

The same instrumentation is used whatever the purpose, although the nature of the measurements made will vary with the circumstances.

5.3.2 Instruments

Field measurements of lighting are usually undertaken with two basic instruments, an illuminance meter and a luminance meter.

5.3.2.1 Illuminance meters

Illuminance meters are available for illuminance from 0.1 lux to 100 000 lux full scale deflection, i.e. from emergency lighting conditions to daylight conditions.

Meters usually consist of a selenium or silicon photovoltaic cell connected directly, or indirectly by an amplifier, to an analogue or digital display. The quality of an illuminance meter is determined by five factors: spectral response, response to light incident on the photocell at different angles, linearity of response, sensitivity to temperature and accuracy.

Spectral response

The basic spectral response of both selenium and silicon photo-voltaic cells differs from that of the eye. Therefore to achieve accurate measurements of illuminance it is necessary to correct the spectral response of the photocell. This can be done either directly, by means of a filter over the photocell, or indirectly by providing correction factors to effectively recalibrate the photocell for different light sources. When filters are used the instrument is described as colour-corrected and can be used for all light sources, either separately or in combination. The accuracy of the result will obviously depend on the quality of the filter. The photocell whose spectral sensitivity is modified by correction factors supplied by the manufacturers, can only be used for those light sources for which correction factors are available and then only for installation of a single lamp type.

Cosine response

The response of illuminance meters to light falling on the photocell from different directions, is termed the cosine response. The measured illuminance E for light incident at an angle θ from the normal n to the photocell should follow the equation $E = E_n \cos \theta$. Illuminance meters which are not cosine corrected can give large measurement errors when used to measure illuminances where an appreciable proportion of the luminous flux comes at large deviations from the normal, e.g. when measuring daylight in side-lit rooms. Most illuminance meters are cosine corrected by means of either transparent hemispheres or flat diffusing covers. It is important that these covers are kept clean.

Linearity of response

The linearity of response of an illuminance meter is determined by the resistance of the circuit into which the output from the photocell is fed; the higher the resistance the greater will be the non-linearity of response at higher illuminances.

Sensitivity to temperature

The sensitivity of illuminance meters to temperature variations is also influenced by the resistance of the circuitry associated with the photocell. When resistance is high then extremes of temperatures will cause errors in measurement. Selenium photocells are considerably more sensitive to temperature than are silicon photocells. Prolonged exposure to temperatures above 50°C will permanently damage selenium photocells. Ideally, photovoltaic cells should be operated in ambient temperatures of about 25°C. They should not be used outside the temperature range of 15°C to 50°C. Within this temperature range errors will occur, but correction factors for different operating temperatures can be supplied by manufacturers.

Accuracy

Standards for two grades of portable photoelectric illuminance meters (Types P1 and P2) are given in *BS 667*[136]. Errors of measurement of ± 10% (Type P1) and ± 15% (Type P2) are permitted. This gives some idea of what is achievable even with a good quality illuminance meter when it is new. The sensitivity of illuminance meters varies with time and should be recalibrated at least once a year. This can be done by any photometric laboratory.

5.3.2.2 Luminance meters

Luminance meters are available which provide measurements over a range of 10^{-4} to 10^{8} cd/m^2 for areas varying from a few seconds of arc to several degrees.

A luminance meter consists of an imaging system, a photoreceptor, and a display. The optical imaging system is used to form an image of the object of interest on the photoreceptor. The photoreceptor produces a signal which is dependent on the average luminance of the image it receives. The object of interest must, therefore, fill the field of view in order to obtain valid readings. This signal is amplified and displayed in either analogue or digital form. By changing the imaging system it is possible to alter the field of view of the photoreceptor to give different areas of measurement. The photoreceptors used in luminance meters may be photovoltaic cells or photomultiplier tubes. The photovoltaic cells, as in illuminance meters, need to be colour corrected and used with associated circuitry to give a linear response and operate acceptably over a range of ambient temperature.

Photomultiplier tubes are more sensitive than photovoltaic cells. They are also more susceptible to vibration and magnetic fields and need a high voltage electrical supply. Like photovoltaic cells, photomultiplier tubes need to be colour corrected. The choice between photovoltaic cells and photomultiplier tubes is essentially one of the balance required between sensitivity and robustness.

5.3.3 Field surveys

5.3.3.1 General

It is essential when making field measurements to keep a complete and accurate record of the state of the lighting installation and the interior in general at the time the measurements are made. Particular attention should be given to the lamp type and age, the level and stability of the supply voltage, the state of maintenance of the lamps and luminaires, the surface reflectances, the degree of obstruction and any other factors which could influence the measurement. Photographs of the interior are a valuable supplement to a written record.

It is necessary to decide on the lighting conditions which are of interest. For example, is daylight to be admitted and, if it is, what type of control is to be used? Are the measurements to be concerned with average values over the interior or only individual workplaces? Should the measurements around the workplace be taken with the people present, etc?

Before starting to take measurements it is necessary to stabilise the performance of the lamps and luminaires and the meters. The time required to stabilise the light output of an installation depends on the nature of the lamp and luminaire. Installations using discharge lamps, including tubular fluorescent, require at least 20 min, and ideally one hour, before measurements are made.

To stabilise the reading of some meters the photocell should be exposed to the approximate levels to be measured for about 5 min before making the first measurement.

Daylight is rarely stable and hence the illuminance and luminance it produces can rapidly vary over a very large range. For this reason when measurements of the electric lighting installation alone are required, daylight must be excluded from the interior.

When carrying out a photometric survey the measurer must ensure that body shadows do not obstruct light reaching the photocell.

5.3.3.2   Average illuminance

The average illuminance over an interior is usually measured to check if an installation has achieved its design specification. For design calculations using computers it is practical to obtain a print out of illuminance over a large number of closely spaced grid points. With site measurements, for logistical reasons, the aim must be to obtain acceptably accurate results from a minimum number of points (see sections 4.5.4.1 and 5.3.3.3). To do this the following procedures are recommended, after the installation has been operating for an appropriate time at the design supply voltage. For discharge lamps this time is 100 hours, but it will be less for incandescent lamps.

Two methods of measurement of average illuminance are recommended. The first is based on a full grid of measurement points (see Figures 4.17, page 167 and 5.1) over the working plane or task areas which may also be used in the measurement of illuminance variation (see section 5.3.3.3). The second is a two-line method of measurement for average illuminance which may be used for a limited range of installations.

Full grid of measurement points

The interior is divided into a number of equal areas which should be as square as possible. The illuminance at the centre of each area is measured and the mean value calculated. This gives an estimate of the average illuminance. The accuracy of the estimate depends on the number of measurement points and the variation of illuminance.

Table 5.7 relates the room index to the number of measurement points necessary to give an error of less than 10%; the data in the Table are valid for spacing-to-height ratios up to 1.5:1[137].

Table 5.7   Relationship between room index and the minimum number of measurement points to obtain a value for average illuminance with an error of less than 10% (using a Type P1 meter, see section 5.3.2.1)

Room index	Number of points
Below 1	9
1 and below 2	16
2 and below 3	25
3 and above	36

The only limitation on the use of Table 5.7 is when the grid of measuring points coincides with the grid of lighting points; large errors are then possible and more points than the number given

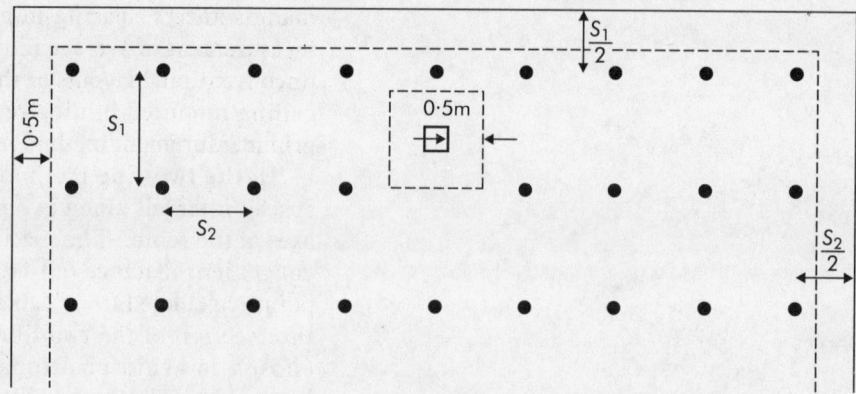

Figure 5.1 Layout of grid points for illuminance measurement (and calculation) over the core area of the working plane. The choice of grid spacings S₁ and S₂ is discussed in section 4.5.4.1.

should be used. The numbers of measurement points suggested are minima, and it may be necessary to increase their number to obtain a symmetrical grid to suit a particular room shape.

The following examples illustrate the use of the method:

(a) An interior measuring 20 m × 20 m and with luminaires mounted 4 m above the working plane has a room index of 2.5. A minimum of 25 points is therefore required, i.e. a 5 × 5 grid spaced at 4 m × 4 m.

(b) If the room measures 20 m × 33 m with the luminaires mounted at the same height, the room index of 3.1 indicates that a minimum of 36 points would suffice. To give a grid which is acceptably 'square', 40 points could be used, spaced at 4 m × 4.125 m.

(c) Re-entrant room shapes may be treated as separate, smaller rectangular areas and the closest spacing arrived at by the above method applied to the whole room. Thus a room of 25 m × 20 m with a 10 m × 10 m re-entrant portion at one corner may be considered as two areas of 20 m × 15 m and 10 m × 10 m. For a luminaire mounting height of 3 m the larger area has a room index of 2.8, indicating a minimum number of points of 4 × 6 = 24 at a grid spacing of 3.75 m × 3.3 m. The smaller area has a room index of 1.7 indicating a minimum number of points as 16 at a spacing of 2.5 m. A grid of points spaced at 2.5 m would be applicable to the whole space.

Measurements should be made at the height of the working plane but if this is not specified the measurements should be taken on a horizontal plane at 0.8 m above the floor. A portable stand or tripod is useful to support the photocell at the required height and inclination. Care should be taken not to cast a shadow over the photocell when taking the readings.

Two-line method of measurement

This method applies to rectangular rooms lit by a regular layout of ceiling-mounted luminaires which are installed at or below the manufacturers' spacing-to-height ratios[138]. It is not suitable for measurement of average illuminance in non-uniform installations, unconventional layouts or those consisting of mixtures of different ceiling mounted luminaires or uplighters. In such cases the full grid measurement method must be used.

In the two-line method, measurements are taken at evenly spaced intervals along two perpendicular lines parallel to the two axes of the room. The spacing of the measurements may be at any convenient distance but must not exceed the spacing of the grid points calculated from Table 5.7 and must include a reading at the intersection of the two lines. The intersection point should be chosen to avoid positions exactly below or midway between luminaires. The average illuminance E_x and E_y along the two lines of measurement are calculated and the average illuminance of the installation is:

$$E_{av} = E_x E_y / E_{is}$$

where E_{is} is the illuminance at the intersection point of the two lines.

5.3.3.3　Measurement of illuminance variation

To confirm compliance with the recommendations in section 2.4.3 requires information on illuminance conditions over the total area of the working plane to calculate illuminance 'diversity' and over task areas and their immediate surrounds to calculate 'uniformity'.

Diversity

For a wide range of commercial and industrial interiors where the visual task may be adversely affected by excessive variations in illuminance, the measurement procedure using a full set of grid points set out in section 5.3.3.2 above can be used. This will provide a coarse grid of points over the whole, or a representative area, of the core working plane. Additional measurements are then required, centred on selected points to check for local maximum and minimum illuminance values. These additional measurements are made on a 3×3 grid of points at about 1 m centres as discussed in section 4.5.4.1. In this procedure any measurement locations within 0.5 of room walls or large fixed obstructions are ignored.

Uniformity

To measure uniformity a 0.25 m square grid of measurement points is established over the task and its immediate surround at a number of representative positions. Task uniformity is assessed using the area-weighted arithmetic average of the measurement points within each task area and the minimum grid point illuminance value within that area. The lowest values of uniformity calculated from the measured values at the selected positions is taken as representative of the whole installation.

For measurement in an unfurnished area where there is no information on the task area and immediate surround dimensions, the grid shown in Figure 4.17 (page 167) should be used at selected positions within the core area (see section 4.5.4.1.)

5.3.3.4 Scalar illuminance

Scalar illuminance can be a useful measure of the lighting conditions when there are no obvious working planes in the interior (see section 5.2.3). For precise measurements of scalar illuminance, instruments based on a photocell with a diffusing sphere attached are available. However, a good approximation can be obtained using a conventional illuminance meter by averaging the illuminances measured on the six faces of a cube centred at the point. A better approximation can be given by the average of the illuminances on four faces of a regular tetrahedron centred at the point.

5.3.3.5 Mean cylindrical illuminance

Where information on the illuminance in vertical or near vertical planes is of interest then the measurement of mean cylindrical illuminance can be useful (see section 5.2.4). For precise measurement of mean cylindrical illuminance instruments based on a photocell with a diffusing cylinder attached are available. However, a good approximation can be obtained using a conventional illuminance meter and by averaging the illuminance measured on the four vertical faces of a cube centred at the point.

5.3.3.6 Illuminance vector

The illuminance vector is a measure of the 'flow of light' in a room. It can be combined with the scalar illuminance to give the vector/scalar ratio which is a measure of the modelling effect of the lighting (see section 4.4.3.3). Precise measurements of the magnitude and direction of the illuminance vector can be made using commercially available equipment based on a matched pair of cosine corrected photovoltaic cells mounted back-to-back. Alternatively, measurements of magnitude and direction can be obtained by the vector addition of the differences in illuminance between the three pairs of opposing faces of a cube centred at the point.

5.3.3.7 Luminance measurements

Luminance measurements are often made in response to complaints of over-brightness. In these circumstances the conditions which are the subject of complaint should be established and luminance measurements made from the position of the people who are complaining. In this way the source of the complaints may be identified. Luminances are most accurately and conveniently measured with a luminance meter. Particularly when measuring the luminance of light sources or luminaires, the meter should be mounted on a tripod and it is essential that the area of interest must fill the complete field of view of the meter. An estimate of the luminance of matt room surfaces can be obtained indirectly by measuring the reflectance of the surface and the illuminance (lux) on it and then calculating the luminance (cd/m^2) as follows:

$$\text{Luminance} = \frac{\text{Illuminance} \times \text{Reflectance}}{\pi}$$

5.3.3.8   Measurement of reflectance

The reflectance of a surface can be most accurately measured by the use of a luminance meter and a standard reflectance surface made from pressed barium sulphate or magnesium oxide. The luminances of the surface of interest and the standard reflectance surface are measured from an appropriate position. Then the reflectance of the surface of interest is given by the expression:

$$R = R_s L_1 / L_s$$

where R is the reflectance of the surface of interest, L_1 is the luminance of the surface of interest (cd/m^2), L_s is the luminance of the standard reflectance surface (cd/m^2), and R_s is the reflectance of the standard reflectance surface.

The above method can be used to obtain the luminance factor (or gloss factor) for non-matt surfaces where local values of luminance, from defined viewing positions, are of interest. This has little or no relevance to the average value of the inter-reflected illuminance received on the working plane or other room surfaces.

If a luminance meter is not available, then an approximate measure of the reflectance of a surface can be obtained by making a match between the surface of interest and a sample from a range of colour samples of known reflectance (see Tables 5.8 and 5.9).

5.3.3.9   Daylight measurements

As stated earlier, the illuminance and luminance produced in an interior by daylight can vary widely and rapidly. For this reason, the daylight available in an interior is usually expressed in terms of daylight factor rather than in terms of illuminance and luminance. If required, the daylight factor can be measured. Full details are given in reference 2.

5.3.4   Tolerances or uncertainty

From the information given in this appendix it will be clear that there are many factors which can cause disparity between the calculated prediction and the measured performance of a lighting installation.

In section 5.3.2.1 the characteristics and accuracy of measurement equipment are described whilst in sections 5.3.3.1–5.3.3.3 guidance is given on the procedure to be followed when conducting a photometric survey. This will reduce measurement uncertainty and noted site conditions may explain certain variations from the predicted performance, particularly in the case of average values.

For point values and diversity, and to a lesser extent uniformity, even when the best survey practice is followed it is still possible to find a disparity. The main reason for this is that, even if the calculation process is of the highest possible accuracy, it is assumed that all the individual lamps, circuits and luminaires provide an identical photometric performance. As this is clearly impossible, some tolerance must be expected. The magnitude of the difference will depend on the type of lighting equipment used and the manufacturer should be asked to advise on the magnitude of variation to be expected. Even then, the random distribution of individual high and low performance equipment within the layout cannot be allowed for except on the basis of probability, as the influence of this on the result is unlikely to be all positive or all negative.

5.4   Glare formulations

5.4.1   Disability glare

Consider a situation where a source of high luminance lies close to a task. The light from the source will be scattered in the eye across the retinal image of the task. The effect of this scattered light is to reduce the contrast of the task and to change the local state of adaptation of the retina. Furthermore, the retinal image of the high luminance source will induce changes in the operating state of the surrounding retinal areas. The net effect of these changes is to reduce the visibility of the task. This phenomenon is known as disability glare.

The extent of disability glare can be quantified by measuring the luminance of a uniform field which, when placed over the task, produces the same reduction in task visibility as does the disability glare. This equivalent veiling luminance, as it is known, can be measured in the laboratory but for field conditions it is more convenient to calculate it. Different experimenters have produced different formulae relating the equivalent veiling luminance to the physical conditions[139, 140, 141] but the most generally accepted formula is:

$$L_v = 10 \sum_{j=1}^{n} \frac{E_j}{\theta_j^2}$$

where L_v is the equivalent veiling luminance (cd/m^2); E_j is the illuminance at the eye on a plane perpendicular to the line of sight, from the jth glare source; and θ_j is the angle between the line of sight and the jth glare source ($^\circ$).

This formula holds for values of θ_j from 1.5° to 60°. For values of θ_j of less than 1.5° a different formula has been proposed[142]. This is:

$$L_v = 9.2 \sum_{j=1}^{n} \frac{E_j}{\theta_j^{3.44}}$$

where the terms have the same meaning and units as above. These two equations demonstrate that disability glare is greatest for glare sources very close to the line of sight, and diminishes rapidly with deviation from the line of sight.

The effect of equivalent veiling luminance on the contrast of a task can be estimated by adding the equivalent veiling luminance to the luminance of task detail and the luminance of the task background equally. The resulting contrast can be considered as the effective task contrast in the presence of disability glare.

The formula for effective task contrast is

$$C_e = \left| \frac{(L_t + L_v) - (L_b + L_v)}{(L_b + L_v)} \right| = \left| \frac{(L_t - L_b)}{(L_b + L_v)} \right|$$

where C_e is the effective task contrast; L_t is the luminance of task detail (cd/m^2); L_b is the luminance of task background (cd/m^2); L_v is the equivalent veiling luminance (cd/m^2).

Note that the vertical lines are a modulus symbol which means that the sign of the contrast is ignored.

It should be noted that this formulation of disability glare assumes a static viewing situation. Furthermore, the magnitude of the disability glare is determined by the illuminance at the eye and not by the luminance of the glare source. Therefore these formulae cannot take account of situations where the luminance of the glare source is sufficient to produce after-images. Fortunately, disability glare is a rare occurrence with interior electric lighting. Light sources which might act as sources of disability glare either tend to be located away from common lines of sight or they create sufficient discomfort to cause remedial action to be taken thus avoiding significant disability glare.

One value of the disability glare formula is that it applies to disability glare from small high luminance sources and large area sources. In many ways large area sources are worse because there may be no discomfort associated with them.

5.4.2 Discomfort glare from electric lighting

Discomfort glare is likely to be experienced whenever some part of the interior has a much higher luminance than occurs in the rest of the interior. By far the most common sources of high luminances in interiors are luminaires and windows. The discomfort glare effect of windows is discussed in section 5.4.3.

The magnitude of the discomfort glare which will be produced by an electric lighting installation can be estimated by calculating the glare index[126]. The basis of this index is a formula for the discomfort glare caused by small area sources[143,144]. The formula for obtaining the glare index for a lighting installation is:

$$\text{Glare index} = 10 \, \log_{10} \frac{0.45}{L_b} \sum_{j=1}^{n} \frac{L_j^{1.6} \, \omega_j^{0.8}}{L_b P_j^{1.6}}$$

where L_j is the luminance of the jth glare source (cd/m^2); L_b is the average luminance of the field of view, excluding the glare source (cd/m^2); ω_j is the subtended area of the jth glare source (steradians); P_j is the position index of the jth glare source which increases with increasing deviation from the line of sight.

This formula can be applied to individual, randomly arranged or regular arrays of luminaires for any specified direction of view. A simplified tabular method based on the above formula applied to a set of standard conditions is given in CIBSE *TM10*[126] as well as advice on computing procedures suitable for use with the basic formula.

The glare index system can be applied to a wide range of conventional luminaires, but it does have some limitations. It cannot be applied to large area light sources such as luminous ceilings because the basic formula is then invalid. It cannot be applied to coffered ceilings and similar large cut-off luminaires because of the difficulty of deciding what constitutes the luminaire. Also it may underestimate the discomfort glare for some ceiling-mounted luminaires, specifically those where the luminaire luminous intensity distribution is such that the luminance of the ceiling immediately adjacent to the luminaire is greater than the luminance of the luminaire itself.

Given that a glare index has been calculated for an installation, the designer still has to decide whether or not the installation will be considered unacceptably glaring. The schedule in section 2.6.4 contains recommended values of limiting glare index for specific applications. These are the values which should not be exceeded if discomfort is to be avoided. These limiting glare indices are based on formal assessments of the level of discomfort glare appropriate for different applications[145] and on field experience. The indices are set three units apart; such a difference being necessary for a significant change in discomfort glare sensation to occur.

International agreement has recently been reached with CIE on an alternative formula, the unified glare rating (UGR) and it is anticipated that this will replace the glare index during the life of this edition of the *Code*.

5.4.3 Discomfort glare from daylight

Visual discomfort from windows can be minimised by the following measures:

— ensuring that the sky, seen through a window, does not lie in the immediate field of view with a visual task

— avoiding specular reflection of windows by VDT screens, desktops, chalkboards or similar surfaces

— reducing the brightness contrast between the sky, seen through a window, and the surrounding window wall; this may be achieved by measures such as splayed window reveals, louvres, translucent curtains, and by increasing the illuminance on the window wall[126] (see section 2.4.5.2).

5.5 Contrast rendering factor

5.5.1 Definition of contrast rendering factor

The luminance contrast of a target is defined as:

$$\text{Luminance contrast} = \left| \frac{L_t - L_b}{L_b} \right|$$

where L_t is the luminance of the target (cd/m^2), L_b is the luminance of the background (cd/m^2).

Note that the vertical lines are a modulus symbol which means that the sign of the contrast is ignored.

In a practical task, such as reading this print, the 'target' would be the black ink and the 'background' the paper on which it is printed. The term 'task' includes both target and background.

The contrast rendering factor is most conveniently defined as a ratio of luminance contrasts for a given task[146,147]. Specifically, the contrast rendering factor of a task occurring at a given position under a particular lighting installation, i.e. 'real' lighting, and viewed from a stated direction is defined as:

$$\text{CRF} = C_1/C_2$$

where CRF is the contrast rendering factor, C_1 is the luminance contrast of the task under the real lighting, C_2 is the luminance contrast of the target under reference lighting viewed from the same direction.

The reference lighting condition is completely diffuse and unpolarised illumination such as can be produced in an integrating sphere[148]. The reference lighting condition is chosen for its ease of replication rather than some inherent quality. Contrast rendering factor can vary from zero to greater than unity. When CRF is less than unity the contrast of the task under the real lighting is reduced from what it is under reference conditions. When CRF is greater than one the contrast of the task is greater under the real lighting and when CRF is equal to one, the contrast of the target is the same under both real and reference lighting conditions.

5.5.2 Features which affect contrast rendering factor

A contrast rendering factor is specific to a particular task at a particular point under a particular real lighting installation, viewed from a particular direction. Changing any one of these features may change the CRF. There is no such thing as a CRF for a particular real lighting installation, there will always be a range of CRF values[149]. To estimate what this range is likely to be in any situation it is necessary to understand the factors which determine the CRF value.

5.5.2.1 Specularity

The greater the specularity of the target the larger the range of CRF values that will occur in an interior. Figure 5.2 shows two samples, one of matt print on matt paper, the other of specular pencil writing on matt paper. Both samples are lit in the way described in the figure captions ((a), (b), (c) and (d)). There are very few reflections in the matt print on the matt paper for either method of lighting but for the pencil writing on paper, when the lighting is above and in front of the observer, the light source is reflected towards the viewer with the consequence that strong veiling reflections occur. This means that the contrast of the writing on the paper is reduced. It will be appreciated that the CRF of the specular pencil writing on matt paper will be much less than the CRF of the matt print on matt paper for the same lighting conditions.

5.5.2.2 Lighting/task/viewer geometry

When a source of high luminance (usually a luminaire) is positioned such that it is specularly reflected towards the viewer, veiling reflections can occur. The light which is specularly reflected from the task to the viewer originates from an area called the offending zone (Figure 5.3).

5.5.2.3 Luminance in offending zone

It is only when a source of relatively high luminance occupies the offending zone that veiling reflections occur. For reference lighting conditions the offending zone has the same luminance as all the other parts of the photometric sphere, so few veiling reflections will occur, but when a conventional ceiling-mounted luminaire occupies the offending zone it will cause veiling reflections because it has a much higher luminance than most other parts of the room.

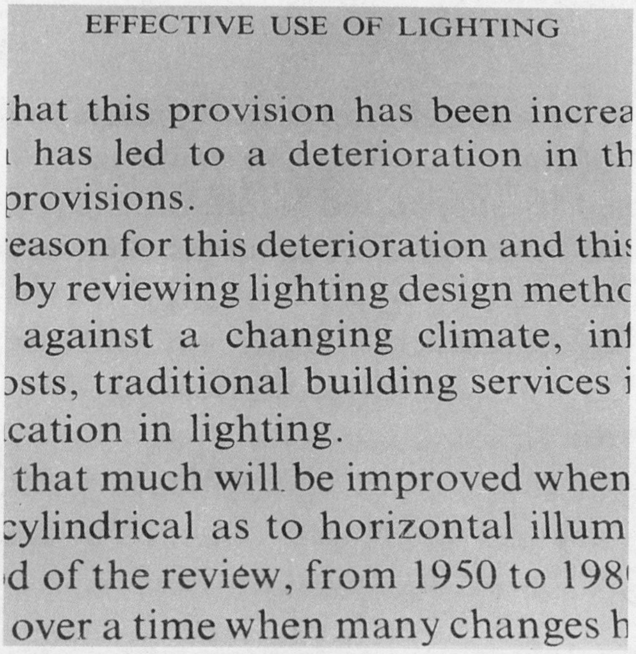

EFFECTIVE USE OF LIGHTING

:hat this provision has been increa
has led to a deterioration in th
provisions.
reason for this deterioration and this
by reviewing lighting design metho
against a changing climate, int
osts, traditional building services i
cation in lighting.
that much will be improved when
cylindrical as to horizontal illum
d of the review, from 1950 to 198(
over a time when many changes h

(a) Matt ink on matt paper lit from above and behind observer

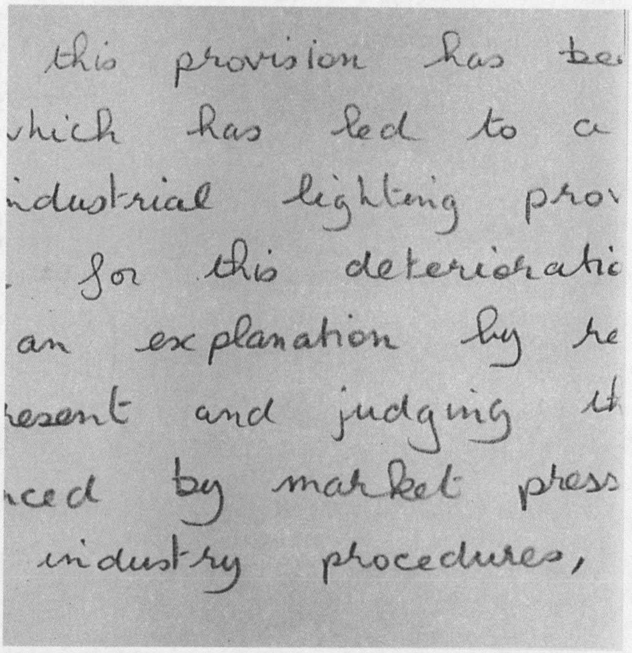

this provision has be
which has led to a
industrial lighting pro
. for this deteriorati
an explanation by he
resent and judging th
ced by market press
industry procedures,

(b) Pencil writing on matt paper lit from above and behind the observer

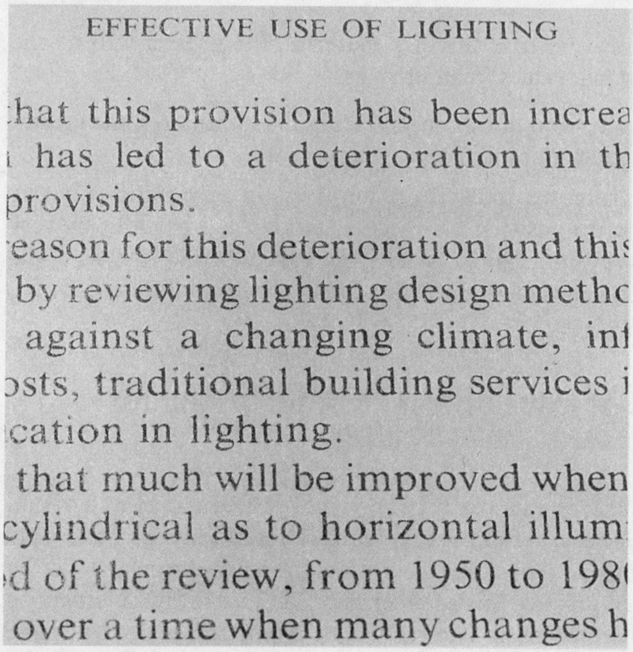

EFFECTIVE USE OF LIGHTING

:hat this provision has been increa
has led to a deterioration in th
provisions.
reason for this deterioration and this
by reviewing lighting design metho
against a changing climate, int
osts, traditional building services i
cation in lighting.
that much will be improved when
cylindrical as to horizontal illum
d of the review, from 1950 to 198(
over a time when many changes h

(c) Matt ink on matt paper lit from above and in front of the observer

this provision has be
which has led to a
industrial lighting pro
n for this deteriorati
an explanation by r
resent and judging t
ced by market pres
industry procedures,

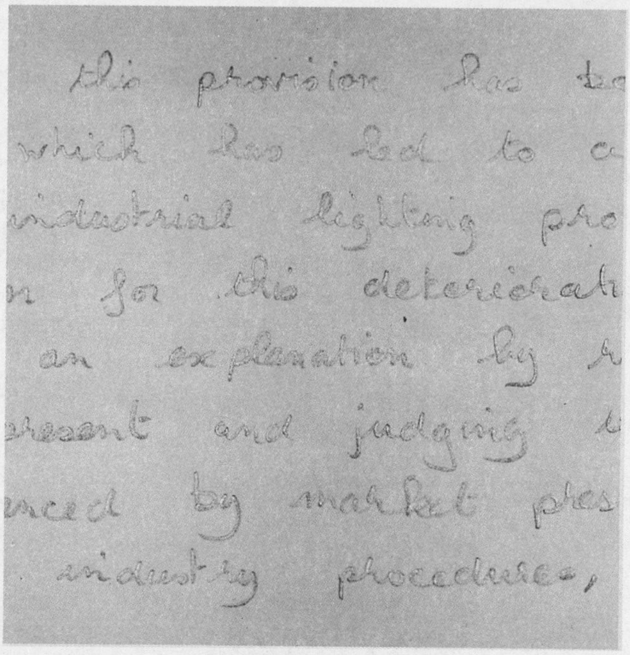

(d) Pencil writing on matt paper lit from above and in front of the observer

Figure 5.2   Differences in specular reflections and hence in visibility for two different lighting arrangements and two different tasks

In practical terms this usually means that the important factors are the specularity of the target, the position and viewing direction of the task, and the luminance of the parts of the luminaires which may occupy the corresponding offending zones.

The practical implications of these aspects are discussed in references[148,149]. However, the conclusions can be summarised in two general rules:

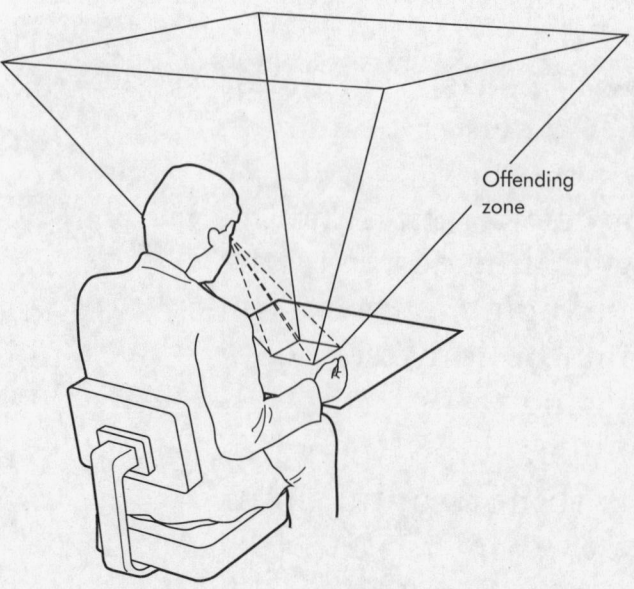

Figure 5.3   Schematic diagram of offending zone

(*a*) The more specular the task material, the greater will be the range of CRF values in an interior

(*b*) The smaller and more concentrating the luminaires, the greater will be the variation of CRF with position.

These two rules act in combination. Very large variations in CRF will occur with position for specular targets in a room lit by very concentrating luminaires. Very little variation in CRF will occur with positions for matt targets in a room lit by very diffuse lighting, e.g. indirect lighting.

5.5.3   Effects of low contrast rendering factor values

Low CRF values can affect both visual performance and visual comfort. Because low CRF values imply reduced contrast, where task performance is dependent on contrast, then performance will be reduced. In practice this occurs rarely, because for most situations either the reduction in contrast is not important or the CRF value can be restored to a higher value by changing the viewing position. However, where the task contrast is critical to the performance of the task and the range of viewing positions restricted, then care should be taken to avoid low CRF values.

The most usual effect of low CRF values is that of visual discomfort. Even when performance can be maintained in the presence of veiling reflections, the knowledge that the lighting is reducing the contrast of the task is irritating and will give rise to complaints about the lighting. Figure 5.4 shows some results of the degree of disturbance felt with different practical materials seen at different levels of CRF[150]. It can be seen that as CRF values decrease the level of disturbance increases.

From these and other results[151,152,153] it can be concluded that a CRF value of 0.7 is the minimum that should occur at work stations if visual discomfort is to be avoided. It should be noted

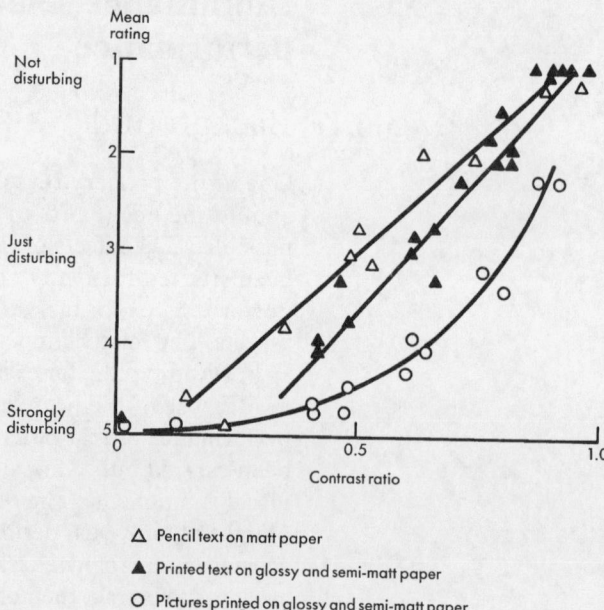

△ Pencil text on matt paper

▲ Printed text on glossy and semi-matt paper

○ Pictures printed on glossy and semi-matt paper

Figure 5.4   Mean ratings of disturbance caused by veiling reflections for various contrast rendering factors

that this criterion does not apply to very glossy materials. For such materials it is possible to have contrast reversal occurring, i.e. glossy black lettering becomes brighter than matt white paper. Contrast reversal will give a high CRF value but it is considered an unsatisfactory aspect of lighting[154].

5.5.4   Prediction of contrast rendering factor

When designing a new installation, the CRF has to be calculated rather than measured. Completely general calculations which can be applied to any task and any installation require computer programs of some complexity, and detailed information about the photometric performance of the luminaire and the reflection characteristics of the target. Such programs exist[155] and the necessary photometric information is available for a few targets. The principles used in the calculation procedure are discussed in reference[156].

However, a limited but more easily applied procedure has been developed[157] which only applies to pencil on a matt background. This results in a diagram analogous to the isolux diagram (Figure 4.18, page 169), but which specifies the CRF at various positions relative to a single luminaire. For a regular array of luminaires, the method can also provide a value of CRF that could be considered as typical for an installation.

5.5.5   Measurements

Exact measurements of contrast rendering factor require accurate measurements of target and background luminance to be made under the actual and reference lighting conditions. From these, the luminance contrast of the task can be calculated and hence the CRF can be obtained. Other approximate measurement techniques are also discussed in the references.

5.6   Illuminance selection based on visual performance

5.6.1   Background

One of the primary reasons for the lighting of work places is to enable the occupants to carry out their work as efficiently as possible. The effects of lighting on the performance of tasks has been studied for many years. As discussed in section 1.3.1 the performance of a task depends on both visual and non-visual aspects. The relative importance of these varies greatly from task to task; audio-typing, for example, is almost entirely non-visual.

Because of the problems associated with the measurement of performance of real tasks, most of the experimental studies have been carried out using simulated tasks designed to have a high visual component. The results have thus demonstrated the effects of lighting on visual performance, measured in terms of speed and accuracy more than on task performance. Some analyses have made attempts to extract the non-visual components to arrive at a purely visual performance function. More or less convincing attempts have then been made to relate the visual performance results to the performance of real tasks.

Major studies in the UK by Weston and his colleagues in the 1930s and 1940s[11] using arrays of Landolt rings produced the familiar relationships showing performance increasing as illuminance or contrast increases, but with diminishing returns (Figure 1.6, page 5). This general relationship has been confirmed in a number of subsequent studies, most recently by Rea[158,159]. He has devised an empirical model, based on studies of reaction times, relating relative visual performance (RVP) to the contrast and size of the task together with the luminance to which the observer is adapted, described by the illuminance on the retina. This model is the best model of visual performance currently available.

As a person ages, less light reaches the retina. This is caused by a decrease in pupil size and a reduction in light transmission through the crystalline lens. These changes affect a person's retinal illuminance and hence relative visual performance. Allowances can be made for these effects[17]. Thus, if the size and contrast of a visual task are known, together with the age of the observer, the task luminance required to achieve a given criterion of relative visual performance may be determined. This approach to illuminance selection is most applicable to tasks with a high visual component and low non-visual component, for example searching for an entry in a telephone directory.

5.6.2   Visual performance model

The model of visual performance developed by Rea is based principally on studies of reaction time[158]. These involved subjects pressing a button as soon as they saw a target appear on a VDT screen. A range of target size and contrast was studied and subject adaptation luminance was also varied. The results are shown in Figure 5.5. This task is almost entirely visual, containing only a very small non-visual component: pressing the button to indicate detection of the target. Rea had previously carried out studies using a task with a slightly larger non-visual component[159]. This required the comparison of lists of numbers to find differences which were then marked using a pencil. He has shown that the results of this, perhaps more realistic, task are compatible with the visual performance model generated from the reaction time study.

5.6.2.1 Limitations of procedure

(*a*) The model of visual performance on which the procedure is based has been developed for simple, highly visual tasks. Its predictions have not been tested against many real tasks which contain significant non-visual components.

(*b*) The task variables included in the visual performance model are size and contrast. While these are important, there may be some

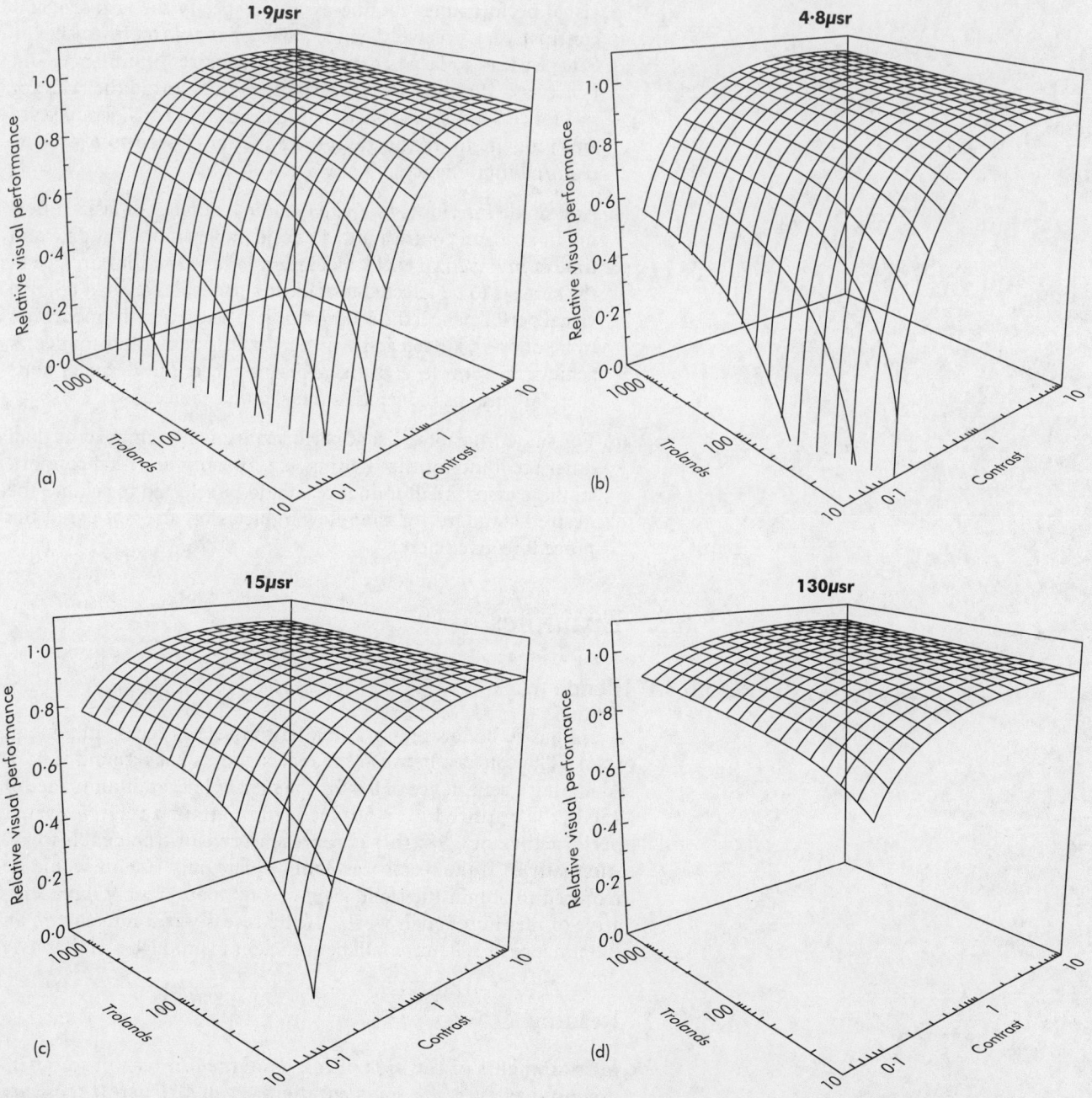

Figure 5.5 Relationship of relative visual performance (RVP) with retinal illuminance in trolands (see section 6.1) and contrast for task size from 1.9 to 130 microsteradians (μsr)[158,159]

tasks which are influenced by other aspects such as movement. Further, the measurement of size is a simple area measure, in steradians; there may be difficulties in defining the relevant area for many real tasks.

(c) The relationship between task size, task contrast, luminance and relative visual performance is shown in Figure 5.5. The shape of the relationships is such that over a wide range of size and contrast, relative visual performance is reasonably insensitive to luminance. This has considerable implications for the use of the model. For a chosen illuminance, and hence luminance, the model can be usefully employed to check that the relative visual performance is acceptable for a particular task size and contrast. Alternatively, if the model is used to determine the task luminance required to obtain a desired relative visual performance, it is necessary to specify the task size and contrast very precisely, since small changes in either size or contrast lead to large changes in the required luminance, and hence task illuminance. Uncertainties in defining the relevant size for real tasks, discussed in (b), means that considerable care and judgement are needed if the model is used to prescribe required illuminances.

(d) Any single interior is likely to contain a number of tasks differing in size and contrast and a considerable amount of data and time is involved in each calculation[160]. If the illuminance of the space is to be selected to achieve a particular level of relative visual performance, the relevant task to be used in the model has to be chosen, since each will need a different illuminance to achieve the same level of visual performance. The designer must therefore use his judgement to make this choice.

(e) For some interiors, visual performance is less important than other attributes of the lighting, e.g. amenity or visual comfort. In these cases the illuminance should be selected to achieve the desired standard for the relevant criterion and not using the procedure given here.

5.6.3 Examples

5.6.3.1 Bench work

A pin has to be located in a small 1mm square recess in a metal plate. The contrast between the recess and its background is 0.25. Assuming a reflectance of 0.4 for the metal plate, an illuminance of 750 lux is required for a 50-year old to attain a relative visual performance of 0.98; this is representative of fine bench work. Alternatively if the recess was 3 mm square only 500 lux would be required to obtain the same level of RVP; more closely representative of medium bench work. If the recess was 5 mm square an illuminance of 300 lux would be sufficient to produce a similar RVP.

5.6.3.2 Reading

Measurements of the area of ink contained in lists of numbers produced an average equivalent digit size of 4.76 μsr. If these are printed with a contrast of 0.7 on paper of reflectance 0.8 and viewed under an illuminance of 500 lux, a 50-year old observer should achieve a relative visual performance of 0.981.

These examples assume that the viewing distance remains constant so that the apparent size of the task increases as its physical size increases. In practice, the worker may well resort to moving closer to a small task to increase its apparent size. This 'peering' at small tasks is to be deprecated on the grounds that it may introduce additional fatigue and increase the risk of injury if machine tools or other moving parts are involved.

5.6.3.3 Conclusions

This approach to illuminance selection has the merit that the assumptions made in arriving at the illuminance are explicit and the consequences of choosing a different illuminance can be examined. However, the illuminance chosen is always a matter of judgement. When the visual performance procedure is employed the designer must make a judgement on factors such as task size and contrast and the likely age of the users of the room. Alternatively the designer may feel more comfortable using his experience of lit spaces to make a judgement on the likely acceptable illuminance for the activities which will be performed in the space. The visual performance model can then be used to check that, for a particular task and observer, the relative visual performance achieved will be acceptable.

In view of the current uncertainties and limitations to this procedure, described above, the recommendations of illuminance contained in the schedule (section 2.6.4 of this *Code*) have been determined by general consensus, as in previous editions of the *Code*. Checks have been carried out using the procedure described in this section. The procedure may prove valuable where a designer wishes to analyse a particular situation involving a specific highly visual task.

5.7 Colour order systems and surface reflectances

The colour of a light source can be specified by its chromaticity co-ordinates in the CIE 1931 xy diagram or the CIE 1976 $u'v'$ uniform chromaticity scale diagram (section 5.7.4). The luminance is also needed for a full specification of the source.

Chromaticity co-ordinates can be used for surface colours together with the luminous reflectance factors but a more usual method is to transform these values into co-ordinates for use in either the 1976 CIELUV or CIELAB colour spaces (section 5.7.4).

Surface colours can also be arranged in a specified way to form a colour solid and four such systems are described in the following sections.

5.7.1 Munsell system

The colours of surfaces are conveniently defined by the Munsell system[161], in terms of three perceptual attributes: hue, value and chroma.

Hue describes the apparently dominant part of the spectrum occupied by the colour, e.g. red, as distinct from yellow or blue. The various hues are located in different sectors of the Munsell colour solid in Figure 5.6. There are five principal hues and five intermediate hues:

— principal hues: red (R), yellow (Y), green (G), blue (B), purple (P)

— intermediate hues: yellow red (YR), green yellow (GY), blue green (BG), purple blue (PB), red purple (RP).

Chroma is the strength of the colour and increases radially in Figure 5.6 from neutral grey (zero chroma) to a maximum which depends upon the hue and reflectance of the surface. Surfaces having zero chroma, and therefore no hue, are denoted Neutral (N).

Value, plotted vertically in Figure 5.6, measures the lightness of the surface from 0 (perfect black) to 10 (perfect white). This is another way of describing reflectance, but differs numerically from reflectance in an important respect: each of the three Munsell scales is divided in such a way that equal intervals of hue, value or chroma denote equal steps in perceived contrast (though the value scale does not have the same spacing as the hue or chroma scales).

The relation between reflectance R (%) and Munsell value V is given by the equation:

$$R = 1.1914V - 0.22533V^2 + 0.23352V^3 - 0.020484V^4 + 0.0008194V^5$$

However the following approximation is easily remembered, and sufficiently accurate for most practical purposes:

$$R = V(V-1)$$

The Munsell co-ordinates for a coloured surface comprise hue, value and chroma, in that order. For example, Munsell reference 2.5GY 6/8 indicates that the hue is 2.5GY, a distinctly yellowish green, the value is 6, which means a reflectance of about 0.3, and the chroma is 8 (moderately saturated but not startling).

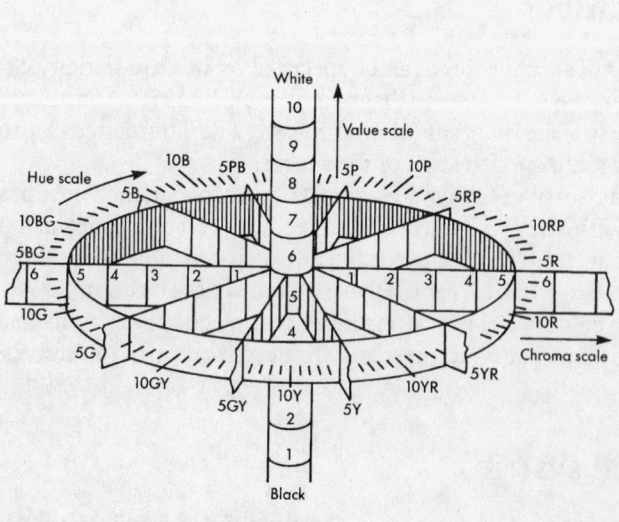
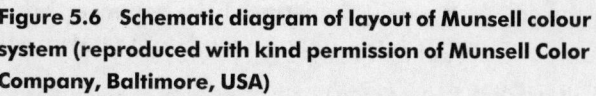

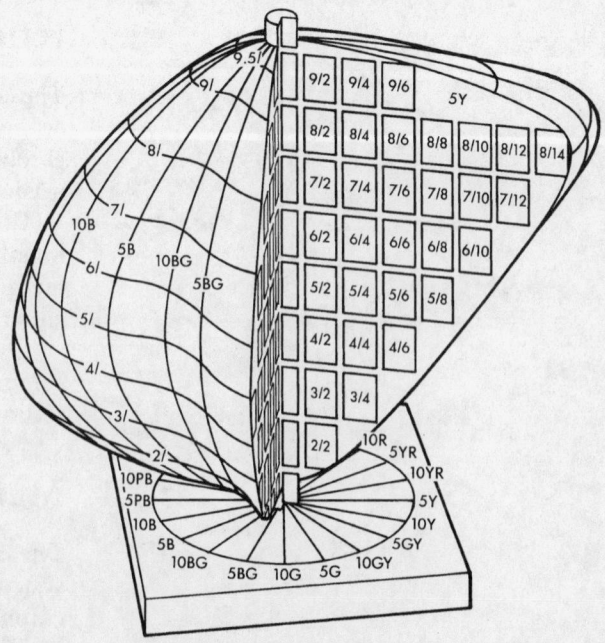

Figure 5.6 Schematic diagram of layout of Munsell colour system (reproduced with kind permission of Munsell Color Company, Baltimore, USA)

Figure 5.7 Munsell colour solid with slice removed, showing boundary of 5Y (yellow) hue plane (reproduced with kind permission of Munsell Color Company, Baltimore, USA)

Figure 5.7 shows the bounding surface of the Munsell colour solid. This indicates the relative positions of the highest possible chromas at each hue and value. Thus high chroma yellows have high value (reflectance) while high chroma reds and blues have low reflectances.

5.7.2 Natural colour system[(162)]

In this system, colours are scaled according to their degree of resemblance to the six elementary colours: white, black, yellow, red, blue and green. Of these, the four chromatic colours are those in which no trace of any other can be seen, e.g. the red that contains no trace of either yellow or blue and so on. These four are placed 90° apart on the hue circle and form the basis for red-green and yellow-blue opponent axes (see Figure 5.8). The white and black are the pure colours of this type that contain no trace of the other or of any of the chromatic elementary colours. Any given colour can have resemblances to no more than two of the chromatic colours plus white and black. For example, an orange hue might be said to bear a 30% resemblance to red and a 70% resemblance to yellow; the sum of the resemblances to the chromatic elementary colour is always 100. The hue of this orange sample would then be Y30R. The degree of resemblance to black is called blackness (s), that to white is called whiteness (w), that to yellow is called yellowness (y), and so on. The degree of resemblance to a maximum, or completely chromatic colour, is called chromaticness (c). By dividing an elementary scale into 100 steps it is possible to get a measure of the degree of resemblance to the elementary colours.

The natural colour system (NCS) triangle (Figure 5.9) is therefore a diagram in which the resemblance of a colour to white, black and the maximum chromatic colour is plotted in terms of whiteness, blackness and chromaticness, and

$$s + w + c = 100$$

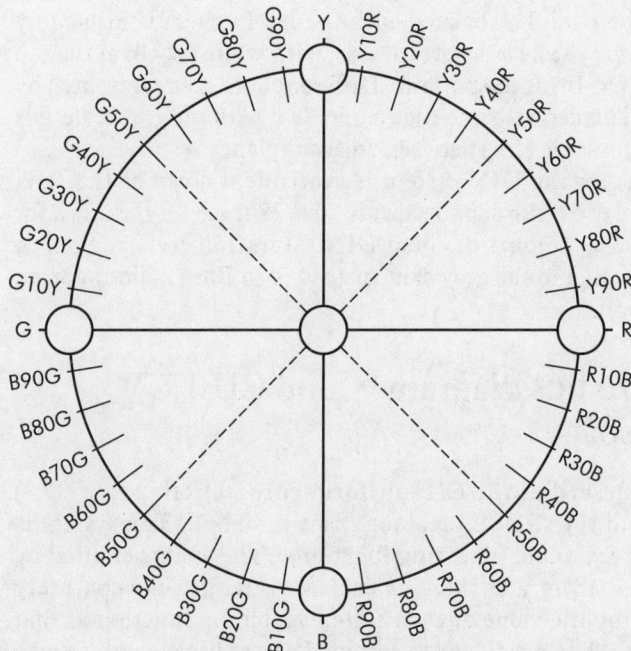

Figure 5.8 Natural colour system hue circle (reproduced with kind permission of the Scandinavian Colour Institute)

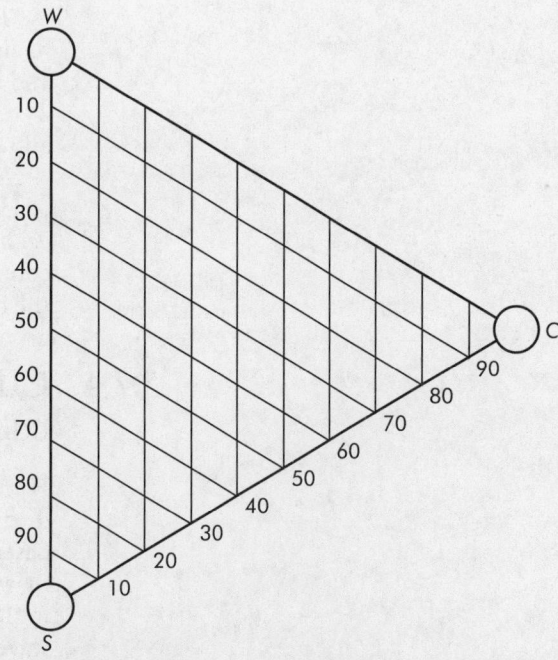

Figure 5.9 NCS constant hue triangle (reproduced with kind permission of the Scandinavian Colour Institute)

The diagram illustrates the arrangement of samples in the NCS Atlas[162] in a constant-hue triangle with corner points w, c and s. Arrays of constant chromaticness (c) are parallel to the vertical axis. Constant blackness (s) and constant whiteness (w) arrays lie on lines parallel to the sloping sides of the triangle and do not pass through the corners unless blackness or whiteness is zero. The hue circle in Figure 5.8 shows the four elementary hues and intermediate notations. It is clear that it is only necessary to specify the hue, s and c in order to specify the colour completely. However, neither the hue circle nor the constant hue triangles show spacings that are close to visual equality. This reflects the very different guiding principles upon which it was based compared with the Munsell system. The Atlas became available in 1979 and contains 1412 colour samples and more recently, ICI (Paints) have introduced an atlas based on the NCS system[163].

5.7.3 DIN system

The DIN (Deutsches Institut für Normung) system (see Figure 5.10) was developed in Germany[164]. The three variables used are hue (T), saturation (S) and darkness (D), quoted in that order. The system uses a standard daylight designated D65, and CIE tristimulus (see section 5.7.4) values for the samples available [165]. There are 24 principal hues, having values of $T=1$ for a yellow, via reds, purples, blues, and greens to a yellow-green of $T=24$. These principal hues were chosen to represent equal hue differences between adjacent pairs all round the hue circle.

The second variable, saturation, is a function of the distance from the point representing the reference white on a chromaticity diagram, and for colours of the same reflectance (not the same darkness) equal saturation represents equal perceptual differences from the grey of the same reflectance.

The third variable is darkness, rather than lightness, and this is not related in a simple way to reflectance.

The colour solid associated with the DIN system is formed by having the grey scale as a vertical axis, with white ($D=0$) at the top and black ($D=10$) at the bottom. Different hues are represented by 24 different planes with one edge coincident with the grey scale axis and the same angle (15°) between adjacent planes.

An atlas for the DIN system is available, known as the DIN Colour Chart[167]: the sample size is 20×28 mm. In the atlas, for each hue page, colours of equal DIN saturation are arranged in columns parallel to the grey axis, instead of in lines radiating from the black point.

5.7.4 CIE 1976 UCS diagram[168] and CIELUV colour space

Hunt[166] describes the CIE uniform chromaticity scale (UCS) diagram and the CIELUV colour space in detail. The system is based on three colour matching functions. The energy emitted by or reflected from a surface at each wavelength is separately multiplied by the value of each colour matching function at that wavelength. The products are summed across wavelength to give three totals, known as 'CIE tristimulus values', one for each of the colour matching functions and these are usually x, y and z. Simple

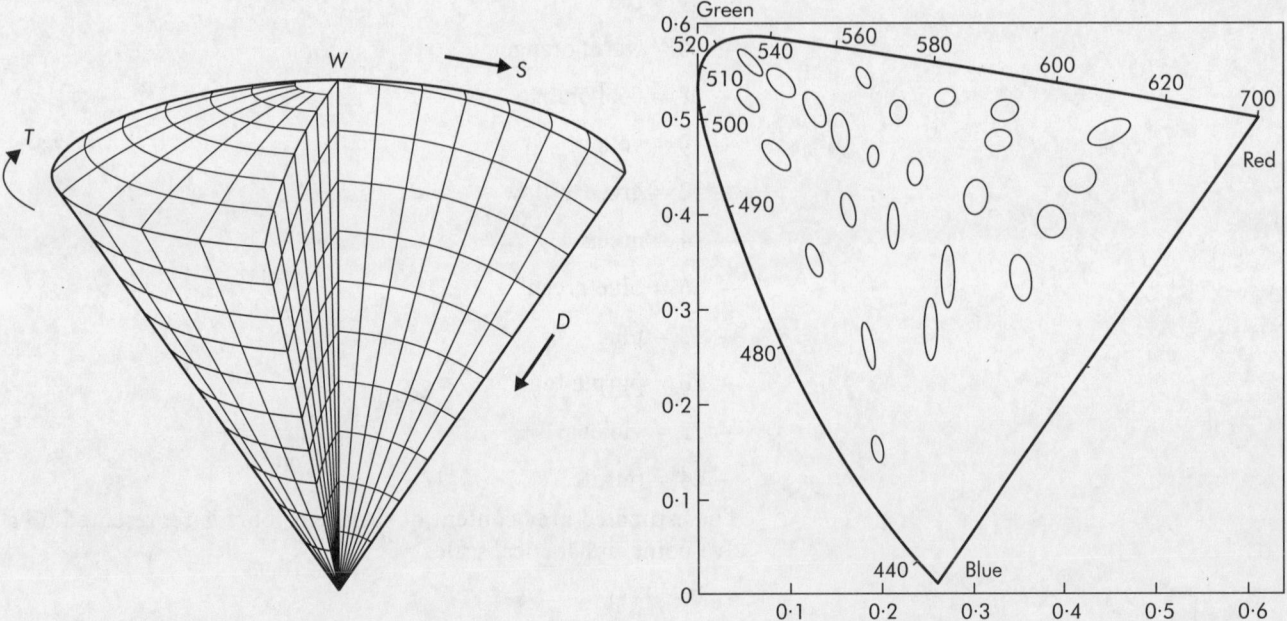

Figure 5.10 Colour solid of the DIN system: *T* = hue, *S* = saturation, *D* = darkness[166] (reproduced with kind permission of Ellis Horwood)

Figure 5.11   CIE 1976 uniform chromaticity scale diagram with MacAdam ellipses (enlarged ×10); these are loci of 10 minimum perceptible colour differences (MPCD)

arithmetic transformations of these totals give values of photopic luminance (L) and values of u' and v', the co-ordinates in the CIE 1976 uniform chromaticity scale (Figure 5.11). To a first approximation, equal distances within the $u'v'$ diagram represent equally discernable colour differences at a given luminance. The colour of any visible source or surface can be represented by a point in the diagram.

Surface colours can also be plotted in colour spaces in which the neutral colour is placed at the centre of the space. The CIE has recommended two such spaces, 1976 CIELUV space and 1976 CIELAB space, the latter being used widely in the colorant industries. The vector to the point representing a surface colour from the reference white has an angle that represents the hue (h) and a length that represents the saturation (s). In addition, the system forms the basis of a sophisticated model[166] for predicting colour appearance under a variety of viewing conditions.

5.7.5   *BS 5252: 1976: Framework for colour co-ordination for building purposes*

BS 5252[169] is a list of 237 surface colours. Though cross-referenced to Munsell co-ordinates *BS 5252* adopts another colour notation specially developed to avoid some of the anomalies of the Munsell system.

The three dimensions of colour in *BS 5252* are: hue, designated by an even number; greyness, designated by a letter; weight, designated by an additional number, usually odd.

12 distinct hues are identified, not counting 'neutral':

— 00 = neutral

— 02 = red-purple

— 04 = red

— 06 = warm orange

— 08 = cool orange

— 10 = yellow

— 12 = green-yellow

— 14 = green

— 16 = blue-green

— 18 = blue

— 20 = purple-blue

— 22 = violet

— 24 = purple.

The estimated grey content of surface colours is represented on a five-point alphabetical scale:

— A = grey

— B = near grey

— C = distinct hue

— D = nearly clear

— E = clear, vivid colour.

Generally, greyness correlates well with chroma but the two concepts are not interchangeable, for black (00E53) and white (00E55), having no greyness content, are clear (Group E) not grey (Group A).

Surfaces having the same weight generally look equally light, but the correlation between weight and reflectance, even within a given greyness group, is uneven. In Groups A and B the correlation is excellent, in Group C it is good, but in D and E it is poor. This is because saturated reds and blues tend to look lighter than yellows or greys of the same reflectance; the phenomenon is known as the Helmholtz–Kohlrausch effect[170].

Individual colours are identified by a combination of a hue number, a greyness group letter and a weight number, in that order. For example, 12B27 means that the hue number is 12 (greenish yellow). The greyness group is B (close to grey) but with a slight hue. The weight number is 27, indicating a darkish tone. The colour is a dark olive green.

Sub-sets of colours suitable for particular applications have been picked from *BS 5252* and published as separate British Standards[171–176]. For example, the *BS 4800* paint colours are listed in Table 5.8 (pages 215–216), with their approximate natural colour system and Munsell equivalents and reflectances.

Reflectances for a selection of typical surface finishes and materials are shown in Table 5.9.

Table 5.8 Approximate NCS and Munsell references and reflectances for colours in *BS 4800: 1981*[171] (continued on page 216)

Greyness Group	Colour designation	Hue	Approximate NCS reference	Approximate Munsell	Approximate reflectance reference
A	00 A 01	Neutral	1501-Y03R	N 8.5	0.68
	00 A 05	Neutral	3101-Y26R	N 7	0.45
	00 A 09	Neutral	5301-R64B	N 5	0.24
	00 A 13	Neutral	7501-R97B	N 3	0.11
	10 A 03	Yellow	2002-Y03R	5Y 8/0.5	0.60
	10 A 07	Yellow	4302-Y09R	5Y 6/0.5	0.33
	10 A 11	Yellow	6702-G98Y	5Y 4/0.5	0.14
B	04 B 15	Red	0906-Y78R	10R 9/1	0.79
	04 B 17	Red	1409-Y83R	10R 8/2	0.62
	04 B 21	Red	3810-Y76R	10R 6/2	0.33
	08 B 15	Yellow-red	0606-Y41R	10YR 9.25/1	0.86
	08 B 17	Yellow-red	1607-Y41R	8.75YR 8/2	0.64
	08 B 21	Yellow-red	4107-Y41R	8.75YR 6/2	0.32
	08 B 25	Yellow-red	6308-Y40R	8.75YR 4/2	0.16
	08 B 29	Yellow-red	8105-Y53R	8.75YR 2/2	0.07
	10 B 15	Yellow	0504-Y21R	5Y 9.25/1	0.87
	10 B 17	Yellow	1811-Y01R	5Y 8/2	0.61
	10 B 21	Yellow	4011-G99Y	5Y 6/2	0.33
	10 B 25	Yellow	6211-G90Y	5Y 4/2	0.16
	10 B 29	Yellow	8305-G89Y	5Y 2/2	0.07
	12 B 15	Green-yellow	0807-G73Y	5GY 9/1	0.81
	12 B 17	Green-yellow	1812-G75Y	2.5GY 8/2	0.61
	12 B 21	Green-yellow	3915-G65Y	2.5GY 6/2	0.33
	12 B 25	Green-yellow	6313-G57Y	2.5GY 4/2	0.15
	12 B 29	Green-yellow	8207-G53Y	2.5GY 2/2	0.07
	18 B 17	Blue	1704-B78G	5B 8/1	0.62
	18 B 21	Blue	4004-B57G	5B 6/1	0.34
	18 B 25	Blue	6405-B14G	5B 4/1	0.16
	18 B 29	Blue	8205-B06G	7.5B 2/1	0.06
	22 B 15	Violet	1000-N	10PB 9/1	0.81
	22 B 17	Violet	1804-R58B	10PB 8/2	0.60
C	02 C 33	Red-purple	1118-R07B	7.5RP 8/4	0.62
	02 C 37	Red-purple	3531-R17B	7.5RP 5/6	0.23
	02 C 39	Red-purple	5331-R21B	7.5RP 3/6	0.10
	02 C 40	Red-purple	7315-R24B	7.5RP 2/4	0.07
	04 C 33	Red	1019-Y86R	7.5R 8/4	0.62
	04 C 37	Red	3632-Y85R	7.5R 5/6	0.23
	04 C 39	Red	5136-Y87R	7.5R 3/6	0.10
	06 C 33	Yellow-red	1517-Y35R	7.5YR 8/4	0.62
	06 C 37	Yellow-red	4034-Y45R	5YR 5/6	0.23
	06 C 39	Yellow-red	6525-Y40R	7.5YR 3/6	0.11
	08 C 31	Yellow-red	0809-Y32R	10YR 9/2	0.81
	08 C 35	Yellow-red	2430-Y24R	10YR 7/6	0.46
	08 C 37	Yellow-red	4340-Y18R	10YR 5/6	0.23
	08 C 39	Yellow-red	6724-Y22R	10YR 3/6	0.10
	10 C 31	Yellow	0811-Y16R	5Y 9/2	0.81
	10 C 33	Yellow	1122-Y03R	5Y 8.5/4	0.71
	10 C 35	Yellow	2536-G99Y	5Y 7/6	0.45
	10 C 39	Yellow	6921-G95Y	5Y 3/4	0.10
	12 C 33	Green-yellow	1623-G72Y	2.5GY 8/4	0.62
	12 C 39	Green-yellow	6626-G49Y	2.5GY 3/4	0.10

Table 5.8   (continued)

Greyness Group	Colour designation	Hue	Approximate NCS reference	Approximate Munsell	Approximate reflectance reference
	14 C 31	Green	0609-G12Y	5G 9/1	0.81
	14 C 35	Green	2610-G06Y	5G 7/2	0.45
	14 C 39	Green	6520-G	5G 3/4	0.10
	14 C 40	Green	8007-G05Y	5G 2/2	0.07
	16 C 33	Blue-green	1613-B68G	7.5BG 8/2	0.60
	16 C 37	Blue-green	4326-B57G	7.5BG 5/4	0.22
	18 C 31	Blue	0704-B97G	5B 9.25/1	0.84
	18 C 35	Blue	2516-B05G	7.5B 7/3	0.42
	18 C 39	Blue	6126-B08G	7.5B 3/4	0.10
	20 C 33	Purple-blue	1117-R83B	5PB 8/4	0.63
	20 C 37	Purple-blue	3827-R87B	5PB 5/6	0.23
	20 C 40	Purple-blue	7415-R82B	5PB 2/4	0.07
	22 C 37	Violet	3928-R60B	10PB 5/6	0.22
	24 C 33	Purple	1514-R35B	7.5P 8/3	0.60
	24 C 39	Purple	5431-R49B	7.5P 3/6	0.10
D	04 D 44	Red	2858-Y88R	7.5R 4/10	0.16
	04 D 45	Red	3657-Y93R	7.5R 3/10	0.10
	06 D 43	Yellow-red	2560-Y27R	7.5YR 6/10	0.33
	06 D 45	Yellow-red	4644-Y47R	5YR 4/8	0.16
	10 D 43	Yellow	2163-G97Y	5Y 7/10	0.45
	10 D 45	Yellow	3952-G98Y	5Y 5/8	0.24
	12 D 43	Green-yellow	2954 G64Y	2.5GY 6/8	0.32
	12 D 45	Green-yellow	5043-G54Y	2.5GY 4/6	0.15
	16 D 45	Blue-green	5536-B51G	7.5BG 3/6	0.10
	18 D 43	Blue	3536-B09G	7.5B 5/6	0.22
	20 D 45	Purple-blue	4938-R88B	5PB 3/8	0.10
	22 D 45	Violet	4542-R63B	10PB 3/8	0.10
E	04 E 49	Red	0314-Y91R	7.5R 9/3	0.80
	04 E 51	Red	0963-Y81R	7.5R 6/12	0.33
	04 E 53	Red	1777-Y81R	7.5R 4.5/16	0.18
	06 E 50	Yellow-red	0742-Y32R	7.5YR 8/8	0.60
	06 E 51	Yellow-red	0860-Y50R	2.5YR 7/11	0.46
	06 E 56	Yellow-red	2962-Y43R	5YR 5/12	0.24
	08 E 51	Yellow-red	1178-Y16R	10YR 7.5/12	0.51
	10 E 49	Yellow	0823-G87Y	10Y 9/4	0.79
	10 E 50	Yellow	0848-Y	5Y 8.5/8	0.64
	10 E 53	Yellow	0875-G95Y	6.25Y 8.5/13	0.64
	12 E 51	Green-yellow	0963-G66Y	2.5GY 8/10	0.60
	12 E 53	Green-yellow	1266-G45Y	5GY 7/11	0.44
	14 E 51	Green	1854-G09Y	2.5G 6.5/8	0.34
	14 E 53	Green	2854-G5G	5/10	0.22
	16 E 53	Blue-green	3049-B50G	7.5BG 5/8	0.22
	18 E 49	Blue	0710-B64G	5B 9/2	0.79
	18 E 50	Blue	0822-B11G	7.5B 8/4	0.60
	18 E 51	Blue	1847-B06G	7.5B 6/8	0.31
	18 E 53	Blue	2959-B	10B 4/10	0.15
	20 E 51	Purple-blue	1548-R89B	5PB 6/10	0.32
	00 E 53	Black	9500-N	N 1.5	0.05
	00 E 55	White	0000-N	N 9.5	0.85

Table 5.9   Approximate reflectances of typical building finishes

Building surface	Reflectance	Material or finish
Ceilings	0.8	White emulsion paint on plain plaster surface
	0.7	White emulsion paint on acoustic tile
	0.6	White emulsion paint on no-fines concrete
	0.5	White emulsion paint on wood-wool slab
Walls	0.8	White emulsion paint on plain plaster surface; Tiles: white glazed
	0.7	Brick, white gault
	0.65	Plaster, pink
	0.4	White asbestos cement; Brick: concrete, light grey; Portland cement, smooth
	0.35	Stainless steel
	0.3	Brick: fletton
	0.25	Concrete, light grey; Portland cement, rough (as board marked); Brick: London stock; Timber panelling: light oak, mahogany, gaboon
	0.2	Timber panelling: teak, afromosia, medium oak; Brick: concrete, dark grey
	0.15	Brick: blue engineering
	0.05	Chalkboard, painted black
Floors and furniture	0.8	Paper, white
	0.45	Cement screed; PVC tiles: cream; Carpet: light grey, middle buff
	0.35	Timber: birch, beech, maple
	0.25	Timber: oak; PVC tiles: brown and cream marbled; Carpet: turquois, sage green
	0.2	Timber: iroko, kerning, medium oak; Tiles: cork, polished
	0.1	Quarry tiles: red, heather brown; Carpet: dark, 'low maintenance'; PVC tiles: dark brown; Timber: dark oak

5.8   CIE colour rendering index

5.8.1   Basis of CIE colour rendering index

The most widely used system for indicating the colour rendering properties of light sources is the CIE general colour rendering index[107]. The index quantifies the accuracy with which test sample colours are reproduced by the light source of interest relative to their colour under a theoretical reference light source. The procedure involves calculating the positions of the test sample colours on the CIE 1960 uniform chromaticity scale diagram when illuminated by a test light source and a reference illuminant. The difference between the positions for a test colour is expressed on a scale that gives a value of 100 for zero difference and reduces as the difference between positions increases. For a single test sample colour the result of this calculation, which also includes a correction for chromatic adaptation, is called the CIE special colour rendering index (R_i).

The CIE recommends a set of test sample colours which cover a hue circle and which include some particularly important colours

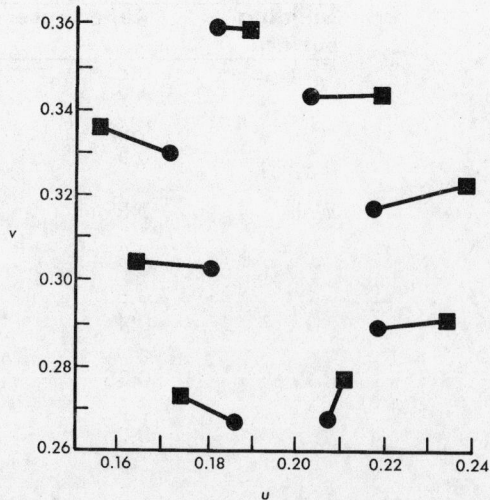

Figure 5.12   Positions of eight CIE test samples are shown on the CIE 1960 uniform chromaticity scale diagram under the reference illuminant (squares) and under the lamp of interest (circles). Note: The CIE 1960 uniform chromaticity scale diagram is used for calculating CRI, not the u'v' diagram (Figure 5.11, page 213) in section 5.7.4.

such as human skin. For general use a set of eight test sample colours is recommended. The average of the CIE special colour rendering indices for these eight test samples is called the CIE general colour rendering index (R_a) (Figure 5.12).

Perfect agreement between the colours of all eight test samples under the test light source and under the reference illuminant gives a CIE general colour rendering index of 100. Differences between the positions will produce lower values of the CIE general colour rendering index, the values being scaled so that a warm white tubular fluorescent lamp has a CIE general colour rendering index of about 50.

The choice of a suitable reference illuminant is obviously important and as the correction for chromatic adaptation in use at the moment is only applicable to small differences in chromaticity; a series of reference illuminants has been recommended[107]. For colour temperatures at or below 5000 K, the reference illuminant is a full radiator; above 5000 K it is one of a series of daylight spectral energy distributions specified by the CIE. The reference illuminant chosen has to be the one closest in chromaticity to the test light source and the colour temperature of the reference illuminant should be quoted with the CIE colour rendering index.

5.8.2   Limitations of CIE colour rendering index

The amount of information available from any procedure that results in a single number index to describe the colour rendering properties of a light source is bound to be limited. The CIE general colour rendering index indicates how the colour rendering of the test light source differs from that of the reference illuminant but it does not describe the differences in detail. To obtain this information a series of CIE special colour rendering indices is required; the greater the number of these, the more accurate the knowledge of the colour rendering properties of the test source.

The following characteristics of the CIE colour rendering index should be noted.

(a) Light sources with the same CIE general colour rendering indices do not necessarily render colours in the same way because the same CIE general colour rendering index may result from very different combinations of CIE special colour rendering indices.

(b) Light sources with the same CIE special colour rendering index for a particular test colour do not necessarily render that colour in the same way. The CIE special colour rendering index does not indicate the direction of the differences in colour.

(c) The CIE colour rendering index is intended for comparing the colour rendering of two white lamps of about the same chromaticity. A lamp with a colour some distance from the full radiator locus cannot be assessed accurately.

(d) Comparison of the colour rendering properties of light sources with different apparent colours is difficult since each CIE colour rendering index refers to a reference illuminant of a chromaticity similar to that of the test light source. The colour rendering effects of illuminants with different apparent colours, e.g. daylight at a correlated colour temperature of 6500 K and an incandescent lamp at a correlated colour temperature of 2700 K are entirely different, although they can both have a CIE general colour rendering index of 100.

5.9 Physiological effects of optical radiation

5.9.1 Introduction

In physical terms 'light' is a small part of the electromagnetic spectrum, lying in the wavelength range 400 nm to 780 nm (Figure 5.13). Adjacent to it are ultra-violet radiation, nominally occupying the wavelength range 100 nm to 400 nm and infra-red radiation, covering the wavelength range 780 nm to 1 mm. The electromagnetic radiation in the complete wavelength range 100 nm to 1 mm is called optical radiation. One effect of the part of optical radiation called light is to allow the human visual system to operate, but the non-visual part of optical radiation can also affect human eye and skin tissue. This section summarises the effects of optical radiation on skin and eye tissue and lists the most widely recognised criteria by which the effects of such radiation may be assessed.

5.9.2 Effects of optical radiation

5.9.2.1 Ultra-violet radiation

The CIE has divided the ultra-violet region of the electromagnetic spectrum into three parts: UV-A (400–315 nm), UV-B (315–280 nm)

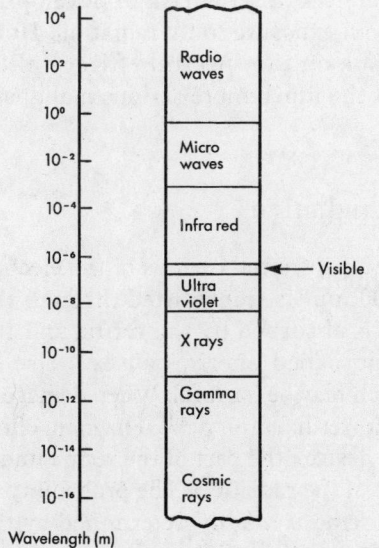

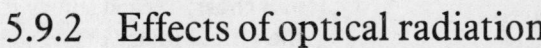

Figure 5.13 Schematic diagram of the electromagnetic spectrum

and UV-C (280–100 nm)[112]. The main hazard to human tissue comes from UV-B and UV-C radiation.

Radiation from these two regions of the ultra-violet spectrum is absorbed by the cornea and conjunctiva of the eye and in sufficient quantities will cause kerato-conjunctivitis. This is an unpleasant but temporary condition involving photo-conjunctivitis and an inflammation of the cornea called photo-keratitis. The action spectrum for photo-conjunctivitis peaks at about 260 nm whilst that for photo-keratitis has a peak sensitivity at about 270 nm[177]. It should be appreciated that the important factor in the incidence of kerato-conjunctivitis is the dose of radiation received, i.e. the product of the irradiance received and the time for which it is received. Therefore both short duration, high irradiance exposures and long duration, low irradiance exposures can be harmful.

Exposure of the skin to ultra-violet radiation produces two distinct effects depending on the wavelength range of the incident radiation. If the skin is exposed to UV-A radiation immediate pigment darkening can occur without any reddening of the skin. This change in pigment is of short duration[177]. If the skin is exposed to UV-B and UV-C radiation reddening of the skin occurs some hours after exposure. This reddening is called erythema, and in an extreme form is known as sunburn[177]. UV-A is also capable of producing erythema but requires exposures about 100 times greater than those for UV-B and UV-C. The CIE have adopted a reference action spectrum, for erythema, which is defined by three separate equations with maximum effectiveness between 250 nm and 298 nm[178]. Frequent, moderate exposures to UV-B and UV-C can lead to tanning. This is because repeated exposures cause changes in the structure of the skin. A new darker pigment is formed near the surface of the skin and the outer layer of the skin thickens. The effect of these changes in the skin structure is to reduce the absorption of ultra-violet radiation by the skin. This can legitimately be called a defence mechanism because chronic exposure to high levels of UV radiation accelerates skin ageing and increases the risk of developing certain types of skin cancer[177,179]. There is general agreement that the reference erythemal action spectrum is acceptable for determining the risk of developing non-melanoma skin cancer from exposure to UV radiation. However, there are no reliable data on the spectral efficacy of UV radiation for the induction of the much more serious malignant melanoma skin cancer.

5.9.2.2   Visible and near infra-red radiation

Radiation in the visible and near infra-red regions of the electro-magnetic spectrum (400–1400 nm) is transmitted through the ocular media of the eye and is absorbed by the retina and the surrounding tissues. The absorbed energy causes a rise in temperature of these areas which may be harmful. When damage is caused the result is called chorio-retinal injury[180]. The main effect of a chorio-retinal injury is to destroy the part of the retina under the retinal image of the source of the radiation. The probability of the chorio-retinal injury occurring is mainly determined by the retinal radiant exposure, i.e. the product of the retinal irradiance and the exposure time. The retinal irradiance is determined by the nature of the radiant source, the pupil size and the transmission of the ocular media. For very bright sources the retinal exposure periods are generally limited to about 0.2 s by the natural aversion responses (blinking, looking away) so that very high retinal irradiances are required to produce radiant exposures large enough to cause injury.

The mechanism which creates chorio-retinal injury is thermal. In addition to this effect there is also evidence[180] that absorption of visible radiation, particularly of that at the blue end of the visible spectrum can cause damage to the retinal receptors[181]. This photo-chemical effect also requires high retinal radiant exposures.

5.9.2.3 Infra-red radiation

The CIE has divided the infra-red region of the electromagnetic spectrum into three parts, IR-A (780–1400 nm), IR-B (1.4–3.0 μm) and IR-C (3.0 μm–1 mm)[112]. The effect of infra-red radiation depends on where the radiation is absorbed. Most of the IR-A radiation is absorbed in the ocular media of the eye but some of it reaches the retina and is absorbed there. IR-B radiation in the wavelength range 1400–1900 nm is almost all absorbed in the cornea and aqueous humour of the eye. Infra-red radiation above 1900 nm does not penetrate the eye, being absorbed by the cornea. The effect of the IR-A radiation that reaches the retina has already been discussed as chorio-retinal injury. The IR-A and IR-B radiation that is absorbed in the ocular media or the cornea will raise the temperature of these tissues. It is believed that elevated temperatures in the lens are related to the development of opacities there, particularly if the exposure is prolonged.

As for damage to the skin caused by visible and infra-red radiation, if the temperature elevation caused by the absorption of radiation is sufficient, burns will occur. The irradiance necessary to cause skin burns depends on the area and reflectance of the exposed skin and the duration of the exposure.

5.9.3 Practical aspects

5.9.3.1 Limits

The above discussion of the effects of optical radiation has shown that it is necessary to protect people from excessive exposure to such radiation. But how much is excessive? The most widely accepted recommendations about safe exposures to the various types of optical radiation are the limits published by the American Conference of Governmental Industrial Hygienists (ACGIH) for visible and infra-red radiation and by the International Non-Ionizing Radiation Committee (INIRC) for ultra-violet exposures[182,183,184]. These limits quantify, in appropriate forms, the optical radiation conditions to which people may be repeatedly exposed without adverse effect. The relevant limits are listed in Tables 5.10 and 5.11. The various weighting functions which are used to specify the spectral sensitivity of the eye or skin to the different hazards are given in Tables 5.12 and 5.13. It should be noted that the limits are established recommendations and are supported by the UK National Radiological Protection Board (NRPB).

5.9.3.2 Light sources

By using the recommended limits listed in Tables 5.10 and 5.11, it is possible to assess the hazards that various light sources pose to people. The light sources commonly used in interiors, when used in conventional ways, are unlikely to exceed any of these limitations[185,186]. However, there exist several very powerful light sources used for floodlighting as well as several different types of source which are designed as sources of optical radiation rather than light; for example, ultra-violet lamps for ink curing or sunbeds, and infra-red lamps for drying. In addition, there occur some applications such as ophthalmological examination, in which large amounts of light are projected into the eye[180]. Whenever such lamps or applications are being considered, care should be taken to check that the limits in Tables 5.10 and 5.11 are not exceeded for realistic conditions of exposure. It should also be noted that the recommendations given in Table 5.10 do not apply to lasers. For these sources of optical radiation a different set of limits is available[187].

5.9.3.3 Exposure control

If the limits in Tables 5.10 and 5.11 are exceeded then the user is left with three choices. The source of the offending radiation can be changed, the method of operation can be changed, or some degree of personal protection can be provided. The first option is the best but it is not always available. The second option is acceptable provided the revised mode of operation is adhered to. Personal protection can take two forms: screening of the source with materials opaque to the hazardous radiation and/or some form of eye filters, helmets, clothing etc. Advice is available on suitable approaches of this type[48,188,189].

Table 5.10 International Non-Ionizing Radiation Committee (INIRC) limits for ultra-violet radiation[183,184]

Wavelength range	Threshold limit value	Notes
Ultra-violet 180–315 nm	Exposure time on skin or eye(s) $$\sum_{180}^{315} \frac{30}{E_\lambda S_\lambda \Delta_\lambda} S$$	E_λ = Spectral irradiance at eye or skin ($Wm^{-2}nm^{-1}$) S_λ = Relative spectral effectiveness (see Table 5.12) Δ_λ = Bandwidth (nm)
Ultra-violet 315–400 nm	Radiant exposure on the eye(s) ≤ 10 000 Jm^{-2}	Within an 8-hour period
Ultra-violet 315–400 nm	Exposure time on skin $$\sum_{315}^{400} \frac{30}{E_\lambda S_\lambda \Delta_\lambda} S$$	E_λ = Spectral irradiance at skin ($Wm^{-2}nm^{-1}$) S_λ = Relative spectral effectiveness (see Table 5.12) Δ_λ = Bandwidth (nm)

Table 5.11   American Conference of Governmental Industrial Hygienists (ACGIH) threshold limit values for visible and infra-red radiation[181, 182, 185]

Wavelength range	Threshold limit value	Notes
Visible and near infra-red 400–1400 nm	$\sum\limits_{400}^{1400} L_\lambda R_\lambda \Delta_\lambda \leq \alpha^{-1} t^{-0.5} \times 10^4 \ \mathrm{Wm^{-2}sr^{-1}}$	L_λ = Spectral radiance of the source in bandwidth Δ_λ ($\mathrm{Wm^{-2}sr^{-1}}$) R_λ = Burn hazard function (see Table 5.13) α = Angular subtense of largest dimension of source (rad) t = Viewing duration (s) (values of t are limited to the range 1 μs to 10 s)
Visible 400–700 nm (305)†	$\sum\limits_{\substack{400 \\ (305)}}^{700} L_\lambda t B_\lambda \Delta_\lambda \leq 10^6 \ \mathrm{Jm^{-2}sr^{-1}}$	For $t \leq 10\,000$s, sources subtending more than 0.011 rad L_λ = Spectral radiance of the source in bandwidth Δ_λ ($\mathrm{Wm^{-2}sr^{-1}}$) B_λ = Blue light hazard function (see Table 5.13) t = Exposure time (s)
Visible 400–700nm (305)†	$\sum\limits_{\substack{400 \\ (305)}}^{700} E_\lambda t B_\lambda \Delta_\lambda \leq 100 \ \mathrm{Jm^{-2}}$	For $t \leq 10\,000$s, sources subtending less than 0.011 rad E_λ = Spectral radiance at the eye ($\mathrm{Wm^{-2}sr^{-1}}$) B_λ = Blue light hazard function (see Table 5.13) t = Exposure time (s) Δ_λ = bandwidth (nm)
Visible 400–700 nm (305)†	$\sum\limits_{\substack{400 \\ (305)}}^{700} L_\lambda B_\lambda \Delta_\lambda \leq 100 \ \mathrm{Wm^{-2}sr^{-1}}$	For $t > 10\,000$s, sources subtending more than 0.011 rad L_λ = Spectral radiance of the source in bandwidth Δ_λ ($\mathrm{Wm^{-2}sr^{-1}}$) B_λ = Blue light hazard function (see Table 5.13)
Visible 400–700 nm (305)†	$\sum\limits_{\substack{400 \\ (305)}}^{700} E_\lambda B_\lambda \Delta_\lambda \leq 0.01 \ \mathrm{Wm^{-2}}$	For $t \leq 10\,000$s, sources subtending less than 0.011 rad E_λ = Spectral irradiance at the eye ($\mathrm{Wm^{-2}nm^{-1}}$) B_λ = Blue light hazard function (see Table 5.13) Δ_λ = bandwidth (nm)
Near infra-red >770 nm§	Irradiance at eye $\leq 100 \ \mathrm{Wm^{-2}}$	
Near infra-red 770–1400 nm§	$\sum\limits_{770}^{1400} L_\lambda \Delta_\lambda = \dfrac{0.6 \times 10^4}{\alpha} \ \mathrm{Wm^{-2}sr^{-1}}$	For infra-red lamps where strong visual stimulus is absent L_λ = Spectral radiance of the source in bandwidth Δ_λ ($\mathrm{Wm^{-2}sr^{-1}}$) α = Angular subtense of source (rad)

†   For aphakes substitute A_λ (aphake photic hazard function) for B_λ and sum from 305–700 nm (See Table 5.13)
§   770 nm is the limit for protection against cataract induction

Table 5.12 Weighting function for INIRC recommendations in Table 5.10[183,184]

Wavelength (mm)†	Relative spectral effectiveness S_λ	Wavelength (mm)†	Relative spectral effectiveness S_λ
180	0.012	310	0.015
190	0.019	313	0.006
200	0.030	315	0.003
205	0.051	316	0.0024
210	0.075	317	0.0020
215	0.095	318	0.0016
220	0.120	319	0.0012
225	0.150	320	0.0010
230	0.190	322	0.00067
235	0.240	323	0.00054
240	0.300	325	0.00050
245§	0.360	328	0.00044
250	0.430	330	0.00041
254	0.500	333	0.00037
255	0.520	335	0.00034
260	0.650	340	0.00028
265	0.810	345	0.00024
270	1.000	350	0.00020
275	0.960	355	0.00016
280§	0.880	360	0.00013
285	0.770	365	0.00011
290	0.640	370	0.000093
295	0.540	375	0.000077
297§	0.460	380	0.000064
300	0.300	385	0.000053
303§	0.190	390	0.000044
305	0.060	395	0.000036
308	0.026	400	0.000030

† The values given are representative and S_λ at other wavelengths can be obtained by interpolation.
§ Emission lines for a mercury discharge spectrum.

Table 5.13 Weighting functions for ACGIH recommendations in Table 5.11[181,182,185]

Wavelength (mm)†	Blue light hazard function B_λ	Aphake photic hazard A_λ§	Burn hazard function R_λ
305	—	6.00	—
310	—	6.00	—
315	—	6.00	—
320	—	6.00	—
325	—	6.00	—
330	—	6.00	—
335	—	6.00	—
340	—	5.88	—
345	—	5.71	—
350	—	5.46	—
355	—	5.22	—
360	—	4.62	—
365	—	4.29	—
370	—	3.75	—
375	—	3.56	—
380	—	3.19	—
385	—	2.31	—
390	—	1.88	—
395	—	1.58	—
400	0.10	1.43	1.0
405	0.20	1.30	2.0
410	0.40	1.25	4.0
415	0.80	1.20	8.0
420	0.90	1.15	9.0
425	0.95	1.11	9.5
430	0.98	1.07	9.8
435	1.0	1.03	10.0
440	1.0	1.0	10.0
445	0.97	0.97	9.7
450	0.94	0.94	9.4
455	0.90	0.90	9.0
460	0.80	0.80	8.0
465	0.70	0.70	7.0
470	0.62	0.62	6.2
475	0.55	0.55	5.5
480	0.45	0.45	4.5
485	0.40	0.40	4.0
490	0.22	0.22	2.2
495	0.16	0.16	1.6
500–600	$10^{[(450-\lambda)/50]}$	$10^{[(450-\lambda)/50]}$	1.0
600–700	0.001	0.001	1.0
700–1049	NA	NA	$10^{[(700-\lambda)/500]}$
1050–1400	NA	NA	0.2

NA = Not applicable
† The values given are representative and S_λ at other wavelengths can be obtained by interpolation.
§ This function relates to subjects who have had the lens of the eye removed by cataract surgery.

5.10 European Community directives and standardisation

5.10.1 Introduction

A European Community (EC) programme intended to eliminate technical barriers to trade was launched in 1969. The aim was to issue directives setting out objectives, together with detailed annexes giving technical requirements, but leaving member states to fulfil them in different ways. It was soon found that keeping these annexes up-to-date posed a major problem. An exception to the normal practice was the 1973 *Low Voltage Directive* which allowed for National Standards, harmonised through CENELEC, to provide detailed criteria for assessing the safety of a wide range of products to meet minimum 'essential requirements'.

This directive formed the precedent for the 'new approach' to technical harmonisation and standards adopted by the EC Council of Ministers in May 1985. New approach directives since that date are based on the following:

(a) legislative harmonisation to be limited to adoption, through directives, of 'essential requirements only'

(b) preparation of supporting technical specifications to be entrusted to standards organisations

(c) such technical specifications to maintain their status as voluntary standards

(d) national authorities being obliged to recognise products conforming with harmonised standards as presumed to conform with the 'essential requirements'.

5.10.2 EC directives affecting lighting

The aim of this section is to give a brief review of the current directives, and other EC activities, which are likely to have a direct impact on lighting design and lighting products. All are in different stages of implementation and are subject to continual revision. The reader should refer to the regular updates which are available from:

— Health and Safety Executive (HSE) or the Department of the Environment (DoE) who are responsible for issuing consultative documents during the drafting of UK legislation to implement the various directives

— British Standards Institution (BSI) who report regularly on the drafting and publication of standards linked to the directives

— adopted directives are also published in the *Official Journal of the European Communities*[190].

Currently there are seven EC directives which have major significance for lighting:

— *The Workplace*

— *Use of Work Equipment*

— *Display Screen Equipment*

— *Safety Signs at Work*

— *Machine Safety (Integrated Lighting)*

— *Construction Products/CE Mark*

— *Electromagnetic Compatibility.*

The first four listed here are 'individual' directives which come under the *Framework Directive* (89/391/EEC)[191] on the introduction of measures to encourage improvements in the safety and health in the workplace.

5.10.2.1 89/654/EEC *Directive Concerning the Minimum Safety and Health Requirements for the Workplace*[29]

Statutory Instrument SI 3004 *Workplace (Health, Safety and Welfare) Regulations 1992*[30] came into force on 1 January 1993 with a three-year transitional period. The *Approved Code of Practice and Guidance L24*[31] provides additional information. Lighting is one of the many factors contributing to safety and well-being in the workplaces covered by this directive. Harmonised lighting design standards are being worked on in CEN/TC/169 and this edition of the CIBSE *Code for interior lighting* takes account of this work (see section 2.1).

5.10.2.2 89/655/EEC *Directive Concerning the Minimum Safety and Health Requirements for the Use of Work Equipment by Workers at Work*[32]

This directive was implemented by member states on 31 December 1992, Statutory Instrument SI 2932 *Provision and Use of Work Equipment Regulations 1992*[33] enforces it in the UK. *Guidance on Regulations L22*[34] gives additional information. The Directive applies to all sectors of work and work 'equipment', defined as 'any machine, apparatus, tool or installation used at work'. The equipment must be appropriate for preventing the risk of fire, overheating, explosion, contact with electricity etc. For this purpose, reference is made to relevant product safety directives.

5.10.2.3 90/270/EEC *Directive on the Minimum Safety and Health Requirements for Work with Display Screen Equipment*[35]

This directive applies to all new work stations since the 1 January 1993 and is enforced by Statutory Instrument SI 2792 *Health and Safety (Display Screen Equipment) Regulations 1992*[36]. *Guidance on Regulations L26*[37] provides additional information. Existing workstations have four years from that date in which to comply. A workstation moved to another location, or altered in any significant way, will be treated as 'new' and must comply immediately.

The Directive requires that employers must analyse every workstation and evaluate the risk to the employee in terms of health and safety including aspects such as mental stress. These findings must then be communicated and acted upon to reduce the risk. Workers are given an entitlement to an appropriate eye and eyesight test before starting display screen work and at regular intervals thereafter or if they experience visual difficulties.

The Directive sets minimum standards. From the lighting point of view it calls for no disturbing reflections in screens, no discomfort glare and so on.

The CIBSE Lighting Guide *LG3*[25] provides excellent guidance about the lighting of areas for visual display terminals. However compliance with *LG3* does not guarantee compliance with the display screen directive, but the use of *LG3* will significantly reduce the probability of a problem arising (see section 3.3.2.9).

5.10.2.4 92/58/EEC *Directive on the Minimum Requirement for the Provision of Safety and/or Health Signs at Work*[192]

Adopted in June 1992, this directive replaces 77/576/EEC, which was implemented in the UK by the *Safety Signs Regulations 1980*[193]. Implementation is due in June 1994 with a further transitional period of 18 months. The Directive primarily concerned with harmonisation of symbols and logos used for safety signs which, for lighting products, has direct influence on self-illuminated emergency lighting signs (section 3.3.2.19). For general lighting, there is also the need to provide adequate visibility and colour rendering of non self-illuminated signs or warning colours used in hazardous locations.

5.10.2.5 89/392/EEC as amended by 91/368/EEC *Directive on the Approximation of the Laws of Member States Relating to Machinery*[194]

Statutory Instrument SI 3073 *Supply of Machinery (Safety) Regulations 1992*[195] came into force in January 1993 with a transitional period of two years. The Directive requires that 'the manufacturer must supply integral lighting suitable for the operation concerned where its lack is likely to cause a risk despite ambient lighting of normal intensity'. 'Integral lighting', as used in the directive, is equivalent to 'local lighting' referred to in this *Code* (see section 4.4.2.3). Harmonised standards are being worked on in CEN/TC/169, but essentially local lighting fitted to the machine by the manufacturer must provide the task illuminance at all material positions, independent of any ambient general lighting, which may be obstructed by the machine or the operator.

5.10.2.6 89/106/EEC *Directive on the Approximation of Laws, Regulations and Administrative Provisions of the Member States Relating to Construction Product/CE Mark*[196]

This officially came into force on 27 December 1991 and is covered in the UK by Statutory Instrument SI 1620 *Construction Products Regulations 1991*[197]. All new approach directives are to be adopted by each EC member state. It will, therefore, be an offence to sell non-conforming products anywhere within the EC.

The CE Mark (see Figure 5.14) is intended to convey information regarding products conformity with these directives to market inspectors. The Mark is not claimed to be a mark of quality or safety for the consumer and is not an approval mark. It is not yet clear whether or not lighting equipment will be viewed as a construction product.

Figure 5.14   CE Mark

5.10.2.7 89/336/EEC *Directive on the Approximation of the Laws of Member States Relating to Electromagnetic Compatibility (EMC)*[50]

This Directive came into force on 1 January 1991 with a transitional period which ends on the 31 of December 1995. The Directive requires that electrical and electronic equipment shall not interfere electrically with other equipment or itself suffer from interference. The International Special Committee on Radio Interference, set up by IEC, has in CISPR 14 and 15 set RFI limits since 1985, but no immunity standards exist. Generic emission and immunity standards are being drafted in IEC TC110 to cover 0–400 GHz in Class 1 EMC environments. Ultimately, the aim is to develop lighting product-specific standards which then take precedence over the generic standards.

5.10.2.8 Other European Community activities

In the area of consumer protection and information there are proposals for energy, ecological (ECO) and waste labelling of products. To achieve a 20% improvement in energy efficiency by 1995, a series of initiatives have also been set up. The SAVE programme provides a framework of recommendations and directives, such as energy labelling for buildings and domestic appliances. The THERMIE programme supports new technologies in member states such that energy efficiency may be promoted.

For energy labelling, there are proposals to indicate lumen/watt efficacies (see Figure 3.4, page 102) on lamp packaging. Consideration is also being given to energy audits for buildings which, for lighting, will be linked with installed and energy use targets (see section 2.5).

By far the greatest environmental impact of lighting is from energy used through life. These environmental aspects of lighting are discussed in section 5.11. Additionally, the use of materials and processes in lamp and luminaire manufacture and the disposal of products at end of life has a small, but important, environmental impact which can be reduced by schemes for recycling of products. Waste labelling has similar aims and includes disposal and recycling of packaging materials.

5.10.3 Standardisation

As stated in section 5.10.2, up-to-date information on all current standards is available from BSI. However, a useful reference to the standards in the field of lighting is jointly published each year by the Builder Group PLC and CIBSE[198].

5.10.3.1 Organisations

The aim of this section is to briefly summarise the international, European and national procedures by which standards are created or revised. From Figure 5.15 it will be seen that there are three international standards organisations:

— IEC: International Electrotechnical Commission (French initials: CEI) dealing with electrical and mechanical safety standards for all electrical equipment. For lighting this in-

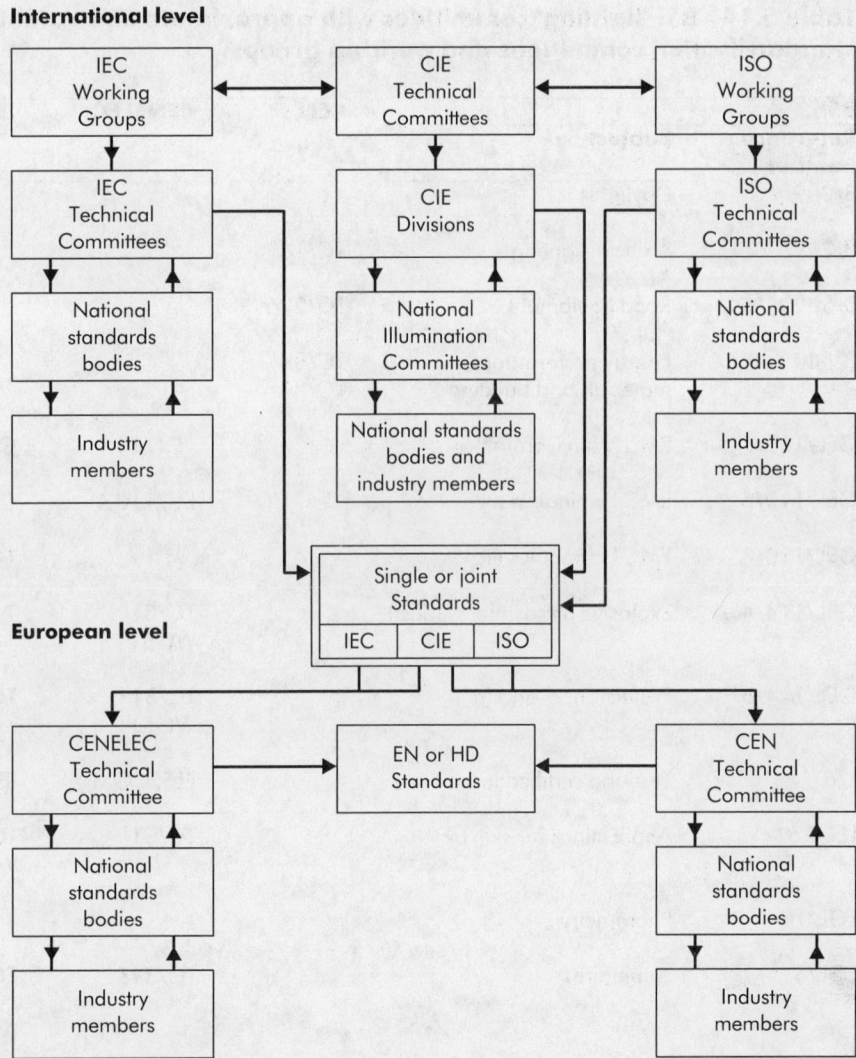

Figure 5.15 Inter-relationships of international, European and national standardisation bodies

cludes all product standards for lamps, control gear, accessories and luminaires.

— ISO: International Organization for Standardization dealing with all non-electrical matters. For lighting, this is primarily in the area of buildings and ergonomics, including daylighting.

— CIE: Commission Internationale de l'Eclairage (International Commission on Illumination) which deals with all matters related to the science, technology and art in all the fields of light and lighting covering vision, colour, photometry, photobiology, photochemistry, daylight and electric lighting application design. As such, CIE maintains specialist liaison with IEC and ISO.

At the European level, CENELEC (European Committee for Electrotechnical Standardisation) is equivalent to IEC and CEN (European Committee for Standardisation) is the counterpart of ISO. CIE has no European equivalent but, when necessary, liaises directly with CEN and CENELEC.

At the national level, in the UK, the BSI is the national member of IEC and ISO and the NIC (National Illumination Committee) is the UK national member of the CIE. BSI is the co-operating organisation member of NIC.

Table 5.14   BSI 'lighting' committees with approximate equivalent European and international standardisation committees and working groups

BSI Reference. number	Subject	CEN	CENELEC	IEC	ISO	CIE Division
B/209/9/1	Daylight				TC/160	3
B/209/9/2	Artificial lighting	TC/169				3
B/509	Road equipment	TC/226				
B/540	Energy performance, materials and building	TC/88 TC/89			TC/163	
GEL/110	EMC Main Committee		TC/110	CISPR		
GEL/110/6	EMC Luminaires etc.		SC/110 A	CISPR/F		
GEL/110/8	EMC Harmonics etc.		TC/77			
GEL/114/4	Explosive atmospheres (dust)		TC/31 WG51	TC/31		
GEL/114/6	Protection 'e' and 'n'		TC/31 WG51	TC/31		
L/6	Test and certification		ELSECOM	IECEE		
LEL/161/15	Applications for skin UV		TC/61	TC/61 WG16	TC/94	6
LGL/1	Photometry					2
LGL/3	Luminaires		TC/34Z	TC/34 (SC/34 D) (WG LUMEX)		
LGL/3/15	Luminaires, street		TC/34Z	TC/34 (SC/34 D) (WG LUMEX)		
LGL/3/19	Luminaires, emergency		BT-TF 62-8	TC/34 (SC/34 D) (WG LUMEX)		
LGL/6	Electric lamps		TC/34Z	TC/34 (SC/34 A) (WG PRESCO)		7
LGL/6/4	Halogen lamps			TC/34 (SC/34 A) (WG PRESCO)		7
LGL/6/5	GLS incandescent			TC/34 (SC/34 A) (WG PRESCO)		7
LGL/6/6	Discharge including fluorescent			TC/34 (SC/34 A) (WG PRESCO)		7
LGL/21	Control gear (ballasts)		TC/34Z	TC/34 (SC/34 C) (WG COMEX)		7

Table 5.14   (continued)

BSI Reference. number	Subject	CEN	CENELEC	IEC	ISO	CIE Division
LGL/22	Lamp caps		TC/34Z	TC/34 (SC/34 B)		
LGL/22/1	Lamp holders			TC/34 (SC/34 B)		
LGL/23	Streetlighting	TC/226 TC/169		TC/34 (SC/34 D) (WG LUMEX)		4
LGL/24	Emergency code	TC/169	BT-TF 62-8			3
LGL/25	Lighting applications	TC/169			TC/159/ SC/4	3,4,5
M/2	Colour equations				TC/187	1
MQE/11	Flameproof luminaires		TC/34Z	TC/34 (SC/34D) (WG LUMEX)		
PEL/122	VLF mains signalling		SC/105 A	TC/57		
RHE/2	Air handling devices	TC/156			TC/144	

5.10.3.2 Working programme

With such a complex multi-national and multi-disciplinary structure, there is a real danger of duplication of effort. To minimise the risk of this, the three international organisations have an agreement to produce joint standards whenever possible and CEN and CENELEC are committed to accepting international standards where possible.

To show the main links between the organisations, Table 5.14 lists the main lighting topics covered by BSI committees together with the approximate equivalent committees in the European and international organisations.

As far as Europe is concerned, the standards which serve as detailed references to the EC directives are issued in the form of EN, HD and ENV documents. These and the various deviations are explained below:

— EN (European Standard): this must be identical (except for language), for all national standards, and is preferred because it is identical. Only special national conditions are allowed as a national deviation.

— HD (Harmonised Document): this is established if transposition into identical national standards is unnecessary, impractical, or particularly if agreement is subject to the acceptance of national deviations. Although not identical, the HD should be technically equivalent in each national standard.

— ENV (prospective standards for provisional application): these are for technical fields where the innovation rate is high, such as information technology.

— prEN, prHD: draft documents for comment/enquiry.

Deviations:

— Common modification: alteration, addition to, or deletion from
the content of the reference document (e.g. IEC standard)
approved by CEN/CENELEC and thus forming part of the EN
or HD.

— Special national condition: national characteristic or practice
that cannot be changed even over a long period, e.g. climatic
conditions, electrical earthing conditions. If it affects harmonisation it forms part of the EN or HD.

— National deviation: modification of, addition to, or deletion
from, the content of an HD made in a national standard within
the same scope as the HD. It does not form part of the HD.

— A deviation: national deviation due to regulations, the alteration of which is, for the time being, outside the competence of
the CEN/CENELEC member.

— B deviation: national deviation due to particular technical
requirements permitted for a specified transitional period.

5.11 Environmental aspects of lighting

5.11.1 Introduction

With the world's population growth estimates of 3.7 thousand
million between 1990 and 2030, demand for food will almost double
and industrial output and energy use will probably treble
worldwide and increase six-fold in developing countries. With
current trends, the result could be appalling global environmental
conditions. This represents both a major challenge and opportunity.

Within the lighting industry, an environmental study has been
carried out on light sources[199]. This study presented a survey of
the environmental impact at all stages of the life cycle of lighting
products in order to formulate proposals for a policy aimed at
reducing environmental pollution throughout the life chain.

5.11.2 Product-orientated environmental study on light sources

The life chain of a product is defined as the whole of the lifespan
including:

(a) exploration and extraction of raw materials

(b) transformation into materials

(c) production

(d) packaging

(e) use

(f) waste disposal.

In the study, only (c) to (f) were looked at in detail. Transport was
also taken into account: the transportation of the materials to the
manufacturing plant is part of the production process (c), transportation between production plant and user is part of the usage (e),

and the transportation from user to the waste treatment plant is part of the waste disposal process (*f*). (*a*) and (*b*) were not analysed in detail, but the environmental effects of these two stages were expressed in index numbers, taken from the literature, for the materials concerned. These index numbers indicate the amount of energy (in kWh or MJ) that is needed to produce 1 kg of the materials in question and the amount of emissions that occur at the extraction and the transformation stages. The energy expenditure for all steps in the life chain was computed, with the emissions involved.

For the energy taken from the electricity supply, the make-up and the emissions of the Dutch supply system was taken as a standard. As the Netherlands has a high proportion of power stations using natural gas and the UK has a predominance of coal-fired generating plant, the mercury emissions for the UK are likely to be higher. The study did not take into account the environmental effects of fuel gathering, reprocessing, refining or building power stations.

The study was carried out for eight principal light sources (section 3.2.4) used throughout the application fields of industrial, commercial and domestic lighting. These were:

— GLS (filament)

— TH (filament)

— MCF (tubular fluorescent)

— CFL-a (compact fluorescent with integral wire-wound gear)

— CFL-b (compact fluorescent without integral gear)

— HPM (high pressure mercury)

— SOX (low pressure sodium)

— HPS (high pressure sodium).

5.11.3 Summary of findings

The resultant emissions to the soil (of mercury, lead and copper) were expressed in milligram per Megalumen hour (mg/Mlm h) and emissions to the air (mercury, non-acidifying and acidifying substances) expressed in units of polluted air (UPA) per Megalumen hour (UPA/Mlm h). For mercury emissions the total quantities for soil and air are given in Figure 5.16.

Figure 5.17 shows the total of all relevant solid waste, which passes to both soil and air and Figure 5.18 shows relevant emissions to air. Both figures show the share of emission resulting from the consumption of energy and those emanating from other factors over the life chain, e.g. transport and waste disposal.

5.11.4 Choice of light source

The results show that the environmental effects of light sources are mainly determined by the energy consumed during the service period of the lamp and the environmental effects of energy production associated with it. The emissions from coal-fired power stations are the major pollutants, due to the many trace elements which are mobilised in the process, one of which is mercury. Therefore, the light source with the least luminous efficacy, the incandescent lamp, is the least acceptable from an environmental

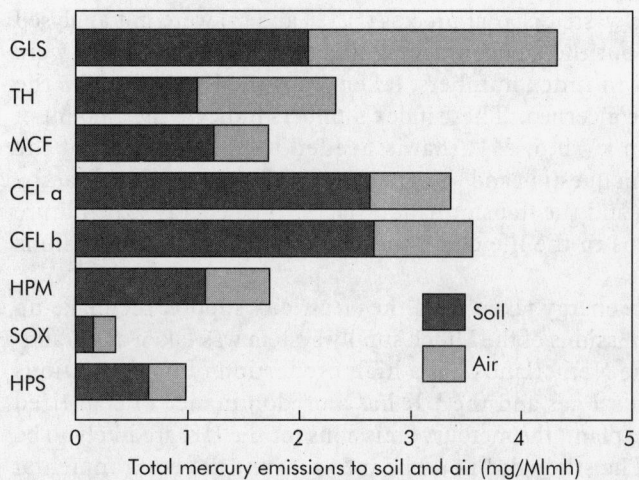

Figure 5.16 Total quantities of mercury emissions to the environment of the eight types of lamp under consideration. The UPAs are converted to milligrammes to express emissions in milligramme per Megalumen hour (mg/Mlm h)

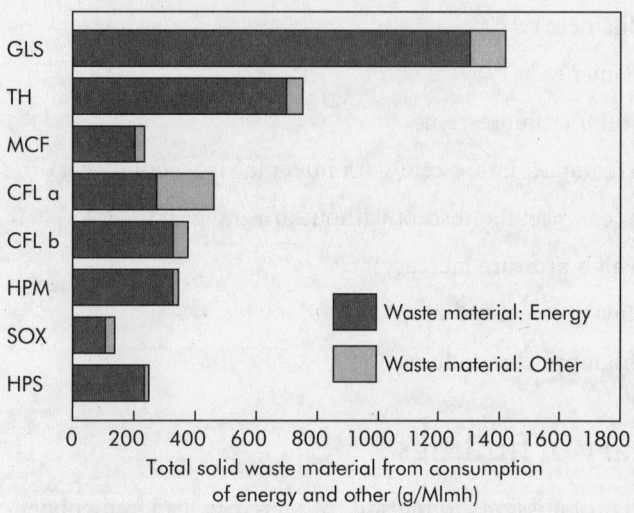

Figure 5.17 Sum total of all relevant solid waste material (in soil and air) in grammes per Megalumen hour (g/Mlm h) for the eight types of lamp, subdivided into the share resulting from the consumption of energy and the share for other factors

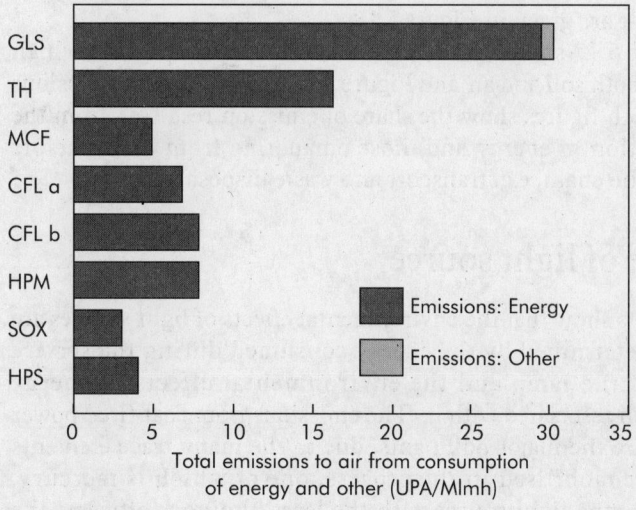

Figure 5.18 Sum total of all relevant emissions to the air in UPAs per Megalumen hour (UPA/Mlm h) for the eight types of lamp, subdivided into the share resulting from the consumption of energy and the share for other factors

point of view. The total emission of mercury (per lumen hour) from such lamps, for instance, is higher, by a factor of two, than that for tubular fluorescent lamps, although incandescent lamps themselves do not contain mercury and tubular fluorescent lamps do. The mercury emissions are due to the generation of electricity. The tungsten–halogen lamp has a slightly higher luminous efficacy than the ordinary incandescent lamp and, for that reason, is more environment friendly.

The lamps can be listed in increasing order of environmental nuisance: the low-pressure sodium lamp, followed by the high pressure sodium lamp, then the tubular fluorescent lamp, followed by the high-pressure mercury lamp. Finally, there are the compact fluorescent lamps, but these are most likely to be used to replace the least efficient filament lamps.

5.11.5 Effect in market areas

It is only possible to estimate the percentage of total electrical energy consumed by lighting as, with the exception of public lighting, it is seldom connected to a separately metered supply. Table 5.15 shows the best estimates available together with the theoretically possible reductions in energy use by employing the equipment and design techniques discussed in Parts 3 and 4 of this *Code*. The information on the number of customers is based on data from 1987/88 for England and Wales. Other estimates suggest that the total energy use for lighting in the UK is 230 500 GWh/annum.

Clearly the domestic section has the largest potential for energy saving, but as this is made up of a very large number of small electrical loads, this saving will be difficult to realise. This *Code* mainly addresses lighting design for the industrial and commercial sectors, where the potential for energy saving and reduction of emissions to air and soil is substantial.

As a result of the replacement of incandescent lamps with compact fluorescent lamps, in the domestic and parts of the commercial sectors, the total waste flow of mercury will decrease, but the proportion to the soil will increase. This is not the case with public lighting and parts of the industrial sectors, where mercury lamps are replaced with sodium lamps.

In general, the change to more energy saving lamps will result in a shift in emissions from the air to the soil, where emissions are easier to control.

Table 5.15 Summary of market sectors and lighting energy use

Market sector	Share of total electricity (about 230 500 GWh) used by lighting (%)	Theoretically possible reduction in electricity use (%)	Number of consumers[200]
Industrial	2–3	30	193 000
Commercial	10–13	30–50	1 638 000
Domestic	3–3.5	50–70	20 077 000
Public	1	30	about 450†

†   Based on the number of UK counties, regions and district authorities (1992)

5.12 Predicting daylight factor at a point[105]

5.12.1 Introduction

The daylight factor, D, may consist of three components:

— D_c, sky component, light reaching a point in a room directly from the sky

— D_e, externally reflected component, light reaching a point directly after reflection from an external surface

— D_i, internally reflected component, light reaching a point after reflection from a surface within the room.

The daylight factor is given as a percentage. It is calculated by adding the three components and applying correction factors:

$$D = c_g c_t c_d (D_c + D_e + c_r D_i)$$

where the correction factors (see section 5.12.5) are as follows: c_g for glazing bars which reduce the window area (Table 5.18); c_t for glazing materials other than clear glass (Table 5.19); c_d for dirt on the glazing (Table 5.20); c_r for dirt on internal surfaces (use Table 4.7, page 155, assuming daylight from side windows is equivalent to luminaire flux distribution of direct/indirect).

Many methods exist for finding the components. The following sections give examples for straightforward cases while the CIBSE Applications Manual: *Window design*[2] has further calculation methods and extensive references. It also covers measurement of daylight factor in actual buildings and in scale models.

5.12.2 Sky component from side windows

The BRE sky component table[201] (Table 5.16) gives the value of D_c from a vertical rectangular window.

To use the table the following information is required:

— h_1 and h_2 are the heights of the window head and sill above the working plane

— w_1 and w_2 are the distances of the window's vertical edges from a line drawn from the reference point for which the daylight factor is to be calculated, normal to the plane of the window.

— d is the distance from the reference point to the plane of the window (this is the plane of the inside of the wall or the outside whichever edge of the window aperture limits the view of the sky).

Given the appropriate values for each of these distances, the sky component can be obtained from Table 5.16. For example, Figure 5.19 shows the procedure for a window with a sill on the working plane and with the reference point on the centre line of the window. For this situation let $h_1 = 8$, $h_2 = 0$, $w_1 = 12$, $w_2 = 12$, $d = 10$. Therefore $h_1/d = 0.8$, $h_2/d = 0$, $w_1/d = 1.2$, $w_2/d = 1.2$. From Table 5.16 the sky component of window area $P = 3.1\%$, the sky component of window area $Q = 3.1\%$, therefore the sky component of window $PQ = 6.2\%$.

Table 5.16   Sky component (CIE standard overcast sky) for vertical glazed rectangular windows[201]

h/d	w/d																					θ
0	0.1	0.2	0.3	0.4	0.5	0.6	0.7	0.8	0.9	1.0	1.2	1.4	1.6	1.8	2.0	2.5	3.0	4.0	6.0	∞		0°
∞	1.3	2.5	3.7	4.9	5.9	6.9	7.7	8.4	9.0	9.6	10.7	11.6	12.2	12.6	13.0	13.7	14.2	14.6	14.9	15.0		90°
5.0	1.2	2.4	3.7	4.8	5.9	6.8	7.6	8.3	8.8	9.4	10.5	11.1	11.7	12.3	12.7	13.3	13.7	14.0	14.1	14.2		79°
4.0	1.2	2.4	3.6	4.7	5.8	6.7	7.4	8.2	8.7	9.2	10.3	10.9	11.4	12.0	12.4	12.9	13.3	13.5	13.6	13.7		76°
3.5	1.2	2.4	3.6	4.6	5.7	6.6	7.3	8.0	8.5	9.0	10.1	10.6	11.1	11.8	12.2	12.6	12.9	13.2	13.2	13.3		74°
3.0	1.2	2.3	3.5	4.5	5.5	6.4	7.1	7.8	8.2	8.7	9.8	10.2	10.7	11.3	11.7	12.0	12.4	12.5	12.6	12.7		72°
2.8	1.1	2.3	3.4	4.5	5.4	6.3	7.0	7.6	8.1	8.6	9.6	10.0	10.5	11.1	11.4	11.7	12.0	12.2	12.3	12.3		70°
2.6	1.1	2.2	3.4	4.4	5.3	6.2	6.8	7.5	7.9	8.4	9.3	9.8	10.2	10.8	11.1	11.4	11.7	11.8	11.9	11.9		69°
2.4	1.1	2.2	3.3	4.3	5.2	6.0	6.6	7.3	7.7	8.1	9.1	9.5	10.0	10.4	10.7	11.0	11.2	11.3	11.4	11.5		67°
2.2	1.1	2.1	3.2	4.1	5.0	5.8	6.4	7.0	7.4	7.9	8.7	9.1	9.6	10.0	10.2	10.5	10.7	10.8	10.9	10.9		66°
2.0	1.0	2.0	3.1	4.0	4.8	5.6	6.2	6.7	7.1	7.5	8.3	8.7	9.1	9.5	9.7	9.9	10.0	10.1	10.2	10.3		63°
1.9	1.0	2.0	3.0	3.9	4.7	5.4	6.0	6.5	6.9	7.3	8.1	8.5	8.8	9.2	9.4	9.6	9.7	9.8	9.9	9.9		62°
1.8	0.97	1.9	2.9	3.8	4.6	5.3	5.8	6.3	6.7	7.1	7.8	8.2	8.5	8.8	9.0	9.2	9.3	9.4	9.5	9.5		61°
1.7	0.94	1.9	2.8	3.6	4.4	5.1	5.6	6.1	6.5	6.8	7.5	7.8	8.2	8.5	8.6	8.8	8.9	9.0	9.1	9.1		60°
1.6	0.90	1.8	2.7	3.5	4.2	4.9	5.4	5.8	6.2	6.5	7.2	7.5	7.8	8.1	8.2	8.4	8.5	8.6	8.6	8.6		58°
1.5	0.86	1.7	2.6	3.3	4.0	4.6	5.1	5.6	5.9	6.2	6.8	7.1	7.4	7.6	7.8	7.9	8.0	8.0	8.1	8.1		56°
1.4	0.82	1.6	2.4	3.2	3.8	4.4	4.8	5.2	5.6	5.9	6.4	6.7	7.0	7.2	7.3	7.4	7.5	7.5	7.6	7.6		54°
1.3	0.77	1.5	2.3	2.9	3.6	4.1	4.5	4.9	5.2	5.5	5.9	6.2	6.4	6.6	6.7	6.8	6.9	6.9	6.9	7.0		52°
1.2	0.71	1.4	2.1	2.7	3.3	3.8	4.2	4.5	4.8	5.0	5.4	5.7	5.9	6.0	6.1	6.2	6.2	6.3	6.3	6.3		50°
1.1	0.65	1.3	1.9	2.5	3.0	3.4	3.8	4.1	4.3	4.6	4.9	5.1	5.3	5.4	5.4	5.5	5.6	5.6	5.7	5.7		48°
1.0	0.57	1.1	1.7	2.2	2.6	3.0	3.3	3.6	3.8	4.0	4.3	4.5	4.6	4.7	4.7	4.8	4.8	4.9	5.0	5.0		45°
0.9	0.50	0.99	1.5	1.9	2.2	2.6	2.8	3.1	3.3	3.4	3.7	3.8	3.9	4.0	4.0	4.0	4.1	4.1	4.2	4.2		42°
0.8	0.42	0.83	1.2	1.6	1.9	2.2	2.4	2.6	2.7	2.9	3.1	3.2	3.3	3.3	3.3	3.3	3.4	3.4	3.4	3.5		39°
0.7	0.33	0.68	0.97	1.3	1.5	1.7	1.9	2.1	2.2	2.3	2.5	2.5	2.6	2.6	2.6	2.6	2.7	2.7	2.8	2.8		35°
0.6	0.24	0.53	0.74	0.98	1.2	1.3	1.5	1.6	1.7	1.8	1.9	1.9	2.0	2.0	2.0	2.1	2.1	2.1	2.1	2.1		31°
0.5	0.16	0.39	0.52	0.70	0.82	0.97	1.0	1.1	1.2	1.3	1.4	1.4	1.4	1.4	1.5	1.5	1.5	1.5	1.5	1.5		27°
0.4	0.10	0.25	0.34	0.45	0.54	0.62	0.70	0.75	0.82	0.89	0.92	0.95	0.95	0.96	0.96	0.96	0.97	0.97	0.98	0.98		22°
0.3	0.06	0.14	0.18	0.26	0.30	0.34	0.38	0.42	0.44	0.47	0.49	0.50	0.50	0.51	0.51	0.52	0.52	0.52	0.53	0.53		17°
0.2	0.03	0.06	0.09	0.11	0.12	0.14	0.16	0.20	0.21	0.21	0.22	0.22	0.22	0.22	0.23	0.23	0.23	0.23	0.24	0.24		11°
0.1	0.01	0.02	0.02	0.03	0.03	0.04	0.04	0.05	0.05	0.05	0.06	0.06	0.06	0.06	0.07	0.07	0.07	0.07	0.08	0.08		6°

Note:

Ratio h/d=Height of window head above working plane: distance from window
Ratio w/d=Width of window to one side of normal: distance from window
θ =Angle of obstruction

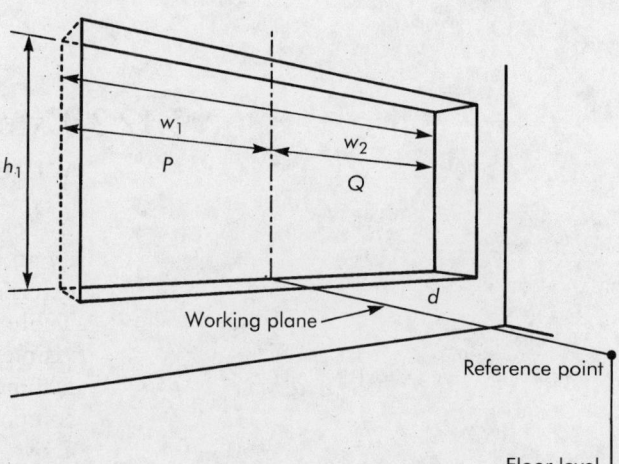

Figure 5.19   A window with the sill on the working plane, and the reference point on the centre line of the window

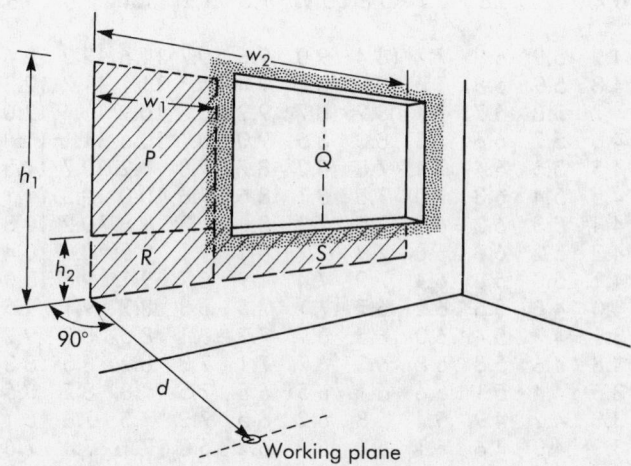

**Figure 5.20   A window with a high sill, and the reference
point outside the width of the window**

In general, the sky component at any reference point can be obtained by addition or subtraction of sky components for appropriate areas. For example, Figure 5.20 shows the procedure for a window with the sill above the working plane and with the reference point off-centre, outside the width of the window. For this situation let $h_1 = 8, h_2 = 2, w_1 = 8, w_2 = 24, d = 10$. Therefore $h_1/d = 0.8, h_2/d = 0.2, w_1/d = 0.8, w_2/d = 2.4$. Then from Table 5.16 the sky component of window area $PQRS = 3.3\%$, the sky component of window area $PR = 2.6\%$, the sky component of window area $RS = 0.23\%$, the sky component of window area $R = 0.20\%$. Therefore the sky component of window Q equals the sky component of $PQRS$ minus the sky component of PR minus sky component of RS plus sky component of R:

$$Q = PQRS - PR - RS + R$$

Therefore,

$$D_c = 3.3 - 2.6 - 0.23 + 0.20 = 0.67\%$$

5.12.3 Externally reflected component from side windows

If the direct entry of light through the window is severely limited by an external obstruction, it will be necessary to calculate the externally reflected component D_e. This can also be done using Table 5.16. The procedure is to treat the external obstruction visible from the reference point as a patch of sky whose luminance is some fraction of that of the sky obscured. In other words, the sky component for the obstructed area is first calculated as described above and is then converted to the externally reflected component by multiplying by the ratio of the luminance of the obstructed area to the sky luminance.

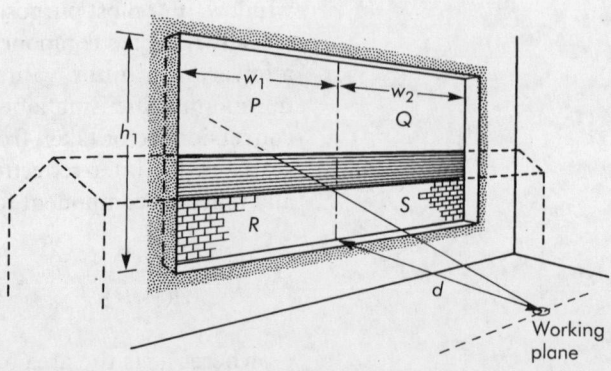

Figure 5.21   A window with the sill on the working plane and the reference point on the centre line of the window; a continuous external obstruction is parallel to the window

Of course, if the external obstruction is sufficient to justify calculating the externally reflected component, it will also be necessary to modify the window area for which the sky component is calculated. Specifically, the average height of the external obstruction viewed from the reference point should be treated as the effective window sill level. Figure 5.21 demonstrates the procedure for calculating the sky component and externally reflected component for a window which is subject to external obstruction. In Figure 5.21 the window sill is on the horizontal plane containing the reference point and the external obstruction is bounded by the roof line.

The sky component is calculated for window area PQ. For window $PQRS$, let $h_1 = 8$, $h_2 = 0$, $w_1 = 12$, $w_2 = 12$, $d = 10$. Therefore $h_1/d = 0.8$, $h_2/d = 0$, $w_1/d = 1.2$, $w_2/d = 1.2$.

From Table 5.16 the sky component of window $PR = 3.1\%$. The sky component of window $QS = 3.1\%$. Therefore the sky component of window $PQRS = 3.1 + 3.1 = 6.2\%$.

For window RS, let $h_1 = 4$, $h_2 = 0$, $w_1 =12$, $w_2=12$, $d = 10$. Therefore $h_1/d = 0.4$, $h_2/d = 0$, $w_1/d=1.2$, $w_2/d = 1.2$.

From Table 5.16, the sky component of window $RS = 0.92 + 0.92 = 1.84\%$.

Therefore the sky component of window $PQ =$ the sky component of window $PQRS$ – the sky component of window RS $= 6.20 - 1.84 = 4.36\%$.

The externally reflected component is calculated for window RS. Assuming the luminance of the obstruction is 1/10th of the luminance of the sky it obstructs, the externally reflected component for window RS is:

$$D_e = RS \times \frac{\text{Luminance of obstruction}}{\text{Luminance of sky}} = 1.84 \times 0.1 = 0.184\%$$

5.12.4 Internally reflected component from side windows

The amount of inter-reflected light varies with distance from the window. For most purposes it is sufficient to assume an average internally reflected component over the greater part of the room with a lower, minimum, value of points far from the window. The minimum value is obtained by multiplying the average value by a conversion factor taken from Table 5.17.

The BRE inter-reflection formula[202] gives the average internally reflected component for side-lit rooms:

$$D_i = \frac{0.85 A_w}{A(1-R)}(CR_{FW} + 5R_{CW})$$

where A_w is the area of window; A is the total area of ceiling, floor and walls, including windows, expressed as a fraction; R is the average reflectance of ceiling, floor and all walls, including windows; R_{FW} is the average reflectance of the floor and those parts of the walls below the plane of the mid-height of the window (excluding the window wall); R_{CW} is the average reflectance of the ceiling and those parts of the walls above the plane of the mid-height of the window (excluding the window wall); C is a coefficient having values dependent on the obstruction outside the window. For a continuous obstruction with an angular height ω degrees above the horizon, measured at the centre of the window:

$$C = 40 - \frac{\omega}{2}$$

Table 5.17   Conversion of average to minimum internally reflected component

Average reflectance R	Conversion factor
0.3	0.54
0.4	0.67
0.5	0.78
0.6	0.85

5.12.5 Correction factors

The proportion of window area obstructed by glazing bars depends on the framing material and the design. Table 5.18 gives examples.

Table 5.18   Correction factors for glazing bars

Type of frame	c_g
Metal patent glazing	0.9
Metal frame	
—large pane	0.8
Wood frame	
—large pane	0.7
—'Georgian panes'	0.6

The BRE tables and formula incorporate the diffuse transmittance of clear glass. When another material is used, the correction factor c_t should be obtained from Table 5.19.

Table 5.19   Mean light transmittance and correction factors of glazing materials

Material	Diffuse light transmittance	c_t
Clear 6 mm glass	0.80	1.0
Body-tinted 6 mm glass		
—bronze	0.46	0.57
—grey	0.39	0.48
—green	0.66	0.83
Strongly reflecting 6 mm glass	0.18	0.23
Sealed unit		
—2 mm x 6 mm clear glass	0.65	0.82
—6 mm clear glass and 6 mm low emissivity neutral	0.63	0.79
—6 mm reflecting and 6 mm clear	0.26	0.33
—6 mm strongly reflecting and 6 mm clear	0.15	0.19
Wired, cast 6 mm glass	0.74	0.92

The correction factor for dirt on window varies with location and slope, as given in Table 5.20.

Table 5.20   Correction factors, c_d, for dirt on glass

Type of location	Angle of glazing		
	Vertical	Sloping	Horizontal
Clean	0.9	0.8	0.7
Industrial	0.7	0.6	0.5
Very dirty	0.6	0.5	0.4

To obtain a correction factor for the deterioration of room surface reflectance (c_r) reference should be made to Table 4.7 (page 155), which gives room surface maintenance factors (RSMF) used for interior lighting design. For daylighting from side windows the equivalent 'luminaire flux distribution' would be 'direct/indirect'.

5.13   Illuminance at a point reference diagrams

5.13.1 Introduction

The following sections contain a series of diagrams (Figures 5.22–5.28). Each diagram shows a particular arrangement of a light source illuminating a point on a surface. The associated formulae necessary for the calculation of illuminance at the point is provided with each diagram.

In order to use the reference diagrams, first determine whether the source is a point, line or area source. To do this, calculate the distance between the centre of the luminaire and the point for which the illuminance is to be calculated. If this distance is D and the width and length of the fitting are W and L respectively, then:

— if $5W \leq D$, and $5L \geq D$, then use the point source formulae (section 5.13.2)

— if $5W \leq D$, but $5L > D$, then use the line source formulae (section 5.13.3)

— if $5W > D$, and $5L > D$, then use the area source formulae (section 5.13.4).

Having established which set of formulae to use, turn to the appropriate section and read the notes, before looking through the individual diagrams to find one which matches the problem.

Notes

Where luminous intensity values are obtained from published photometric data they will normally be quoted in candelas per 1000 lamp lumens. These should be corrected by multiplying by the total bare lamp luminous flux of the luminaire divided by 1000.

When calculating the maintained illuminance the maintenance factor must be included in all the formulae (section 4.5.2).

The inter-reflected illuminance must be calculated separately (section 4.5.5.4) and added to the value obtained from these formulae.

5.13.2 Point source formulae

Three applications of the inverse square and cosine laws are given:

(a) the general case from which the others are derived (Figure 5.22)

(b) the illuminance on a horizontal surface (Figure 5.23)

(c) the illuminance on a vertical surface (Figure 5.24).

In each of the formulae the luminous intensity $I(\theta)$ in candelas at the angle of elevation (θ) is required. This can be found from the luminous intensity distribution of the luminaire.

5.13.3 Line source formulae

The basis and limitations of this method are discussed in section 4.5.5.2.

Line source formulae are given here for four situations (Figures 5.25–5.28) with three variations ((a), (b) and (c)) for each case according to the position of the point of illumination relative to the end of the luminaire.

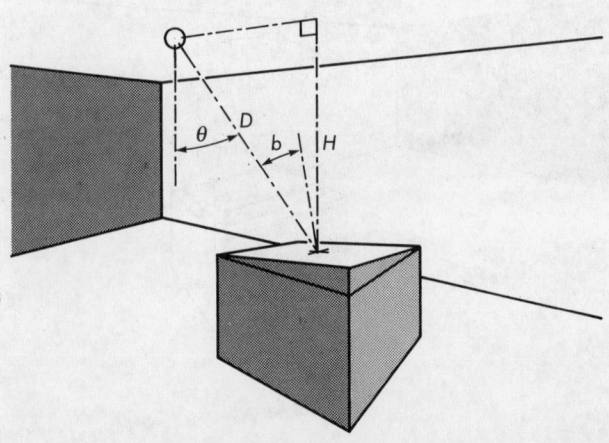

Figure 5.22 Illuminance on a plane at angle b to the source.
Point source formulae, general case:

$$E = \frac{I(\theta)\cos b}{D^2}$$

or

$$E = \frac{I(\theta)\cos^2(\theta)\cos b}{H^2}$$

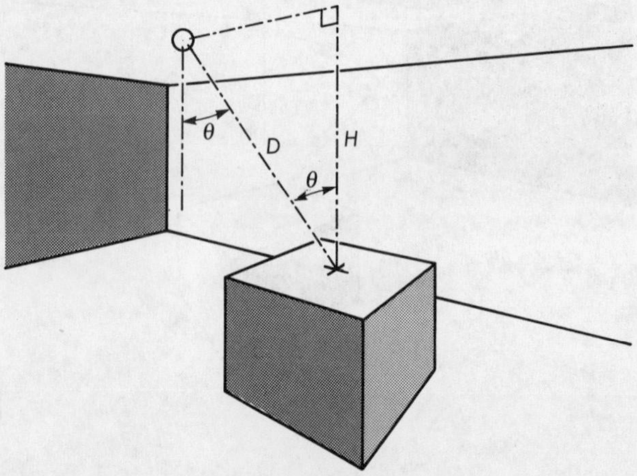

Figure 5.23 Illuminance on a horizontal plane.
Point source formulae:

$$E = \frac{I(\theta)\cos(\theta)}{D^2}$$

or

$$E = \frac{I(\theta)\cos^3(\theta)}{H^2}$$

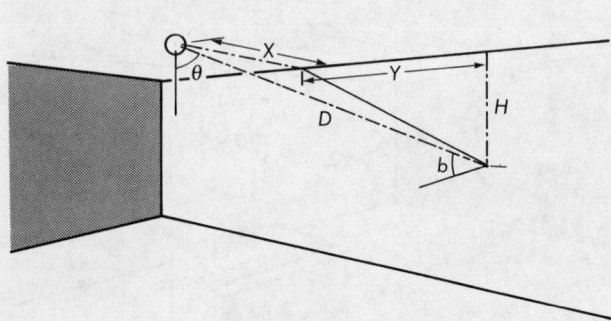

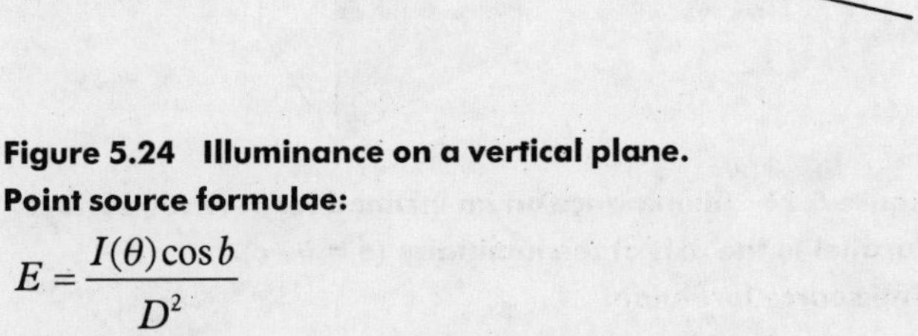

Figure 5.24 Illuminance on a vertical plane.
Point source formulae:

$$E = \frac{I(\theta)\cos b}{D^2}$$

or

$$E = \frac{I(\theta)\sin a}{D^2}$$

where $\sin a = \dfrac{X}{D}$

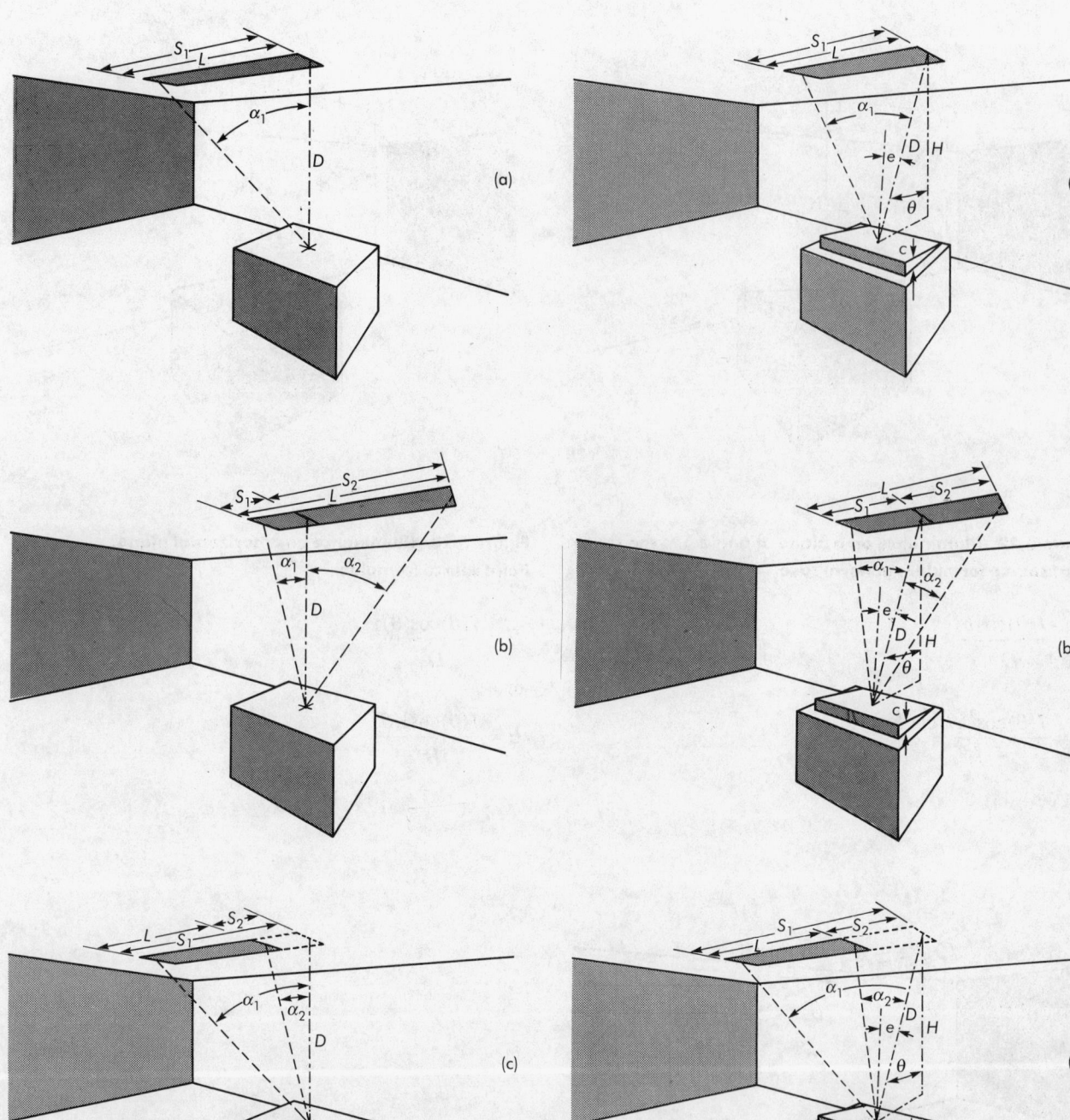

Figure 5.25 Illuminance on a horizontal surface.
Line source formulae:

(a) $E = \dfrac{I(\theta)\mathrm{AF}(\alpha_1)}{LD}$

(b) $E = \dfrac{I(\theta)[\mathrm{AF}(\alpha_1) + \mathrm{AF}(\alpha_2)]}{LD}$

(c) $E = \dfrac{I(\theta)[\mathrm{AF}(\alpha_1) - \mathrm{AF}(\alpha_2)]}{LD}$

Figure 5.26 Illuminance on an inclined (or vertical) surface parallel to the axis of the luminaire ($e = \theta - c$).
Line source formulae:

(a) $E = \dfrac{I(\theta)\cos e\,\mathrm{AF}(\alpha_1)}{LD}$

(b) $E = \dfrac{I(\theta)\cos e[\mathrm{AF}(\alpha_1) + \mathrm{AF}(\alpha_2)]}{LD}$

(c) $E = \dfrac{I(\theta)\cos e[\mathrm{AF}(\alpha_1) - \mathrm{AF}(\alpha_2)]}{LD}$

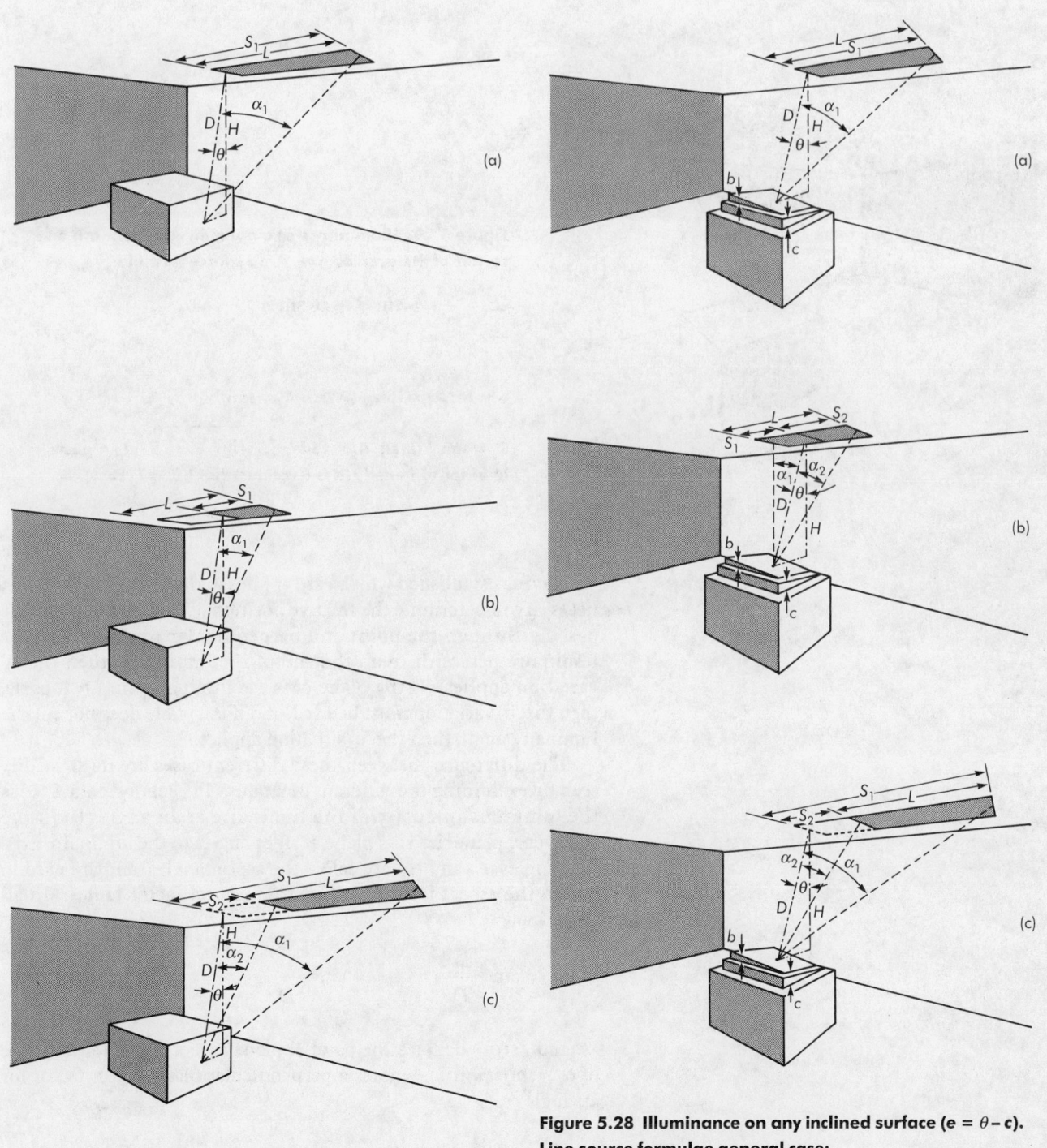

Figure 5.28 Illuminance on any inclined surface (e = θ − c).
Line source formulae general case:

(a) $E = \dfrac{I(\theta)\cos e \cos b \,\mathrm{AF}(\alpha_1) + I(\theta)\sin b \, af(\alpha_1)}{LD}$

(b) $E = \dfrac{I(\theta)\cos e \cos b[\mathrm{AF}(\alpha_1) + \mathrm{AF}(\alpha_2)] + I(\theta)\sin b[\, af(\alpha_1) + af(\alpha_2)]}{LD}$

(c) $E = \dfrac{I(\theta)\cos e \cos b[\mathrm{AF}(\alpha_1) - \mathrm{AF}(\alpha_2)] + I(\theta)\sin b[\, af(\alpha_1) - af(\alpha_2)]}{LD}$

Figure 5.27 Illuminance on a vertical surface
perpendicular to the axis of the luminaire.
Line source formulae:

(a) $E = \dfrac{I(\theta)af(\alpha_1)}{LD}$

(b) $E = \dfrac{I(\theta)af(\alpha_1)}{LD}$

(c) $E = \dfrac{I(\theta)[af(\alpha_1) - af(\alpha_2)]}{LD}$

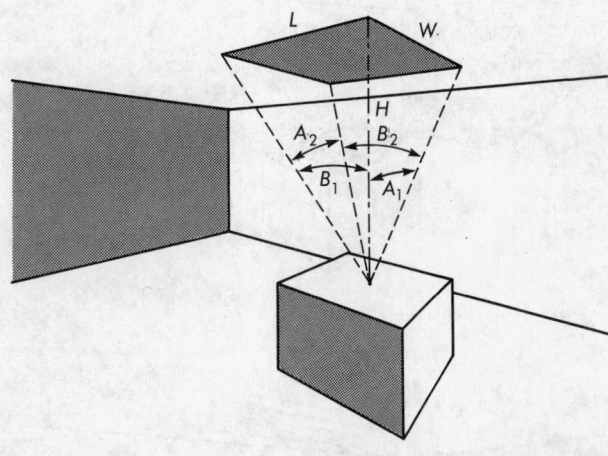

Figure 5.29   Illuminance at a point directly beneath one corner of the area source. Area source formula:

$$E = \frac{I_\mathrm{p}}{2}(A_2 \sin B_1 + B_2 \sin A_1)$$

where: $A_1 = \tan^{-1}(W/H)$; $A_2 = \tan^{-1}[W\sqrt{(L^2 + H^2)}]$;

$B_1 = \tan^{-1}(L/H)$; $B_2 = \tan^{-1}[L\sqrt{(W^2 + H^2)}]$; I_p = peak luminous intensity (it is assumed that $I(\theta) = I_\mathrm{p}\cos\theta$).

Having established which case applies to the situation, it is then necessary to determine the relative position of the source. If a plane passing through the point and perpendicular to the axis of the luminaire passes through the end of the luminaire, then the 'a' variation applies. If the plane cuts the luminaire into two parts, then the 'b' variation must be used, and if the plane does not cut the luminaire at all, then the 'c' situation applies.

The differences between these different cases are most readily seen by examining the different diagrams. In each formula, $I(\theta)$ is the luminous intensity of the luminaire at an angle (θ) in the transverse plane; i.e. in a plane at right angles to the luminaire axis. The angles α_1 and α_2 are called the aspect angles' and are used to obtain the aspect factors (AF, *af*) from aspect factor tables. In all cases:

$$\alpha_1 = \tan^{-1}\frac{S_1}{D} \qquad \alpha_2 = \tan^{-1}\frac{S_2}{D}$$

and $AF(\alpha_1)$ denotes the parallel plane aspect factor for an angle of α_1, whilst $af(\alpha_2)$ denotes a perpendicular plane aspect factor for an angle α_2.

5.13.4 Area source formulae

The basic formula for a uniform area source with a cosine distribution gives the illuminance at a point directly beneath one corner. The geometry is given in Figure 5.29.

To obtain the illuminance at a point that is not directly beneath one corner, it is necessary to add or subtract contributions from four imaginary area sources, each with a corner over the point to obtain the resultant.

5.14   Uplighting design

5.14.1 Introduction

The technique of uplighting involves illuminating the ceiling and upper walls of an interior, which then serve as large diffuse sources illuminating the room. The lighting effect from a large diffuse source is softer than that from direct lighting, with no harsh shadows, giving good visual conditions, and a reduction in problems of reflections in VDT screens and keyboards.

Before designing an uplighting scheme, the purpose of the lighting and the suitability of the interior should be considered. Because the ceiling and upper walls are directly illuminated, uplighting will often be chosen to provide a decorative function, to highlight the building structure or accentuate an important architectural feature. It can be used to reveal the character and texture of an ornately decorated ceiling, for example, but if the ceiling is of low reflectance uplighting alone is not likely to be an efficient means of providing the room lighting, and should be used in combination with some direct lighting.

5.14.2 Design criteria

5.14.2.1 Illuminance and uniformity

Illuminance should be selected from the recommendations for the activity or task given in this *Code* (see section 2.6.4). Uplighting can be designed to provide general lighting, or localised lighting (section 4.4.2). The uplighting can either provide a uniform background level of illuminance, supplemented by separate local task lighting, or the uplights can be placed adjacent to work stations, producing a variation in illuminance between task and background. This localised arrangement is the most energy efficient, and, as changes in illuminance from task to background are smooth, the resulting diversity is acceptable.

Uplights are usually designed with a wide spread of light, to produce a large illuminated patch on the ceiling. It is not normally desirable to attempt to light the ceiling uniformly, but the ceiling luminance should be within recommended luminance limits.

5.14.2.2 Glare

Direct glare will be avoided by the choice of a properly designed luminaire and correct selection of mounting height and position. Free standing luminaires are usually about 1.8 m high, i.e. above normal eye height for a person standing nearby. When positioning uplights in areas with more than one level, the risk of a direct view into the uplight, for example by a person descending a staircase, should be avoided.

The luminance of the ceiling should be controlled to avoid reflected glare from the ceiling, and problems with excessively bright reflections in VDT screens. The average ceiling luminance should not be more than 500 cd/m^2 with a maximum of 1500 cd/m^2.

5.14.2.3 General requirements

To maximise efficiency, the reflectance of the ceiling should be as high as possible, preferably greater than 70% (see Table 5.9, page 217). The upper walls should be treated in the same way as the ceiling, especially if the uplights are some distance below the ceiling.

Ceilings should be near-white, as strongly coloured ceilings will influence the colour of the light reflected into the room, apart from reducing the system efficiency.

Surfaces should preferably be matt, as gloss finishes will produce bright images of the uplight in the ceiling, creating a potential glare source, and tending to reduce the uniformity of illuminance on the working plane. A small degree of specularity, however can usually be tolerated.

Ceilings can be plain or textured, flat or coffered, but obstructions such as beams or girders should be avoided if possible as they will reduce the installation efficiency.

Uplighting in rooms where the uplights are some distance below the ceiling will be less efficient than in rooms with large, shallow ceiling cavities, although the uniformity of ceiling luminance will usually be higher.

Overall system efficiency normally requires well designed, high efficiency optics used with high efficacy light sources such as high pressure sodium or metal halide, although fluorescent lamps are suitable for installations with very low ceilings, or where lower levels of illuminance are required. Uplighters with tungsten halogen lamps tend to be limited to decorative applications due to the relatively low lamp efficacy.

5.14.3 Calculations

5.14.3.1 Cavity reflectance

In an uplighting installation, all upward light from the luminaires is directed into the ceiling cavity. Light is absorbed by interreflection in the cavity, depending on the surface reflectances and the shape and size of the cavity. The result is to reduce the effective reflectance of the cavity to less than the actual ceiling reflectance, and an accurate assessment of the reflectance of the cavity is necessary to ensure that calculations are correct (see section 4.5.3.3).

Table 4.10 (page 164–165) gives the effective reflectances of cavities, R_C, for a range of actual surface reflectances and cavity indices.

5.14.3.2 UF calculation

The lumen method can be used to calculate the average illuminance from an array of uplights, or the number of uplights required to achieve a particular average illuminance. Using the lumen method formula given in section 4.5.3.5(f):

$$UF_F = ULOR \times TF_{C,F}$$

Table 5.21 Transfer factor table, $\text{TF}_{C,F}$ (for R_F other than 20% refer to Table 5.24)

Reflectance			Room index (K)									
R_C	R_W	R_F	0.75	1.00	1.25	1.50	2.00	2.50	3.00	4.00	5.00	∞
80	50	20	0.406	0.492	0.556	0.605	0.674	0.721	0.754	0.798	0.826	0.886
80	30	20	0.333	0.418	0.485	0.537	0.613	0.665	0.704	0.756	0.790	0.865
80	10	20	0.281	0.364	0.430	0.483	0.562	0.618	0.660	0.719	0.758	0.846
70	50	20	0.349	0.423	0.477	0.519	0.578	0.617	0.645	0.683	0.707	0.758
70	30	20	0.288	0.362	0.419	0.463	0.528	0.573	0.605	0.649	0.678	0.741
70	10	20	0.245	0.317	0.373	0.419	0.487	0.535	0.570	0.620	0.652	0.726
60	50	20	0.294	0.356	0.401	0.436	0.485	0.518	0.542	0.573	0.593	0.635
60	30	20	0.245	0.307	0.354	0.392	0.446	0.483	0.510	0.547	0.570	0.622
60	10	20	0.209	0.270	0.318	0.356	0.413	0.453	0.482	0.523	0.550	0.610
50	50	20	0.241	0.291	0.328	0.357	0.396	0.423	0.442	0.467	0.483	0.518
50	30	20	0.202	0.253	0.292	0.322	0.366	0.396	0.418	0.447	0.467	0.508
50	10	20	0.173	0.224	0.263	0.294	0.340	0.373	0.397	0.430	0.451	0.499

Table 5.21 gives transfer factors $\text{TF}_{C,F}$ for a range of reflectance and room index (K) values.

Note: To calculate K, the value of h_m is as shown on Figure 5.30.

5.14.3.3 Ceiling luminance calculations

The average and maximum ceiling luminances are given by:

$$L_{ave} = \frac{N \times F \times \text{ULOR} \times R_C}{\pi \times A}$$

$$L_{max} = \frac{I_{180°-\theta} \times \cos^3 \theta \times R_C}{\pi \times h_o^2}$$

See Figure 5.30.

This method is valid if the distance between uplight and ceiling is at least three times the maximum luminous dimension of the up-lighter optic, e.g. 1.2 m for 400 mm diameter reflector.

To ensure compliance throughout the life of the installation, calculations should be based on initial lamp lumens (F) and no maintenance factor.

The minimum ceiling height necessary to achieve compliance with the maximum luminance limit for a given R_C can also be calculated for a particular uplight.

5.14.3.4 Illuminance distribution

A simple method, suitable for manual calculation, to predict illuminance values from uplights, is provided by the 'equivalent point source' technique[203]. This separates the uplighting into two parts:

(a) illuminance E_d from the first reflection from the ceiling, which is considered to be produced by an imaginary point source above the ceiling

(b) illuminance E_i from all subsequent inter-reflections, which is considered to be uniformly distributed over the working plans.

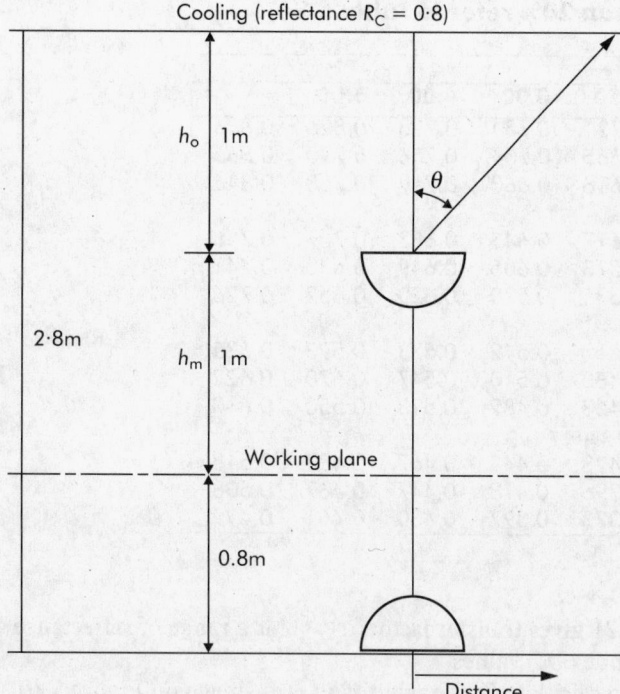

Table 5.22 Scale correction factors for illuminance curve (uplight height of 1.8 m and working plane height of 0.8 m)

Ceiling height (m)	D_k	E_k
2.4	0.73	1.86
2.6	0.87	1.33
2.8	1.00	1.00
3.0	1.13	0.78
3.2	1.27	0.62
3.4	1.40	0.51
3.6	1.53	0.43
3.8	1.67	0.36
4.0	1.80	0.31

Figure 5.30   Uplighter calculations and standard conditions for published data in Figure 5.31

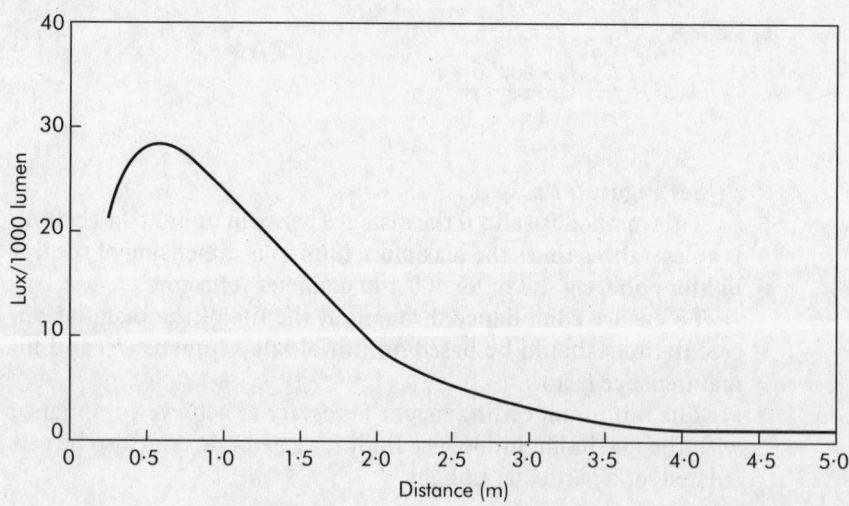

Figure 5.31   Example of illuminance curve for uplighter

First reflection—use of illuminance curves

Standard conditions for published curves are shown in Figure 5.30, and an example curve is shown in Figure 5.31.

The illuminance curves can be converted for other values of ceiling reflectance and ceiling height.

Table 5.22 gives scale correction factors D_k and E_k for various ceiling heights for a 0.8 m working plane and a 1.8 m uplighter height. D_k is applied to the horizontal (distance) axis and E_k to the vertical (lux per 1000 lamp lumens) axis on Figure 5.31.

Multiply the horizontal (distance) axis by D_k.

Multiply the vertical (illuminance) axis by:

$$\frac{R_C}{0.8} \times \frac{F}{1000} \times E_k = E_d$$

where R_C is the actual ceiling reflectance, and F is the actual lamp lumens.

The scale correction factors for other uplighter heights and working planes can be calculated from:

$$D_k = \frac{h_m + 2h_o}{3}$$

and

$$E_k = \left(\frac{3}{h_m + 2h_o}\right)^2$$

Subsequent inter-reflections

The contribution from all subsequent inter-reflections is considered to be distributed uniformly over the whole uplit area. The value of E_i is added to the values of the first reflection illuminance values at each point of interest, and is calculated as follows:

$$E_i = \frac{N \times F \times UI_F \times ULOR}{A}$$

Table 5.23 gives values of indirect utilance UI_F.

Note: to calculate K the value of h_m is as shown in Figure 5.30. The value of maintained illuminance (E) is therefore:

$$E = MF\,(E_d + E_i)$$

Table 5.23   Utilance table for 'indirect' light, UI_F (for R_F values other than 20% refer to Table 5.24)

Reflectances			Room index (K)									
R_C	R_W	R_F	0.75	1.00	1.25	1.50	2.00	2.50	3.00	4.00	5.00	∞
80	50	20	0.150	0.160	0.165	0.167	0.169	0.168	0.168	0.166	0.164	0.152
80	30	20	0.077	0.086	0.093	0.099	0.107	0.113	0.117	0.124	0.129	0.152
80	10	20	0.025	0.032	0.038	0.045	0.056	0.066	0.074	0.087	0.096	0.152
70	50	20	0.125	0.132	0.135	0.136	0.135	0.134	0.133	0.130	0.128	0.114
70	30	20	0.064	0.071	0.076	0.080	0.085	0.089	0.092	0.096	0.099	0.114
70	10	20	0.021	0.026	0.031	0.036	0.044	0.051	0.057	0.067	0.073	0.114
60	50	20	0.102	0.107	0.108	0.108	0.106	0.104	0.102	0.099	0.096	0.082
60	30	20	0.053	0.058	0.061	0.063	0.067	0.069	0.070	0.073	0.074	0.082
60	10	20	0.017	0.021	0.024	0.028	0.034	0.039	0.043	0.049	0.054	0.082
50	50	20	0.081	0.084	0.084	0.083	0.080	0.078	0.076	0.072	0.070	0.056
50	30	20	0.042	0.045	0.047	0.048	0.050	0.051	0.052	0.053	0.053	0.056
50	10	20	0.013	0.016	0.018	0.021	0.024	0.028	0.030	0.035	0.038	0.056

Table 5.24 Correction factor to convert UF_F values for 0.20 floor reflectance to other values of floor reflectance. Multiply the published UF_F value by the appropriate factor.

$R_F = 0.0$

Reflectances			Room index (K)								
R_C	R_W	R_F	0.75	1.00	1.25	1.50	2.00	2.50	3.00	4.00	5.00
0.70	0.50		0.948	0.937	0.928	0.921	0.910	0.902	0.896	0.889	0.888
	0.30	0.00	0.966	0.955	0.946	0.938	0.925	0.916	0.909	0.899	0.892
	0.10		0.980	0.970	0.961	0.951	0.938	0.928	0.920	0.908	0.900
0.50	0.50		0.957	0.950	0.943	0.939	0.932	0.927	0.923	0.918	0.915
	0.30	0.00	0.973	0.965	0.959	0.953	0.944	0.938	0.934	0.927	0.923
	0.10		0.985	0.978	0.971	0.965	0.955	0.948	0.943	0.934	0.929
0.30	0.50		0.965	0.962	0.959	0.957	0.953	0.951	0.950	0.948	0.946
	0.30	00.0	0.978	0.975	0.971	0.968	0.963	0.960	0.958	0.954	0.951
	0.10		0.989	0.985	0.981	0.978	0.972	0.968	0.964	0.960	0.957

$R_F = 0.10$

Reflectances			Room index (K)								
R_C	R_W	R_F	0.75	1.00	1.25	1.50	2.00	2.50	3.00	4.00	5.00
0.70	0.50		0.973	0.968	0.962	0.959	0.953	0.948	0.945	0.941	0.938
	0.30	0.10	0.983	0.977	0.973	0.968	0.961	0.956	0.953	0.947	0.943
	0.10		0.990	0.984	0.980	0.975	0.968	0.962	0.959	0.952	0.947
0.50	0.50		0.978	0.974	0.971	0.969	0.965	0.962	0.960	0.957	0.955
	0.30	0.10	0.986	0.983	0.979	0.976	0.972	0.968	0.965	0.962	0.960
	0.10		0.993	0.988	0.985	0.983	0.977	0.973	0.971	0.965	0.963
0.30	0.50		0.983	0.981	0.979	0.978	0.976	0.975	0.974	0.973	0.973
	0.30	0.10	0.989	0.987	0.985	0.984	0.982	0.979	0.979	0.977	0.975
	0.10		0.994	0.992	0.991	0.988	0.985	0.984	0.982	0.980	0.978

$R_F = 0.30$

Reflectances			Room index (K)								
R_C	R_W	R_F	0.75	1.00	1.25	1.50	2.00	2.50	3.00	4.00	5.00
0.70	0.50		1.027	1.035	1.040	1.045	1.053	1.057	1.061	1.067	1.070
	0.30	0.30	1.017	1.024	1.029	1.035	1.043	1.048	1.053	1.060	1.063
	0.10		1.011	1.016	1.021	1.026	1.034	1.040	1.046	1.054	1.059
0.50	0.50		1.023	1.028	1.030	1.034	1.038	1.041	1.043	1.046	1.048
	0.30	0.30	1.014	1.018	1.022	1.026	1.030	1.034	1.037	1.042	1.044
	0.10		1.008	1.012	1.016	1.019	1.024	1.028	1.032	1.036	1.040
0.30	0.50		1.018	1.020	1.022	1.024	1.025	1.027	1.027	1.028	1.029
	0.30	0.30	1.011	1.014	1.016	1.016	1.019	1.021	1.023	1.025	1.026
	0.10		1.005	1.008	1.010	1.012	1.015	1.017	1.018	1.021	1.024

Part 6

Glossary, abbreviations, bibliography and references

6.1 Glossary

The explanations and definitions given in this Glossary are intended to help readers to understand the Code. They are based on *BS 4727: Part 4: Glossary of terms particular to lighting and colour* (1971/1972)[204] and on the *International Lighting Vocabulary 1987*[112] issued jointly by the Commission Internationale de l'Eclairage (CIE) and the International Electrotechnical Commission (IEC). These documents should be consulted if more precise definitions are required.

Action spectrum

Any physiological or biological response to different wavelengths of radiation (not necessarily limited to the visual spectrum) can be plotted to give an action spectrum. The most familiar is the V_λ function, giving the sensitivity of the eye to stimuli throughout the visible spectrum. However, others, such as those for plant growth or sun tanning, are also important.

Adaptation

The process which takes place as the visual system adjusts itself to the brightness or the colour (chromatic adaptation) of the visual field. The term is also used, usually qualified, to denote the final state of this process. For example 'dark adaptation' denotes the state of the visual system when it has become adapted to a very low luminance.

Apostilb (asb)

A non-SI unit of luminance. One apostilb is the luminance of a uniform diffuser emitting one lumen per square metre (see Table 6.1, page 263).

Apparent colour

Of a light source; subjectively the hue of the source or of a white surface illuminated by the source; the degree of warmth associated with the source colour. Lamps of low correlated colour temperatures are usually described as having a warm apparent colour, and lamps of high correlated colour temperature as having a cold apparent colour.

Aspect factor (AF, *af*)

A function of the angle subtended at a point by the length of a linear source, and of the axial distribution of luminous intensity from the source; used in the calculation of illuminance at a point.

Average illuminance (E_{ave})

The arithmetic mean illuminance over the specified surface.

Black body

See *Full radiator*.

Brightness

The subjective response to luminance in the field of view dependent upon the adaptation of the eye.

Brightness constancy

Sometimes referred to as 'lightness' or 'whiteness' constancy. The condition achieved under adequate illuminance where the perceived 'lightness' of objects is relatively unchanged through fairly large changes of illuminance. For example, a dimly lit sheet of matt white paper may have a lower luminance than a brightly lit sheet of matt black paper but the former will still look white and the latter black. See also *Colour constancy*.

BZ (British Zonal) System (obsolescent)

A system for classifying luminaires, as described in CIBSE *TM5*[100], in terms of the flux from a conventional installation directly incident on the working plane, relative to the total flux emitted below the horizontal (the direct ratio). The BZ class number (e.g. BZ3) is, however, no longer used.

Candela (cd)

The SI unit of luminous intensity, equal to one lumen per steradian.

Cavity index (CI)

A term, indicating the proportions of boundary surfaces, used in determining the effective reflectances of room, floor or ceiling cavities for interior lighting design: defined for a cavity of length L, width W, and height h, as $LW/[h(L+W)]$.

Ceiling cavity reflectance (RE_C, R_C)

Effective reflectance of the room volume above the plane of the luminaires.

Chroma

In the Munsell system, an index of saturation of colour ranging from 0 for neutral grey to 10 or over for strong colours. A low chroma implies a pastel shade.

Chromatic adaptation

The process which takes place as the visual system adjusts to changes in the colour of different light sources.

Chromaticity

The colour quality of a stimulus, usually defined by coordinates on a plane diagram in the CIE colorimetric system (CIE publication 15.2[205]) or by the combination of dominant wavelength and purity.

CIE chromaticity diagram

A plane diagram showing the effect of mixtures of colour stimuli, each chromaticity being represented unambiguously by a single point on the diagram (see Figure 5.11, page 213).

CIE standard photometric observer

A receptor of radiation whose relative spectral sensitivity curve conforms to either the V_λ (photopic) or the V'_λ (scotopic) curve (see CIE publication 41 (1978)[206] and *ISO/CIE 10527*[207]).

Colour atlas

A collection of colour samples arranged according to specified rules.

Colour constancy

The condition resulting from the process of chromatic adaptation whereby the colour of objects is not perceived to change greatly under a wide range of lighting conditions both in terms of colour quality and luminance. See also *Brightness constancy*.

Colour rendering

A general expression for the appearance of surface colours when illuminated by light from a given source compared, consciously or unconsciously, with their appearance under light from some reference source. 'Good colour rendering' implies similarity of appearance to that under an acceptable light source, such as daylight.

Colour rendering index (CRI)

A measure of the degree to which the colours of surfaces illuminated by a given light source conform to those of the same surfaces under a reference illuminant, suitable allowance having been made for the state of chromatic adaptation (see also *Adaptation* and CIE publication 13.2[208]).

Colour solid

That part of a colour space that is occupied by surface colours.

Colour space

A geometric representation of colours in space, usually of three dimensions.

Colour temperature (T_c, unit: K)

The temperature of a 'full radiator' which emits radiation of the same chromaticity as the radiator being considered.

Constancy

See *Brightness constancy* and *Colour constancy*.

Contrast

A term that is used subjectively and objectively. Subjectively it describes the difference in appearance of two parts of a visual field seen simultaneously or successively. The difference may be one of brightness or colour or both. Objectively, the term expresses the luminance difference between the two parts of the field by such relationships as:

$$\text{Contrast} = \left| \frac{L - L_1}{L_1} \right|$$

Quantitatively, the sign of the contrast is ignored. L_1 is the dominant or background luminance. L is the task luminance.

Contrast rendering factor (CRF)

The ratio of the contrast of a task under a given lighting installation to its contrast under reference lighting conditions (see section 5.5).

Contrast sensititivy

The reciprocal of the minimum perceptible contrast.

Correlated colour temperature (CCT, T_{cp}, unit: K)

The temperature of a full radiator which emits radiation having a chromaticity nearest to that of the light source being considered, e.g., the colour of a full radiator at 3500 K is the nearest match to that of a white tubular fluorescent lamp.

Cylindrical illuminance (E_c, E_{ez}, E_z, unit: lux)

Total luminous flux falling on the curved surface of a very small cylinder located at the specified point divided by the curved surface area of the cylinder. The axis of the cylinder is taken to be vertical unless stated otherwise. See also CIE publication 17.4 845-09-49[112].

Daylight factor (D)

The illuminance received at a point indoors, from a sky of known or assumed luminance distribution, expressed as a percentage of the horizontal illuminance outdoors from an unobstructed hemisphere of the same sky. Direct sunlight is excluded from both values of illuminance.

Daylight factor, externally reflected component (D_e)

The illuminance received directly at a point indoors from a sky of known or assumed luminance distribution after reflection from an external reflecting surface, expressed as a percentage of the horizontal illuminance outdoors from an unobstructed hemisphere of the same sky. Direct sunlight is excluded from both illuminances. See also *Daylight factor, internally reflected component*.

Daylight factor, internally reflected component (D_i)

The illuminance received at a point indoors from a sky of known or assumed luminance distribution after reflection within the interior, expressed as a percentage of the horizontal illuminance outdoors from an unobstructed hemisphere of the same sky. Direct sunlight is excluded from both illuminances. See also *Daylight factor, externally reflected component*.

Design maintained illuminance

The maintained illuminance used in a lighting specification. Design maintained illuminance is derived from the standard maintained illuminance by taking account of the modifying factors contained in the flow chart (see Figure 2.3, page 43).

Design service illuminance (obsolete)

See *Design maintained illuminance*.

Diffuse reflection

Reflection in which the reflected light is diffused and there is no significant specular reflection, as from a matt paint.

Diffuse lighting

Lighting in which the luminous flux comes from many directions, none of which predominates.

Direct lighting

Lighting in which the greater part of the luminous flux from the luminaires reaches the surface (usually the working plane) directly, i.e. without reflection from surrounding surfaces. Luminaires with a flux fraction ratio less than 0.1 are usually regarded as direct.

Direct ratio (DR)

The proportion of the total downward luminous flux from a conventional installation of luminaires which is directly incident on the working plane.

Directional lighting

Lighting designed to illuminate a task or surface predominantly from one direction.

Disability glare

Glare produced directly or by reflection that impairs the vision of objects without necessarily causing discomfort. See also CIE publication 17.4 845-02-57[112].

Discharge lamp

A lamp in which the light is produced either directly or by the excitation of phosphors by an electric discharge through a gas, a metal vapour or a mixture of several gases and vapours.

Discomfort glare

Glare which causes visual discomfort.

Display illuminance ratio (DIR)

The ratio between the value of local illuminance in the plane of the object to be displayed and the general horizontal plane illuminance in a room (see section 2.4.8).

Diversity (illuminance (D_E) luminance (D_L))

The ratio of minimum to maximum illuminance (or luminance) over a specified area.

Downlighter

Direct lighting luminaire from which light is emitted only within relatively small angles to the downward vertical.

Downward light output ratio (DLOR)

The ratio of the total light output of a luminaire below the horizontal under stated practical conditions to that of the lamp or lamps under reference conditions.

Effective reflectance

Estimated reflectance of a surface, based on the relative areas and the reflectances of the materials forming the surface. Thus, 'effective wall reflectance' takes account of the reflectances of the wall surface, the windows, the filing cabinets etc., that comprise the sides of a room.

Efficacy

See *Luminous efficacy*.

Emergency lighting

Lighting provided for use when the main lighting installation fails.

Energy efficiency

See *Installed efficacy* and *Installed power density*.

Energy management systems (EMS)

Computer base systems for controlling the energy use of the installed load of a complete site, a single building or a section of the building. The signals which initiate the controls may be related to time of year, month, week or day, maximum demand or power factor, daylight availability, occupancy etc. Building energy management systems (BEMS) provide control commands for all equipment on a site, whilst a lighting energy management system (LEMS) will be dedicated to the lighting installation. The LEMS can be independent or linked into the BEMS. Such systems can also be linked to security, fire warning and maintenance systems.

Escape lighting

Emergency lighting provided to ensure that the means of escape can be safely and effectively used at all material times.

Exitance

See *Radiant exitance*.

Flashed (luminous) area

See *Luminous area*.

Flicker

Visible modulation of luminous flux.

Floor cavity reflectance (RE_F, R_F)

Effective reflectance of the room volume below the working plane (see *Cavity index*).

Flux fraction

The proportion of luminous flux emitted from a luminaire in the upper or lower hemisphere (upper and lower flux fractions).

Flux fraction ratio (FFR)

The ratio of the upward luminous flux to the downward luminous flux from a luminaire. It is also the ratio of the upper flux fraction to the lower flux fraction and the ratio of the upward light output ratio to the downward light output ratio.

Foot-candle (fc)

A non-SI unit of illuminance, until recently used in the USA, having the same value as the lumen per square foot (1 foot-candle = 10.76 lm/m^2).

Foot-lambert (fL)

A non-SI unit of luminance based on the same concept as the apostilb. One foot lambert is the luminance of a uniform diffuser emitting one lumen per square foot (see Table 6.1).

Full radiator

A thermal radiator obeying Planck's radiation law and having the maximum possible radiant exitance for all wavelengths for a given temperature; also called a 'black body' to emphasise its absorption of all incident radiation.

Full radiator locus

The curve on a chromaticity diagram representing the colour of the radiation from a full radiator as a function of its temperature.

General lighting

Lighting designed to illuminate the whole of an area without provision for special local requirements.

General surround lighting

Lighting designed to illuminate the non-working parts of a working interior.

Glare

The discomfort or impairment of vision experienced when parts of the visual field are excessively bright in relation to the general surroundings.

Glare index system

A system which produces a numerical index calculated according to the method described in CIBSE *TM10*[126]. It enables the discomfort glare from lighting installations to be ranked in order of severity and the permissible limit of discomfort glare from an installation to be prescribed quantitatively.

Glare rating system

See *Glare index system*.

Gloss factor

See *Luminance factor*.

Greyness

The estimated grey content of surface colours on a scale from maximum greyness to zero greyness (from *BS 5252*[169]).

Group lamp replacement

A maintenance procedure where all lamps are replaced at one time. The lumen maintenance characteristics and probability of lamp failure dictate the period after which bulk replacement, usually linked with luminaire cleaning, will take place. This method has visual, electrical and financial advantages over the alternative of 'spot replacement'.

Hazardous environment

An environment in which there exists risk of fire or explosion.

Hostile environment

An environment in which the lighting equipment may be subject to chemical, thermal or mechanical attack.

Hue

Colour in the sense of red, or yellow or green etc. (see section 5.7).

Ingress protection (IP) number

A two-digit number associated with a luminaire. The first digit classifies the degree of protection the luminaire provides against the ingress of solid foreign bodies. The second digit classifies the degree of protection the luminaire provides against the ingress of moisture (see section 3.3.1).

Illuminance (E, units: lm/m^2, lux)

The luminous flux density at a surface, i.e. the luminous flux incident per unit area. This quantity was formerly known as the illumination value or illumination level. See also *Average illuminance*, *Maintained illuminance*, *Maximum illuminance* and *Minimum illuminance*.

Illuminance diversity

See *Diversity*.

Illumination

The process of lighting.

Illumination vector ($\overrightarrow{E}$, unit: lux)

A term used to describe the directional characteristics of light at a point. Its magnitude is the difference in the illuminances on opposite sides of a flat surface which is so orientated that this difference is a maximum. Its direction is normal to this surface; the positive direction of the vector is from the higher illuminance to the lower illuminance.

Incandescent lamp

A lamp in which light is produced by a filament heated to incandescence by the passage of an electric current.

Indirect lighting

Lighting in which the greater part of the flux reaches the surface (usually the working plane) only after reflection at other surfaces, usually a roof or ceiling. Luminaires with a flux fraction ratio greater than 10 are usually regarded as indirect.

Initial illuminance (E_{avi}, units: lm/m^2, lux)

Average illuminance for a new installation when lamps, luminaires and room surfaces are clean.

$$E_{avi} = \frac{E_m(\text{maintained illuminance})}{MF(\text{maintenance factor})}$$

Initial light output (unit: lm)

The luminous flux from a new lamp. In the case of discharge lamps this is usually the output after 100 hours of operation.

Installed efficacy (unit: lm/W)

A factor which quantifies the effectiveness of a lighting installation in converting electrical power to light. Specifically it is the product of the lamp circuit luminous efficacy and the utilisation factor. Note that this term, used in the 1984 *Code for interior lighting*, is now replaced by *Installed power density*.

Installed power density (W/m^2/100 lux)

The installed power density per 100 lux is the power needed per square metre of floor area to achieve 100 lux on a horizontal plane with general lighting.

Intensity

See *Luminous intensity*.

Irradiance (E_e, E, unit: W/m^2)

The radiant flux density at a surface, i.e. the radiant flux incident per unit area of the surface.

Isolux diagram

A diagram showing contours of equal illuminance.

Lambert (L)

A non-SI unit of luminance based on the same concept as the apostilb; one lambert is the luminance of a uniform diffuser emitting one lumen per square centimetre (see Table 6.1, page 263).

Lamp luminous flux (lumen) maintenance factor (LLMF)

The proportion of the initial light output of a lamp that is produced after a stated period of operation.

Lamp life survival factor (LSF)

The percentage of functioning lamps in an installation after a stated period of operation.

Light loss factor (LLF)

See *Maintenance factor*.

Light output ratio (LOR)

The ratio of the total light output of a luminaire under stated practical conditions to that of the lamp or lamps under reference conditions. For the luminaire, the output is usually measured in the designated operating position at 25°C ambient temperature with control gear of the type usually supplied in a luminaire and operated at its normal voltage. For the lamp the output is measured at 25°C ambient temperature and with control gear of standard properties. This is a practical basis for evaluating the total light output to be expected under service conditions. Note: previously, measurement of lamp flux was also made with a practical ballast and required correction using a 'ballast lumen factor'.

Lighting design lumens (LDL, unit:lumen) (obsolete)

A nominal value which is representative of the average light output of a lamp throughout its life. This term is now obsolete with the introduction of lighting design recommendations in terms of maintained illuminance.

Lightness

A subjective estimate of the proportion of light diffusely reflected by a body or surface.

Lightness constancy

See *Brightness constancy*.

Limiting glare rating

The maximum value of the glare rating which is recommended for a specific lighting application. See *Glare index system*.

Load factor

The ratio of the energy actually consumed by a lighting installation with controls over a specified period of time to the energy that would have been consumed had the lighting installation been operated without controls during the same period of time.

Local lighting

Lighting designed to illuminate a particular small area which usually does not extend far beyond the visual task, e.g. a desk light.

Localised lighting

Lighting designed to illuminate an interior and at the same time to provide higher illuminances over a particular part, or parts, of the interior.

Lumen (lm)

The SI unit of luminous flux, used in describing a quantity of light emitted by a source or received by a surface. A small source which has a uniform luminous intensity of one candela emits a total of 4π lumens in all directions and emits one lumen within a unit solid angle, i.e. 1 steradian.

Luminaire

An apparatus which controls the distribution of light given by a lamp or lamps and which includes all the components necessary for fixing and protecting the lamps and for connecting them to the supply circuit. Luminaire has officially superseded the term 'lighting fitting' which is still used colloquially.

Luminaire maintenance factor (LMF)

The proportion of the initial light output from the luminaire that occurs after a set time due to dirt deposition on and in the luminaire. Lamp luminous flux (lumen) maintenance is not included.

Luminance (L, unit: cd/m^2)

The physical measure of the stimulus which produces the sensation of brightness measured by the luminous intensity of the light emitted or reflected in a given direction from a surface element, divided by the projected area of the element in the same direction. The SI unit of luminance is the candela per square metre. The relationship between luminance and illuminance is given by the equation:

$$\text{Luminance} = \frac{\text{Illuminance} \times \text{Reflectance factor}}{\pi}$$

This equation applies to a matt surface. For a non-matt surface, the reflectance is replaced by the luminance factor.

The luminance of the sky (and other sources that cannot be visualised as surfaces) may be described in terms of the illuminance produced on a surface.

Luminance of a small zone of sky

$$= \frac{\text{Illuminance on a surface directly facing sky zone}}{\pi \times \text{Angular size of zone}}$$

(See Table 6.1, page 263.)

Luminance coefficient

The ratio of the luminance of an element of surface to the illuminance on it for given angles of viewing and incident light.

Luminance factor (β_v, β)

Also known as gloss factor. The ratio of the luminance of a reflecting surface, viewed in a given direction, to that of an identically illuminated 'perfect white' uniform diffusing surface. For a non-matt surface the luminance factor may be greater or less than the reflectance.

Luminous area

The area of a lamp or luminaire which emits light. For a flat surface the projected area varies with the cosine of the angle between the direction of view and the normal to the surface. For a spherical surface the projected area is constant for all directions of view. For less regular solids, e.g. a surface diffuser luminaire, the luminous surfaces in various planes must be calculated separately. For specular reflectors or prismatic optics the 'flashed luminous area' varies with viewing angle and no simple relationship applies in practice.

Luminous efficacy (η_v, η, unit: lm/W)

The ratio of the luminous flux emitted by a lamp to the power consumed by the lamp. When the power consumed by control gear is taken into account this term is sometimes knows and lamp circuit luminous efficacy and is expressed in lumens per circuit watt.

Luminous efficiency (v)

The ratio of the radiant flux weighted according to the CIE standard photometric observer to the corresponding radiant flux at a given wavelength (*ISO/CIE 10527*[207]).

Luminous flux (ϕ_v, ϕ, unit: lm)

The light emitted by a source, or received by a surface. The quantity is derived from radiant flux by evaluating the radiation in accordance with the spectral sensitivity of the standard eye as described by the CIE standard photometric observer (*ISO/CIE 10527*[207]).

Luminous intensity (I, unit: cd)

A quantity which describes the power of a source or illuminated surface to emit light in a given direction. It is the luminous flux emitted in a very narrow cone containing the given direction divided by the solid angle of the cone. Intensity is given by the product of illuminance multiplied by distance-squared, when distance is large compared with the source dimensions.

Luminous intensity distribution

The distribution of the luminous intensity of a lamp or luminaire in all directions. Luminous intensity distributions are usually shown in the form of a polar diagram, or a table, for a single vertical plane, in terms of candelas per 1000 lumens of lamp luminous flux.

Lux (lux)

The SI unit of illuminance, equal to one lumen per square metre (lm/m^2).

Maintained illuminance (E_m, unit: lux)

The average illuminance over the reference surface at the time maintenance has to be carried out by replacing lamps and/or cleaning the equipment and room surfaces. See also *Design maintained illuminance* and *Standard maintained illuminance*.

Maintenance factor (MF)

The ratio of the illuminance provided by an installation at some stated time, with respect to the initial illuminance, i.e. that after 100 hours of operation. The maintenance factor is the product of the lamp lumen maintenance factor, the lamp survival factor (where group lamp replacement without spot replacement is carried out), the luminaire maintenance factor and the room surface maintenance factor. Note: the introduction of maintained illuminance has fundamentally changed the definition of this term which was formally associated with service illuminance. Because of this recent change, the definition in the *International Lighting Vocabulary*, CIE publication 17.4 895-09-59[112], is now incorrect.

Maximum illuminance (E_{max}, unit: lux)

The highest value found by calculation or measurement at any point over a stated grid. Note: a search for the absolute maximum value is rarely, if ever, justified.

Maximum spacing-to-height ratio (SHR$_{max}$)

The SHR for a four-by-four square array of luminaires that gives a ratio of minimum to maximum direct illuminance of 0.7 over the central region between the four innermost luminaires. For the majority of luminaires SHR$_{max}$ is the spacing-to-height ratio at which the mid-point (or mid-area) ratio is 0.7.

Maximum transverse spacing-to-height ratio (SHR$_{max\ tr}$)

The SHR in the transverse plane for continuous lines of luminaires that gives a ratio of minimum to maximum direct illuminance of 0.7 over the central region between the two inner rows.

Mean cylindrical illuminance

See *Cylindrical illuminance*.

Metamerism

The phenomenon occurring when coloured objects which match under one illuminant do not match under another (object metamerism) or when illuminants of the same apparent colour do not have the same colour rendering properties (illuminant metamerism).

Mid-area ratio (MAR)

The ratio of the minimum to maximum direct illuminance values found within or on the boundaries of an 81-point grid under the inner four luminaires of a four-by-four luminaire array.

Mid-point ratio (MPR)

The ratio of the direct illuminance at the centre of a four-by-four square array of luminaires to the direct illuminance under the centre of one of the inner four luminaires. This is a simpler method than the mid-area method for calculating the maximum spacing-to-height ratio. However, it is only suited to luminaires with a relatively smooth intensity distribution and the MAR is generally preferred.

Minimum illuminance (E_{min}, unit: lux)

The lowest value found by calculation or measurement on any points of a stated grid. Note: a search for the absolute minimum value is rarely, if ever, justified.

Mixed reflection

Partly specular and partly diffused reflection, as from smooth, glossy paint. *See Luminance factor.*

Modulation (of luminous flux)

The variation of light output of any light source operated on an AC supply. The percentage modulation is given by:

$$\frac{\phi_{max} - \phi_{min}}{\phi_{max} + \phi_{min}} \times 100$$

Mounting height (h_m)

Usually the vertical distance between a luminaire and the working plane. In some cases the floor may be the effective working plane.

Munsell system

A system of surface colour classification using uniform colour scales of hue, value and chroma. A typical Munsell designation of a colour is 7.5 BG6/2, where 7.5 BG (blue green) is the hue reference, 6 is the value and 2 is the chroma reference number (see section 5.7).

Nominal spacing-to-height ratio SHR$_{nom}$

The highest value of SHR in the series 0.5, 0.75, 1.0 etc., that is not greater than SHR$_{max}$. Utilisation factor tables are normally calculated at a spacing-to-height ratio of SHR$_{nom}$.

No-sky line

The position on the reference plane from which, because of external obstructions, there is no direct view of the sky.

Operating efficacy (unit: lm/W)

A term which quantifies the efficacy of a lighting installation in use. Specifically operating efficacy is the product of the installed efficacy of the installation and the load factor.

Optical radiation

That part of the electromagnetic spectrum from 100 nm to 1 mm.

Power density

See *Installed power density*.

Power factor

In an electric circuit, the power factor is equal to the ratio of the root mean square power in watts to the product of the root mean square values of voltage and current; for sinusoidal waveforms the power factor is also equal to the cosine of the angle of phase difference between voltage and current.

Projected area

See *Luminous area*.

Purity

A measure of the proportions of the amounts of the monochromatic and specified achromatic light stimuli that, when additively mixed, match the colour stimulus. The proportions can be measured in different ways yielding either colorimetric purity or excitation purity.

Radiance (unit: $W/m^2/sr$)

At a point on a surface, the quotient of the radiant intensity emitted from an element of the surface in a given direction divided by the projected area of the element in the same direction.

Radiant efficiency (η_e, η)

The ratio of the radiant flux to the power consumed.

Radiant exitance (M_e, M, unit: W/m^2)

At a point on a surface, the product of the radiant flux leaving the surface.

Radiant exposure (H_e, H, unit: J/m^2)

At a point on a surface, the product of the irradiance and its duration (seconds).

Radiant flux (ϕ_e, ϕ, P, unit: W)

The power emitted, transferred or received as radiation.

Radiant intensity (I_e, I, unit: W/sr)

Of a source in a given direction; the quotient of the radiant flux emitted in a narrow cone containing the direction divided by the solid angle of that cone.

Rated maximum ambient temperature (t_a)

The temperature assigned to a luminaire, or component, by the manufacturer to indicate the highest sustained temperature in which the equipment may be operated under normal conditions to achieve stated luminous performance, life and safety claims.

Reference lighting

Perfectly diffuse and unpolarised lighting by CIE standard illuminant (source) A (see *ISO/CIE 10526*[209]).

Reference surface

The surface on which the visual task lies. See also *Working plane* and *Task area*. Note that the reference surface may be horizontal, vertical or inclined. Since the surface of the detector when measuring illuminance is supposed to coincide with the reference surface, the terms vertical illuminance and horizontal illuminance are also defined by the reference surface.

Reflectance (factor) (R, ρ)

The ratio of the luminous flux reflected from a surface to the luminous flux incident on it. Except for matt surfaces, reflectance depends on how the surface is illuminated but especially on the direction of the incident light and its spectral distribution. The value is always less than unity and is expressed as either a decimal or as a percentage.

Reflection factor

See *Reflectance*.

Relative spectral sensitivity (curve) V_λ

The visual effect of light energy at a particular wavelength is not uniform across the visible spectrum. The V_λ curve shows the relative effect of light at each wavelength, with that at 560 nm being equated to unity (*ISO/IEC 10527*[207]). See also CIE publication 17.4, 845-05-57[112].

Retinal illuminance

See *Troland*.

Room index (K)

An index related to the dimensions of a room and used when calculating the utilisation factor and other characteristics of the lighting installation:

$$\text{Room index} = \frac{L \times W}{h_m (L + W)}$$

where L is the length of the room, W the width and h_m the height of the luminaires above the working plane.

Room surface maintenance factor (RSMF)

The proportion of the illuminance provided by a lighting installation in a room after a set time compared with that when the room was clean. Depreciation in lumen output of lamps and the effect of dirt deposition on luminaires is not included.

Saturation

The subjective estimate of the amount of pure chromatic colour present in a sample, judged in proportion to its brightness.

Scalar (spherical) illuminance (E_s, $E_{v,o}$, unit: lux)

Total luminous flux falling on the whole surface of a very small sphere located at the specified point divided by the surface area of the sphere. See also CIE publication 17.4, 845-01-40[112].

Scalloping

A regular pattern of light and shade caused by luminaires, with a narrow light distribution, mounted close to vertical room surfaces.

Semi-cylindrical illuminance (E_{sc}, unit: lux)

Total luminous flux falling on the curved surface of a very small semi-cylinder located at the specified point, divided by the curved surface area of the semi-cylinder. The axis of the semi-cylinder is taken to be vertical unless stated otherwise.

Service illuminance (obsolete)

See *Maintained illuminance*.

Sky component of the daylight factor (D_c)

The illuminance received directly at a point indoors from a sky of known or assumed luminance distribution expressed as a percentage of the horizontal illuminance outdoors from an unobstructed hemisphere of the same sky. Direct sunlight is excluded from both values of illuminance.

Solid angle (unit: sr)

The angle subtended by an area at a point and equal to the quotient of the projected area on a sphere, centred on the point, by the square of the radius of the sphere; expressed in steradians.

Spacing-to-height ratio (SHR)

This ratio describes the distance between luminaire centres in relation to their height above the working plane. For a regular square arrangement of luminaires, it is the distance between adjacent luminaires divided by their height above the working plane. More generally,

$$\text{SHR} = \frac{1}{h_m} \sqrt{\frac{A}{N}}$$

where A is the total floor area, N is the number of luminaires and h_m is their height above the working plane.

Spectral (power or energy) distribution

Sometimes referred to as 'spectral composition'. The variation of radiant power (or energy) over a range of wavelengths.

Spectral luminous distribution

The result of applying the V_λ function to the spectral power distribution of a light source.

Spectral luminous efficiency

See *Relative spectral sensitivity*.

Specular reflection

Reflection without diffusion in accordance with the laws of optical reflection as in a mirror.

Spherical illuminance

See *Scalar illuminance*.

Spot lamp replacement

A maintenance procedure where individual lamps are replaced only when they fail. Particularly with discharge lamps, this is likely to result in a large proportion of the lamps operating well below their optimum economic efficacy and therefore a greater number of luminaires will need to be installed to achieve the required maintained illuminance during the operational life of the installation. Some spot lamp replacement may be necessary when group lamp replacement is adopted to replace early lamp failure occuring between initial installation and the bulk lamp change.

Standard maintained illuminance

The maintained illuminance recommended for the assumed standard conditions of the application. See *Design maintained illuminance*.

Standard photometric observer

See *CIE standard photometric observer*.

Standby lighting

Emergency lighting provided to enable normal activities to continue.

Steradian (sr)

The unit of solid angle. A complete sphere subtends 4π sr from the centre.

Stilb

A non-SI unit of luminance equal to one candela per square centimetre (cd/cm^2) (see Table 6.1, page 263).

Stroboscopic effect

An illusion caused by modulation of luminous flux, that makes a moving object appear as stationary or as moving in a manner different from that in which it is truly moving.

Task area

See also *Working plane* and *Reference plane*. The area containing those details and objects that must be seen for the performance of a given activity, and includes the immediate background of the details or objects. In the absence of precise dimensions the task area is assumed to be a 0.5 m square, which is placed within a 1 m square surround (see Figure 4.17, page 167).

Temperature rating (t_a)

See *Rated maximum ambient temperature*.

Transmission

The passing of radiation through a medium.

Transmittance (τ)

The ratio of luminous flux transmitted by a material to the incident luminous flux.

Trigger illuminance

The value of daylighting illuminance at the task at which a lighting control system switches the electric lighting on or off (see section 4.5.1.5).

Troland (Td)

Unit used to express a quantity proportional to retinal illuminance produced by a light stimulus. When the eye is viewing a surface of uniform luminance, the number of trolands is equal to the product of the area of pupil (mm²) and the luminance of the surface in cd/m².

Unified glare rating (UGR) system

A proposed CIE system which, at the time of publication, is not finalised. It is intended to provide and international agreed numerical rating. This value of UGR will enable the discomfort glare from lighting installations to be ranked in order of severity and the permissable limit of discomfort glare from an installation to be prescribed quantitively in the form of a limiting unified glare rating. See also *Glare index system*.

Uniform diffuser

A surface that emits a cosine intensity distribution.

Uniform chromaticity scale (UCS) diagram

A chromaticity diagram in which co-ordinate scales are chosen with the intention of making equal intervals represent approximately equal steps of discrimination for colours of the same luminance at all parts of the diagram (see CIE publication 15[168]).

Uniformity (illuminance (U_E) luminance (U_L))

The ratio of the minimum illuminance (or luminance) to the average illuminance (or luminance) over a specified surface. The ratio usually applies to values on the task area over the working plane. See also *Diversity* and CIE publication 17.4, 845-09-58[112].

Uplighter

Luminaires which direct most of the light upwards onto the ceiling or upper walls in order to illuminate the working plane by reflection. See also *Indirect lighting*.

Upward light output ratio (ULOR)

The ratio of the total light output of a luminaire above the horizontal under stated practical conditions to that of the lamp or lamps under reference conditions.

Utilance (U)

The proportion of luminous flux leaving the luminaires which reaches the working plane.

Utilisation factor (UF)

The proportion of the luminous flux emitted by the lamps which reaches the working plane.

V_λ function

See *Relative spectral sensitivity*.

Value

In the Munsell system, an index of the lightness of a surface ranging from 0 (black) to 10 (white). Approximately related to percentage reflectance by the relationship

$$R = V(V-1)$$

where R is reflectance (%) and V is value.

Vector/scalar ratio

The ratio of the magnitude of the illumination vector to the scalar illuminance.

Visual acuity

The capacity for discriminating between objects which are very close together. Quantitatively, it can be expressed by the reciprocal of the angular separation in minutes of arc between two lines or points which are just separable by the eye. The expression more commonly used for an individual's visual acuity is the ratio of the distance at which the individual can read a line on a standard optician's chart to the standard distance at which a person of normal sight can read that line (e.g. 6/12 means that the individual can just read at 6 m the line which a normally sighted person can just read at 12 m).

Visual disability

A disability is any restriction or lack (resulting from an impairment) of ability to perform an activity in the manner or within the range considered normal for a human being[210].

Visual environment

The environment either indoors or outdoors as seen by an observer.

Visual field

The full extent in space of what can be seen when looking in a given direction.

Visual handicap

A handicap is a disadvantage for a given individual, resulting from an impairment or a disability, that limits or prevents the fulfilment of a role that is normal for that individual[211]. This may be due to the arrangement of lighting or task and would apply to any individual in the same situation. It may also be peculiar to the individual. Where this is a physical disability the individual is said to have 'low vision' and may benefit from special lighting or some optical aid.

Visual task

The visual element of the work being done.

Visual impairment

An impairment is any loss or abnormality of psychological, physiological, or anatomical structure or function[210].

Weight

An approximate correlation of Munsell value modified to give in conjunction with greyness, subjective equality of brightness in the various hues (from *BS 5252*[169]).

Whiteness constancy

See Brightness constancy.

Working plane

See also *Reference surface* and *Task area*. The horizontal, vertical, or inclined plane in which the visual task lies. If no information is available, the working plane may be considered to be horizontal and at 0.8 m above the floor.

Table 6.1 Conversion of luminance units; to convert a value expressed in units in the first column to a unit in the top line, multiply by the appropriate factor

	cd/m^2	stilb (cd/cm^2)	cd/in^2	apostilb (lm/m^2)	lambert (lm/cm^2)	foot-lambert (lm/ft^2)
cd/m^2	1	0.0001	0.000645	3.14	0.000314	0.292
stilb (cd/cm^2)	10000	1	6.452	31416	3.14	2919
cd/in^2	1550	0.155	1	4869	0.487	452
apostilb (lm/m^2)†	0.318	0.0000318	0.000205	1	0.0001	0.0929
lambert (lm/cm^2)†	3183	0.318	2.054	10000	1	929
foot-lambert (lm/ft^2)†	3.426	0.0003426	0.00221	10.76	0.001076	1

† Units related to a uniform diffuser emitting 1 lm per unit area

6.2   Abbreviations and symbols for quantities, units and notation

AF, af	Aspect factor	L	Luminance or lambert
BEMS	Building energy management system	LDL	Lighting design lumens
cd	Candela	LEMS	Lighting energy management system
CI	Cavity index	LLF	Light loss factor
CRF	Contrast rendering factor	LLMF	Lamp luminous flux (lumen) maintenance factor
CRI	Colour rendering index		
D	Daylight factor	lm	Lumen
D_c	Sky component of daylight factor	LMF	Luminaire maintenance factor
D_E	Illuminance diversity	LOR	Light output ratio
D_e	Externally reflected component of daylight factor	LSF	Lamp survival factor
		lx	Lux
D_i	Internally reflected component of daylight factor	MAR	Mid-area ratio
		M_e, M	Radiant exitance
D_L	Luminance diversity	MF	Maintenance factor
DIR	Display illuminance ratio	R, ρ	Reflectance
DLOR	Downard light output ratio	RE_C, R_C	Ceiling cavity reflectance
DR	Direct ratio	RE_F, R_F	Floor cavity reflectance
E	Illuminance	RSMF	Room surface maintenance factor
$\overline{E}$	Illuminance vector	SHR	Spacing-to-height ratio
E_{ave}	Average illuminance	sr	Steradian
$E_c, E_{e,z}, E_z$	Cylindrical illuminance	t_a	Temperature rating (control gear)
E_e, E	Irradiance	T_c	Colour temperature
E_h	Horizontal plane illuminance	T_{cp}, CCT	Correlated colour temperature
E_{avi}	Initial illuminance	Td	Troland
E_m	Maintained illuminance	U	Utilance
E_{max}	Maximum illuminance	U_E	Illuminance uniformity
E_{min}	Minimum illuminance	U_L	Luminance uniformity
EMS	Energy management system	UCS	Uniform chromaticity scale
$E_s, E_{v,o}$	Scalar (spherical) illuminance	UF	Utilisation factor
E_{sc}	Semi-cylindrical illuminance	UGR	Unified glare rating (system)
E_v	Vertical plane illuminance	ULOR	Upward light output ratio
fc	Foot-candle	V	Luminous efficiency
FFR	Flux fraction ratio	V_λ, V'_λ	(Relative) spectral luminous efficiency (sensitivity)
fL	Foot lambert		
H_e, H	Radiant exposure	β_v, β	Luminance factor (gloss factor)
h_m	Mounting height	η_e, η	Radiant efficacy
I	Luminous intensity	η_v, η	Luminous efficacy (of source)
I_e, I	Radiant intensity	τ	Transmittance
IP	Ingress protection	ϕ_e, ϕ, P	Radiant flux
K	Kelvin (colour temperature)	ϕ_v, ϕ	Luminous flux
K	Room index		

6.3   Bibliography

This bibliography has been split into four parts: books; papers; guides and standards; and a classified index of guides and standards. It is hoped that these classifications will make the bibliography useful to professionals wishing to maintain a technical library as well as those wishing to learn more about lighting.

Books have been given the following classifications: effects of lighting conditions; general; light; lighting applications; lighting equipment; and vision.

Papers have been given the following classifications: Calculations; colour; contrast rendering; controls; daylight; directional effects of lighting; emergency lighting; flicker; general; glare; integrated lighting; maintenance; preferred conditions; and task performance.

Guides and standards have been listed by their publishing organisation and their number. They have been given the following classifications: calculations; colour; daylight; effects of lighting conditions; emergency lighting; general; general lighting applications; general lighting equipment; glare; lamps and controls; light; luminaires; maintenance; public lighting; signs; sunlight; and vision.

The following letters have been used for guides and standards:

BS	British Standard normal series.
BSCP	British Standard Code of Practice.
BSDD	British Standard Draft for Development.
BSEN	British Standard Euronorm.
CIBSEAM	CIBSE Application Manual
CIBSEG	CIBSE general publication.
CIBSETM	CIBSE Technical Memorandum.
CIE	Commission Internationale de l'Eclairage normal series.
CIED	CIE publication on diskette.
CIES	CIE special report.
CIEX	CIE divisional proceeding.
ICEL	Industry Committee for Emergency Lighting.
ILEG	Institution of Lighting Engineers general publication.
ILETR	ILE Technical Report.
LIFF	Lighting Industry Federation Factfinder.
LIFG	LIF general publication.

British Standards are available from BSI, Linford Wood, Milton Keynes, MK14 6LE (telephone 0908 221166). CIBSE and CIE publications are available from CIBSE, Delta House, 222 Balham High Road, London SW12 9BS (telephone 081 675 5211). ICEL and LIF publications are available from LIF, 207 Balham High Road, London SW17 7BQ (telephone 081 675 5432). ILE publications are available from ILE, Lennox House, 9 Lawford Road, Rugby, Warwickshire CV21 2DZ (telephone 0788 576492).

6.3.1   Books

Effects of lighting conditions

Attridge T H *Light and plant responses* (London: Edward Arnold) (1990)
Boyce P R *Human factors in lighting* (London: Applied Science) (1981)
Cronly-Dillon J, Rosen S and Marshall J (ed.) *Hazards of light* (Oxford: Pergamon) (1986)
Hopkinson R G and Collins J B *The ergonomics of lighting* (London: McDonald) (1970)
Hunter R S and Harrold R W *The measurement of appearance* 2nd edn (New York: Wiley–Interscience) (1987)
Lam W M C *Perception and lighting as formgivers for architecture* (New York: McGraw Hill) (1977)
McKinlay A F, Harlen F and Whillock *Hazards of optical radiation: a guide to sources, uses and safety* (London: Hilger) (1988)
Rasmussen S E *Experiencing architecture* 2nd edn (Cambridge MA.: MIT Press) (1962)

General

Interior Lighting Design (London: Lighting Industry Federation and the Electricity Council) (1977)
Lighting Handbook (New York: Illuminating Engineering Society of North America) (1981)
Lighting and wiring of churches 4th edn (London: Church House Publishing) (1988)
Birren F *Light, colour and environment* (Schiffer) (1988)
Boud J *Lighting design in buildings* (Stevenage: Peregrinus) (1973)
Bowers B *A history of electric light and power* (London: Peregrinus) (1982)
Cayless M A and Marsden A M (ed.) *Lamps and lighting* (London: Edward Arnold) (1983)
de Boer J B and Fischer D *Interior Lighting* (Antwerp: Philips Technical Library) (1978)
de Boer J B, and Fischer D *Interior lighting* 2nd edn (Antwerp: Philips Technical Library) (1981)
Deyan Sudjic *The lighting book: a complete guide to lighting your home* (London: Mitchell Beazley) (1985)

Flynn J E, Segil A W and Steffy G R *Architectural interior systems — lighting/acoustics/air conditioning* 2nd edn (New York: Van Nostrand) (1988)

Greif M *The lighting book: a buyer's guide to locating almost every kind of lighting device* (Pittstown: The Main Street Press) (1986)

Hopkinson R G *Architectural Physics — Lighting* (London: HMSO) (1963)

Hughes G J (ed.) *Electricity and buildings* (London: Peregrinus) (1984)

Jankowski W *The best of lighting design* (New York: PBC International) (1987)

Lumsden W K, Aldworth R C and Tate R L C *Outdoor lighting handbook* (Epping: Gower Press) (1974)

Lynes J A (ed.) *Developments in lighting – 1* (London: Applied Science) (1978)

Moon P *The scientific basis of illuminating engineering* (New York: Dover) (1961)

Murdoch J B *Illuminating engineering – from Edison's lamp to laser* (New York: Macmillan) (1985)

Neville M *Emergency and security lighting handbook* (Oxford: Heinemann Newnes) (1988)

Pilbrow R *Stage lighting* (London: Cassell) (1982)

Pritchard D C *Lighting* (London: Longman) (1978)

Pritchard D C (ed.) *Developments in lighting – 2* (London: Applied Science) (1982)

Reid F *The stage lighting handbook* 3rd edn (London: A and C Black) (1987)

Thomson G *The museum environment* 2nd edn (London: Butterworth) (1986)

van Bommel W J M and de Boer J B *Road lighting* (Antwerp: Philips Technical Library) (1980)

Walsh J W T *Textbook of Illuminating Engineering* (London: Pitman) (1947)

Watson L *Lighting design handbook* (New York: McGraw Hill) (1990)

Weston H C *Light sight and work* (London: H K Lewis) (1962)

Light

Ditchburn R W *Light* (2 volumes) (London: Academic Press) (1976)

Grum F and Bartleson C J (ed.) *Optical radiation measurements – 1 Radiometry* (London: Academic Press) (1980)

Grum F and Bartleson C J (ed.) *Optical radiation measurements – 2 Colour measurement* (London: Academic Press) (1980)

Henderson S T *Daylight and its spectrum* (Bristol: Hilger) (1977)

Koller K R *Ultraviolet radiation* (New York: J Wiley) (1967)

Seliger H H and McElroy W D *Light: physical and biological action* (New York: Academic Press) (1965)

Sobel M I *Light* (Chicago: University of Chicago Press) (1987)

Walsh J W T *Photometry* (London: Constable and Co.) (1958)

Wysecki G and Stiles W S *Colour science* (New York: J Wiley) (1967)

Lighting applications

Agostan G A *Colour theory and its application in art and design* 2nd edn (Berlin: Springer-Verlay) (1987)

Anstey J *Rights of light and how to deal with them* (London: Royal Institution of Chartered Surveyors) (1988)

Blakey R R *Measuring colour* (BTP Tioxide Ltd.) (1980)

Chamberlain G J and Chamberlain D G *Colour, its measurement, computation and application* (London: Heyden) (1980)

Evans B H *Daylight in architecture* (New York: McGraw Hill) (1981)

Gloag H L and Gold M J *Colour co-ordination handbook* (London: HMSO) (1978)

Hopkinson R G, Petherbridge P and Longmore J *Daylighting* (London: Heinemann) (1963)

Hunt R W G *Measuring colour* 2nd edn (New York: Wiley–Interscience) (1991)

Keitz H A *Lighting calculations and measurements* (London: McMillan) (1971)

Lam W M C *Sunlighting as formgiver for architecture* (New York: Van Nostrand Reinhold) (1986)

Longmore J *BRS daylight protractors* (London: HMSO) (1968)

Lynes J A *Principles of natural lighting* (London: Elsevier) (1968)

Lyons S L *Exterior lighting for industry and security* (London: Applied Science) (1981)

Lyons S L *Handbook of industrial lighting* (London: Butterworths) (1981)

MacAdam D L *Colour measurement, themes and variations* (Berlin: Springer-Verlay) (1981)

Moore F *Concepts and prcatice of architectural daylighting* (New York: Van Nostrand Reinhold) (1985)

Olgyay A and Olgyay V *Solar control and shading devices* (Princeton: Princeton University Press) (1976)

Petherbridge P *Sunpath diagrams and overlays for solar heat gain calculations* (London: HMSO) (1969)

Robbins C L *Daylighting – design and analysis* (New York: Van Nostrand Reinhold) (1986)

Turner D P (ed.) *Window glass design guide* (London: Architectural Press) (1977)

Van Bommel W J M and de Boer J B *Road lighting* (Antwerp: Philips technical library) (1980)

Wright W D *Measurement of colour* 4th edn (London: Hilger) (1969)

Lighting equipment

Bean A R and Simons R H *Light fittings, performance and design* (Oxford: Pergamon) (1968)

Cayless M A and Marsden A M (ed.) *Lamps and Lighting* (London: Edward Arnold) (1983)

de Groot J and van Vliet J *The high pressure sodium lamp* (Antwerp: Philips Technical Library) (1986)

Elenbas W *Light sources* (London: McMillan) (1972)

Jolley L B W, Waldram J M, Wilson G H *The theory and design of illuminating engineering equipment* (Chapman Hall) (1930)

Weymouth J R *Electric discharge lamps* (Cambridge, MA.: MIT Press) (1971)

Vision

The psychology of vision (London: The Royal Society) (1980)

Barlow H B and Mollon J D *The senses* (Cambridge: Cambridge University Press) (1982)

Bruce V and Green P *Visual perception physiology, psychology and ecology* (Erlbaum) (1985)

Cornsweet T N *Visual Perception* (New York: Academic Press) (1970)

Gregory R L *The intelligent eye* (London: Weidenfield and Nicholson) (1971)

Gregory R L *Eye and Brain* (London: Weidenfield and Nicholson) (1977)

Hubel D H *Eye, Brain and Vision* (New York: Scientific American Library) (1988)

Marr D *Vision: a computational investigation into the human representation and processing of visual information* (San Francisco: W H Freeman) (1982)

Overington I *Vision and acquisition* (London: Pentech Press) (1976)

Padgham C A and Saunders J E *The perception of light and colour* (London: G Bell and Sons) (1975)

Weale R A *The ageing eye* (London: H K Lewis and sons) (1963)
Weale R A *Focus on vision* (London: Hodder and Stoughton) (1982)

6.3.2   Papers

Calculations

Bean A R Utilance values and uniformity in a model room *Lighting Res. Technol.* **7** 169 (1975)
Bean A R The calculation of utilization factors *Lighting Res. Technol.* **8** 200 (1976)
Bell R I A method for the calculation of direct illuminance due to area sources of various distributions *Lighting Res. Technol.* **5** 99 (1973)
Bellchambers H E and Godby A C Illuminance and utilance calculation for luminous ceilings *Lighting Res. Technol.* **5** 195 (1973)
Cuttle C Yes, but which illuminance? *Light and Lighting* **66** 349 (1973)
Hopkinson R G The indirect component of illumination in artificially lit interiors *Light and Lighting* **48** 315 (1955)
Jones J R and Neidhart J J The zonal method of computing coefficients of utilization and illumination on room surfaces *Illum. Eng.* **48** 141 (1953)
Jones J R and Sampson F K Lighting design and luminance coefficients *Illum. Eng.* **61** 221 (1966)
Lynes J A The concept of luminaire domain *Lighting Res. Technol.* **7** 185 (1975)
O'Brien P F and Howard J A Predetermination of luminance by finite difference equations *Illum. Eng.* **54** 209 (1959)
Zijl H Large size perfect diffusers *Philips Technical Library* (1960)

Colour

Bellchambers H E and Godby A C Illumination, colour rendering and visual clarity *Lighting Res. Technol.* **4** 104 (1972)
Boyce P R An investigation of the subjective balance between illuminances and lamp colour properties *Lighting Res. Technol.* **9** 11 (1978)
Cockram A H, Collins J B and Langdon F J A study of user preferences for fluorescent lamp colours for daytime and nighttime lighting *Lighting Res. Technol.* **2** 249 (1970)
Gloag H L Hue, greyness and weight *Building Materials* **29** 7 (1969)
Halstead M B Colour rendering systems and their applications *Light and Lighting* **69** 244 (1976)
Halstead M B, Morley D I, Palmer D A and Stainsby A G Colour rendering tolerances in the CIE system *Lighting Res. Technol.* **3** 99 (1971)
Holmes J G A lighting engineer looks at colour *Trans. Illum. Eng.* **30** 117 (1965)
Tikkanen K T A study of emotional reactions to light and colour in a school environment *Lighting Res. Technol.* **8** 27 (1976)
Whitfield T W H and Wiltshire T J The aesthetic function of colour in buildings: a critique *Lighting Res. Technol.* **12** 129 (1980)

Contrast rendering

Office lighting for good visual task conditions *Building Research Establishment Digest 256* (1981)
Boyce P R Is equivalent sphere illuminance the future? *Lighting Res. Technol.* **10** 179 (1978)

Boyce P R and Slater A I The application of contrast rendering factor to office lighting design *Lighting Res. Technol.* **13** 65 (1981)
de Boer J B Performance and comfort in the presence of veiling relections *Lighting Res. Technol.* **9** 179 (1978)
Reitmaier J Some effects of veiling relections in papers *Lighting Res. Technol.* **11** 204 (1979)

Controls

Energy conservation in artificial lighting Building Research Establishment Digest 232 (1979)
Boyce P R Observation of manual switching of lighting *Lighting Res. Technol.* **12** 195 (1980)
Crisp V H C The light switch in buildings *Lighting Res. Technol.* **10** 69 (1978)
Crisp V H C and Henderson G The energy management of artificial lighting *Lighting Res. Technol.* **14** 193 (1982)
Hunt D R G Simple expressions for predicting energy saving from photoelectric control of buildings *Lighting Res. Technol.* **9** 93 (1978)
Hunt D R G Improved daylight data for predicting energy savings from photoelectric controls *Lighting Res. Technol.* **11** 9 (1979)
Hunt D R G Predicting artificial lighting use — a method based upon observed patterns of behaviour *Lighting Res. Technol.* **12** 7 (1980)
Littlefair P The luminance distribution of an average sky *Lighting Res. Technol.* **13** 169 (1981)

Daylight

Bell J A M Development and practice with daylighting of buildings *Lighting Res. Technol.* **5** 173 (1973)
Hunt D R G Improved daylight data for predicting energy savings from photoelectric controls *Lighting Res. Technol.* **11** 9 (1979)
Krochmann J, and Seidl M Quantitative data on daylight for illuminating engineering *Lighting Res. Technol.* **6** 165 (1974)
Lynes J A Sequences for daylight design *Lighting Res. Technol.* **11** 102 (1979)
Ne'eman E Visual aspects of sunlight in buildings *Lighting Res. Technol.* **6** 159 (1974)

Directional effects of lighting

Cuttle C Lighting patterns and the flow of light *Lighting Res. Technol.* **3** 171 (1971)
Lynes J A Lighting for texture *Lighting Res. Technol.* **11** 67 (1979)
Lynes J A, Burt W, Jackson G K and Cuttle C The flow of light into buildings *Trans. Illum. Eng. Soc.* **31** 65 (1966)
Waldram J M Studies in interior lighting *Trans. Illum. Eng. Soc.* **19** 95 (1954)

Emergency lighting

Heatlie-Jackson *et al.* Emergency lighting *Light and Lighting* **65** 226 (1972)
Jaschinski W Conditions of emergency lighting *Ergonomics* **25** 363 (1982)
Simmons R C Illuminance, diversity and disability glare in emergency lighting *Lighting Res. Technol.* **7** 125 (1975)

Flicker

Brundrett G W   Human sensitivity to flicker *Lighting Res. Technol.* **6** 127 (1974)
Brundrett G W, Griffiths I D and Boyce P R   Subjective response to AC and DC fluorescent lighting *Lighting Res. Technol.* **5** 160 (1973)

General

Bell R I and Page R K   The need for a unified approach to interior lighting design parameters *Lighting Res. Technol.* **13** 49 (1981)
Fischer D   Comparison of some european interior lighting recommendations *Lighting Res. Technol.* **5** 186 (1972)
Jay P A   Inter-relationship of the design criteria for lighting installations *Trans. Illum. Eng. Soc.* **33** 47 (1968)
Jay P A   Lighting and visual perception *Lighting Res. Technol.* **3** 133 (1971)
Weston H C   Rationally recommended illumination levels *Trans. Illum. Eng. Soc.* **26** 1 (1961)
Yonemura G   Criteria for recommending lighting levels *Lighting Res. Technol.* **13** 113 (1981)

Glare

The development of the IES glare index systems *Trans. Illum. Eng. Soc.* **27** 9 (1962)
Glare from overall diffusing ceilings *Trans. Illum. Eng. Soc.* **30** 21 (1965)
Bellchambers H E, Collins J B and Crisp V H C   Relationship between two systems of glare limitation *Lighting Res. Technol.* **7** 106 (1975)
Bedocs L and Simons R H   The accuracy of the IES glare index system *Lighting Res. Technol.* **4** 80 (1972)
Betts P C and Pritchard D C   Discomfort glare from ceiling mounted luminaires *Lighting Res. Technol.* **6** 230 (1974)
Boyce P R   A comparison of the accuracy of methods of calculating IES glare index *Lighting Res. Technol.* **4** 31 (1972)
Chauvel P, Collins J B, Dogniaux R, and Longmore J   Glare from windows: current views of the problem *Lighting Res. Technol.* **14** 31 (1982)
Lowson J C   A simplified method of estimating glare index *Light and Lighting* **55** 291 (1962)
Stone P T and Harker S D P   Individual and group differences in discomfort glare responses *Lighting Res. Technol.* **5** 41 (1973)

Integrated lighting

Bedocs L and Pinniger M J H   Development of integrated ceiling systems *Lighting Res. Technol.* **7** 69 (1975)
Crichton J and Wood-Robinson M   Integrated services in modern office buildings *Lighting Res. Technol.* **5** 69 (1973)
McIntyre D A   Lighting and thermal comfort *Lighting Res. Technol.* **8** 121 (1976)
Smith P W and Bunker N   The installed performance of integrated ceiling systems *Lighting Res. Technol.* **13** 58 (1981)

Maintenance

McNeill V   Economics of planned lighting maintenance *Light and Lighting* **59** 225 (1966)
Robinson W, and Strange J W   The maintenance of lighting installations *Trans. Illum. Eng. Soc.* **20** 157 (1955)

Preferred conditions

Bean A R and Hopkins A G   Task and background lighting *Lighting Res. Technol.* **12** 135 (1980)
Boyce P R   User attitudes to some types of local lighting *Lighting Res. Technol.* **11** 158 (1979)
Collins J B and Plant C G H   Preferred illuminance distribution in windowless spaces *Lighting Res. Technol.* **3** 219 (1971)
Romaya S M, Dawe S P, Heap L J and Tuck B   Consistency and variation in preferences for office lighting *Lighting Res. Technol.* **6** 205 (1974)
Saunders J E   The role of the level and diversity of horizontal illumination in an appraisal of a simple office task *Lighting Res. Technol.* **1** 37 (1969)
Stone P, Parsons K C and Harker S D P   Subjective judgements of lighting in lecture rooms *Lighting Res. Technol.* **7** 259 (1975)
Waldram J M   Design of the visual field as a routine method *Trans. Illum. Eng. Soc.* **23** 113 (1958)

Task performance

Boyce P R   The influence of illumination level on prolonged work performance *Lighting Res. Technol.* **2** 74 (1970)
Boyce P R   Age, illuminance, visual performance and preference *Lighting Res. Technol.* **5** 125 (1973)
Boyce P R   Illuminance, difficulty, complexity and visual performance *Lighting Res. Technol.* **6** 222 (1974)
Boyce P R and Simons R H   Hue discrimination and light sources *Lighting Res. Technol.* **9** 125 (1978)

6.3.3   Guides and standards

BS 161 Specification for tungsten filament lamps for domestic and similar general lighting purposes. Performance requirements
BS 559 Specification for electric signs and high-voltage luminous-discharge-tube installations
BS 667 Specification for portable photoelectric photometers
BS 873 Road traffic signs and internally illuminated bollards
BS 889 Specification for flameproof electric lighting fittings
BS 950 Specification for artificial daylight for the assessment of colour
BS 1853 Tubular fluuorescent lamps for general lighting service
BS 2049 Specification for paraffin lighting appliances for domestic use
BS 2818 Ballasts for tubular fluorescent lamps
BS 2977 Domestic lighting appliances for use with liquefied petroleum gases
BS 3224 Lighting fittings for civil land aerodromes
BS 3456 Specification for safety of household and similar electrical appliances (Section 102.27 Ultra-violet and infra-red radiation skin treatment appliances for household use)
BS 3677 Specification for high-pressure mercury vapour lamps
BS 3767 Specification for low-pressure sodium vapour lamps
BS 3772 Specification for for starters for fluorescent lamps
BS 3944 Specification for colour filters for theatre lighting and other purposes
BS 4533 Luminaires: Part 101 Specification for general requirements and tests
BS 4533 Luminaires: Part 102 Particular requirements
BS 4533 Luminaires: Part 103 Performance requirements
BS 4647 Specification for lighting sets for christmas trees and decorative purposes for indoor use
BS 4683 Specification for electrical apparatus for explosive atmospheres
BS 4727 Glossary of electrotechnical, power, telecommunications, electronics, lighting and colour terms (Part 4: Terms particular to lighting and colour)

BS 4800 Schedule of paint colours for building purposes
BS 4900 Specification for vitreous enamel colours for building purposes
BS 4901 Specification for plastic colours for building purposes
BS 4902 Specification for sheet and tile flooring colours for building purposes
BS 4904 Specification for external cladding colours for building purposes
BS 5042 Specification for bayonet lampholders
BS 5101 Specification for lamp caps and holders together with gauges for the control of interchangeability and safety
BS 5225 Photometric data for luminaires
BS 5266 Emergency lighting
BS 5345 Code of practice for selection, installation and maintenance of electrical apparatus for use in potentially explosive atmospheres (other than mining applications or explosive processing and manufacture)
BS 5371 Standard method of measurement of lamp cap temperature rise
BS 5394 Specification for limits and methods of measurement of radio interference characteristics of fluorescent lamps and luminaires
BS 5481 Photographic flash equipment
BS 5489 Road lighting
BS 5501 Electical apparatus for potentially explosive atmospheres
BS 5550 Cinematography (Section 7.1 Light sources and lighting)
BS 5649 Lighting columns
BS 5971 Specification for safety of tungsten filament lamps for domestic and similar domestic purposes
BS 5972 Specification for photoelectric control units for road lighting
BS 6012 Specification for heat test source (HTS) lamps for carrying out heating tests on luminaires
BS 6345 Method for measurement of radio interference terminal voltage of lighting equipment
BS 6702 Specification for lampholders for tubular fluorescent lamps and starterholders
BS 6726 Specification for festoon and temporary lighting cables and cords
BS 6776 Specification for Edison screw lampholders
BS 7132 Nomenclature for glass bulb designation system for lamps
BS 7216 Classification and interpretation of new lighting products
BS 8206 Lighting for buildings
BSCP 153 Windows and rooflights
BSCP 1003 Electrical apparatus and associated equipment for use in explosive atmospheres of gas or vapour other than mining applications
BSCP 1007 Maintained lighting for cinemas
BSDD 67 Basic data for the design of buildings: sunlight BSDD 73 Basic data for the design of buildings: daylight
BSEN 40 Lighting columns
BSEN 60920 Specification for ballasts for tubular fluorescent lamps General and safety requirements
BSEN 60921 Specification for ballasts for tubular fluorescent lamps Performance requirements
BSEN 60922 Specification for general and safety requirements for ballasts for discharge lamps (excluding tubular fluorescent lamps)
BSEN 60923 Specification for performance requirements for ballasts for discharge lamps (excluding tubular fluorescent lamps)
BSEN 60924 Specification for general and safety requirements for dc supplied electronic ballasts for tubular fluorescent lamps
BSEN 60926 Specification for general and safety requirements for starting devices (other than glow starters)
BSEN 60927 Specification for performance requirements for starting devices (other than glow starters)
BSEN 60928 Specification for ac supplied electronic ballasts for tubular fluorescent lamps General and safety requirements
CIBSEAM 2 Window design
CIBSEG 1 Lighting for museums and art galleries
CIBSEG 2 Lighting for shipbuilding and ship repair
CIBSEG 3 Lighting in hostile and hazardous environments
CIBSEG 4 A review of the National Lighting Awards 1986
CIBSEG 5 Perspective for lighting engineers
CIBSELG 1 The industrial environment
CIBSELG 2 Hospitals and health care buildings
CIBSELG 3 Areas for visual display terminals
CIBSELG 4 Sports
CIBSELG 5 Lecture, teaching and conference rooms
CIBSELG 6 The outdoor environment
CIBSETM 5 The calculation and use of utilisation factors
CIBSETM 10 Calculation of glare indices
CIBSETM 12 Emergency lighting
CIBSETM 14 CIBSE standard file format for the electronic transfer of luminaire photometric data
CIE 2.2 Colours of light signals
CIE 8 Street lighting and accidents
CIE 9 History of CIE
CIE 12.2 International recommendations for the lighting of public thoroughfares
CIE 13.2 Method of measuring and specifying colour rendering of light sources
CIE 15.1 Special metamerism index: change in illuminant
CIE 16 Daylighting
CIE 17.4 International lighting vocabulary
CIE 18.2 The basis of physical photometry
CIE 19 /2 An analytical model for describing the influence of lighting parameters upon visual performance 19/2.1 Technical foundations 19/2.2 Summary and application guidelines
CIE 22 Standardisation of luminance distribution on clear skies
CIE 24 Photometry of indoor type luminaires with tubular fluorescent lamps
CIE 27 Photometry of luminaires for street lighting
CIE 28 The lighting of sports events for colour television broadcasting
CIE 29.2 Guide on interior lighting
CIE 30.2 Calculation and measurement of luminance and illuminance in road lighting
CIE 31 Glare and uniformity in road lighting installations
CIE 32 Report on public lighting (in situations requiring special care) Version A in French, Version B in English
CIE 33 Report on depreceation of public lighting installations and their maintenance Version A in French, Version B in English
CIE 34 Road lighting, lantern and installation data, photometrics classification and performance
CIE 35 Lighting traffic signs
CIE 36 Proceedings of the 18th CIE Session, London, 1975
CIE 37 Exterior lighting in the environment
CIE 38 Radiometric and photometric characteristics of materials and their measurement
CIE 39.2 Surface colours for visual signalling
CIE 40 Calculations for interior lighting basic method
CIE 41 Light as a true visual quantity: principles of measurement
CIE 42 Lighting for tennis
CIE 43 Photometry of floodlights CIE 44 Absolute methods for relection measurements
CIE 45 Lighting for ice sports
CIE 46 A review of publications on properties and reflection values of material reflection standards
CIE 47 Road lighting for wet conditions
CIE 48 Lighting signals for road traffic control
CIE 49 Guide on emergency lighting of building interiors
CIE 50 Proceedings of the CIE Session in Kyoto
CIE 51 A method of assessing the quality of daylight simulators for colorimetry
CIE 52 Calculations for interior lighting: Applied method
CIE 53 Methods of characterizing the performance of radiometers and photometers
CIE 54 Retroreflection: Definition and measurement
CIE 55 Discomfort glare in the interior working environment
CIE 56 Proceedings of the CIE Session in Amsterdam, 1983
CIE 57 Lighting for football
CIE 58 Lighting for sports halls

CIE 59 Polarization: Definitions and nomenclature, instrument polarization
CIE 60 Vision and the visual display unit work station
CIE 61 Tunnel entrance lighting: A survey of fundamentals for determining the luminance of the threshold zone
CIE 62 Lighting for swimming pools
CIE 63 The spectroradiometric measurement of light sources
CIE 64 Determination of the spectral responsivity of optical radiation detectors
CIE 65 Electrically calibrated thermal detectors of optical radiation (absolute radiometers)
CIE 66 Road surfaces and lighting
CIE 67 Guide for the photometric specification and measurement of sports lighting installations
CIE 68 Guide to the lighting of exterior working areas
CIE 69 Methods of characterizing illuminance meters and luminance meters: peformance characteristics and specifications
CIE 70 The measurement of absolute luminance intensity distributions
CIE 71 Proceedings of the CIE Session in Venice
CIE 72 Guide to the properties and uses of relectors at night
CIE 73 Visual aspects of road markings
CIE 74 Roadsigns
CIE 75 Spectral luminous efficiency functions based upon brightness matching for monochromatic point sources, 2 and 10 fields
CIE 76 Intercomparison on measurement of (total) spectral radiance factor of luminescent specimens
CIE 77 Electric lights sources: state of the art 1987
CIE 78 Brightness-luminance relations: classified bibliography
CIE 79 A guide for the design of road traffic lights
CIE 80 Special metamerism index: change in observer
CIE 81 Mesopic photometry: history, special problems and practical solutions
CIE 82 CIE History 1913 - 1988
CIE 83 Guide for the lighting of sports events for colour televison and film systems
CIE 84 Measurement of luminous flux
CIE 85 Solar spectral irradiance
CIE 86 CIE 1988 2 spectral luminous efficency function for photopic vision
CIE 87 Colorimetry of self-luminous dispalays - a bibliography
CIE 88 Guide for the lighting of road tunnels and underpasses
CIED 1 Disc version of CIE photometric and colorimetric data
CIED 2 CIE colorimetry and colour rendering tables
CIES 1 Colorimetric illuminants
CIES 2 Colorimetric observers
CIEX 1 Aktuelle Themen der Aussenbeleuchtung (SLG CIE Division 5 Symposium proceeding, Fribourg 1989
CIEX 2 Tunnel entrance zone lighting (SLG CIE Division 4 Symposium proceeding, Agno/Lugano 1989
CIEX 3 Daylight and Solar Radiation Measurement (CIE-WMO Symposium proceeding, Berlin 1989
ICEL 1001 Industry standard for the construction and performance of battery-operated emergency lighting equipment Part 1 Equipment for central systems
ICEL 1001 Industry standard for the construction and performance of battery-operated emergency lighting equipment Part 2 Self-contained luminaires and associated equipment
ICEL 1002 Photometry of battery-operated emergency lighting luminaires ICEL 1003 Emergency lighting - Applications guide
ICEL 1004 Guide to the use of emergency lighting modification units
ILEG 1 Code of practice for electrical safety in public lighting operations
ILEG 2 The lighting and crime file
ILETR 5 Brightness of illumianted advertisements
ILETR 8 Maintenance of public lantern output depreciation
ILETR 12 Lighting of pedestrian crossings
ILETR 13 Lighting of pedestrian subways
ILETR 14 The cost effectiveness of night-time patrolling

ILETR 17 Study of lamp replacement for discharge sources
ILETR 18 The planned replacemnt of lighting columns
ILETR 19 The effectiveness of lantern cleaning
ILETR 20 A guide to the use of compact fluorescent lamps
LIFF 3 LIF Lamp Guide
LIFF 4 Lighting and energy
LIFF 5 The benefits of certification
LIFF 6 Hazardous area lighting
LIFG 1 Better lighting at work
LIFG 2 Energy managers lighting handbook
LIFG 3 High frequency ballasts for tubular fluorescent lamps
LIFG 4 Interior lighting design handbook 6th ed.
LIFG 5 LIF Buyer's guide
LIFG 6 PCBs lighting guide

6.3.4 Classified index of guides and standards

Calculations

BS 5225; CIBSEG 5; CIBSETM 5; CIBSETM 10; CIBSETM 14; CIE 18; CIE 19; CIE 24; CIE 27; CIE 30; CIE 38; CIE 40; CIE 41; CIE 43; CIE 44; CIE 46; CIE 52; CIE 53; CIE 54; CIE 63; CIE 64; CIE 65; CIE 67; CIE 70; CIE 72; CIE 75; CIE 81; CIE 84; CIE 85; CIE 86; CIED 1; CIED 2; ICEL 1002.

Colour

BS 3944; BS 4800; BS 4900; BS 4901; BS 4902; BS 4904; CIE 2; CIE 13; CIE 15; CIE 28; CIE 39; CIE 51; CIE 64; CIE 80; CIE 87; CIED 1; CIED 2; CIES 1; CIES 2.

Daylight

BS 950; BSCP 153; BSDD 73; CIBSEAM 2; CIE 16; CIE 22; CIE 51; CIEX 3; ILETR 20.

Effects of lighting conditions

BS 3456; CIE 60; CIE 73; LIFG 1.

Emergency lighting

BS 5266; BSCP 1007; CIBSETM 12; CIE 49; ICEL 1001; ICEL 1001; ICEL 1002; ICEL 1003; ICEL 1004.

General

BS 4727; BS 7132; BS 7216; BS 8206; CIE 9; CIE 17; CIE 29; CIE 36; CIE 40; CIE 50; CIE 56; CIE 71; CIE 82; CIEX 1; LIFF 4; LIFF 5; LIFG 2; LIFG 4; LIFG 5.

General lighting applications

BS 3224; BS 5550; BSCP 1007; CIBSEG 1; CIBSEG 2; CIBSEG 3; CIBSEG 4; CIBSEG 5; CIBSELG 1; CIBSELG 2; CIBSELG 3; CIBSELG 4; CIBSELG 5; CIBSELG 6; CIE 28; CIE 42; CIE 45; CIE 57; CIE 58; CIE 62; CIE 67; CIE 68; CIE 83; LIFF 6; LIFG 6.

General lighting equipment

BS 161; BS 559; BS 667; BS 2049; BS 2977; BS 4647; BS 4683; BS 5345; BS 5394; BS 5481; BS 5501; BS 6345; BS 6726; BSCP 1003; CIE 37; CIE 69.

Glare

CIBSETM 10; CIE 31; CIE 55.

Lamps and controls

BS 161; BS 1853; BS 2818; BS 3677; BS 3767; BS 3772; BS 5042; BS 5101; BS 5371; BS 5971; BS 6702; BS 6776; BS 7132; BSEN 60920; BSEN 60921; BSEN 60922; BSEN 60923; BSEN 60924; BSEN 60926; BSEN 60927; BSEN 60928; CIE 13; CIE 77; ILETR 17; LIFF 3; LIFG 3.

Light

CIE 41; CIE 59; CIE 63; CIE 65; CIE 75; CIE 76; CIE 78; CIED 1.

Luminaires

BS 873; BS 889; BS 3224; BS 4533; BS 4533; BS 4533; BS 5225; BS 6012; CIE 24.

Maintenance

CIE 33; CIE 34; ILETR 8; ILETR 18; ILETR 19.

Public lighting

BS 873; BS 5489; BS 5649; BS 5972; BSEN 40; CIE 8; CIE 12; CIE 27; CIE 30; CIE 31; CIE 32; CIE 33; CIE 34; CIE 35; CIE 37; CIE 39; CIE 43; CIE 47; CIE 48; CIE 61; CIE 66; CIE 72; CIE 73; CIE 88; CIEX 2; ILEG 1; ILEG 2; ILETR 8; ILETR 12; ILETR 13; ILETR 14; ILETR 17; ILETR 18; ILETR 19.

Signs

BS 559; CIE 35; CIE 48; CIE 73; CIE 74; CIE 79; CIE 87; ILETR 5.

Sunlight

BSCP 153; BSDD 67; CIBSEAM 2; CIE 22; CIE 85; CIEX 3.

Vision

CIE 19; CIE 60; CIE 75; CIE 80; CIE 81; CIE 86; CIES 2.

6.4   References

1   *BS 820: Part 2: 1992: Code of practice for daylighting* (London: British Standards Institution) (1992)

2   *Window design* Applications Manual **AM1** (London: Chartered Institution of Building Services Engineers) (1987)

3   Weston H C *Industrial Health Research Board Report 87* (London: HMSO) (1945)

4   Bean A R and Bell R I The CSP index: A practical measure of office lighting quality as perceived by the office worker *Lighting Res. Technol.* **24**(4) 215–224 (1992)

5   Saunders J E The role of level and diversity of horizontal illuminance in an appraisal of a simple office task *Lighting. Res. Technol.* **1**(1) 39 (1969)

6   Cayless M A and Marsden A M (ed.) *Lamps and Lighting* 3rd edn 36–40 (London: Arnold) (1983)

7   *The Industrial Environment* Lighting Guide **LG1** (London: The Chartered Institution of Building Services Engineers) (1989)

8   Williams P C The effects of surface colour on apparent surface distance *Lighting Res. Technol.* **4**(1) 27–30 (1972)

9   *BS 1710: 1984 (1991) Specification for identification of pipelines and services* (London: British Standards Institution) (1991)

10   *BS 5378: Safety signs and colours* (London: British Standards Instiution) (1976–84)

11   *Guide on interior lighting* CIE Publication **29.2** 2nd edn (Paris: Commission Internationale de l'Eclairage) (1986)

12   *Method of measuring and specifying colour rendering of light sources* CIE Publication **13.2** 2nd edn (corrected reprint) (Paris: Commission Internationale de l'Eclairage) (1988)

13   Wilkins A S and Clark C Modulation of light from fluorescent lamps *Lighting Res. Technol.* **22**(2) 103–109 (1990)

14   Dakin S R G, Hargroves R A, Ruddock K H and Simons R H *Visual sensitivity to high frequency flicker* (unpublished paper) (October 1993)

15   Wilkins A J, Nimmo-Smith I, Slater A I and Bedocs L Fluorescent lighting, headaches and eyestrain *Lighting Res. Technol.* **21**(1) 11–18 (1989)

16   Cockram A H, Collins J N and Langdon F J A study of user preferences for fluorescent lamp colours for daytime and night-time lighting *Lighting Res. Technol.* **2**(4) 249–256 (1970)

17   Weale R A *The ageing eye* (London: H K Lewis and Sons) (1963)

18   *Lighting for Partial Sight Handbook* (London: Iridian)

19   Davies R G and Ginthner D N Correlated colour temperature illuminance level and the Kruithof curve *J. Illum. Eng. Soc.* (Winter 1990)

20   Boyce P R and Cuttle C Effect of correlated colour temperature on the perception of interiors and colour discrimination performance *Lighting. Res. Technol.* **22**(1) 19–36 (1990)

21   *BS 950: 1967: Specification for artificial daylight for the assessment of colour* (Parts 1 and 2) (London: British Standards Institution) (1967)

22   *Health and Safety at Work etc. Act 1974* (London: HMSO) (1974)

23   *Factories Act 1961* (London: HMSO) (1961)

24   *Electricity at Work Act 1989* (London: HMSO) (1969)

25   *Areas for visual display terminals* Lighting Guide **LG3** (London: Chartered Institution of Building Services Engineers) (1989)

26   *Outdoor environment* Lighting Guide **LG6** (London: Chartered Institution of Building Services Engineers) (1992)

27   *Lighting for offices* Lighting Guide **LG7** (London: Chartered Institution of Building Services Engineers) (1993)

28   *Recommended practice for lighting of railway premises* (London: British Railways Board) (1969)

29   *Directive concerning the minimum safety and health requirements for the workplace* EC Directive 89/654/EEC (Brussels: Commission for the European Communities) (1989)

30   *Workplace (Health, Safety and Welfare) Regulations 1992* SI 3004 (London: HMSO) (1992)

31   *Workplace (Health, Safety and Welfare) Regulations: Guidance on regulations* HSE Approved Code of Practice **L24** (London: Health and Safety Executive/HMSO) (1992)

32   *Directive concerning the minimum safety and health requirements for the use of work equipment by workers at work* EC Directive 89/655/EEC (Brussels: Commission for the European Communities) (1989)

33   *Provision and Use of Work Equipment Regulations 1992* SI 2932 (London: HMSO) (1992)

34   *Work equipment: Guidance on regulations* HSE Approved Code of Practice **L22** (London: Health and Safety Executive/HMSO) (1992)

35 *Directive on the minimum safety and health requirements for work with display screen equipment* EC Directive 90/270/EEC (Brussels: Commission for the European Communities) (1990)

36 *Health and Safety (Display Screen Equipment) Regulations 1992* (London: HMSO) (1992)

37 *Display screen equipment work: Guidance on regulations* HSE Approved Code of Practice **L26** (London: Health and Safety Executive/HMSO) (1992)

38 *BS 5655: Part 1: 1979: Safety rules for the construction and installation of electric lifts* (London: British Standards Institution) (1979)

39 *Safety in the use of escalators* HSE Guidance Note **PM34** (London: Health and Safety Executive) (1983)

40 *Food Safety Act 1990* (London: HMSO) (1990)

41 *BS 5489: Road lighting: Part 9: 1992: Code of practice for lighting for urban centres and public amentuy areas* (London: British Standards Institution) (1992)

42 *Lighting in hostile and hazardous environments* Lighting Guide (London: Chartered Institution of Building Services Engineers) (1983)

43 *Ship building and ship repair* Lighting Guide (London: Chartered Institution of Building Services Engineers) (1979)

44 *Guide to the lighting of exterior working areas* CIE Publication **68** (Paris: Commission Internationale de l'Eclairage) (1986)

45 *Guide for floodlighting* CIE Publication **94** (Paris: Commission Internationale de l'Eclairage) (1993)

46 *Guidance notes for the reduction of light pollution* (Rugby: Institution of Lighting Engineers) (1992)

47 *Security engineering* Applications Manual **AM4** (London: Chartered Institution of Building Services Engineers) (1991)

48 *Protection against ultra-violet radiation in the workplace* (Didcot: National Radiological Protection Board) (1977)

49 BS 5345: Code of practice for selection, installation and maintenance of electrical apparatus in potentially explosive atmospheres (London: British Standards Institution) (1977–1990)

50 *Directive on the approximation of the laws of the member states relating to electromagentic compatibility* EC Directive 89/336/EEC (Brussels: Commission for the European Communities) (1989)

51 *BS 6467: Electrical apparatus with protection by enclosure for use in the presence of combustible dusts* (London: British Standards Institution) (1985–1988)

52 *Food Hygiene (General) Regulations 1970* (London: HMSO) (1970)

53 *Slaughterhouse (Hygiene) Regulations 1955* (London: HMSO) (1955)

54 *Lighting in printing works* (London: British Printing Industries Federation) (1980)

55 *Essentials of farm lighting* (Capenhurst : Electricity Association Technology Ltd)

56 *Lighting for horticultural production* (Capenhurst: Electricity Association Technology Ltd)

57 *BS 5502: Buildings and structures for agriculture* (London: British Standards Institution) (1987–1992)

58 *Underground lighting recommendations* (Cheltenham: National Coal Board/Coal Research Establishment)

59 *Design guide for coal preparation plants* (Cheltenham: National Coal Board/Coal Research Establishment)

60 *Building and civil engineering sites* Lighting Guide (London: Chartered Institution of Building Services Engineers) (1975)

61 *Emergency lighting* Technical Memoranda **TM12** (London: Chartered Institution of Building Services Engineers) (1986)

62 *Construction (General Provisions) Regulations 1961* (London: HMSO) (1961)

63 *BS 7375: 1991: Code of practice for distribution of electricity on construction and building sites* (London: British Standards Institution) (1991)

64 *BS 7671: 1992: Requirements for electrical installations* (London: British Standards Institution) (1992)

65 *Libraries* Lighting Guide (London: Chartered Institution of Building Services Engineers) (1982)

66 *Lecture, teaching and conference rooms* Lighting Guide **LG5** (London: Chartered Institution of Building Services Engineers) (1991)

67 *Museums and art galleries* Lighting Guide (London: Chartered Institution of Building Services Engineers) (1980)

68 *Lighting and wiring of churches* (London: Church of England/Church Information Office)

69 *BS CP 1007: 1955: Maintained lighting for cinemas* (London: British Standards Institution) (1955)

70 *ABTT Theatres planning guidance for design and adaptation* (London: Architectural Press)

71 *Sports* Lighting Guide **LG4** (London: Chartered Institution of Building Services Engineers) (1990)

72 *Guidelines for environmental design and fuel conservation in educational buildings* DES Design Note **17** (London: Department of Education and Science) (1981)

73 *Education (School Premises) Regulations 1981* (London: HMSO) (1981)

74 *Hospitals and health care buildings* Lighting Guide **LG2** (London: Chartered Institution of Building Services Engineers) (1989)

75 *BS 4533: Section 102.55: 1986: Specification for luminaires for hospitals and health care buildings* (London: British Standards Institution) (1986)

76 *Hospital Technical Memorandum* **TM6** (London: Department of Health/HMSO)

77 *BS 4533: Section 103.2: 1986: Specification for photometric characteristics of luminaires for hospitals and health care buildings* (London: British Standards Institution) (1986)

78 *Special requirements of light sources for clinical purposes* MRC Memorandum **43** (London: Medical Research Council)

79 *Handbook of sports and recreational building design* (London: Sports Council)

80 *Lighting in small multi-purpose sports halls* (London: Sports Council)

81 *Energy data sheets* (London: Sports Council)

82 *Data sheets* (London: Sports Council)

83 *Lighting for swimming pools* CIE Publication **62** (Paris: Commission Internationale de l'Eclairage) (1984)

84 *Guide to photometric specifications and management of sports lighting installations* CIE Publication **67** (Paris: Commission Internationale de l'Eclairage) (1986)

85 *Guide to the lighting of sports events for CTV and film systems* CIE Publication **83** (Paris: Commission Internationale de l'Eclairage) (1989)

86 *LIF Lamp Guide* (London: Lighting Industry Federation) (1990)

87 *Regulations for Electrical Installations* 16th edn (London: Institution of Electrical Engineers) (1992)

88 *BS 4533: Luminaires* (London: British Standards Institution) (1986-1990)

89 *EN 60 598-1* (Brussels: Comité Européen de Normalisation) (1989) published in UK as *BS4533: Part 101: 1993* (London: British Standards Institution) (1993)

90 *IEC 598* (Geneva: International Electrotechncial Commission) published in UK as *BS 4533* (London: British Standards Institution) (1993)

91 *Low Voltage Electrical Equipment (Safety) Regulations 1989* (London: HMSO) (1989)

92 *Electricity (Factories Act) Special Regulations 1944* (London: HMSO) (1944)

93 *IEC 529* (Geneva: International Electrotechnical Commission) (also available from British Standards Institution)

94 *BS 5490: 1977: Specification for classification of degrees of protection provided by enclosures* (London: British Standards Institution) (1977)

95 *UTE C20 010* (French Standard) (Paris: AFNOR)

96 *BS 5750: Quality systems* (London: British Standards Institution) (1981–1987)

97 *ISO 9000: Quality systems* (Geneva: International Standards Organisation) (1987)

98 *EN 29000: Quality systems* (Brussels: Comité Européen de Normalisation) (1987)

99 *BS 5225: Photometric data for luminaires: Parts 1 and 2: 1985* (London: British Standards Institution) (1985)

100 *Calculation and use of utilization factors* Technical Memoranda **TM5** (London: Chartered Institution of Building Services Engineers) (1980)

101 *Technical Guidance Note* **10** (London: Lighting Industry Federation) (1991)

102 *Control of Substances Hazardous to Health Regulations 1988* (London: HMSO) (1988)

103 *The Environmental Protection (Duty of Care) Regulations 1991* (London: HMSO) (1991)

104 Lynes J A and Littlefair P J Lighting energy savings from daylight: Estimation at the sketch design stage *Lighting Res. Technol.* **22**(3) 129–137 (1990)

105 Littlefair P J *Average daylight factor: a simple basis for daylight design* (Garston: Building Research Establishment) (1988)

106 Tregenza P R Modification of the split-flux formulae for mean daylight factor and internal reflected component with large external obstructions *Lighting Res. Technol.* **21**(3) 125–128 (1989)

107 Secker S M and Littlefair P J Daylight availability and lighting use: Geographical variations *Lighting Res. Technol.* **19**(2) 25–34 (1987)

108 Flynn J E and Spencer T J Effect of light source colour on user *J. Illum. Eng. Soc.* (April 1977)

109 *Multiple criterion design: a design method for interior electric lighting installation* Technical Report **15** (London: Illuminating Engineering Society/Chartered Institution of Building Services Engineers) (1977)

110 *Lighting controls and energy management systems* LIF Application Guide (London: Lighting Industry Federation) (1989)

111 *Lighting controls and daylight use* BRE Digest **272** (Garston: Building Research Establishment) (1985)

112 *CIE International lighting vocabulary* CIE Publication **17.4** (Paris: Commission Internationale de l'Eclairage) (1987) (also *IEC 50(845)* (Geneva: International Electrotechnical Commission)

113   *Maintenance of indoor electric lighting systems* CIE
      Publication **97** (Paris: Commission Internationale de
      l'Eclairage) (1992)

114   *IES Lighting handbook* HB-SET-87-1987 (New York:
      Illuminating Engineering Society of North America)
      (1987)

115   *Aanbevelingen voor binnenverlichting* (Nederlandse
      Stichting voor Verlichtingskunde) (1981)

116   *Technical Code JIEC-001-1980* (Tokyo: Illuminating
      Engineering Institute of Japan) (1980)

117   *DIN 5035 Innenraumbeleuchtung mit kunstlichen Licht*
      (Berlin: Deutsches Institut für Normung)

118   *Belsoteri Mesterseges Vilagitas MSZ6290/1-86* (Hungary:
      Magyar Tudomanyos Akademia Vilagitastechnikai
      Bizottsag)

119   Aizenberg J B, and Rozhkova I B Constructional
      Standards and Instructions U-4-79 Part U, Chapter 4
      Natural and Artificial Lighting (Moscow) (1980)

120   Clark F Accurate Maintenance Factors *Illum. Eng.* **58**
      124 (March 1963)

121   Clark F Accurate Maintenance Factors Part Two
      Illum. Eng. **61** 37 (January 1966)

122   Clark F Light Loss Factors in the Design Process
      Illum. Eng. **63** 575 (November 1968)

123   Marsden A M *The economics of interior lighting
      maintenance* CIE Publication **103**/5 37–46 (1993)

124   Carter D J and Boughdah H Lumen design method for
      constructed interiors *Lighting Res. Technol.* **24**(1) 15–24
      (1992)

125   Raitelli M R and Carter D J A designer's guide to
      electric lighting in obstructed interiors *Proc. 7th Lux
      Europa Conference, Edinburgh* **1** 220–233 (1993)

126   *Calculation of glare indices* Technical Memoranda
      TM10 (London: Chartered Institution of Building
      Services Engineers) (1985)

127   *Fire Precautions Act 1971* (London: HMSO) (1971)

128   *BS 5266: Emergency lighting of premises* (London:
      British Standards Institution) (1981–1988)

129   Boyce P R Movement under emergency lighting: the
      effect of illuminance: Part 1 *Lighting Res. Technol.*
      17(2) (1985)

130   Boyce P R Movement under emergency lighting: the
      effect of illuminance: Part 2 *Lighting Res. Technol.*
      18(1) Part 2 (1986)

131   *BS 5499: Fire safety signs, notices and graphic symbols*
      (London: British Standards Institution) (189–1990)

132   *Owning and operating costs* CIBSE Guide Section B18
      (London: Chartered Institution of Building Services
      Engineers) (1986)

133   Lynes J A, Burt W, Jackson G K and Cuttle C C The
      flow of light in buildings *Trans. Illum. Eng. Soc.*
      (London) **31** 65 (1966)

134   Epaneshnikov M M, Obrosova N A, Sidorova T N and
      Undasynov G N New characteristics of lighting
      conditions for the appearance of public buildings and
      methods for their calculation *Proc. CIE 17th Session,
      Barcelona* (1971)

135   Carlton J W Effective use of lighting *Developments in
      lighting 2* D C Pritchard (ed.) (London: Applied
      Science Publishers) (1982)

136   *BS 667: 1985: Photo-electric photometers* (London:
      British Standards Institution) (1985)

137   Carter D J, Secton R C and Millar M Field
      measurement of illuminance *Lighting Res. Technol.*
      21(1) 29 (1989)

138   Einhorn H D Average iluminance: Two-line method
      of measurement *Lighting Res. Technol.* **22**(1) 43 (1990)

139   Stiles W S The effect of glare on the brightness
      difference threshold *Proc. Royal Soc.* **B104** 322 (1929)

140   Holladay L L The fundamentals of glare and visibility
      J. Opt. Soc. Amer. **12** 271 (1926)

141   *Glare and uniformity in road lighting installations* CIE
      Publication **31** (Paris: Commission Internationale de
      l'Eclairage) (1976)

142   Hills B L Visibility under night driving conditions:
      derivation of $(\Delta L, A)$ characteristics and factors in
      their application *Lighting Res. Technol.* **8**(1) 11 (1976)

143   *Discomfort glare in the interior working environment* CIE
      Publication **55** (Paris: Commission Internationale de
      l'Eclairage) (1983)

144   Petherbridge P and Hopkinson R Discomfort glare
      and the lighting of buildings *Trans. Illum. Eng. Soc.*
      (London) **15** 39 (1950)

145   Luminance study panel of IES Technical Committee:
      The development of the IES Glare Index System
      Trans. Illum. Eng. Soc. (London) **27** (1962)

146   *An analytic model for describing the influence of lighting
      parameters upon visual performance* Volume **1** 2nd edn
      CIE Publication **19.21** (Paris: Commission
      Internationale de l'Eclairage) (1981)

147   *An analytic model for describing the influence of lighting
      parameters upon visual performance* Volume **2** 2nd edn
      CIE Publication **19.22** (Paris: Commission
      Internationale de l'Eclairage) (1981)

148   Boyce P R The variability of contrast rendering factor
      in lighting installations *Lighting Res. Technol.* **10**
      94–105 (1978)

149 Boyce P R and Slater A I The application of contrast rendering factor to office lighting design *Lighting Res. Technol.* **13** 65–79 (1981)

150 De Boer J B Performance and comfort in the presence of veiling reflections *Lighting Res. Technol.* **9** 169–176 (1977)

151 Bjorset H H and Frederiksen E A proposal for recommendations for the limitation of contrast reduction in office lighting *Proc. CIE 19th Session, Kyoto* (1979)

152 Boyce P R *Veiling reflections: an experimental study of their effect on office work* **M1230** (Capenhurst: Electricity Council Research Centre) (1979)

153 Fisher C Suitable quality classes for the contrast rendering factor *CIE Journal* **1**(1) 15–17 (1982)

154 Reitmieir J Some effects of veiling reflections in papers *Lighting Res. Technol.* **11** 204–209 (1979)

155 Slater A I Variation and use of contrast rendering factor and equivalent sphere illumination *Lighting Res. Technol.* **11** 117–139 (1979)

156 *IES Lighting Handbook* 6th edn Reference Volume **9-63** (New York: Illuminating Engineering Society of North America) (1981)

157 Lynes J A Designing for contrast rendition *Lighting Res. Technol.* **14** (1) (1982)

158 Rea M S and Ouellette M J Visual performance using reaction times *Lighting Res. Technol.* **20**(4) 139–153 (1988)

159 Rea M S and Ouellette M J Relative visual performance: a basis for application *Lighting Res. Technol.* **23**(3) 135–144 (1991)

160 Rea M S Practical implications of a new visual perfomance model *Lighting Res. Technol.* **18**(3) 113–118 (1986)

161 *Munsell Book of Color* (Baltimore, USA: Munsell Color Corporation) (1973) (Salisbury: D G Color Ltd)

162 Hard A and Sivak L NCS: Natural Colour System: A Swedish standard for colour notation *Color Res. Applic.* **6** 128–138 (1981)

163 *NCS atlas* (Slough: ICI Paints Division)

164 Richter M and Witt K The story of the DIN colour system *Color Res. Applic.* **11** 138–145 (1986)

165 Wyszecki G and Stiles W S *Color science* 2nd edn (New York: Wiley) (1982)

166 Hunt R W G *Measuring colour* 2nd edn (Chichester: Ellis Horwood) (1991)

167 *DIN Colour Chart* (Berlin: Deutches Institüt fur Normung)

168 *CIE 1976 uniform chromaticity scale diagram* (Paris: Commission Internationale de l'Eclairage) (1976)

169 *BS 5252: 1976: Framework for colour coordination for building purpose* (London: British Standards Institution) (1976)

170 Padgham C A and Saunders J E *The perception of light and colour* (London: G Bell and Sons) (1975)

171 *BS 4800: 1981: Specification for paint colours for building purposes* (London: British Standards Institution) (1981)

172 *BS 4900: 1976 Specification for vitreous enamel colours for building purposes* (London: British Standards Institution) (1976)

173 *BS 4901: 1976: Specification for plastics colours for building purposes* (London: British Standards Institution) (1976)

174 *BS 4901: 1976: Specification for sheet and tile flooring colours for building purposes* (London: British Standards Institution) (1976)

175 *BS 4903: 1979: Specification for external colours for farm buildings* (London: British Standards Institution) (1979)

176 *BS 4904: 1978: Specification for external cladding colours for building purposes* (London: British Standards Institution) (1978)

177 Steck B Effects of optical radiation on man *Lighting Res. Technol.* **14** 130 (1982)

178 *Reference action spectra for UV induced erythema and pigmentation of different types of human skin types: Report of CIE Technical Committee 6-10* Publication **103.3** 15–21 (1993)

179 Parrish J A, Anderson R R, Urbach F and Pitts D *UV-A, Biological effects of ultra-violet radiation with emphasis on human responses to longwave ultra-violet* (Chichester: J Wiley and Sons) (1978)

180 Wolbarsht M L and Sliney D H Ocular effects of non-ionising radiation *Proc. Soc. Photo-Optical Instrumentation Engineers* (Washington, USA) 229 (1980)

181 McKinlay A F, Harlen F and Whillock M J *Hazards of Optical Radiation: A guide to sources, uses and safety* (Bristol: Adam Hilger) (1988)

182 *Threshold limit values for chemical substances and physical agents for 1991–1992* (Cincinatti, USA: American Conference of Governmental Industrial Hygienists) (1991)

183 International Non-ionizing Radiation Committee of the International Radiation Protection Association: Guidelines on limits of exposure to ultraviolet radiation of wavelengths between 180 nm and 400 nm (incoherent optical radiation) *Health Physics* **49** (2) pp331–340 (August 1985)

184 International Non-ionizing Radiation Committee of the International Radiation Protection Association: Proposed changes to the IRPA 1985 guidelines on limits of exposure to ultraviolet radiation *Health Physics* **56** (6) pp971–972 (June 1989)

185 Sliney D H Optical radiation safety *Lighting Res. Technol.* **14** 142 (1982)

186 Spears G R Radiant flux measurements of ultra-violet emitting light sources *J. Illum. Eng. Soc.* **4** 36 (1974)

187 BS EN 825: Radiation safety of laser products (London: British Standards Institution)

188 Sliney D H Non-ionising radiation *Industrial Environmental Health* L V Cralley (ed.) (London: Academic Press) (1972)

189 Sliney D H and Wolbarsht M L *Safety with lasers and other optical sources* (London: Plenum Press) (1985)

190 *Official Journal of the European Communities* (Brussels: Commission for the European Communities) (periodical)

191 *Framework Directive* EC Directive 89/391/EEC (Brussels: Commission for the European Communities) (1989)

192 *Directive on the minimum requirement for the provision of safety and/or health signs at work* EC Directive 92/58/EEC (Brussels: Commission for the European Communities) (1992)

193 *Safety Signs Regulations 1980* (London: HMSO) (1980)

194 *Directive 89/392/EEC as amended by Directive on the approximation of the laws of member states relating to machinery* EC Directive 91/368/EEC (Brussels: Commission for the European Communities) (1991)

195 *Supply of Machinery (Safety) Regulations 1992* SI 3073 (London: HMSO) (1992)

196 *Directive on the approximation of laws, regulations and administrative provisions of the member states relating to the construction product/CE Mark* EC Directive 89/106/EEC (Brussels: Commission for the European Communities) (1989)

197 *Construction Products Regulations 1991* SI 1620 (London: HMSO) (1991)

198 *Opus: Building services design file* (London: Building Services Publications Ltd/Chartered Institution of Building Services Engineers) (annual)

199 Muis, Posthumus, Slob, van der Sluis *Environmental aspects of lighting — A product orientated approach* (1990)

200 *Handbook of electricity supply statistics* (Capenhurst: Electricity Association Technology Ltd) (1988)

201 *Estimating daylight in buildings: Part 1* BRE Digest **309** (Garston: Building Research Establishment) (1986)

202 *Estimating daylight in buildings: Part 2* BRE Digest **310** (Garston: Building Research Establishment) (1986)

203 Bedocs L, Hugill J and Lynes J Point-by-point illuminance from uplighters *Lighting Res. Technol.* **16** (4) 187–192 (1984)

204 *BS 4727: Part 4: Glossary of terms particular to lighting and colour* (London: British Standards Institution) (1971–72)

205 *Colorimetry* CIE Publication **15.2** (Paris: Commission Internationale de l'Eclairage) (1986)

206 *Light as a true visual quantity: principles of measurement* CIE Publication **41** (Paris: Commission Internationale de l'Eclairage) (1978)

207 *ISO/CIE 10527* (Geneva: International Standards Organisation) (also available from British Standards Institution)

208 *Method of measuring and specifying colour rendering of light sources* CIE Publication **13.2** (Paris: Commission Internationale de l'Eclairage) (1988)

209 *ISO/CIE 10526* (Geneva: International Standards Organisation) (also available from British Standards Institution)

210 *International classification of impairments, disabilities and handicaps* (Geneva: World Health Organisation) (1980)

Index